ROMAN CATHOLIC CHURCH MUSIC IN ENGLAND, 1791–1914: A HANDMAID OF THE LITURGY?

Roman Catholic Church Music in England, 1791–1914: A Handmaid of the Liturgy?

T.E. MUIR

ASHGATE

ML
3031
.M85
2008

Published by
Ashgate Publishing Limited
Gower House
Croft Road
Aldershot
Hampshire GU11 3HR
England

Ashgate Publishing Company
Suite 420
101 Cherry Street
Burlington, VT 05401-4405
USA

www.ashgate.com

British Library Cataloguing in Publication Data
Muir, T.E.
  Roman Catholic church music in England, 1791–1914: a handmaid of the liturgy? – (Music in nineteenth-century Britain)
  1. Church music – England – 19th century 2. Church music – Catholic Church
  I. Title
  781.7'12'00942'09034

Library of Congress Cataloging-in-Publication Data
Muir, T.E., 1954–
  Roman Catholic church music in England, 1791–1914: a handmaid of the liturgy? / by T.E. Muir.
     p. cm– (Music in nineteenth-century Britain)
  Includes bibliographical references (p.   ), discography (p.   ), and index.
  ISBN 978-0-7546-6105-4 (alk. paper)
  1. Church music–England–19th century. 2. Church music–Catholic Church. I. Title.
  ML3031.M85 2008
  781.71'200942–dc22

                                                                              2007044478

ISBN 978-0-7546-6105-4

Bach musicological font developed by (c) Yo Tomita.

Mixed Sources
Product group from well-managed forests and other controlled sources
www.fsc.org Cert no. SA-COC-1565
© 1996 Forest Stewardship Council

Printed and bound in Great Britain by
MPG Books Ltd, Bodmin, Cornwall.

Contents

V   THE IRON FRAME: CATHOLIC MUSIC DURING
THE EARLY TWENTIETH CENTURY

List of Figures

List of Tables

List of Music Examples

Acknowledgements

This book could not have been completed without the help and encouragement of many people and organisations. First I must thank Dr Bennett Zon, who supervised the doctoral thesis on which much of this book is based. Next, I must thank all those who gave me access to archives and documentation for my research, and the following in particular: M. Theresa Arrowsmith of the Bar Convent, York; Dom Aidan Bellenger, Dom Philip Jebb and Dom Dunstan O'Keefe of Downside Abbey; Fr Robert Canavan and Michael Dolan at the Talbot Library, Preston; Fr Anselm Cramer and Fr Adrian Convery, of Ampleforth Abbey; Dr Ian Dickie at the Westminster Archdiocesan Archives; Fr Mark Hartley of Mount Saint Bernard Abbey; Frank Hickey, ex-organist of St Wilfrid's Church, Bishop Auckland; Fr Emmanuel Gribben of Ushaw College, Nr Durham; Fr David Lannon at the Salford Diocesan Archives; Fr Peter Leighton of St Cuthbert's Church, Durham; Sr Mary Therese and Sr Mary Magdalene of the Canonesses of the Holy Sepulchre, Colchester; Fr John Mills of St Dominic's Priory, Newcastle; Fr Thomas McCoog of the Farm Street Archives, London; Jack Moon organist at St Mary's Church, Chipping; Anne Moynihan at the Franciscan Study Centre, Canterbury; Mary Pethicka at Long Crendon presbytery, Bucks (formerly the repository of the CMA collection); Sr M. Peter, of Oulton Abbey, Nr Stone, Staffs; the late Dom Alan Rees and Br Raphael Aspinall, of Belmont Abbey; Phyllis Rigby, Organist at Our Lady and St Michael's Church, Alston Lane; F.L. Salvin of Croxdale Hall, Nr Durham; Fr Geoffrey Scott and John Rowntree, at Douai Abbey, Nr Reading; Fr John Southworth, Our Lady of Mount Carmel Church, Liverpool, Sr. Margaret Truran, of Stanbrook Abbey, Nr Worcester; the late Fr Frederick Turner, David Knight, Robin Highcock, Gregory Mann and Kevin Morgan at Stonyhurst College, Nr Blackburn.

List of Abbreviations and Terminology

Abbreviations

AJ	*Ampleforth Journal* (Ampleforth Abbey, North Yorkshire)
CJM	*Crown of Jesus Music* (London: Thomas Richardson and Son, 1864)
CM	*Church Music* (n.p.: Church Music Association)
CRS	*Catholic Record Society* (n.p.)
CTS	*The Catholic Truth Society* (London)
DM	*Douai Magazine* (Reading: Douai Abbey)
DR	*Downside Review* (Stratton on the Fosse: Downside Abbey)
DubR	*Dublin Review* (London: Burns and Oates)
EG	*Études Grégoriènnes* (Solesmes)
EM	*Early Music* (London: Oxford University Press)
IER	*Irish Ecclesiastical Record* (Dublin: Browne and Nolan Ltd.)
LN	*Letters and Notices* (Roehampton: Manresa Press, Society of Jesus (English Province))
ML	*Music and Liturgy* (n.p.: Society of St Gregory. Some issues though were published under the title *Liturgy* and have been referred to as such)
MQ	*Musical Quarterly* (Oxford: Oxford University Press)
MT	*Musical Times* (London: Novello)
MLet	*Music and Letters* (London: Oxford University Press)
NCH	*Northern Catholic History* (n.p.: journal of the North-East Catholic History Society)
NPOR	*National Pipe Organ Register* (www.bios.org.uk)
NWCH	*North-West Catholic History* (n.p.: journal of the North-West Catholic History Society)
OC	*Organist and Choirmaster* (London)
OJ	*Orthodox Journal* (London: E. Andrews/P. and M. Andrews)
PM	*Paléographie musicale* (Solesmes: Imprimerie de St Pierre. Later Paris, Rome, Tournai: Desclée et Cie)
PMM	*Plainsong and Medieval Music* (Cambridge: Cambridge University Press)
PMMN	*Panel of Monastic Musicians Newsletter*
PP	*Past and Present* (Oxford: Past and Present Society)
RH	*Recusant History* (CRS)
SAA	*Stanbrook Abbey Archives*
SM	*Stonyhurst Magazine* (Stonyhurst College, Lancashire)

Tablet	*The Tablet* (London: Burns Oates and Washbourne. Vol. nos follow the New Series up to 1948, after which the editors reverted to the 'Old Series' numbering)
TCM	*Tudor Church Music* (London: Oxford University Press).
UM	*Ushaw Magazine* (Ushaw College, Nr Durham)
WCC	*Westminster Cathedral Chronicle* (Westminster Cathedral, London)
WH	*The Westminster Hymnal* (London: R. and T. Washbourne, 1912)

Terminology

CMA	Church Music Association
EBC	English Benedictine Congregation
SSG	Society of St Gregory
TLS	*Tra Le Sollectudini*. Motu proprio by Pius X (1903). English translation in Terry, Richard, *Music of the Roman Rite* (London: Burns Oates and Washbourne, 1931), pp. 253–69.
Vatican II	The Second Vatican Council
WH	ed. Richard Terry et al., *The Westminster Hymnal* (London: R. and T. Washbourne, 1912)

The term 'Catholic' always refers to the Roman Catholic Church. The term 'Anglican' refers to the Anglican Church of England. The noun 'Protestant' refers to any Christian who is a member of any Protestant denomination, including the Anglican Church of England.

Preface

This book is the first major study of music performed by the English Catholics during the nineteenth century, a period bounded by the 1791 Catholic Relief Act and the onset of the Great War. The field is enormous, for such music served the needs of a vigorous, vibrant and multi-faceted community that grew from about 70,000 to 1.7 million people. Contemporary literature of all kinds abounds; and, in addition, collections of mainly uncatalogued sheet music survive all around the country, some running to hundreds, occasionally even thousands, of separate pieces, many of which have since been forgotten. Moreover, much of the music performed constituted a revival or imitation of older musical genres, especially plainchant and Renaissance polyphony. The latter music – which was originally intended to be performed by professional musicians for the benefit of privileged royal, aristocratic or high ecclesiastical elites – was repackaged for rendition by amateurs before largely working- or lower-middle-class congregations, many of them Irish. Whatever the qualms about musical quality, such facts constitute a socio-musical phenomenon of first-class importance. No assessment of the British musical experience is complete without it.

Yet, outside the Catholic orbit, little attention has been paid to the subject. Consequently, the achievements and widespread popularity of many composers within the English Catholic community have passed largely unnoticed. Worse, much of the evidence is rapidly disappearing, partly because so much of it is not stored in academic institutions, but mainly because it no longer seems relevant to the needs of the modern Catholic Church. However, such neglect has not stopped rival groups from appealing to imagined conceptions about what this musical tradition consisted of. On the contrary, it provides a subconscious touchstone in current controversies about the future shape of Catholic church music in the twenty-first century.

This book aims to set the record straight before it is too late. It is based on developments from research for my doctoral thesis.[1] Naturally, the vast quantity of material means that any conclusions must, of necessity, be of a provisional nature, especially regarding the relationship between what contemporaries thought was happening and what was actually occurring on the ground. Nonetheless, the main landmarks can be delineated, and some of the supporting detail filled in. One can show how and why Catholic music in England evolved in the way that it did, and this can be set in its proper historical, liturgical and legal context. Indeed, the music itself is evidence for the changing character of English Catholicism. In turn this means we are in a much better position to understand the nature of English Catholic music in the early to mid twentieth century and the extent to which ordinary Catholics really 'toed the line' laid down by their ecclesiastical superiors.

T.E. Muir

---

1   Thomas Muir: *'Full in the panting heart of Rome'*: Roman Catholic Church Music in England 1850–1962 (Durham: PhD thesis, 2004).

General Editor's Series Preface

Music in nineteenth-century Britain has been studied as a topic of musicology for over two hundred years. It was explored widely in the nineteenth century itself, and in the twentieth century grew into research with strong methodological and theoretical import. Today, the topic has burgeoned into a broad, yet incisive, cultural study with critical potential for scholars in a wide range of disciplines. Indeed, it is largely because of its interdisciplinary qualities that music in nineteenth-century Britain has become such a prominent part of the modern musicological landscape.

This series aims to explore the wealth of music and musical culture of Britain in the nineteenth century and surrounding years. It does this by covering an extensive array of music-related topics and situating them within the most up-to-date interpretative frameworks. All books provide relevant contextual background and detailed source investigations, as well as considerable bibliographical material of use for further study. Areas included in the series reflect its widely interdisciplinary aims and, although principally designed for musicologists, the series is also intended to be accessible to scholars working outside of music, in areas such as history, literature, science, philosophy, poetry and performing arts. Topics include criticism and aesthetics; musical genres; music and the church; music education; composers and performers; analysis; concert venues, promoters and organisations; the reception of foreign music in Britain; instrumental repertoire, manufacture and pedagogy; music hall and dance; gender studies; and music in literature, poetry and letters.

Although the nineteenth century has often been viewed as a fallow period in British musical culture, it is clear from the vast extent of current scholarship that this view is entirely erroneous. Far from being a 'land without music', nineteenth-century Britain abounded with musical activity. All society was affected by it, and everyone in that society recognised its importance in some way or other. It remains for us today to trace the significance of music and musical culture in that period, and to bring it alive for scholars to study and interpret. This is the principal aim of the Music in Nineteenth-Century Britain series – to advance scholarship in the area and expand our understanding of its importance in the wider cultural context of the time.

Bennett Zon
Durham University, UK

Introduction
Nineteenth-Century English Catholic Music: A Neglected Heritage

> There is little to be said about music in the Roman Catholic Church in this country until the 1960s and the Second Vatican Council.
>
> *In Tune with Heaven* (London, 1992), p. 45 (clause 89).[1]

Roman Catholic church music in nineteenth-century England is a neglected subject. This applies not just to Anglicans, represented by *In Tune With Heaven*; it extends to members of other Christian denominations, the world of musical scholarship and, indeed, to Catholics themselves. Why is this so? The reasons appear to be simple. In the first place, English Catholic music before the Second Vatican Council (or Vatican II) generally has a low reputation, both in terms of its aesthetic quality and in its standards of performance. *In Tune with Heaven*, for instance, states that:

> In parish churches... there was a long period of stagnation, although there were improvements in standards and taste [a reference to work in the twentieth century by the Society of St Gregory, Richard Terry and Henry Washington], and until the time of Vatican II there had been few developments in the liturgy and its music. There was little vocal participation by the people in the Mass, and such music as they had was generally in the context of other services or devotions.[2]

Many Catholics agreed. 'Why is church music so bad?' is the title of one article in a collection of essays published by Richard Terry (1865–1938), Director of Music at Westminster Cathedral between 1901 and 1923.[3] Elsewhere, in his book *English Catholic Music*, published in 1907, he declared that, 'whatever may be the case in other countries, it is a certain fact that congregational singing is not cultivated in Catholic churches as it deserves to be'.[4]

Secondly, Catholic music in England appears, at times, to lack a clear national identity. After all, the Catholic Church is a supra-national body, so people expect its music to have an international character: hence the paradox. The Catholic music of composers such as Beethoven, Haydn, Mozart and Palestrina is well known, but that

---

1   *In Tune with Heaven: The Report of the Archbishops' Commission on Church Music* (London, 1992).

2   Ibid., 94 (clause 253).

3   Richard Terry, 'Why is church music so bad?', in Richard Terry (ed.), *A Forgotten Psalter and Other Essays* (London, 1929), pp. 105–25.

4   Richard Terry, *English Catholic Music* (London, 1907), p. 121.

of many of their English Catholic equivalents is largely ignored. For instance, even now, music by John Crookhall (1821–87), John Richardson (1816–79), William Sewell (b. 1863), Joseph Egbert Turner (1853–97) and Francis M. De Zulueta (1853–1937), which was frequently performed by English Catholics during the late nineteenth and early twentieth centuries, receives no mention in the latest edition of *Grove's Dictionary of Music and Musicians*. By contrast, the Anglican Church since the Reformation has been the official state church. So, naturally enough, the history of English Church music, with due acknowledgement to the native Nonconformist hymn-singing tradition, has been viewed largely from this perspective. It is also understandable that members of one religious denomination should pay little attention to the music of another. Eric Routley's *A Short History of English Church Music*, with additional material by Lionel Dakers, is typical. All its musical examples come from *A Treasury of English Church Music*, edited by William Read and Gerald Knight, a former president of the Royal School of Church Music (RSCM). Here, nineteenth-century *Continental* themes, such as the Cecilian movement and developments in plainchant, are discussed; but they are interpreted within an English Protestant perspective. For example, as regards plainchant from Solesmes, Routley states that the 'most potent interpreters of its principles to England were G.H. Palmer and J.H. Arnold', both of whom worked in the Anglican tradition. When it comes to hymnody, Protestant developments are described, but there is no hint that English Catholics developed a substantial vernacular tradition of their own.[5]

Thirdly, the music of the era before Vatican II seems irrelevant to many English Catholics, especially those born after 1962, the year when that council opened. Music from before that year was largely composed for the Latin Tridentine liturgy, and it was meant primarily to be sung by clerics and choirs. Its values, then, appear to be diametrically opposed to today's imperatives, with their emphasis on congregational participation in a vernacular liturgy. In his final public interview, the late James Crichton, the influential Catholic liturgist, asserted that 'Latin and Plainchant are not exactly popular; they are foreign'. He then went on to declare that 'most of the great Classical Polyphony [meaning the Renaissance polyphony epitomised by composers such as Palestrina] does not fit the present rite. A seven-minute *Kyrie* is a distortion, not a prayer.'[6] Such statements are remarkable, not just in themselves, but because they were made by the former editor of *Music and Liturgy*, the magazine produced by the Society of St Gregory – originally founded in 1929, specifically to promote plainchant and 'Classical Polyphony'.

Why, then, should people study the English Catholic musical culture of the nineteenth century? Basically the answer is fourfold. First, this was the music heard on an at least weekly basis by a community that grew from about 70,000 to 1.7 million

---

5   Eric Routley, with a concluding chapter by Lionel Dakers, *A Short History of English Church Music* (London, 1979/R1997), pp. 79, 66–74, 97, 101–102. William Read and Gerald Knight (eds), *A Treasury of English Church Music* (London, 1965).

6   'The Liturgy of the Roman Catholic Church over one hundred years – an interview with Monsignor James D Crichton', *ML*, 27/2 (No. 302) (Summer 2001): 19.

people between 1770 and 1913.[7] Moreover, as shall be shown in the next chapter, this was a community that had a national infrastructure that became progressively more elaborate and wide reaching. In 1913, it was well on the way to becoming the largest single religious denomination across the country by the late twentieth century, despite the fact that it was not the official state church.[8] Music played an essential part in that process. Not only did it set the mood, it was often the medium through which the Catholic liturgy was presented to congregations. Whatever the doubts about its aesthetic quality, the standard of its performance and the nature of its English identity, this is a socio-musical phenomenon that cannot be ignored. It is an essential component in the study of the history of English music.

Second, there is the sheer scale and variety of the music that survives, illustrated in Tables I.1 and I.2. These summarise the nineteenth-century contents of a cross-section of sheet music collections from the North East and Lancashire, the traditional heartland of English Catholicism. Taken together, they produce a repertoire of 2,669 separate compositions. Their mere existence shows that they had enduring value for the communities that used them. Their variety is indicated by the fact that only 811, or roughly a third of that repertoire, appear in more than one collection. No item can be found in all eight collections, and only eighteen in a maximum of five collections. It is certain, then, that other compositions will be found in other collections of music, and this is a fact confirmed by hard on-the-ground experience. The chapel of the Sacred Heart attached to Broughton Hall, near Skipton, is a good example. This has a rare copy of *Cantiones Ecclesiasticae, Opus 93* containing works by the Cecilian composer Michael Haller (b. 1840) and Joseph Auer (1856–1911). Haller's works also appear in an equally rare volume of *Cantica Sacra Vol. II, Opus 54*, whilst other Cecilian works by Bernhard Kothe (1826–97) and Johann Singenberger (1848–73) were copied into a manuscript organ book there.[9]

---

7   Statistics on Catholic numbers, as with all denominations, are a complex subject, mainly because of the distinction between figures derived from those attending a service on a particular day and those arrived at by applying a multiplier of 3–5 to those figures to account for the ill and more casual visitors who may still think of themselves as 'Catholics'. The figure of 70,000 for 1770 is taken from John Bossy, *The English Catholic Community* (London, 1975), pp. 298–9. This is derived from the government-sponsored 'Return of Papists' conducted by Anglican parish clergy in 1767, giving a figure of 69,376 (which Bossy considered to be an underestimate of 5 per cent) a survey by the Vicars Apostolic in 1773, giving a figure of 59,500 and calculations by J.-A. Lesourd, *Les Catholics dans la societé anglaise de 1765–1865* (Strasbourg, PhD thesis). The figure for 1913 comes straight from *The Catholic Directory* of that year (London), p. 600D. This is based on a single count made by Catholic priests on one Sunday.

8   Adrian Hastings, *A History of British Christianity 1920–1985* (London, 1986), pp. 134–5, 276–7, 473–6. For discussion of Protestant numbers see pp. 35–40, 265, 473–8 and 444.

9   *Cantiones Ecclesiasticae, Opus 43* (Ratisbon, 1903). *Cantica Sacra Vol. II* (Ratisbon, 1893). The manuscript organ book also has works by Elgar, Reger, Haller and Koenen. This has no date; but the script, as well as its contents, implies a late nineteenth or early twentieth-century provenance.

Table I.1   Catholic music copied or published between c.1750 and c.1914 in a selection of Catholic centres[a]

Name of Centre	Number of Compositions
Church of Our Lady and St Michael, Alstone, Nr Longridge, Lancs.	132
Church of St Mary and the Angels, Bolton Le Sands, Lancs.[b]	24
Church of St Mary, Chipping, Lancs.	78
Church of St Cuthbert, Durham	785
Chapel of St Mary and St Everilda, Everingham, E. Yorks[c]	1,121
Church of St Augustine, Preston, Lancs.[d]	230
Stonyhurst College, Lancs.	923
Ushaw College, Nr Durham	475

[a]   These figures, and those presented in subsequent tables, are derived from details of the music in each collection that have been placed on a Microsoft Access relational database which has then been interrogated using 'filter' and 'query' tools. This is a larger and more complete version of the database used in Thomas Muir, 'Full in the Panting Heart of Rome': Roman Catholic Church Music in England: 1850–1962 (Durham: PhD thesis, 2004). However, the methodology is the same. For details of this see vol. 2, pp. 409–72.

[b]   The music from this collection is stored, along with other music, at the Talbot Library, Preston. It has been identified by cross-referencing items that have been stamped with the church insignia along with items signed by the choirmaster and members of the choir.

[c]   The music from Everingham is now stored in a cupboard in one of the conference rooms of the Bar Convent, York.

[d]   Music from St Augustine's is stored at the Talbot Library, Preston.

Table I.2   Music found in more than one of the collections listed in Table I.1

Compositions in 2 collections	206
Compositions in 3 collections	330
Compositions in 4 collections	57
Compositions in 5 collections	18
Total number of compositions in all 8 collections	2,669

Such variety flies in the face of a picture of centralised uniformity conveyed by other sources. The reasons for this phenomenon are largely structural. In the first place, the figures do not include the contents of the standardised printed volumes that appeared in increasing numbers during the late nineteenth century, such as liturgical books, hymnals and Albert Tozer's New and Complete Manual of Benediction of 1898.[10] As shall be seen in later chapters, these increased the size of the available repertoire by many times, and, in so doing, they give a greater degree of uniformity. Against this it should be noted that the more variegated selection of loose sheet and manuscript music underlines the inherent independence displayed by most choirs,

10 Albert E. Tozer (ed.), New and Complete Manual of Benediction (London, 1898).

past and present. By definition, they are likely to go in a separate direction, not just because some may wish to distinguish themselves from, or in front of, their congregational audience, but because their specialist musical skills – honed during separate rehearsals – mean that they have an incentive to acquire music that can only be performed by themselves. Moreover, the variety of repertoire this produces will have been further enhanced by the many different types of institution within the English Catholic Church. In this sample, for instance, there is a fundamental divide between the seminaries with schools, such as Stonyhurst and Ushaw Colleges, and the other missions (English Catholic parishes were not recognised as such by the Papacy before 1908). Within the missions there is another division between what was essentially a private household chapel (Everingham) – albeit serving the local area – and what were, in effect, public churches. With the latter, in some cases, they had only moved out from household centres with a centuries-long tradition in the late eighteenth century (such as Alston and Chipping), others were offshoots from existing Catholic communities (for example St Augustine, Preston), and some were brand new establishments dating from the late nineteenth century (Bolton Le Sands, for example). Furthermore, there was the separation between centres run by regulars (Stonyhurst and Chipping) and those by secular priests (Alston, St Augustine, Bolton Le Sands, St Cuthbert, Everingham and Ushaw). On top of that there were variations in socio-geographical location. St Augustine's, for example, was a classic urban industrial centre serving a predominantly working-class, and mainly Irish, Catholic community. St Cuthbert's, Durham, is located in a cathedral city, but otherwise catered for a very similar sort of population. By contrast, Chipping and Bolton Le Sands are still utterly rural, whilst Alston, because of its location near Longridge, on the frontier between industrial and rural Lancashire, was something of a hybrid between the two. Nor, it should be stressed, does this list cover the whole gamut of variety. For instance, it does not include such categories as cathedrals, enclosed monastic houses (such as communities in the English Benedictine Congregation) or female religious orders that ran schools – such as the Sisters of Notre Dame or the Institute of the Blessed Virgin Mary.

Third, such evidence is not just important in itself; it exposes the nature of the Catholic community that produced and used it. Music is not merely a product of its historical time, it can enhance our knowledge of that past. In this case, it is well suited for revealing the subconscious soul of the Catholic body. For example, Tables I.3 and I.4 show the balance in these centres between Continental and native British composers, and between music composed in different historical periods. Two points stand out. First, apart from the plainchant found in liturgical books, the repertoire was substantially contemporary. So nineteenth-century Catholics were often up to date, and many were prepared to make use of the latest developments in a rapidly changing world. Second, the largest single block of music was composed by British composers, followed by Austro-Germans and Italians. At the very least this shows that, musically speaking, the Catholic Church in this country had a British inflexion, even if one accepts the proposition that it was influenced by Continental styles. On the other hand, much of the Italian music would have had specifically Papal overtones. For example, when the church of St Peter's, Stonyhurst as opened in

Table I.3   Classification of repertoire listed in Table I.1 by national origin

Country of origin[a]	Number of compositions
Britain	818 (plus 16 by Anglo-Americans)
Austria-Germany	463 (plus 7 by German-Americans and 4 by German-speaking Croats)
Italy	352 (plus 6 others of possible Italian origin and 5 by British-Italians)[b]
France	50
Spain	29
Portugal	13
Flemish[c]	16
Belgian	7
Total repertoire	2,669

[a]   For the sake of simplicity the much smaller contributions by composers from other countries have not been included here.
[b]   This figure does not include compositions by Vincent Novello, who has been classified as a 'British' composer.
[c]   Flemish composers have been distinguished from those living in Holland, after the Dutch Revolt of the late sixteenth century, and those living in Belgium after it attained independence in the 1820s.

Table I.4   Classification of repertoire listed in Table I.1 by period of composition[*]

Period of composition	Number of compositions
No data	861
Pre-1500 (excluding plainchant)	2
1501–1650	127
(1601–1700)	(6)
1651–1750	79
(1701–1800)	(109)
1751–1900	1,219
(1851–1950)	(123)
Total repertoire	2,669

[*]   The figures are given here in simplified form. The additional figures in brackets cover composers active at times that straddled the period divisions. The figures for 1851–1950 do not include the works of composers active only after 1900.

1835, the Jesuits commissioned a *Mass in D* from Salvatore Meluzzi (fl. 1835), director of the Papal choir at St Peter's, Rome to celebrate the occasion. This, then, was a declaration of the special connection between the English Province of the Society of Jesus and the Holy See. Yet the existence of a substantial body of Austro-German music shows that English Catholics looked to other Continental traditions lacking such overtones. Such differences did not necessarily mean that the British and other different Continental traditions were antagonistic to one another. On the contrary, they were often perceived to be compatible. Meluzzi's Mass, for example, uses the prevailing Classical Viennese style deployed by Haydn and Mozart. Many British Masses, for example compositions by Henry George Nixon (1796–1849) and Henry Farmer SJ (1849–1928) (who trained at Stonyhurst) do the same. The varied national origins of a given repertoire may therefore be symptomatic of the place occupied by English Catholics in an international religious community. By the same token, they show how they attempted to balance or blend the claims of that religious community against or with the demands of nineteenth-century British nationalism.

By any standard, material of this sort constitutes a massive cultural legacy. Unfortunately it is in danger of being lost. Usually such music is not stored and catalogued in libraries. It is the surviving detritus of music used by working musicians, and, due to its apparent liturgical irrelevance since Vatican II, much of it has been or is being disposed of. Symptomatic are the huge differences in the size of each collection. This is not necessarily the product of varied levels of musical interest in different centres during the nineteenth century. Were this the case, what survives at Stonyhurst and Ushaw would be a significantly larger collection than that from Everingham as they were much larger establishments. It can be the consequence of subsequent accident. For example, the music from St Augustine's, Preston, survives because it was transferred to the Talbot Library in the same town when the church was substantially demolished in 2002–03. On the other hand, material from St Mary's, Richmond and St Dominic's, Newcastle has almost entirely disappeared. Yet it is known they had substantial musical traditions. Richmond was where Henry Farmer worked as a parish priest, whilst Richard Terry was employed briefly by St Dominic's in 1896–97. Policy, too, can play a part. A curious feature of the collection at St Cuthbert's, Durham is the comparative paucity of music copied or purchased between the Great War and the 1960s. Either its flourishing nineteenth-century tradition declined, or the post-1918 material was largely disposed of after Vatican II but the earlier material survived because it was stored in a different place and missed.

The threat of such destruction makes the analysis of such music an urgent necessity, and not simply as a matter of socio-cultural record. Assumptions about Catholic music from the past are being used to influence current controversy over policy, not just in music, but in the ethos of the Catholic body as a whole. This is the fourth, and most immediate, reason why such music needs to be studied. On one side, there are those who want to maintain and develop the status quo established after Vatican II, with its emphasis on a participatory vernacular liturgy. Many also appreciate the greater independence enjoyed by local communities since the 1960s; a point reinforced by the fact that the increasing shortage of clergy forces such communities to rely more on lay helpers. On the other side, there are the traditionalist conservatives, who want a less populist, more centralised and more uniform church. Some, notably members of the Latin Mass Society, advocate the return of the Latin, and even the pre-Vatican II Tridentine Mass.[11] Music is an essential ingredient in the debate.

As has been seen, for many music before Vatican II is irrelevant, and it also represents much that was wrong with the Catholic Church at that time. For them the obscure, difficult and alien style of plainchant, to say nothing of the anti-congregational character of Renaissance polyphony, is mirrored by similar exclusionary qualities inherent in any non-vernacular liturgy. Moreover, such people are unlikely to take kindly to the re-imposition of centralised uniformity implied by a reassertion of the dominant official place held by such styles. Traditionalists argue the reverse. Plainchant and Renaissance polyphony are symbols of an aesthetic and spiritual excellence that is supposed to lie at the heart of the Tridentine rite. That excellence, moreover, is believed to be in glaring contrast with much of the music that has replaced it. 'Bad Church music to be outlawed. "Dumbed-down" folk Masses could disappear as Vatican tells bishops to re-introduce Gregorian Chant' is a typical recent headline from *The Catholic Herald*.[12] Offence is also taken at the way many post-Vatican II composers have wilfully altered the text in church services or introduced new texts whose sentiments are at odds with what is supposed to be Catholic doctrine, to say nothing of the taste and belief of many in Catholic congregations. In addition, to counter the claim that plainchant and the Latin Mass lack popular appeal, traditionalists can draw attention to the special 'New Age' attraction plainchant is supposed to have for the young; they repeat the pre-Vatican II claim that it *can* be learnt by congregations, and they argue that the resulting uniformity enables people to go into any Catholic church and not be baffled by an unfamiliar repertoire. Thus, as Helen Phelan states: 'On the one hand Gregorian Chant has been increasingly hijacked as the ideological repertoire of those critical of liturgical reforms and harking back to a pre-Vatican II liturgy. On the other it has experienced a wave of non-liturgical popularity associated with New Age spirituality and techno-music mixes'.[13]

Such concerns find resonance at the highest level. For example, the Post Synodal Apostolic Exhortation *Sacramentum Caritatis* makes a careful balance between 'respecting various styles and different praiseworthy traditions' and the desire that 'Gregorian Chant be suitably esteemed and employed as the chant proper to the Roman Liturgy'.[14] On the other hand the encyclical *Liturgiam Authenticam*, produced

---

11 See, for example, Dietrich Von Hildebrand, 'The case for the Latin Mass', reprinted from the October 1996 issue of *Triumph*, and 'A homily preached at the launch of CIEL UK at St James, Spanish Place, London by a priest of the Oratory' (1 March 1977) on www.latin-mass-society.org/canon.htm. Viewed on 8 March 2001.

12 Freddy Gray, 'Bad Church music to be outlawed…' *The Catholic Herald* No. 6210 (29 July 2005): 1. In the same issue see the editorial 'Sing to the Lord': 11.

13 Helen Phelan, 'Gregorian Chant and Contemporary Liturgy', *ML*, 28/1 (No. 305) (Spring 2001): 20. For discussion of plainchant's appeal for New Age spirituality see Katherine Le Mee, *Chant: The Origins, Form, Practice and Healing Power of Gregorian Chant* (London, 1994), esp. pp. 1–11 and 107–46.

14 www.vatican.va/holy_father/benedict_xvi/apostolicexhortations/documents/Benedictxvihf_ben-xvi_(exh_20070…) clause 42. Viewed on 26 March 2007.

in 2001, demands strict adherence to the liturgical text.[15] Under this ruling, an anonymous popular 'folk' setting such as the 'Peruvian Gloria' cannot be substituted for the Gloria text in the Mass Ordinary.[16] The revised *General Instruction of the Roman Missal (GIRM)* goes further. Amongst other things this promotes new texts for the Mass Proper.[17] The music recommended to match it will be of two kinds: plainchant taken from the *Graduale Simplex* and *Graduale Romanum*, or a selection of new settings officially approved by the bishops. As Anthony Boylan has pointed out, if executed, this will sweep away the 'four hymn sandwich' that has hitherto dominated post-Vatican II liturgical music. It will reassert the musical importance of the Proper within the Mass; and, if expressed through plainchant, it will be done in a traditional pre-Vatican II manner. It also marks a return to the centralising authoritarian policies of the early 1900s.[18]

The most direct connection with the past is made in the *Chirograph of the Supreme Pontiff John Paul II for the Centenary of the Motu Proprio 'Tra Le Sollectudini' on sacred music*, issued in 2003.[19] As the title shows, this is directly inspired by the contents of Pope Pius X's Motu Proprio decree *Tra Le Sollectudini (TLS)* of 1903. Here music was declared to be 'the handmaid of the liturgy'. Consequently it had to express sacred and spiritual values, which were best delivered by plainchant and Renaissance polyphony. By contrast, music of a secular or operatic character – for example Masses in the Viennese-Classical tradition – was excoriated.[20] The chirograph therefore seems to signal a return to pre-Vatican II musical policies. In addition, it reminds readers that the same sentiments were expressed in *Sacrosanctum Consilium*, the first document issued by the Second Vatican Council. Vernacular liturgies, for example, were only to be permitted with permission from the local bishop.[21] The implication, then, is that liberals had hijacked this document to produce a liturgical-musical scene that was at odds with what had been originally intended.

Such debates are not new. A vast body of polemic survives from the nineteenth and early twentieth centuries. Indeed, as the contents of *TLS* demonstrate, some of the issues are strikingly similar. Then, as now, there were the competing claims of local diversity versus centralised uniformity. For example, Cecilian Societies pioneered the drafting of lists of officially approved music, a policy to some extent

---

15 *Liturgiam Authenticam*, www.Vatican.va/roman_curia/congregations/ccdds/documents/ cc com_doc_liturgiam-authenticam_en.html (2001). Viewed on 12 August 2005.

16 This was first published in Kevin Mayhew (compiler), *20th Century Folk Hymnal Vol. 2* (Great Wakering, Essex, 1975), no. 75.

17 In other words, The Entrance Antiphon (Introit), Responsorial Psalm and Gospel Acclamation (an expanded version of the old Latin Gradual and Alleluia), the Offertory and Communion antiphons.

18 Anthony Boylan, 'Renewing the Renewal 2 – Music. The new General Instruction on the Roman Missal', *ML*, 31/3 (No. 319) (Autumn 2005): 7–8.

19 This can be found at www.vatican.va/holy_father/john_paul_ii/letters/2003/documents/ hf_jp_let_en.html (2003). Viewed on 12 August 2005.

20 *TLS*, clauses 6 and 23.

21 Walter M. Abbott (ed.), Joseph Gallagher (trans.), *The Message and Meaning of the Ecumenical Council* (London and Dublin, 1966) pp. 116–17, 137–8.

implemented by diocesan music committees created as a result of *TLS*.[22] Cecilians also vigorously promoted the claims of plainchant and Renaissance polyphony against those of up-to-date Mass settings by Classical-Viennese composers and their successors. In the mid- and late nineteenth century the equivalent of present-day 'folk' hymnals can be found in Henri Hemy's *Crown of Jesus Music* and the Notre Dame Hymnal.[23] Likewise, just as some people today object to the use of guitars and electronic instruments in church, so *TLS* banned the use of orchestral instruments in church unless authorised for a specific occasion by the local bishop. The only thing that appears not to be an issue now is the campaign by some to exclude women from choirs; but, even here, that has not stopped some people today continuing to advocate the virtues of all-male choirs with boy singers, as the continued survival of the Pueri Cantores movement demonstrates.[24]

The crucial difference lies in the level of informed knowledge. In the nineteenth century Catholics could measure the claims of polemicists against their own musical experience. Today, when anyone cites the evidence of music from the past to support a given policy, by and large no such check exists. This is because, as was stated at the beginning, actual factual knowledge about past practice is very limited, and what there is tends to be refracted through received personal impressions and thus riddled with misconceptions.[25] Take, for example, the alleged contrast between the excellence of plainchant or Renaissance polyphony and more recent material. First, it ignores the vast quantity of music composed in the past that was perceived to be low grade at that time. Richard Terry, for example, roundly condemned the contents of the *Crown of Jesus Music* and compositions imitating the Renaissance polyphonic style by many Cecilian composers.[26] Second, in terms of performance the comparison

---

22 Sybille Mager, *'Music becomes a prayer': The movement for the reform of Catholic Church music in late nineteenth-century Germany and Austria* (Cambridge, MPhil Thesis, 1994), p. 8.

23 Henri Hemy (ed.), *Crown of Jesus Music Parts I–III* (London and Dublin, 1864). Later editions, with a fourth part were published by Burns and Oates. The individual parts were also published separately. *Convent Hymns and Music by the Sisters of Notre Dame* (Liverpool, 1891).

24 *TLS*, clauses 13 and 20. For examples of local efforts by the diocese of Salford in this direction see the *Acta Salfordiensum* (Synod XX, allocution No. 2., 26 April 1887): 164. For the same diocese see also Bishop Louis Cassertelli's *A Letter on Church Music* (26 January 1906). The Foederatio Internationali Pueri Cantores, as its title implies, is an international organisation with a strong presence in Italy, France, Holland, Poland, Canada and USA. The British branch is relatively small. Annual international congresses have been held since 1947. Although primarily intended to promote male choirs, in a few cases choirs with girls or women have been permitted. For further details see www/pueri cantors.org.

25 Useful introductions, albeit based to a substantial degree on personal memories and tilted towards the twentieth-century scene, are given by John Ainslie, 'English Liturgical Music before Vatican II', in John Ainslie, James Crichton and Harold Winstone (eds), *English Catholic Worship: Liturgical Renewal in England since 1900* (London, 1979) pp. 47–59, and by Brian Plumb, 'Dead, buried and scorned? Catholic Church Music 1791–1960', *NWCH*, 26 (1999): 70–95. For a didactic historical book of instruction produced just before Vatican II see Alec Robertson, *Music of the Catholic Church* (London, 1961).

26 Terry, 'Why is church music so bad? pp. 110–11 and 115–16.

is intrinsically unfair. Today plainchant and Renaissance polyphony are primarily known through performances by professional musicians. Such performances do not take place during the church service; they occur at public concerts or in the privacy of the home through radio, TV, CDs or other electronic media. There is little appreciation of the fact that, before Vatican II, plainchant and Renaissance polyphony were rendered by amateur choirs – in other words by musicians of a similar calibre to those now performing music in the modern 'folk' idiom.[27] Like is not being compared with like.

Next, there is little appreciation of the degree of change between English Catholic music in the early nineteenth century and that of the early twentieth. As has been seen, in the current debate the tendency has been to look at the early and mid-twentieth-century scene when, officially at least, plainchant and Renaissance polyphony were supposed to hold sway.

Yet, by definition, the existence of a significantly different pattern of emphasis in the nineteenth century alters the nature of any argument predicated on alleged contrasts between pre- and post-Vatican II music. The key areas are as follows. First, the nature of plainchant was quite different. It was not plainchant in the style advocated by Solesmes, characterised by smooth flowing undulating lines and built around the principle of a single indivisible note length. Most nineteenth-century plainchant was the chunky, slow-moving 'measured' chant developed during the late Middle Ages and consolidated in the late sixteenth and early seventeenth centuries by musicians such as Palestrina, Guidetti, Anerio and Soriano. Moreover, up till the mid-nineteenth century, new music continued to be written in that style. It was a living, rather than an artificially resuscitated tradition.

Second, Renaissance polyphony was not a dominant musical style. That position was held by music composed in the Classical Viennese and grand modern styles associated with such composers as Haydn, Mozart, Beethoven, Gounod and Turner. At a simpler level it was matched by a native tradition represented by the two Samuel Webbes (1740–1816 and 1770–1843) and Vincent Novello (1781–1861).

However, it is true that there was a development of interest in Renaissance polyphony during the late nineteenth century, and for this much of the credit must go to the work of the Cecilian movement. Yet, as with plainchant, the nature of that interest was different from that pertaining in the twentieth century or today. It had a strong Ultramontane, or pro-Papal, bias; so the polyphony that was promoted had the 'Roman' connotations associated with composers such as Palestrina and Victoria. It was only in the late 1890s and early 1900s that Richard Terry, in particular, promoted the cause of native English practitioners, for example Byrd, Phillips and Tallis. In so doing he suggested that in this genre national traditions were compatible with international Catholic values. Moreover, Cecilians did not just revive Renaissance polyphony, they composed numerous imitations of it. This repertoire, represented by the works of composers such as Joseph Seymour (fl. 1890), Johann Molitor

---

27 An example of a choir still performing pre-Vatican repertoire in this way can still be heard occasionally at St Mary's church, Oswaldtwistle, Lancashire. Twentieth-century recordings of such groups can also occasionally be found. See, for example *The Choir of 1966, St Albans* [Blackburn] (Lancaster, 1966).

(1834–1906), Franz Xavier Witt (1834–88) and Lorenso Perosi (1872–1956), had been almost completely discarded by the 1920s, thereby altering the context in which its late sixteenth- and early seventeenth-century exemplars were viewed. In addition, a hybrid style, combining elements of the modern and Renaissance idiom, can be found in compositions by, for example, Crookall, Richardson, Sewall, Zulueta and, above all, Terry.

Finally, during the mid- and late nineteenth centuries there was a vast growth in Catholic vernacular hymnody, paralleled by a similar expansion in music composed for Benediction and other extra-liturgical services. However, as shall be seen later on, the nature of such developments can be easily misunderstood. This is because hymnody is associated with present-day ideas of congregational participation, largely derived from Protestant denominational practice. Nineteenth-century vernacular Catholic hymnody did not evolve in the same way. In the first place it was driven out of the Mass and Office and largely confined to outdoor processions and extra-liturgical services. The latter had a strong devotional streak, which militated against active congregational participation. As a result, for a long time hymns were often the preserve of the choir and treated like anthems or motets.[28] It was only from the late nineteenth century onwards that stronger efforts were made to develop a tradition of congregational hymn singing.

These and other related subjects have to be analysed and discussed if any clear understanding of Catholic music in nineteenth-century England can be attained. Above all, it must be recognised that such musical developments did not occur in a vacuum. They were the product of socio-historical change, which, in turn, shaped the liturgical ambience in which such music was performed. For example, the rising popularity of extra-liturgical services – on which the growth of vernacular hymnody and Benediction music depended – can only be understood by reference to demographic shifts in the geographical and class composition of the Catholic community in the mid-nineteenth century. It is this developing social and liturgical framework, then, that will be described and discussed in the next two chapters.

---

28 For example, the copy of *The Crown of Jesus Music* at St Cuthbert's church, Durham is marked 'IV' and 'for the use of the choir', implying that there were originally four copies – one for each part in an SATB singing group.

PART I
Heritage, History and Liturgy

Chapter 1

The Historical Background

Faith of our fathers! Living still
In spite of dungeon, fire and sword[1]

'Faith of our fathers', by Frederick William Faber, was one of the most popular – and notorious – hymns of the pre-Vatican II era; and it bears witness to the strong sense of history pervading the character of the English Catholic community at that time. It also demonstrates how much music can reflect and promote such attitudes. Any study of English Catholic music then has to be set against an appropriate historical background, though this need not be a comprehensive survey. Rather, what is required is the isolation of factors shaping the compilation, selection and performance of music in the period. For this purpose you have to go back to the late sixteenth century. Viewed from this perspective English Catholic history can be divided into three eras: a Recusant period between the establishment of the Elizabethan church settlement in 1559 and the first Catholic Relief Act of 1778; a period of transition from that time till the more or less full granting of Catholic Emancipation in 1829; and a period of expansion thereafter.

The Recusant period 1559–1778

The Recusant period takes its name from those Catholics who refused (*recusare*) to conform to the Anglican Church. It is an era of disinheritance and disconnection. Catholics were driven out of the Medieval English church and forced to set up their own organisation. In one sense then they occupied the same position as other Nonconformist denominations. The difference of course lay in their ties with the Papacy; and, unlike with Catholics on the Continent, such a relationship was untrammelled by association with a Church officially recognised by the State.

Connections with the Papacy immediately raised the question of loyalty, and there was also the persistent fear that a revived Catholicism would enforce the restitution of dissolved monastic lands.[2] The Papal excommunication of Elizabeth I in 1569 thus acted as the trigger for a spate of punitive legislation, forcing waverers to choose between the Anglican and Catholic communions; and, if they chose the latter, if nothing else to keep a low profile. It was unlawful for a priest to enter the country or say Mass; it was illegal for Catholics to shelter them or keep Catholic

---

1   *WH*, No. 138.

2   This remained an issue as late as 1688. John Miller, *Popery and politics in England 1660–1688* (Cambridge, 1973), p. 71.

objects and literature; and a refusal to attend Anglican church services could be penalised by swingeing fines. Catholics were also excluded from entering the professions, running schools, or, after 1673, from holding government office. Later obstacles were placed in the way of them bequeathing or inheriting property.[3]

Had the law been consistently enforced it is unlikely that Catholicism could have survived in England. Instead, in normal times, local magistrates were often reluctant to prosecute their Catholic neighbours, and statute was often seen as a weapon only to be used in times of national emergency.[4] As it was, the efficiency of the Anglican Church and the Tudor regime in different regions determined the Catholic geographical and social balance.[5] In the south and east it was reduced to pockets around the households of the Recusant gentry; in the north and west, Catholics were more numerous, especially in Lancashire.

At the same time, to cope with persecution, a new decentralised system with dual control was developed, initially by the Society of Jesus, then by other religious orders and secular priests. Under this administration priests were trained in seminaries – most of them English – on the Continent and then distributed – mainly through gentry households – in provinces across the country.[6] Since the gentry provided most of the money and protection through their households it was they who exerted effective control, and under their influence some places became centres of musical excellence. William Byrd's activity for the Petre family is a notable example.[7]

In addition, for much of the seventeenth century the Stuart court – especially the entourage of Henrietta Maria and Catherine de Braganza, Charles I's and Charles II's Catholic queens – provided a focus for religious activity. This had a musical expression, since works performed in the Queen's chapel and that of the Catholic James II used the latest *Secunda Pratica* styles from Italy, providing models for English Catholic composers such as Richard Dering, Henry Lawes, Matthew

---

3   See for example the following anti-Catholic statutes, in addition to the ones mentioned so far: the Act of Treason 5 Eliz. Cap 1 (1570), the Act to retain the Queen's subjects in obedience 23 Eliz. Cap 23 (1581), the Act against Seditious Acts and Rumours 23 Eliz. Cap 2 (1581), the Act for the surety of the Queen's person 27 Eliz. Cap 1(1585), the Act against Popish Recusants 35 Eliz. Cap 2 (1593), the Act for the discovery and repressing of Popish Recusants 3 and 4 James. Cap 4 (1606), the Act to prevent dangers from Popish Recusants 3 and 4 James I. Cap 5 (1606), the first Test Act (1673). 25 Car II Cap 2, the second Test Act 30 Car. II. Cap 1 (1678), and the Act against Popery. 11 William III. Cap 4 (1700).

4   Miller, pp. 51–66.

5   For discussion of the issue see John Bossy, *The English Catholic community 1570– 1850* (London, 1975), pp. 78–107, 182–94, 405–413 and 423–7. For a different interpretation see Christopher Haigh, 'The Continuity of Catholicism in the English Reformation', *PP*, 93 (November 1981): 37–69.

6   The most important seminaries for secular priests were at Douai (founded 1567), the English College in Rome (1577), Valladolid (1589), Lisbon and Seville. Jesuit establishments were at Liège, Louvain, Watten and Ghent. Male Benedictine houses were founded at Dieulouard (1606), Douai (1605), Chelles (1611), Paris (1615), St Malo (1611) and Lambspring (in Germany) (1644).

7   John Harlay, *William Byrd: Gentleman of the Chapel Royal* (Aldershot, 1997), pp. 141–4. For a discussion of the influence of the gentry see Bossy, pp. 149–81.

Locke and Henry Purcell to follow.[8] When James II was driven into exile by the Revolution of 1688 his court and that of his son, James III (the 'Old Pretender') at Saint-Germain-en-Laye and Urbino remained an important centre of Catholic activity. Once again the latest Italian music – and, for that matter, French styles, which had gained a foothold at the court of Charles II – was an important aspect of this. François Couperin (1668–1733) was regularly employed there between 1692 and 1712. It has also been argued by Bennett Zon that the hymn *Adeste Fideles* may be a coded expression of Jacobite propaganda.[9]

On the other hand, in contrast to such symptoms of positive achievement, the late sixteenth and early seventeenth centuries were marred by a series of vicious disputes between secular and regular clergy – notably the Wisbech Stirs and the Archpriest Controversy – which had damaging effects that lasted right into the late nineteenth century.[10] Such disputes concerned not just matters of internal ecclesiastical organisation; they extended to the relationship between Catholics and the English government. Some secular priests thought it might be possible to negotiate an oath of allegiance to the state while allowing Catholics freedom of worship. In turn this meant that limitations on what the government regarded as foreign Papal control had to be imposed through the selection of an English bishop by a semi-autonomous chapter or committee representing the interests of the secular clergy. Naturally, such a scheme was unacceptable to the Papacy and religious orders, especially the Society of Jesus, who prided themselves on their loyalty to the Holy See. It also conflicted with gentry interests, since it involved relinquishing to any such bishop their *de*

---

8 Richard Dering was Henrietta Maria's chapel organist. Matthew Locke also worked at her household in the 1650s during her exile in the Netherlands. Dering's compositions were revived by Richard Terry in performances at Westminster Cathedral between 1917 and 1922. Hilda Andrews, *Westminster retrospect: A memoir of Sir Richard Terry* (London, 1948), pp. 124–5 and 130. For full details of the introduction and survival of Italian seventeenth-century music see Jonathan P. Wainwright, *Musical patronage in seventeenth-century England: Christopher, First Baron Hatton 1605–1670* (Aldershot, 1997). See also the CDs *Queen of Heavenly Virtue: Sacred Music for Henrietta Maria's Chapel in Oxford* (Concertare, dir. Jonathan P. Wainwright, 1997) and *A Music Strange: Anthems and Devotional Songs by George Jeffreys* (Yvonne Seymour and others, dir. P. Aston, 1980/R1995). For details about Matthew Locke see Anthony Lewis, 'English Church Music', in Ian Spink (ed.), *The Blackwell history of music in Britain: The seventeenth century* (Oxford, 1992), pp. 506–12. For Italian Catholic influences on Purcell see Graham Dixon, 'Purcell's Italianate Circle' and Jonathan P. Wainwright, 'Purcell and the English Baroque' in Richard Burden (ed.), *The Purcell companion* (London, 1995) pp. 38–51 and 21–37.

9 Music at James II's and James III's courts is discussed by Edward Corp, 'The Court as a centre of Italian music', in Edward Corp and others, *A court in exile: The Stuarts in France 1689–1718* (Cambridge, 2004), pp. 234–56. See also his 'Music at the Stuart Court at Urbino 1717–1718', *MLet*, 81/3 (August 2000): 351–63. For Jacobite readings of *Adeste Fideles* see Bennett Zon, 'Plainchant in the eighteenth-century English Catholic Church', *RH*, 21/3 (May 1993): 373.

10 P. Renold (ed.), *The Wisbech Stirs 1595–1598*, CRS, 51 (1958). Raymond Stanfield (comp.), 'The Archpriest Controversy', in *Miscellanea XII*. CRS 22 (1921): 132–87. John Warner, *The history of the English persecution of Catholics and the Presbyterian plot*, CRS, 47& 48 (1953 & 1955), ed. T.A. Birrell, trans. John Bligh.

facto control over clerical appointments to their households. The result was that, up till the appointment of four Vicars Apostolic in 1688, there was no effective form of episcopal control; and even after that date the influence bishops could exert over religious orders was very limited.

Despite such problems, the system of dual control and training ensured that an otherwise highly circumscribed clergy kept in touch with the international Catholic scene on the Continent. In addition, the foundation overseas of nunneries and schools such as the Jesuit-run St Omers College (which had a formidable musical tradition) coupled with the social effects of the Grand Tour, produced the same effects for the Catholic gentry and some women.[11] Nevertheless, musically speaking, in the early to mid-eighteenth century the effect was to create a divide between a sophisticated Continental culture and, except in the London Catholic embassy chapels, a simpler, more rudimentary scene in England, especially for those of lower social status who could not travel.

The effects of disconnection and disinheritance were long lasting. For example, in the nineteenth century they surface in the text of Bishop Ambrose Burton's hymn 'Lover of Christ's Immortal Bride'. This is a summary of events from the conversion of Anglo-Saxon England up to his own lifetime.[12] The desire to reconnect with the Medieval past is also exemplified by the 'Downside Movement' for the reform of the English Benedictine Congregation (EBC) in the 1880s and 1890s.[13] Meanwhile, disinheritance fuelled a determination to recover losses and dethrone the Anglican Church as the dominant denomination through conversions, as verses from the hymn 'Faith of Our Fathers' illustrate.

> Faith of Our Fathers! Mary's prayers
> Shall win our country back to thee;
> And through the truth that comes from God
> England shall then indeed be free.

Note though that the hymn, especially the opening lines quoted at the start of this chapter, also contains reminders of past persecutions. The didactic purpose then is defensive as well as offensive. Memories of persecution were a tool for confirming Catholics in their faith and in reinforcing their sense as a separate beleaguered community.

The period of emancipation 1778–1829

In 1778, however, a new phase opened with the first Catholic Relief Act (18 George III Cap. 60), allowing Catholics a limited freedom of worship, the ability to establish schools and the right to convey property. In addition, by requiring Catholics to pray

---

11   Thomas Muir, *Stonyhurst* (Cirencester, 1992/R2006), chs. 1, 2 and 3. For musical details see pp. 37–8. [Kathleeen Corrigan,] *In a great tradition: The life of Dame Laurentia McLachlan by the Benedictines of Stanbrook* (New York/London, 1956), pp. 3–33.

12   *WH*, no. 249.

13   Aidan Bellenger, 'The English Benedictines: the search for a monastic identity', in Judith Loades (ed.), *Monastic studies: The continuity of tradition* (Bangor, 1990) pp. 299–321.

for the monarch at Mass, it signalled the end of their ties with the Jacobite cause. Musically, this resulted in the composition of several settings of the *Domine Salvum Fac* text during the course of the next century.[14] In 1791 a second Relief Act (31 George III Cap. 33) allowed Catholics to build chapels (provided they did not have a steeple) and admitted them to the professions. Restrictions on the size of chapels, however, placed limitations on the scope available for liturgical music. Finally, after much negotiation, complete freedom of worship was granted by the Catholic Emancipation Act of 1829 (10 George IV Cap. 7).[15]

During this period there were three major developments. First, between 1773 and 1815 the Society of Jesus was suppressed, resulting in a temporary weakening of their administrative system. However, despite this, in the guise of 'The Gentlemen of Liège' and 'The Gentlemen of Stonyhurst' the English Province continued to operate in disguised form, enabling them to engage in substantial musical activity at Stonyhurst from 1811 onwards.[16] Second, the French Revolutionary Wars, temporarily at least, curtailed the international dimension of English Catholicism. Yet, at the same time, the arrival of thousands of exiled French Catholic clergy gave a temporary boost to English Catholicism, especially since it underlined the point that Catholics and other Englishmen had a common cause against the French Revolutionary government.[17] As far as the Catholic aristocracy were concerned, wartime restrictions did not prevent them from maintaining close connections with the colleges and seminaries where so many were educated. This was because, in most cases, such institutions were driven to take permanent refuge in England.[18] Moreover, if it proved harder to travel abroad, they could continue to pay periodic visits to London. As a result, in terms of music, the wars enhanced the effects of cross-fertilisation between embassy chapels in London, gentry household centres, and the big seminaries and colleges, especially Stonyhurst and Ushaw. For instance, publications by Samuel Webbe the Elder and Vincent Novello, who worked at the Sardinian and Portuguese embassy chapels respectively, can be found at Ushaw, Stonyhurst and the Constable-Maxwell

---

14 B.C. Foley, *Some other people of the penal times: Aspects of a unique social and religious phenomenon* (Lancaster, 1991), Appendix 16 ('Directions from the Vicars Apostolic following the First Catholic Relief Act'), p. 185.

15 Edward Norman, *The English Catholic Church in the nineteenth century* (Oxford, 1984) ,pp. 35, 63–6. The 1829 Catholic Emancipation Act though prohibited religious orders from taking new recruits. However this prohibition was never enforced.

16 The Society was formally restored by the Papacy in 1815; but this was not formally recognised in England by the Vicars Apostolic till 1829. Muir, *Stonyhurst*, pp. 94–7. For their early musical activities at Stonyhurst see Muir, 'Music for St Peter's Church 1811–1940, *SM*, 52 (2002): 279–82.

17 Aidan Bellenger, *The French exiled clergy in the British Isles after 1789: A historical introduction and working list* (Bath, 1986).

18 For instance, members of the seminary at Douai settled at Ushaw, nr Durham and St Edmund's, Ware; the Jesuit school and seminary from Liège (before that the school had been at St Omer and Bruges) came to Stonyhurst; Benedictines from Dieulouard and Douai settled at Ampleforth and Downside; while those from Paris moved to the old Benedictine premises at Douai. This community finally left for Woolhampton, nr Reading – but retained the name of Douai – in 1903.

household chapel at Everingham, in East Yorkshire.[19] The male members of the Constable-Maxwell family all went to Stonyhurst. Novello's collection of *Twelve Easy Masses calculated for small choirs*, copies of which survive at Stonyhurst and Ushaw, is dedicated to James Everard, Lord Arundell of Wardour Castle; and he, an ex-pupil of Stonyhurst, left his entire library to the College in 1837.[20] Similarly the sole surviving manuscript of one of Thomas Arne's two masses, which we know from the Mawhood Diary were performed at the Sardinian and Bavarian Embassy chapels, surfaced at Thomas Weld's chapel at Lulworth in Dorset; and it was Thomas Weld who was responsible for bringing the Jesuits to Stonyhurst.[21]

Third, the negotiations for emancipation exposed divisions between the Cisalpine and Ultramontane wings of the English Catholic community. The Cisalpine Club, formed in 1792, while including some clergy amongst its supporters, by and large represented the interests of the Catholic aristocracy. Like some secular priests in the seventeenth century they believed that the best way to achieve freedom of worship was to negotiate an oath of allegiance to the state coupled with limitations on Papal authority over English Catholics. Moreover, as shall be seen in chapter 2, in their concern to show the compatibility between Catholicism and English society, some were prepared to experiment with vernacular elements in the liturgy. Ultramontanes, who emphasised Papal supremacy and the way it underwrote clerical authority, would have none of this. The passage of the Catholic Emancipation Act without such limitations (other than the denial of any Papal power to depose the government or claim any form of temporal or civil jurisdiction) therefore marked a shift in the balance of power away from the gentry to the clergy. Partly this was due to an alliance between John Milner, Vicar Apostolic of the Midland District, and the Irish Catholic leadership; but it was also because during the eighteenth century, and especially after the passage of the Catholic Relief Acts, the Catholic population in towns steadily grew. By definition, the new missions that were being established in the towns were less likely to be amenable to control by a rural Catholic aristocracy. Moreover, the senior clergy were successful in defeating any nascent attempts by prominent laity,

---

19 See the contents of the *Bar Convent* ('Everingham' table), *Stonyhurst* and *Ushaw* databases in Muir, *Full in the Panting Heart of Rome*. For a late example, see the copy of *Plainchant for the chief Masses and Vespers... compiled for the use of W-D-R Chapel* (London, J.P. Coghlan, 1787) now held at Douai, which is signed 'J. Crookall, Wardour Castle, April 9th, 1856'. Given that Crookall directed all the music at the seminary of St Edmunds, Ware, this shows a direct connection between that institution, a gentleman's household and the London ex-embassy chapel scene with which Coghlan, who was a subscriber to Samuel Webbe the elder's *A Collections of Motets and Antiphons* (London, 1785), had been intimately connected.

20 *Twelve Easy Masses calculated for small choirs* (London, 1816).

21 John P. Rowntree, 'Lulworth Chapel and a missing Arne Mass', *MT*, 128 (1987): 347–9. E.E. Reynolds (ed.), *The Mawhood Diary 1724–1797.* CRS (1956): 34, 36, 46 for performances of Arne's Mass in 1770, 1771 and 1773. Muir, *Stonyhurst* pp. 80, 90–1 for gifts and sales to the College by the Weld family. For further details of the musical connections see Muir, 'Music for St Peter's Church': 280–81.

in the manner of Nonconformist churches, to exert effective control over priestly appointments and religious policy in these new congregations.[22]

A period of growth 1829–1914

The full effects of these developments though only became apparent after Emancipation. The basic theme is one of expansion; not just of numbers, which rose from 252,783 to 1,793,038 between 1851 and 1913, but in bread-and-butter operations to create a national infrastructure of churches, schools, guilds and other supporting confraternities.[23] (See Table 1.1).

Such progress was recognised at the highest level. In 1850 the Papacy restored the Episcopal hierarchy in England; and in 1908, under the decree *Sapienti Consilio*, Britain ceased to be a missionary territory.

Table 1.1   Numbers of Catholic clergy and churches, 1850–1900*

Date	No. of priests	No. of churches
1850	788	587
1870	1,528	1,152
1900	2,812	1,529

*   Norman, citing data from issues of the *Catholic Directory*, pp. 205–206. For data of the financial costs see pp. 78–81; for education see pp. 181–3.

Of particular significance was the arrival of the Irish. For example, at the mission of St Cuthbert, Durham they caused a tripling of the Catholic congregation in under twenty years (see Table 1.2).

Table 1.2   The Catholic congregation at St Cuthbert, Durham*

Year	Easter communions	Estimated population
1848	411	1,220
1852	526	1,307
1855	675	1,460
1861	1,100	2,425

*   J.M. Tweedy, *Popish Elvet: The History of St Cuthbert's, Durham* (Durham,n.d.) Part 1, pp. 126, 128 and 132–5.

---

22 Bossy, pp. 282–6 (Catholic population in the eighteenth century), pp. 322–30 (the decline of the Catholic gentry), pp. 330–37 (the role of the Catholic gentry and clergy in the emancipation negotiations). Norman, pp. 45–64.

23 1851: National Religious Census. 1913: *Catholic Directory*. Norman (pp. 203–6) reckons though that the first figure is a gross underestimate, as it is based on Mass attendances on a single day in March that year. According to him 700,000 would be nearer the mark.

The result was that the existing shift in the centre of gravity towards the towns was reinforced; and the musical evidence reflects this. In effect, major urban churches gradually superseded rural aristocratic chapels as centres of music, whilst in London itself the former embassy chapels were increasingly challenged by centres such as the Church of the Immaculate Conception, Farm Street or the Brompton Oratory.[24] Simultaneously there was a substantial increase in the quantity of published music, thanks to the transition from engraving to lithography and improved musical type (see Figure 1.1). For example, at Ushaw 20 publications survive from the period 1801–1849, as opposed to 263 from 1850–1900.[25] As a result Catholic music came to be dominated by large publishing companies based in London, such as Boosey and Co, Thomas Richardson and son, Burns, Lambert and Oates, Cary and Co, and J.A. Novello and its successors. This meant that some embassy chapel music, far from being neglected, was exported throughout the English Catholic world during the nineteenth century. For example, the collection of music from St Cuthbert's church, Durham contains works by Samuel Webbe the elder, Joachim De Natividad, Peter Von Winter, John Danby, Stephen Paxton, Henry Nixon, Joseph Haydn, Wolfgang Mozart and many other composers associated with the London embassy chapel tradition. The presence of works by Luigi Cherubini and Carl Maria von Weber shows how extensions from this Classical style were being picked up here too. In a different fashion, the fortunes of Vincent Novello's own editions confirm the changing picture. His first publication, *A Collection of Sacred Music* (1811), states directly that this was music performed at the Portuguese Embassy Chapel, where Novello worked; and the subscription list includes names from the Catholic aristocratic families, as well as Jesuits working at Stonyhurst.[26] This, then, was the market aimed at in these and subsequent publications. However, under the management of his son, Joseph Alfred Novello, many of these publications appeared as new editions, notably in the *Cheap Musical Classics* series inaugurated in 1849. Examples include *The Celebrated Arrangement of Haydn's Masses* and *The Celebrated Arrangement of Mozart's Masses*, as well as Vincent Novello's editions (with full keyboard realisations) of Webbe's *A Collection of Sacred Music* and *A Collection of Motets and Antiphons*, which originally had been published in 1785 and 1791 respectively. As the series title suggests, the emphasis was on cheap mass production, showing that urban Catholic choirs and the Choral Society movement were the principal commercial targets.

At the same time music from the major Seminaries exerted a major influence on the new urban churches. St Mary's, Oscott, for instance, was a major proponent of plainchant and Renaissance polyphony. The classic example is Charles Newsham's edition of *A Collection of Music suitable for the rite of Benediction*, published in the mid-nineteenth century by Burns, Lambert and Oates. Newsham was President at Ushaw College, so not only does his collection contain his own works, but also

---

24 The passage of Catholic relief acts reduced the need for chapels attached to the embassies of Catholic powers, and they were gradually replaced by regular missions. For further details, see chapter 4.

25 Two other items cannot be given more than a general nineteenth-century attribution.

26 Vincent Novello (ed.), *A Collection of Sacred Music* (London, 1811).

AT THE REDUCED PRICES.

Selections from the Catalogue of SACRED MUSIC with LATIN WORDS, Published by J. ALFRED NOVELLO.

The Orchestral and Vocal Parts are published to those Works marked with an *, and the Vocal Parts only to those marked with a †. A Catalogue of the prices may be had separately.

LARGE HYMNS, PSALMS, MOTETTS, ORATORIOS WITH FOREIGN WORDS, &c.

*Buhler, Jesu Dulcis memoria, a Motett in full score for four voices, violins, flutes, clarinets, horns, double bass, with accompaniment for organ or pianoforte by V. Novello ... 2 0

†Beethoven, The Music (in full score) performed at Beethoven's Funeral Consisting of Beethoven's "Miserere mei," and Seyfried's "Libera me Domine." ... 2 0

*Hummel, Quod quod in orbe, four voices ... 1 6

*Haydn, Insanæ et vanæ, four voices ... 1 6

†— Passione, or seven last words, arranged with an accompaniment for organ or pianoforte by V. Novello ... 8 0

Each movement may be had separate.

Separate movements—

No. 1. Pater dimitte illis, and Padre celeste	1	6
2. Amen dico tibi, and Tu di gratia	1	6
3. Mulier ecce filius, and Virgin Madre	1	6
4. Eli, Eli, and Perchè m'hai	1	8
5. Gesu esclama, ...	1	8
6. Consummatum est ...	1	8
7. Pater in manus tuas, and Nel tua man	2	0

— Ne pulvis et cinis superbe, for four voices, with organ or pianoforte accompaniment by V. Novello ... 9 0

Separate movements—

O quam tristis, A. solo	0	6
Quis non posset, S. solo	0	6
Pro peccatis, B. solo	0	6
Vidit suum, T. solo	0	9
Sancta Mater, Duet S.T.	0	9
Fac me vere, A. solo	0	6
Flammis ored, B. solo	0	6
Fac me cruce, T. solo; and Paradisi Gloria, Fugue, 4 voices.	1	9

Haydn's Te Deum for four voices, with organ accompaniment by M. Conran ... 5 0

*Mozart, Litany, in B flat, for four voices with accompaniment for organ or pianoforte by V. Novello ... 5 0

Separate movements—

Panis virus, S. Solo	0	6
Panis Omnipotentis, T. Solo	0	6
Pignus Futuræ, Choral Fugue	0	9
Agnus Dei, S. Solo		

*Mozart, Beatus Vir, a psalm for four voices, Vespero Intero, in full score for the Vespero, two violins, violoncello, and double bass, with accomp. for organ or P.F. ... 2 0

Quis te comprehendat, a chorus in full score for four voices, violins, viola horns, organ, and double bass, with accomp. for organ or pianoforte ... 2 0

Sancta Maria, in full score for four voices, violins, viola, and double bass, with accomp. for organ or pianoforte ... 1 6

*— Splendente te Deus, for four voices, with accomp. for organ or pianoforte ... 2 0

*— Amavit eum Dominus, in full score for four voices, violins, and bass, with an accomp. for organ or piano-forte ... 2 0

*— Sancte et justi, an offertorium, in full score for four voices, violins, and bass, with accomp. for organ or pianoforte ... 2 0

*— Deus tibi Laus et honor, for four voices, with accomp. for organ or P.F. ... 2 6

*— Alma Dei creatoris, an offertorium in full score for four voices, violins and bass, with accomp. for organ or P.F. ... 2 0

*Mendelssohn, Ave Maria (in full score), for 8 v., 2 clarinets, 2 bassoons, and double bass, with accompaniment for organ ... 2 6

Ravalli, Stabat Mater, for soprano, tenore, e basso (dedicated to Dr. Wiseman) ... 7 6

*Rossini, Stabat Mater, for s.s.a.t.b., with accompaniment for pianoforte ... 10

Each movement may be had separate.

No. 1. Stabat Mater, coro	1	6
2. Cujus animam, T. solo	1	0
3. Quis est homo, Duet S.S.	1	0
4. Pro peccatis, B. solo	1	0
5. Eia Mater, B. recit and coro, without accompaniment	1	0
6. Sancta Mater, S.S.T.B.	0	9
7. Fac ut portem, A. solo	0	9
8. Inflammatus, S. solo and coro	1	6
9. Quando corpus, S.S.T.B., without accompaniment	1	0
10. In sempiterna sæcula, coro	1	9

*Romberg, Te Deum, four voices, with accompaniment for organ or pianoforte ... 2 6

Separate movements—

Te ergo quæsumus, S.A.T.B.	0	9
Quem admodum, fugue	0	9

TANTUM ERGO.

186	Bach, J.S., (quartett) Sacred Music, vol. 2	0	6
182	Cherubini, quintett (s.s.a.t.b.) Evening Service, book 8	0	6
	De Angioli, (n. solo and chorus)	0	6
32	Evans, (a. solo and quartett) Motetts, bk. 5	0	6
62	Gluck, (quartett and chos.) Motett, bk. 10	0	6
	Guttenberg, (s. solo and chorus) with violin or flute obligato	3	0
36	Handel, (t. solo and Quartett) Motetta, book 6	0	6
	Le Jeune, A. Jun. (4 voices)	0	9
33	Leal Moreira, (quartett and chorus) Motetta, book 5	0	6
	Mozart, quintett (s.s.a.t.b.) Convent Music	0	6
	Novello, in D Minor (Convent Music)	0	6
56	— (s. solo and cora fugato) Motetta, book 9	0	9
124	— (t. solo and chorus) Sacred Music, volume 2	0	6
98	— (s.s. and chorus) Evening Service, book 10	0	6
37	— Quartett in E minor, and quartett in E major	0	6
119	Novello, Quintett (s.a.t.b.) Sacred Music, volume 1	1	9
	— Tantum in E flat, quartett—Tantum in D, quartett (Vienna)—Tantum, s. solo and quartett (Righini)—s. solo and quartett (Vogler)	1	0
	Panzi, S. (s. solo and chorus)	0	9
	Ricci, four voices, with Domine, by V. Novello	1	0
68	Spohr, (quartett) Motetts, book 11	2	0
268	Winter, (quartett) Evening Service, bk. 5	0	6
		0	3

LONDON SACRED MUSIC WAREHOUSE, 69, DEAN STREET, SOHO, & 24, POULTRY; ALSO IN NEW YORK, AT 389, BROADWAY.

(ORDER NOVELLO'S EDITIONS.)

Figure 1.1   The growth in the Catholic music market. Select list of works advertised on the back of J. Alfred Novello's publication of Samuel Webbe the elder's *Mass in D* arranged and edited by Vincent Novello, and published c. 1850, as Vol. 50 of the *Cheap Musical Classics* (this particular list is curious because of the paucity of liturgical, especially Mass, settings).

those by other Ushaw luminaries such as Charles Youens, and Richard and Robert Gillow. In addition there are compositions by John Crookall, who worked at St Edmund's College, Ware. Newsham's publication was revised by John Richardson, who added many of his own compositions. Richardson was organist at Liverpool Pro-Cathedral. So the revised edition demonstrates how works from this seminary tradition were penetrating the new urban churches.[27] The same point surfaces in the important publication series of Masses, motets and antiphons known as *The Choir: A Collection of Sacred Music for Churches, Church Societies and Families*. This was also edited by John Richardson. It includes works by Crookall and Richardson himself, as well as a limited number of items in the Renaissance polyphonic style.[28]

Such stylistic competition was symptomatic of wider tensions exposed by this growth. Culturally, these were expressed by the divide between 'Ancient' and 'Modern' genres, and not just in music. 'Ancients' favoured Gothic and Renaissance architecture, whereas 'Moderns' employed the current utilitarian Classical idiom. Their musical equivalents were protagonists for plainchant and a revival of Renaissance polyphony, as opposed to practitioners of the Classical Viennese style and its successors. Thus, it is significant that Augustus Welby Pugin, the leading 'Gothic' protagonist in architecture and interior design, wrote the pamphlet *An Earnest Plea for the Revival of the Ancient Plain Song*.[29] Likewise in liturgy, as shall be seen, some wanted a full Latin rite, whilst others were prepared to import vernacular elements. In short, 'Ancient' styles appealed to those seeking connections with the imagined religious certainties of the past. They also coalesced around the Victorian Romantic interest in things Medieval; and they reacted against the massive changes unleashed by the Industrial Revolution and the onset of Liberal ideas. 'Moderns', by contrast, sought to adapt precisely these forces for religious purposes. The 'Ancient-Modern' divide was therefore one aspect of the difference between two strategic approaches: namely, a defensive siege mentality cocooning Catholics from pernicious secular and Protestant influences, versus a more open policy, made feasible by Catholic Emancipation, of outreach towards potential converts.

In the event Irish immigration pushed Catholics in a defensive direction. The principal concern was 'wastage'. For example, the 1851 census showed that there were 519,919 people of Irish birth in England and Wales as against 252,783 Catholics.[30] No one stopped to consider how many Irish might have been Protestants from Ulster; Irish were Catholics who had to be 'rescued' from the perils of heresy and secular indifference. Hence the drive to establish new missions, schools, confraternities and guilds, in effect providing a spiritual service 'from the cradle to the grave'. Consider, for example, the implications of the following hymn.

---

27 Thomas Muir, 'Charles Newsham, Henri Hemy, John Richardson and the rise of Benediction music in nineteenth-century Catholic England', *NCH*, 47 (2006): 10–22.

28 Both volumes were published by Burns, Lambert and Oates.

29 London, 1850.

30 Norman, p. 205.

I am a faithful Catholic,
I love my holy Faith,
I will be true to Holy Church,
and steadfast unto death.

I shun the haunts of those who seek
to ensnare poor Catholic youth:
No Church I own, no schools I know
but those that teach the truth.[31]

Such separatism was further reinforced by continued, though diminishing, outbursts of 'No Popery' throughout the century, notably in connection with the Restoration of the Hierarchy and the 1908 Eucharistic Congress at Westminster. The concomitant hardening of attitudes is also illustrated by the increasingly hostile stance taken by the Hierarchy against 'mixed' marriages between Catholics and non-Catholics.[32]

Yet, it is precisely at such points that there is some ambivalence. For example, 'I am a faithful Catholic' was set by Henri Hemy to the melody for 'Ein machchen oder weibchen wünocht Papageno sich' – Papageno's theme in Mozart's opera *The Magic Flute*. Here, a relatively modern secular tune was applied to an inward-looking religious text. 'Faith of our fathers' shows the same ambivalence in another way. Not only was it set to what Hemy called a 'Swiss Air', it was sung at public parades designed to demonstrate Catholic unity *and* advertise the faith. Another musical response to 'No Popery' agitation is equally revealing. Numerous settings of *Domine Salvum Fac*, the prayer for the monarch instituted at Mass after the 1778 Relief Act, show that Catholics were desperate to assert their national loyalty.[33]

Inward- and outward-looking strategies were therefore by no means incompatible; they could be complementary. After all, conversion must be followed by confirmation in the faith. The Romantic appeal of the past implied that a backward-looking approach could have popular resonance, especially among High Church Anglican converts such as Faber. Gothic or Renaissance architecture in a Classical cityscape was, by definition, distinctive. It openly proclaimed that here was an alternative to secular values. In any case their interior layout often reveals compromises between authenticity and practical requirements. A Puginesque church with rood screens and a long chancel, such as St Giles, Cheadle (opened in 1846), did not meet the needs of teeming Irish congregations; big open spaces with a clear view of the altar were required. St Walbuge's, Preston, opened in 1854, is an extreme example. Its double hammer beam roof allows side aisles to be dispensed with, and there is an apse

---

31 Henri Hemy (ed.), *Crown of Jesus Music* (London and Dublin, 1863), no. 63.

32 Paul Van Arx, 'Ultramontanism and the Catholic Church in British politics', *RH*, 19/3 (May 1989): 322–47. Thomas Harwood, 'Public Opinion and the 1908 Eucharistic Congress', *RH*, 25/1 (May 2000): 120–33. Peter Doyle, 'Family and Marriage' and Sheridan Gilley, 'The Years of Equipoise 1892–1953', in Vivian A. McClelland and Michael Hodgetts (eds), *From without the Flaminian Gate: 150 Years of Catholic History in England and Wales 1850–2000* (London: Darton, Longman and Todd, 1999), pp. 39–40 and 195–6.

33 For example, 12 and 21 such settings survive in collections from St Cuthbert's, Durham and Everingham, East Yorkshire respectively.

instead of a chancel. In such churches the choir remained in a 'west gallery' at the back of the nave, giving them a semi-independent status. This helps explain why, despite ecclesiastical pressure, Classical-Viennese Masses often remained the norm up till the end of the century.

Similar ambivalence surrounds plainchant and Renaissance polyphony. As shall be seen later, plainchant did not just appeal to the Romantic Medievalist; some aspired to its rendition by congregations. Moreover, methods of performance, including diatonic note-for-note harmonisations brought it into closer affinity with later styles. Many composers, for example Joseph Seymour and Terry, used it as a starting point for new compositions. Here, they were being both 'Ancient' and 'Modern'. This was because such practices were not new; they had been employed in Medieval and Renaissance times. The only difference was that the plainchant was being planted within a 'modern' nineteenth-century idiom. Similarly, as William Sewell's works illustrate, there evolved a hybrid style where current chromatic harmony was used within an idiom owing more to Renaissance than Classical-Viennese genres.

Nowhere is the symbiosis between inward and outward mentalities more apparent than in the phenomenal growth of monasticism. For example, between 1800 and 1917 the number of women's orders working in England and Wales rose from 9 to 161. Many came from the Continent, thereby temporarily accentuating the alien element within English Catholicism. However, Table 1.3 shows that they were predominantly 'active' rather than 'contemplative', given that they served the needs of urban missions, providing schools, hospitals and other religious social services.[34] In one sense, then, the object was defensive, given the perceived need to 'rescue' Catholics. On the other hand they had to engage with the local community. *The Notre Dame Hymn Book* is symptomatic. As shall be seen, its crude application of popular style tunes and accompaniments to simple – and often rather sentimental – religious texts was an appeal to the perceived tastes of urban Catholic schoolgirls.[35]

Table 1.3   The balance between 'active' and 'contemplative' women's orders, 1857–1917*

Date	'Active' houses	'Mixed' houses	'Contemplative' houses	No data	Total no. of houses
1857	65	18	14	3	100
1917	605	149	45	1	800

*   Walsh, p. 177.

The behaviour of 'Contemplatives' is in complete contrast. For example, in Recusant times the EBC had been organised on centralised Jesuit lines to serve the practical needs of missions. However, after Emancipation pressure grew for the adoption of a more communal life. In the end supporters of this 'Downside

34 Barbara Walsh, *Roman Catholic nuns in England and Wales. 1800–1937. A social history* (Dublin and Portland, OR, 2002), Appendix II, Table 2 pp. 170–71.

35 See chapter 7.

Movement' got their way. As a result of the Apostolic Letter *Religiosus Ordo* (1890) and the Bull *Diu Quidem* (1899) priories, hitherto subject to an elected President and Regimen, or council, became virtually autonomous abbeys and the Benedictine missions were shared out between them. Henceforth the accent shifted from a relatively solitary existence on the mission to a fully coenobitic life centred round the Office. By definition, such a life is inward-looking. Moreover, it is significant that most Benedictine abbeys were located in the countryside. In this context plainchant acquired a new significance, and the style adopted was that purveyed by Solesmes. Abbot Prosper Guéranger, its founder, consciously rejected the French Revolution and the liberal nationalistic values associated with it. Instead, he sought to reconnect with the Medieval antecedents of the *ancien régime*. Plainchant was part of a liturgical regime designed to make this a living monastic reality.[36] The 'Downside Movement' attempted the same thing, but the gap to be bridged was far wider, since it reached back to the English monastic world that had been virtually obliterated by the Reformation. It is no accident then, to find English Benedictine monks, such as Cardinal Francis Gasquet, in the forefront of monastic historical research at this time.

This tilt in an inward-looking direction can be found in many parts of the English Catholic church. It is literally visible in architecture, as the data in Table 1.4 shows. Moreover, it is closely bound up with the association made between Ultramontanism and episcopal authority. For a start the Ultramontane stress on Papal supremacy, buttressed by the definition of Papal Infallibility at the First Vatican Council (1870), appealed to those wanting certainty within a clearly defined chain of command. This was not simply a matter of dogma, based on the historical concept of an Apostolic Succession. There were practical considerations. If, to prevent 'wastage', an urban infrastructure was needed, then scarce financial and clerical resources had to be deployed with great care. In Recusant times many of these had been tied up under gentry control in the countryside. Now some aristocrats, notably the Earl of Shrewsbury, gave generously to new missions; but many other missions depended heavily on contributions from the urban poor. Moreover the gentry, naturally enough, wanted to retain 'their' chaplains, not just in household chapels, but in other establishments built on their estates. This, then, was the case for strong episcopal control, especially as regards the deployment of clergy across their dioceses. The issue was further exacerbated by the debilitating effects of continuing squabbles between secular priests and independently minded regulars. These were not finally settled to the bishops' satisfaction until the promulgation of the bull *Romanos Pontifices* in 1883.

In such situations the ideological power of an appeal to Papal supremacy, underwriting episcopal authority, was strong. Little wonder that Nicholas Wiseman, Henry Manning and Herbert Vaughan – successive Cardinal Archbishops of

---

36 Katherine Bergeron, *Decadent enchantments: The revival of Gregorian chant at Solesmes* (Berkeley, Los Angeles, London), pp. 10–11.

Table 1.4   Catholic churches in London 1928, classified by architectural style[a]

Style	Number of churches
Genuine Medieval	1[b]
Gothic	39[c]
'Romanesque'[d]	8
'Transition style'[e]	1
'Italian or Roman style'	6
'Oriental type on Roman lines'	4[f]
'Byzantine'	1[g]
'Classical'	14
No category given	12

[a]   Material taken from Alexander Rottman, *London Catholic Churches: A Historical and Artistic Record* (London, 1928).
[b]   This is St Etheldreda, Ely Place, a medieval church restored to Roman Catholic worship in 1879. Rottman, pp. 142–52.
[c]   This does not include the church of the Sacred Heart, Wimbledon, which is omitted from the description.
[d]   This includes St Joseph, Highgate. However, the photograph suggests that Florence Cathedral may have been the inspiration. Rottman, pp. 216–17.
[e]   That is, between the Romanesque and Early Gothic styles: for example, St Francis of Assisi, Notting Hill. Rottman, pp. 118–23.
[f]   Described in Rotrman, p. xii.
[g]   That is, Westminster Cathedral. Rottman, p. xii.

Westminster – were fervent Ultramontanes.[37] Moreover, its psychological impact could be enhanced by the imposition of 'Roman' ways of doing things – in liturgy, through the institution of Italianate cults and devotions such as the Quarante D'Ore, and in music. In this way, the sense of difference between English Catholics and their compatriots would be reinforced. For instance, the Fourth Synod of Westminster, convened by Manning in 1873, asserted the primacy of plainchant and Renaissance polyphony. At that time both had 'Roman' connotations. Renaissance polyphony meant music by Palestrina or Victoria; plainchant meant the music found in the Ratisbon editions, which were based on the Medician Gradual of 1614–15 and supported by a Papal grant of monopoly. Later, in accordance with *Tra le Sollectudini*, official lists of approved church music were published, and these were followed up by an official list of authorised hymns in 1910.[38]

Thus, as the twentieth century opened, authoritarian, backward-looking and separatist attitudes appeared to predominate, at least at an official level. Yet, as has

37 Norman, pp. 110–57, 244–86, 345–63. James Pereiro, '"Truth before Peace": Manning and Infallibility', *RH: Henry Edward Manning (1808–1892)*, 21/2 (October 1992): 218–53. Note that bishops with full ordinary powers had a greater degree of independence from the Papacy than the Vicars Apostolic.
38 See chapters 7 and 12.

been seen, even within the conservative camp there was considerable ambivalence. Moreover, as Tables I.3 and I.4 have shown, in the nineteenth century nearly half the choral repertoire was composed after 1750, and British composers contributed more than any other national group. Thus, in practice – as opposed to theory – the musical evidence suggests that English Catholics were willing to adopt contemporary methods. In addition, except for campaigns to maintain Catholic education, the Catholic Church leadership in England was largely apolitical.

Such dichotomy seemed vindicated by continued growth in the ensuing decades. Between 1913 and 1963 numbers rose from 1,793,038 to 3,726,500, the supply of priests grew from 3,838 to 7,591, and the provision of churches increased from 1,797 to 7,591.[39] Moreover, at the same time other religious denominations experienced serious decline. In other words, 'wastage' was curtailed as numbers more than kept pace with the general growth of the national population. As a result Catholics became the largest single denomination in the country. For the first time since the Reformation they acquired a truly national spread. They were no longer concentrated in Lancashire, industrial centres across the north, parts of the Midlands and London. Nor were they largely confined to the proletarian Irish with a small elite of aristocratic families at the top. They could be found in the south and east, in the suburbs, and among the middle classes. This meant they were better educated, especially since the supply of talented converts – including musicians such as Terry and Edmund Rubbra (1901–1986) continued to flow.[40] Yet, in the long run, despite the defeat of Modernism in the 1890s and the hostility evinced by the hierarchy towards Communism and Socialism in the 1920s and 1930s, this meant that a questioning attitude among the laity was bound, sooner or later, to appear. That event occurred after the great changes unleashed by the Second Vatican Council (1962–63). Whether this would have happened without them, it is impossible to say. What, perhaps, is surprising is that it took so long to surface. Such official conservatism is reflected in music. Renaissance polyphony and plainchant retained the established status they had acquired by the 1900s. Indeed, the shift to Solesmes chant after 1904 imbued the style with inward-looking self-abnegating contemplative monastic values. Simultaneously, there seems to have been an ossification in the repertoire of many choirs. For example, the surviving collection Our Lady of Mount Carmel, Liverpool and an analysis of music programmes from St Dominic's, Newcastle show that in both cases the music acquired between 1890 and 1914 remained the basic staple in the 1920s and 1930s.[41] Worse still, during the 1950s there are numerous examples of publishers offering music in editions that had been laid down before 1914. Clearly, they believed that Catholic musicians were still willing to buy them. As a result a repertoire that was largely contemporary in 1914 had become symbolic of backward-looking attitudes by the early 1960s. This, in a nutshell, was

---

39 Sources: *Catholic Directory* (London, 1913), pp. 56 and 100, (1933), p. 580, (1963), p. 763. The figures do not include Wales.

40 Hastings, pp. 134–5, 275–8, 473–6, 561. Gilley, in McClelland and Hodgetts (eds), p. 40.

41 Thomas Muir, 'Sir Richard Terry and the music for St Dominic's Church, Newcastle: 1930–1939', *NCH*, 48 (2007).

the problem facing English Catholics as Vatican II opened. The unspoken balance between inward- and outward-looking viewpoints that had seemed appropriate in 1900 might no longer be relevant in a very different age.

Chapter 2

The Liturgical Framework

No study of Catholic church music can ignore liturgy. In theory, it provides the basic framework within which music is performed, and it supplies the text with which musicians have to work. In practice the relationship is more complex, and, at the outset, it must be recognised that the study of liturgical theory and theology as an academic discipline did not emerge till the late nineteenth century. This means that much liturgical thinking before that time is implicit rather than explicit in contemporary statements. Moreover, the development of liturgy as an academic discipline signified a change in its character and the sources of authority that underpinned it. This chapter, then, considers five aspects:

1. the liturgical structure and place of music in the principal services;
2. liturgical books;
3. the nature and function of liturgy;
4. the relationship between liturgy and music; and
5. patterns of liturgical change.

Music in liturgical and extra-liturgical services

In the Catholic Church there is a basic distinction between liturgical and extra-liturgical services, although this does not seem to have been formally recognised before the end of the nineteenth century. Liturgical services, such as the Mass or the Office, are public and official; theoretically, at least, the text is subject to tight control; frequently they are propitiatory or sacrificial in character; and, except with the Office, they are often sacramental. Extra-liturgical services are different, although some, such as Benediction and Corpus Christi, are derived from the Mass. They are not sacramental; for instance, at Benediction the host is adored but not received. They are more informal, with greater scope for adaptation of the text. Indoors, they tend to be private and devotional; outside, especially with processions, they promote solidarity and advertise the Catholic Church to the outside world. In various ways, then, greater efforts were made to involve the laity.[1]

Within the liturgy proper music has mainly been composed for the Mass and the Office. Nonetheless, with other services, such as the ceremonies surrounding the

---

1   The distinction between private and public prayer is made in Charles Borromeo (ed.), *The Catechism of the Council of Trent for Parish Priests*, Rockford, IL (1923/1982R), p. 498. For a general extension of this to liturgical and extra-liturgical services see Adrian Fortescue, 'Liturgy', in *The Catholic Encyclopaedia* (London, 1910), vol. 9, p. 306.

burial of the dead, consecration, confirmation, ordination and marriage, the musical element should not be forgotten.

The Mass came in various forms. These are listed in Table 2.1.

Table 2.1   Forms of the Mass[a]

Basic type (with variations)	Subcategories	Distinguishing features
Pontifical High Mass	At the throne At the footstool For the dead	A sung Mass offered by a bishop, assisted by Deacon and Subdeacon reading the lessons.
Solemn High Mass	Standard form In the presence of a prelate For the dead	This has the same features as a Pontifical High Mass but is offered by a Priest.
Low Mass	Standard form In the presence of a prelate For the dead	This is a Mass whose text is spoken by the celebrant without the assistance of a Deacon or Subdeacon.
Missa Cantata	Solemn form Simple form	This is a Low Mass offered without the assistance of a Deacon or Subdeacon with a sung Proper and Ordinary (defined below).
Missa Cum Cantu		This is a Low Mass spoken by the priest but with the choir singing the Ordinary while the priest utters the text. It does not appear in the rubrics for the Roman Missal.[b]
Conventual	High Mass	This is a Mass sung in the House of a Religious Order. Its form can vary according to the particular order (for example, Benedictine, Dominican or Cistercian). The distinction between High and Low Mass is basically the same as for that given above.
Private Mass		This is usually a Low Mass sung in a private chapel or household.

[a] Based on Adrian Fortescue, *The ceremonies of the Roman Rite described* (London, 1918) pp. 69–75, 82–148, 163–98.

[b] James D. Crichton, *As it was: reminiscences and prophecies* (Mildenhall, 1999), p. 31.

The sung parts of a High Mass or a Missa Cantata were as shown in Table 2.2. The sung parts of a Requiem Mass were a compound of elements from the Ordinary and Proper, as shown in Table 2.3.

It is important to recognise that Low Mass was the most popular form of Mass attended by English Catholics. Usually, however, this had no music; and this meant that only the minority who attended some form of sung Mass had any real

Table 2.2   Sung parts of the Mass[a]

Principal elements		Notes
The Ordinary		The sung parts of the Mass whose text remains unchanged from week to week. From the fifteenth century onwards, musically speaking, these were often composed as a single group to form a 'Mass'. Following this precedent similar groupings took place to form plainchant Masses.
	Kyrie	
	Gloria	
	Credo	
	Sanctus-Benedictus	
	Agnus Dei	
Other parts of the Ordinary that might be sung:		
	Responses at the start and conclusion	
	Responses at the Preface	
	Responses at the Epistle and Gospel	
	The *Asperges* (or *Vidi Aquam* in Lent)	
	The 'Great Amen' after the Canon	
	The *Pater Noster*	
The Proper		The sung parts of the Mass whose texts vary according to the day in the liturgical calendar. This comes in two forms: The Calendar of the Year (*Temporale*) and the Calendar of the Saints (*Sanctorale*). In addition, a motet could be sung after the Offertory antiphon and/or the *Benedictus*.[b]
	Introit	
	Gradual after the Epistle	
	Alleluia and verse after the Gradual.	
	Offertory antiphon	
	Communion antiphon	
In addition on certain feast days a Tract (or extract from a Psalm) might be substituted for a Gradual. On certain occasions a Sequence would follow the Alleluia and verse thus:		
	Victimae Paschali (Easter)	
	Veni Sancte Spiritus (Whitsun)	
	Lauda Sion (Corpus Christi)	
	Dies Irae (Requiem Masses)	
	Stabat Mater (Feast of the Seven Douleurs)[c]	

[a]   Richard Terry, *The Music of the Roman Rite* (London, 1931), pp. 127–45 (Offices and Mass), 145–56 (Holy Week), 157–86 occasional services – Terry describes them as Offices – requiring a Bishop.

[b]   *TLS*, clause 8.

[c]   The vast number of sequences known in the Middle Ages was reduced to four in the 1570 revision of the Missal. The *Stabat Mater* was added by Benedict XIV in the eighteenth century. William O'Shea, *The worship of the church: a companion to liturgical studies* (London, 1960R), p. 357.

Table 2.3   Principal sung elements in a Requiem Mass*

Item	Text
Introit	*Requiem Aeternam*
Kyrie	
Gradual	*Requiem Aeternam*
Sequence	*Dies Irae*
Tract	*Absolve Domine*
Offertory	*Domine Jesu Christe*
Sanctus- Benedictus	
Agnus Dei	
Communion	*Lux Aeterna*
Conclusion	*Libera Me Domine* followed by *Kyrie*

*   Alec Robertson, *Requiem: Music of Mourning and Consolation* (London, 1967), esp. pp. 8–24.

experience of Catholic music. Yet the regulations pertaining to music at Low Mass were a good deal more flexible than for High Mass, since they were dependent on rulings by the local bishop, rather than directives from Rome. Music here could even include vernacular texts. It is curious then to observe how little use was made of such opportunities.[2]

Traditionally, Office services occurred at three-hour intervals. However, the times were frequently adjusted to suit local convenience (Table 2.4).

Table 2.4   Office services

*Matins**	Sext (Midday Office)
Lauds	None
Prime	*Vespers*
Terce	Compline

*   Greater Hours are given in italics, Lesser Hours in normal type.

The key ingredients were readings from the scripture, a monastic rule or a martyrology, the singing of psalms, a canticle (the *Benedictus*, *Magnificat* and *Nunc Dimittis* at Lauds, Vespers and Compline respectively), a hymn, and prayers or petitions. Traditionally, most Psalm texts came from the Itala, rather than the Vulgate Bible.[3] Compline was usually concluded with Marian antiphons fixed according to the time in the liturgical calendar (see Table 2.5).

---

2   For a contemporary discussion of music permitted at Low Mass see P. Morrisroe, 'The character of music at Low Mass', *IER* 21(4th series) (1907): 201–202. The key point was that 'there is no general law of the Church that regulates the character of the music, or singing, that may be rendered during a Low Mass'.

3   Vilma Little, *The Sacrifice of Praise: An introduction to the meaning and use of the Divine Office* (London, 1957), p. 23.

Table 2.5   Marian antiphons

Period	Title of antiphon
First Sunday of Advent to the Feast of the Purification	*Alma Redemptoris Mater*
Feast of the Purification to Wednesday of Holy Week	*Ave Regina Coelorum*
Holy Saturday to Pentecost	*Regina Coeli Laetare*
Trinity Sunday to the First Sunday of Advent	*Salve Regina*

The celebration of Holy Week, especially the Triduum (Maundy Thursday, Good Friday and Holy Saturday) constituted the oldest part of the liturgy and was a major showcase, musically as well as liturgically, for the Catholic faith. These were a compound of Masses and Office services (see Table 2.6). Musically speaking, its centrepiece were the three services of Tenebrae, a combination of Matins and Lauds, held on the eve of their assigned day. Similar services were held on the eve of Christmas and Pentecost.

Table 2.6   The celebration of Holy Week

Day	Principal events
Palm Sunday	Procession of Palms Mass, including the *St Matthew Passion*
Monday of Holy Week	Usual Mass and Offices
Tuesday of Holy Week	Mass, including the *St Mark Passion*
	Usual Offices
Wednesday of Holy Week	Mass, including the *St Luke Passion*
	Usual Offices
	Maundy Thursday Tenebrae:
	Three nocturnes, each containing a reading from the Lamentations of Jeremiah and three Responsories
	Miserere Mei Deus
	Christus Factus Est
Maundy Thursday	Ceremony of the Washing of the Feet (Mandatum)
	Mass
	Good Friday Tenebrae on the same lines as Tenebrae for Maundy Thursday
Good Friday	Mass of the Presanctified, including the *St John Passion*, *Improperia* (Reproaches), and the Procession to the Cross (accompanied by the hymns *Pange Lingua* and *Crux Fidelis*)
Holy Saturday	Twelve Prophecies read interspersed with Tracts in the morning Tenebrae (on the same lines as above)

Non-liturgical services can be divided into outdoor processions, such as Corpus Christi, and indoor devotions, such as Stations of the Cross, the Forty Hours Devotion, Rosaries and, above all, Benediction. Musically speaking this consisted of the *O Salutaris*, a Litany (of the Saints, Loreto or the Virgin Mary), and the *Tantum Ergo*. Music for these texts was sometimes composed as a single 'Benediction Service'. In addition the *Adoremus in Aeternum* and motets, such as *Ave Verum*, might be sung. The whole was often introduced and concluded with a vernacular hymn. The *O Salutaris* and *Tantum Ergo* texts, it should be noted, derive from the Office of Corpus Christi.

In most parishes, on Sunday afternoons and evenings, there was a tendency to string together a sequence of extra-liturgical services, sometimes interlarded with Vespers and Compline. In such circumstances vernacular hymns, which were meant to be chosen according to themes in the liturgical calendar, were used to link the different services together.[4]

A curious survival from days when the vernacular could be used in the Office was the devotion known as 'Psalms'. Following the authorised version of the *Manual of Prayer* this consisted of two psalms in English, the canticle *Benedicite*, the *Benedictus* from St Luke's Gospel and prayers.[5]

Liturgical books

Superficially the liturgical book scene was complex and confused. There were various reasons for this. For a start, with most liturgical books there were at least three sets of variables:

1. The Roman rite, as opposed to the Ambrosian, Mozarabic and Gallican Rites, to say nothing of variations pertaining to separate religious orders (such as Benedictines, Cistercians, Dominicans and Franciscans). Within a rite there could be variations known as Uses, of which the Sarum Rite is the most famous in medieval England.[6] In addition, supplements with texts and music appropriate for feast days of saints and martyrs especially associated with particular religious congregations, regions or nations might be added.
2. Differences in the language of rubrics: Latin, English, French or other vernacular languages. This led to the publication of numerous sub-editions from the same basic publication.
3. Differences in musical notation. For instance, in the early twentieth century some plainchant books added the Solesmes rhythmical signs developed by

---

4   James D. Crichton, *As it was: Reminiscences and Prophecies* (Mildenhall: Decani Press, 1991), p. 46.

5   Ibid., pp. 43–4.

6   For a simple account of the emergence in the Middle Ages of different monastic liturgies see Lancelot C. Sheppard, *The Mass In The West* (London, 1962), pp. 61–7 (Carthusians), 67–81 (Cistercians), 81–5 (Premonstratensians), 85–90 (Carmelites) and 90–94 (Dominicans). Sarum Rite is covered on pp. 100–102. See also David Hiley, *Western Plainchant: A handbook* (Oxford, 1993), pp. 608–15.

Mocquereau; others, following the Vatican Typical editions, did not. In addition, mainly for the benefit of organists expected to improvise accompaniments at sight, as well as for schools, there were books with plainchant in modern notation.

Secondly, there were differences between Medieval and nineteenth-century liturgical books. Thus, books that in medieval times were essentially composite compilations, such as the Missal or the Breviary, became recognised as distinct volumes in their own right.[7] Moreover, due to the development of printing, the supply of books had been transformed. As Harper notes, there were few copies of books in the Middle Ages, so much reliance was placed on memory and rote learning. In such circumstances it was also sensible to issue each clerical official with a relevant specialist book. For instance, a Deacon would have a Lectionary, the principal cantor a Gradual (at Mass) or an Antiphoner (for the Office). The development of Private, and then Low Masses in the later Middle Ages, where the celebrant combined the functions of Priest, Deacon and Subdeacon, then led to the introduction of the Missal without music. Likewise, the need to recite the Office in private, encouraged by the emergence of mendicant orders, resulted in the introduction of the Breviary, again without music.[8] The printing press then facilitated the supply of multiple copies of all liturgical books, not solely to the clergy, but to the choir and eventually many members of the congregation. This meant that the books could be used in a different way.[9] Even so the sheer size of some books made it convenient to produce smaller volumes containing excerpts from the main collections.

Thirdly, up till the 1850s the full effects of printing were limited in England, especially as regards liturgical-musical books. In Recusant times it was difficult to operate a printing press, so most books were produced abroad. Moreover, even after Catholic Relief, it was hard to obtain moveable type suitable for plainchant neumes, despite valiant efforts by James Peter Coghlan in the 1790s. The result was a divide between English religious houses on the Continent, which had access to printed liturgical-musical books, and centres in England, where the supply was more restricted. Manuscript copying therefore remained an important activity. It even played a part on the Continent. For example, John Francis Wade (1711–86), the best known of the mid-eighteenth-century copyists, had connections with Douai, in France, and Bornhem, in the Austrian Netherlands. This was because, prior to technological improvements in the mid-nineteenth century, mass production of cheap copies was impossible.

The effects of such limitations were compounded by the dislocation caused by the French Revolution and Napoleonic Wars. Continental production collapsed and

---

7   The Missal is a combination of the texts from the Sacramentary and Lectionary. James O'Connell, *The Celebration of Mass: A study of the rubrics of the Roman Missal* (London, 1940), p. 6. The Breviary combines the Antiphoner with the other texts of the Office. Its twelfth-century origins are discussed in Little, *The Sacrifice of Praise*, pp. 20–22.

8   John Harper, *The Forms and Orders of Western Liturgy from the Fourth to the Eighteenth Century. A historical introduction and guide for students and musicians* (London, 1991), pp. 58–9. O'Shea, p. 469.

9   Harper, p. 64.

many English Continental communities lost some, or virtually all their liturgical books (sometimes only temporarily) during their hurried flight to England. This explains, for example, the rushed compilation of what is effectively a manuscript *Liber Usualis* by the English Benedictine nuns of Ghent, during their brief stay at Fernyhalgh, near Preston, in 1794–95.[10]

After the Napoleonic Wars, Continental production of liturgical books resumed. Even so, there seems to have been much confusion. Partly this was due to the multiplicity of different editions, but there were also shortages.[11] For example, Stonyhurst obtained a second-hand copy of J.P. Boursay's *Graduale Romanum*, originally published from Lyons in 1816, as late as 1858. Similarly, when Mount St Bernard Abbey, in Leicestershire, was founded in 1837, the Cistercians obtained, amongst other things, a thirteenth-century French Dominican Antiphoner, two copies of M. Nicolle's Cistercian Gradual of 1545, produced in Paris, and another Cistercian Gradual of 1696.[12] Manuscript interpolations show that they were used alongside other early-mid-nineteenth-century volumes, such as a *Processionale Cistercien* published by Merson of Paris in 1843 and still in use during the 1950s.[13] In addition their 1858 copy of an *Antiphonale Cisterciense*, published at Westmallen, Belgium, is in fact a second edition of an antiphoner produced in 1787.

However, from the mid-nineteenth century onwards, the situation was transformed. In 1843 the Mechlin Gradual, edited by Edmund Duval and printed by P.J. Hanicq, appeared. It was the first of a complete series of mass-produced liturgical-musical volumes to become available at affordable prices. Mass production produces standardisation. Moreover, the capital costs of editing and typesetting such mammoth undertakings impelled the Papacy to offer publishing monopolies. Papal support for the Medicean *Gradual* of 1614–15 and Pustet editions produced between 1868 and 1901 were classic examples of this. With the Vatican Typical editions of the early twentieth century the Papacy allowed other companies to publish equivalent volumes, provided that they kept exclusively to the Vatican text.[14]

Such trends were reinforced by the dominance of Latin and the promotion of the Roman liturgy. The Roman Breviary and Missal of 1568 and 1570 did not just reform the Medieval liturgy and prune the liturgical calendar; they were intended to be used uniformly across the whole Church. However, at that time the full effects of this were undermined by the permission given for dioceses and religious orders to retain their own liturgies, provided that they were more than 200 years old. The mid-nineteenth-century Ultramontane promotion of all things Roman largely put a stop to this, especially in France, where Prosper Guéranger, the founding abbot of Solesmes, was chiefly instrumental in persuading dioceses to abandon their Gallican

---

10 This is part of the Fernyhalgh collection in the Talbot Library, Preston. No catalogue number.

11 See Robert Hayburn, *Papal Legislation on Sacred Music 95AD to 1977AD* (Collegeville, MN, 1979), pp. 145–6 for a list of some of these.

12 No other publication data provided.

13 I owe this information to Fr Mark Hartley of Mount St Bernard Abbey.

14 'Sacerdos', ' Article IX – Plainchant', *DubR*, 1874 (2): 172–204. Hayburn, 151–67 (Pustet monopoly) and 251–71 (Vatican Typical editions).

liturgies. Thus, a liturgical book produced by, for example, Desclée in Belgium could be used in England, as the presence of numerous copies with French or Latin rubrics in different English collections attests.

The result was that, by the early twentieth century, beneath the surface clutter, there were basically four types of liturgical book:

1. Principal volumes, such as the Missal or Breviary, with texts only (see Table 2.7).
2. Principal volumes, such as Graduals or Antiphoners, with text and music (see Table 2.8).
3. Books, such as the Liber Usualis, that are composites of other basic volumes.
4. Smaller books consisting of excerpts from the larger basic compilation (see Table 2.9).

The most important example of a composite volume was the Liber Usualis, combining the Kyriale, Antiphoner and Gradual. In addition, throughout the nineteenth century several smaller and handier volumes with materials extracted from larger collections were produced, whilst for extra-liturgical services the principal official volume in England was the Ritus Servandus.

Table 2.7   Principal liturgical books with texts only[a]

Title	Purpose	Standardised versions available before 1914
Missal	The Mass	1570 rev. 1604, 1634, 1884
Breviary	The Office	1568 rev.1602, 1632, 1882, 1914
Ritual	Administration of other sacraments[b]	1614 rev. 1752
Pontifical	For services conducted by bishops	1595 rev. 1645, 1752, 1888
Martyrology	This is a calendar of saints and martyrs with short biographies intended to be read at the Office[c]	1584, rev. 1628, 1675, 1680, 1748, 1913
Ceremonial	Intended as a reference work for bishops	1600, rev. 1650, 1752, 1886

[a]   See also other less well known books from the Middle Ages e.g. The Ordo, giving directions for liturgical Offices, the Ordinal, giving a liturgical directory for each Diocese, Collegiate church or monastery, and the Sacramentary, giving the text of Propers used by the celebrant at Mass. Joseph Dyer in Stanley Sadie (ed.) *The New Grove Dictionary of Music and Musicians* (London, 2001), vol. 15, pp. 4–6.

[b]   From the late nineteenth century onwards this gradually replaced Bishop Challoner's *Ordo Administrandi Sacramenta*. James D. Crichton, '1920–1940: The Dawn of a Liturgical Movement', in James D. Crichton, Harold Winstone and John Ainslie, *English Catholic Worship* (London, 1979), p. 361.

[c]   Based on substantial work conducted under Benedict XIV in the eighteenth century. O'Shea, p. 56.

Table 2.8   Principal liturgical books with texts and music*

Volume	Purpose	Publication date of the official version in 1914
Gradual	Proper of the Mass	1907
Antiphoner	Antiphons for the Office	1913
Kyriale (often incorporated in the Gradual)	Ordinary of the Mass	1905

*   Reference might also be made to the *Directorum Chori*, defined by Laurentia McLachlan as a 'standard textbook for all the tones of the Mass and Office, such as Collects, Epistles, Gospels'. [Laurentia McLachlan], *Grammar of Plainsong in two parts by the Benedictines of Stanbrook Abbey* (London, Chicago, Cincinnati, New York, 1905), p. 79.

Table 2.9   Examples of books with materials extracted from larger collections[a]

Volume	Purpose
Lectionary: (1) for the Mass	Lessons
(2) for the Office	
Officium Majoris Hebdomadae[b]	Holy Week services
Hymnale	A collection of Latin hymns in plainchant usually organised according to the liturgical calendar for the Office
Responsory	A collection of Responsories organised according to the Liturgical calendar

[a]   Other examples are the Homiliary, containing excerpts from Church Fathers to be read at Matins; and the Benedictional, a collection of Blessings pronounced at Mass. Dyer, in *New Grove* (2001) 15: 4–6.
[b]   Italicised items contain substantial amounts of music as well as text.

Liturgy: its nature and usage

Liturgy does two things. First, it presents dogma and instructs, for example in the Creed. As such it is an instrument for conversion. Second, it is an act of worship. Looked at this way it constitutes a fundamental aspect of Catholic belief. It is something for the committed faithful. The Mass, for instance, is regarded as a means to salvation. At its heart lies the doctrine of transubstantiation, as a result of which Catholics believe that they receive the body and blood of Christ given for the remission of sin.[15] Transubstantiation also forms the basis of priestly power, since Catholics accept that this power has been granted through a chain of authority

---

15 Borromeo (ed.), *Catechism of the Council of Trent*, pp. 218, 226–8, 233–45, 253–9.

consisting of bishops, Popes, St Peter and, ultimately, Christ himself. Such authority underwrites not just claims of Papal primacy, but the Church's right to teach.[16]

Transubstantiation therefore illustrates the connection between instruction and worship. Indeed, the one is an essential preparation for the other. Moreover, instruction is something from which even the faithful can benefit. The concept appears, in peculiar form, in Guéranger's concept of the monastic Office. Guéranger took his cue from Romans, chapter 8, vv 14–15 and 26–27, where St Paul states that people can only speak God's word and pray properly when moved by the spirit. Guéranger held that God, through Christ, gave his word to Christ's bride – the Church. The word, as such, is a means of instruction *and* a form of grace. It is presented to people through the liturgy, especially the Office, and through that medium it is returned to God in an endless cycle of praise. Note, though, that in this scenario the Office is not just something performed by committed believers – monks – but that Guéranger's theology makes it an act of worship where conversion of the outsider plays little part.[17]

This shows that much depended on how the liturgy was used. In particular, there was a divide between the claims of public communal celebration and private devotion. In the late nineteenth century, following Guéranger, many regarded the Mass and Office as acts of public celebration, in contrast to extra-liturgical services where, as has already been suggested, the devotional aspect had greater scope. Yet, not only are there Private Masses, but the Office can be recited alone by individuals from the Breviary. Indeed, during Recusant times, the circumstances of 'hidden worship' made this inherently more likely. In such guises the Mass and the Office looked very like acts of personal devotion.

The key, then, was in the level of public participation. Viewed in this light it is obvious that some parts of the Mass were more conducive to it than others. Moreover, there were clear distinctions between the roles (spelt out by the rubrics) performed by officiating clergy, their colleagues and congregations. The first two were the most active and public participants. On the other hand the role of the congregation was more ambiguous. In theory, certain portions – for example, the Ordinary – were their preserve. Other parts, notably the Canon, when the act of transubstantiation takes place, could only be performed by the priest. At such points everyone else appeared to be little more than bystanders. Yet even here it was possible to argue that people could still participate by making the responses, through gestures – such as kneeling or making the sign of the cross, as witnesses, and through parallel reflections on the text, even if that meant little more than following a translation or paraphrase.

---

16 Daniel Rock, rev. W.H. James Weale, *Hierugia or the Holy Sacrifice of the Mass* (London, 1892R) pp. 246–9

17 Prosper Guéranger, trans. Laurence Shepherd, *The Liturgical Year* (Worcester, 1867/R1895) pp. 1–11. Dom Baudot, trans. The Benedictines of Stanbrook, *The Breviary: Its history and contents* London, Edinburgh, St Louis (USA), 1907/1929R), pp. 17, 76–7, 99–102 (here there is the idea that the Chanter is Christ's mouthpiece), 110 and 153 (where he states that 'The Holy Mass is the centre of the Daily Office'). See also Cuthbert Hedley's sermon, 'The monastic Office' delivered at the opening of the Choir of Downside Abbey in 1905, *Tablet*, 106 (July–December 1905): 492–4.

However, there can be little doubt that 'silent' participation of this sort could easily spill over into personal devotions that were only loosely connected with the public action. For example, *The Crown of Jesus* manual, in a section entitled 'Different modes of hearing Mass' states:

> Some read with devotion from their prayer book during the whole time, others recite their beads, others remain with their mind contemplating the sacred mysteries of the Passion of Jesus Christ.[18]

Hence the need to attract attention at the moment of consecration by ringing the Sanctus bell. Worse still, those parts of the service designated for the congregation were often delegated to specialists, such as the altar server or other attendant clergy, who recited the responses, or the choir, who took over the Proper and Ordinary. In the process the choir acquired a status mid-way between the officiating clergy and congregation. Indeed, *Tre Le Sollectudini* (*TLS*) even recognised it to have 'a real liturgical office'; and, like the clergy, it occupied a separately designated space, discouraging congregational participation still further.[19]

The result was the well-known propensity for Catholic congregations to use the Mass and other services as occasions for pursuing private devotions. This was not new. As Harper and others have shown, it was endemic in the Middle Ages, and, as shall be seen, in Recusant times the necessity for 'hidden worship' perpetuated old habits.[20] What is striking is their continuance after Catholic emancipation and the mass production of liturgical books had removed such pressures.

Limited congregational participation, combined with private devotions, had two important effects. First, as volumes such as Daniel Rock's *Hierugia* and Adrian Fortescue's *The Ceremonies of the Roman Rite* illustrate, it enhanced an emphasis on ritual and rubrics at the expense of understanding. Second, it underlined the emphasis on the sanctity of liturgical texts resulting from Guéranger's concept of the cycle of praise. Indeed, such sanctity was an added reason for delegating participatory roles to specialist executants. Moreover, if the texts were sacred, then many thought they should be fixed, thereby ensuring historical continuity with the earliest days of Christianity. Hence the insistence by some liturgists that language should not be corrupted, for musical or other reasons, by excessive repetitions or alterations to the wording.[21] Such attitudes also struck at usage of the vernacular, banned at High Mass and the Office by the Vicars Apostolic in 1838. As a result some, like Rock, argued that laity were not obliged to understand the language of the Mass; this could be explained to them separately by means of the catechism. In other words worship and instruction were separated.[22] Yet, despite this, it was felt that music had to present a plain intelligible text, not so much for the people, because it was in Latin, but for God. After all, it was his word that was being recycled. Thus,

18 [Alban Groom, Raymund Palmer, Robert Suffield (eds)], *The Crown of Jesus. A complete Catholic manual of devotion, doctrine and instruction* (London, Dublin and Derby, 1862), p. 237.
19 *TLS*, clauses 12–15.
20 Harper, p. 162.
21 *TLS*, clause 15.
22 Rock, pp. 294–6.

whereas some Missals with texts, but no music, might have English translations alongside the Latin, liturgical-musical books, such as Graduals and Antiphoners, almost never had a vernacular underlay.[23] In addition, Guéranger, Joseph Pothier and some (but not all) Solesmes scholars and their supporters argued that plainchant originated from oratorical inflections of the spoken text.[24] In that sense, it was not music at all. Indeed, since it was the divine word, plainchant had sacred attributes; hence Solesmes's citation of medieval manuscripts showing Pope Gregory receiving it from God in the form of a dove (see Figure 10.2). This gave additional force to the 'sing as you speak' doctrine applied to plainchant not just by Pothier, but by Franz Xavier Haberl, editor of the Pustet editions so vigorously attacked by Solesmes.[25]

The relationship between liturgy and music

The nature of liturgical usage and understanding therefore did much to shape music. This had several effects. First, at a structural level, it explains the emerging theoretical distinction between different sorts of sacred music. There was liturgical music, where the text is taken from the Missal or the Breviary; there was extra-liturgical music, such as would be used in processions and devotions; and then there was music that was merely religious in character, such as Handel's *The Messiah*, which is not associated with any service. Here, although the text may have a sacred character, it is primarily a work of art. In practice, such distinctions were not absolute. For example, Marian motets might be sung at Mass or during Benediction; and choral numbers from Oratorios were often performed as motets in the Mass.

Second, as already noted, liturgy, in the narrowest sense, was almost entirely in Latin.[26] It therefore opened the way for an international Catholic musical scene, and this helps explain why so much music performed in English Catholic churches was composed by foreigners. Conversely, tightening restrictions on the use of the vernacular in Mass or the Office excluded most of the English Protestant repertoire and confined English hymns to extra-liturgical functions. For instance, the ban on the singing of vernacular psalms by the Vicars Apostolic in 1838 eventually led to the abandonment of Anglican psalm chants in the nineteenth-century repertories of Everingham and St Cuthbert's, Durham.[27] This may help explain why extra-liturgical devotions became so popular at the expense of the Office at parish level.

---

23 An exception is the advertisement of Henri Dumont's Masses in French as well as Latin versions by Desclée in the back of [McLachlan], *The Grammar of Plainsong*, n.p. The Desclée reference codes are 2285, 2285B, 2286, 2286B, 2281 and 2282.

24 Joseph Pothier, *Les Mélodies Grégoriennes d'après la tradition* (Rome, Tournai, 1881), esp. ch. 4.

25 Franz Xavier Haberl, trans. N. Donnelly, *Magister Choralis: A theoretical and practical manual of Gregorian Chant* (Ratisbon, 1877, 4th edn).

26 *TLS*, clause 15 bans the use of the vernacular at 'Solemn liturgical functions'.

27 J.M. Tweedy, *Popish Elvet: The History of St Cuthbert's, Durham* (Durham, 1981), Part 2, pp. 14–15 describes the vigorous rearguard action fought by the local parish priest Edward Consitt in defence of psalm singing in English there in the 1860s and 1870s.

Third, there was always much cross-fertilisation between liturgists and musicians. For instance, Guéranger's liturgical programme at Solesmes led to the systematic researches into plainchant conducted by Joseph Pothier and Paul Jaussons. Abbess Laurentia McLachlan of Stanbrook Abbey is an example of the process in reverse. Not only did she play a key role promoting the Solesmes style of plainchant in England; later in life she concentrated on the editing of medieval liturgical books that threw light on the way a Benedictine monastic life for nuns should be recreated.[28]

In all these ways, then, music was the 'handmaid of the liturgy', as *TLS* stated. For example, clause 27 states that the priest should not be kept waiting at the altar by the music.[29] Yet the presence of such regulations indicates that at times music was apt to assume preponderance over liturgy. The underlying philosophy for this could be quite respectable. It was argued that music, by generating 'atmosphere', could heighten devotion;[30] it was a way of advertising the faith to the non-believer; and there was also the argument, attributed to St Augustine, that the person who sings prays twice. Music therefore had the potential to acquire a life of its own, even with plainchant. André Mocquereau (1849–1930), Pothier's successor at Solesmes, tried to show through his researches that its musical rhythms could be different from those of the text. Thus, the tension between the musical and textual rhythm is the leading characteristic of the Solesmes style that he and, to a lesser extent, Laurentia McLachlan promoted. As shall be shown in chapter 10, the clash between the Pothier and Mocquereau principles lies at the heart of the controversy surrounding the publication of the Vatican editions of plainchant in the early twentieth century.

Even more fundamentally, the development of music as an independent force lies behind a division between liturgical musical books and scores of religious music from the late medieval period onwards. Such a division could even affect the way music is stored. Then, as now, liturgical books were usually held in the sanctuary and sacristy of a church; or, in the case of a monastery, in monks' or nuns' choir stalls. Sheet music was mainly kept in the choir loft or a music room where liturgical-musical books, though sometimes present, did not constitute a majority of the publications. What is startling too is the sheer scale of the divide. For example, copies of Wade's *Antiphonale Romanum*, *Graduale Romanum* and *Cantus Diversi* used by the Montargis nuns contain 1,039 musical items (see Table 2.10). This is as large, or larger, than most of the collections of scores listed in Table I.1, and it is several times the size of any vernacular Catholic hymnal.

---

28 Laurentia McLachlan and J.B.L. Tolhurst (eds), *The Ordinale and Customary of the Benedictine Nuns at Barking Abbey* (Henry Bradshawe Society, vols 65 and 66 (1927–28). See also, by the same editors, *Ordinale and Customary of the Abbey of St Mary, York* (Henry Bradshaw Society, vols 73, 75 and 84 (1936–51) cited in Harper, pp. 227, 231–3. For further information about her scholarly activity see The Benedictines of Stanbrook [Felicitas Corrigan], *In A Great Tradition: Tribute to Dame Laurentia McLachlan* (London and New York, 1956), pp. 152–77.

29 See also *TLS*, clause 23: 'In general it must be considered a very grave abuse when the liturgy in ecclesiastical functions is made to appear secondary to and in a manner at the service of the music'.

30 O'Shea, pp. 92–3.

Table 2.10   Musical materials in liturgical books copied by John Francis Wade

Short title	Date of copying	Number of musical items
Graduale Romanum (Douai Mss 55 (Fernham))	1765	454
Cantus Diversi (Douai Mss 6 (Fernham))	1761	91
Mass Ordinaries appearing in both collections		-13
Subtotal		**532**
Antiphonarium Romanum (Douai Mss 57 (Fernham))	1763	507
Grand total		**1,039**

Such a divide is not just physical, but psychological. For instance, only ten items relate to Benediction, all of them in the *Cantus Diversi*. Partly this was because at that time the service was less popular than it became later in the nineteenth century; but even then liturgical books paid little attention to the genre. The focus was almost entirely on the Mass and the Office, the basic staples of the Catholic liturgy. Such a focus helps explain why so much Benediction music survives in collections of musical scores. It was not simply a case of Benediction being popular; no significant place was found for it in the principal liturgical-music books.

Second, all the items in these volumes are plainchant, and, as was usually the case, they are set using neumes. The contrast with the 'modern' notation prevalent in other musical scores is striking. It underlines the divide between the celebrating clergy and the choir, though the latter, of course, could sing plainchant from liturgical musical books too. Often the choir was placed, not in the chancel, but in a 'West Gallery'. Alternatively, in some churches that were served by a religious order there was a lay choir in the West Gallery and a community of religious chanting the Office in the chancel, a gallery, or even a side aisle, as at St Dominic's church, Stone, in Staffordshire. As a result there then emerged the concept of a separate 'liturgical choir' consisting of canons and other religious deployed near the altar, who might not even be expected to sing.[31] Practical factors do much to explain the situation. Music could only be one of the activities performed by the celebrating clergy; the vast number of liturgical texts specific to particular services and days of the liturgical calendar meant that they were daily confronted with music that had to be sight read; moreover, not all the clergy could be expected to be musically expert. There was also a limit to the size of volumes containing huge amounts of musical text and music. The music in them therefore had to be relatively simple and monodic. By contrast a lay choir pure and simple was a specialist body whose sole function was to deliver music. It could be rehearsed extensively; and it could be equipped with books that only contained music. Such choirs therefore had the capacity to tackle more elaborate pieces. The music could be polyphonic, and to ensure congruence of parts it was best to lay it out in a score using 'modern' notation.[32] Furthermore, since

31 Fortescue, *The Ceremonies of the Roman Rite described*, p. 28.
32 The history of the emergence of the modern type of score is briefly summarised by David Charlton in Sadie, vol. 22, pp. 894–7. Charlton argues that the first attempts to

the criteria for selection were musical rather than liturgical competence, the way was open to recruit laity.

The result was that in the nineteenth century there was a tendency to create a 'holy concert', which the custom of hiring pews to individuals reinforced. Not for nothing was the Bavarian Embassy chapel known as the 'Shilling Opera'.[33] In short Catholic Relief and Emancipation led to the emergence of choirs independent not just of the congregation but, to some extent, of the clergy as well. Indeed, during the late eighteenth and early nineteenth centuries at times the latter seemed to have connived at this. After all, Pope Benedict XIV's encyclical *Annus Qui* (1749) permitted the use of the tuba, lyres, lutes and violins 'provided they serve to strengthen and support the voices'.[34] Symptomatic are the numerous instances when professional choirs and bands were hired to celebrate the opening of new churches. By definition, such groups contained non-Catholics. Their employment shows that, even before Catholic choirs were formed, there was a thirst for ostentatious parade after the cultural privations of the Recusant period. In such circumstances Benedict's ban on percussion, flutes, horns, trumpets, harps, guitars 'and in general all instruments that give a theatrical swing to music' were quietly ignored, as the widespread orchestral performances of Classical Viennese Masses show.

Inevitably this produced a reaction. Hence the attacks by many on secular profane elements in church music, including the use of instruments other than the Organ. *TLS*, for instance, declared that they could only be used on special occasions with express permission from the local bishop.[35] Similarly, in 1873, the Fourth Synod of Westminster discouraged any advertising of musical programmes and performers or the reporting of the quality of any performances.[36] Strenuous efforts were also made to exclude women from choirs. Some even argued that because women were often more proficient at singing than boys they would want to show off in an individualistic and therefore un-liturgical manner.[37]

Related to this were arguments about the position occupied by the choir. Some thought that a closer tie between music and liturgy would result if it was moved to the chancel; hence Adrian Fortescue's idealised layouts of the Choir and Sanctuary in parish and cathedral churches, although he admitted that in most buildings choirs were placed in a West Gallery (see Figure 2.1). Women could then be excluded

---

score polyphonically began as early as the eleventh century; between the thirteenth and mid-seventeenth century it was usual to write out each part separately rather than in 'full score'.

33 Anon., 'Sketch of the State of Music in London', *The Quarterly Musical Magazine and Review*, 2 (April 1820) cited by Rosemarie Darby, *The Music of the Roman Catholic Embassy Chapels in London. 1765 to 1825* (Manchester, MMus thesis, 1984), p. 126.

34 Hayburn, p. 103.

35 *TLS*, clauses 15–20. Further examples of Papal legislation on the subject are given in clause 4.

36 Robert Guy (arranger), *The Synods in English: Being the text of the four synods in English translated into English* (Stratford on Avon, 1886) p. 188, clause 3.

37 See, for example, the anonymous article 'Music as a part of education', *The Rambler*, 3/13 (January 1849): 311–17. See also F. Clement Egerton, *A Handbook of Church Music* (London, 1909), pp. 72 and O'Connell, p. 52.

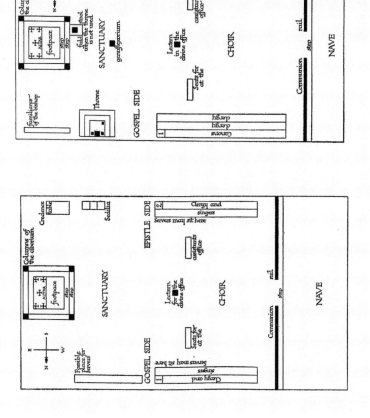

Figure 2.1   Adrian Fortescue's idealised layouts for the Choir and Sanctuary in parish and cathedral churches (Fortescue, *The ceremonies of the Roman Rite described*, pp. 4–5)

because they were not supposed to be in the sanctuary area, particularly as they could not be celebrating clergy.

All these were elements in what was, in effect, an effort from the mid-nineteenth century onwards by Ultramontanes and liturgists to bring choirs under control. For instance, a common pattern was for the choir to be directed by a clergyman, assisted by a lay professional at the organ, as indeed was the pattern usually adopted at Stonyhurst. The difficulty was that virtually all choirs were composed of volunteers. Such recruitment enabled the services of non-Catholic professionals to be dispensed with, but in all other respects restrictions on the membership, especially the female element, were inherently counterproductive. Thus, whereas in 1906 Louis Cassertelli, bishop of Salford demanded that large churches substitute all male choirs for mixed groups, he conceded that 'there are still many smaller churches where the changes would be impossible under present circumstances'.[38] One way round this, as the First and Fourth Synods of Westminster declared, was to train boy singers in schools.[39] Yet this could not obviate an obvious inconsistency, namely the fact that nuns sang the Office and, when they ran schools, they formed girls' choirs. In such circumstances compromises had to be made, given that often the alternative was to have no choir at all. Choirs were an important element in the presentation of the liturgy as a show to attract converts, even if simultaneously they inhibited participation by such people. For instance Moses Heap, a Nonconformist minister from Rossendale, declared after a visit to Stonyhurst in 1852 that 'if religion depended on all this kind of rig-a-mi-jig, they [the Catholics] would have a splendid chance, while many of us would be left a long way in the rear'.[40] At the same time, by taking over the participatory roles allocated to the laity, choirs allowed the committed faithful to pursue their devotions. In many instances, then, the most that could be expected was to push choral repertoire in a more sacred, and less profane, direction.

Patterns of liturgical change

The implication, so far, is that liturgy was supposed to be unchanging. Yet, in reality, this has never really been so.[41] From the sixteenth century onwards, there was a series of official revisions, supplemented by numerous *ad hoc* accretions, mainly in the form of new feast days. It is important to recognise that the rate of change varied for different parts of the liturgy at different times; and, even if apparently no alterations were being made to the formal texts or structures, patterns of usage,

---

38 Louis Cassertelli, 'A Letter on Church Music' (Pastoral Letter), *The Harvest* (26 January 1906): 25.

39 Guy, p. 187, clause 2.

40 *My Life and Times – Moses Heap of Rossendale (1824–1913)*. Mss transcript, Rawtenstall Public Library (1904), p. 61.

41 For an extended discussion of the nature of legitimate and illegitimate liturgical change see Alcuin Reid, *The Organic Development of the Liturgy: The principles of liturgical reform and their relation to the Twentieth-Century liturgical movement prior to the Second Vatican Council* (Farnborough, 2004). Reid argues that liturgy ought to develop organically according to traditions laid down between the first and fourth centuries AD.

for example the balance between the Mass and the Office, or between the liturgy proper and extra-liturgical devotions, could vary considerably. Basically there were four major phases of liturgical change between the sixteenth century and the Great War: the period of Tridentine reform; an era of experimentation with the use of the vernacular in liturgies by some English Catholics in Recusant times, the late eighteenth and early nineteenth centuries; a change in the balance between liturgical services proper (such as the Mass and the Office) and extra-liturgical devotions in nineteenth-century England; and the reforms of the early twentieth century. In addition there must be some consideration of developments in liturgical philosophy towards the end of the period.

Tridentine reform, as noted earlier, was dominated by the revision of the Roman Missal and Breviary. In addition a new body, the Sacred Congregation of Rites, was established in 1588 to supervise all future developments.[42] The new Roman Missal was first issued by Pius V in 1570 under the bull *Quo Primum Tempore*, followed by revisions in 1604 and 1634 under Clement VIII and Urban VIII respectively. It was intended to supersede all other versions that had not been in use for over two hundred years. Under this ruling Sarum and other English Medieval Uses could, theoretically, have been retained.[43] In general this option was not taken, but it did allow English medieval chants using such texts to be performed. This, as shall be seen in chapter 10, was something that happened within the EBC. The new Roman Breviary, meanwhile, was first issued in 1568 and revised in 1602. Its most noteworthy feature was the revision of the liturgical calendar and reclassification of feast days (see Table 2.11).

Table 2.11   Feast days in the Roman Breviary of 1568 and 1602*

Type of Feast	1568	1602
1st Class Double	19	19
2nd Class Double	17	18
Greater Double	0	16
Double	53	43
Semi-Double	60	68
Simple	All the others	All the others

*   Based on Harper, p. 157.

In Recusant times, the late eighteenth and early nineteenth centuries, the formal elements in the liturgy were not just received directly by English laity through sight and sound. They were mediated through a variety of devotional books, manuals, guides and other forms of printed instruction. James D. Crichton has shown that this tradition had Medieval origins, the initial catalyst being the gradual emergence

---

42 O'Shea, p. 133.

43 Joseph Jungmann, *The Mass of the Roman Rite* (New York, Cincinnati, 1950), vol. 1. pp. 130–40. O'Connell 1940, pp. 7–8. Harper, pp. 156–64.

of an educated laity who could read English.[44] However, a decisive step was the publication in 1593 of the *Manual of Prayer*, initially drafted by Richard Verstegan. By 1614 this had run through 15 editions, and a further 83 came out between 1614 and 1800, albeit with many modifications. These, along with *Primers*, were therefore standard items for use by the laity throughout this period.[45] Early editions were semi-Medieval in character, incorporating elements from the Sarum rite and other English Medieval customs.[46] The emphasis was strongly devotional, and the prayers were recited or meditated upon *while* the formal service was going on. Such practices therefore militated against active vocal lay participation in services, and perhaps this may be one of the origins for why many English Catholic congregations, even now, are reluctant to sing. For example, the 1614 *Manual* consists of prayers for every day of the week; prayers before, during and after Mass; hymns and prayers for chief feasts of the year; and an appendix of miscellaneous items such as the Jesus Psalter, the Golden Litany, the Litany of the Saints and the seven Penitential Psalms.[47] However, English translations of the Gloria, Sanctus and the Common Preface are supplied and many of the other prayers are paraphrases of the relevant Latin liturgical texts used during the Mass. This meant that a congregation could at least follow what was going on. In addition both *Primers* and *Manuals* incorporated English translations of several hymns.[48]

During the seventeenth century numerous other books of a similar nature were produced. In most cases the principal purpose was to enable the laity to understand as well as follow the services. Sometimes there was also a tendency to make direct translations of a higher proportion of liturgical texts. For example, *A devout exposition of the holy Mass* (Douai, 1614) gives a complete translation of the ordinary. Later, James Dymock, in *The Great Sacrifice of the New Law*, translated the whole canon as well as the ordinary, despite Pope Alexander VII's 1661 decree prohibiting translations of the Missal. Dymock, in effect, wanted more active congregational participation.[49]

Dymock prepared the way for the work of John Gother (d. 1704) and his followers in the eighteenth century. Gother's ideas about congregational participation are set out in his *Instructions and Devotions for hearing Mass* (1699). His liturgical

---

44 James D. Crichton, *Worship in a Hidden Church* (Blackrock, 1988) pp. 7–24. See especially his discussion of *The Lay Folks Mass Book*, produced sometime in the twelfth or thirteenth centuries.

45 Ibid., p. 30. The standard work on Primers is Joannes Maria Blom, *The Post-Tridentine English Primer* (Krips Repro. B.V. Meppel, 1979).

46 Crichton, *Worship in a Hidden Church*, pp. 37–9.

47 Ibid., pp. 34–5.

48 Ibid., pp. 46–8. Blom, pp. 78–103, 138–61 and 197–238.

49 Crichton, *Worship in a Hidden Church*, pp. 55–8 (Dymock, using the 8th edition of 1687), 52–5 and 60–62 (for a discussion of other seventeenth-century volumes). Dymock's attitudes may also reflect the situation in France, where, after the Revocation of the Edict of Nantes in 1685, the Catholic church needed to incorporate thousands of reluctant Huguenots into its community. For further discussion of Continental developments in liturgical piety combined with congregational participation in the seventeenth, eighteenth and nineteenth centuries see Reid, pp. 52–3.

translations were incorporated into William Crathorne's *The Holy Mass in Latin and English* (1718), which remained in use till the end of the century. Much more elaborate was Charles Cardell's (d. 1791) *The Divine Office for the use of the laity*, published in 1763. In effect this was a Missal for every day of the year. However, as it appeared in no fewer than four expensively bound volumes, its circulation must have been limited.[50]

Parallel to this were several publications by Bishop Richard Challoner, notably *The Catholic Christian* (1737) and *The Garden of the Soul* (1740). The latter remained in use, with numerous additions and modifications, up till Vatican II. Although a follower of Gother, in practice Challoner proved more conservative. In particular he had reservations about the laity reading the canon. Thus *The Catholic Christian* gave translations of the ordinary of the Mass but, except for the dialogues at the Preface, it substituted paraphrases for the canon.[51]

Vernacular traditions continued to develop in the early nineteenth century. For example *A Missal or Roman Catholic devotions for the use of the laity*, printed by Thomas Billing of Liverpool in 1809, was almost entirely in English.[52] More significant, perhaps, was F.C. Husenbeth's *The Missal for the use of the laity*, characterised by highly Latinised English translations. This was published in 1837, and reprinted in 1840, 1845, 1849, 1850 and 1853. As such, it remained in use till the 1890s. In 1842 Husenbeth also produced a *Vesper Book for the use of the laity*, with English translations of the text. The 1844 edition incorporated Gregorian tones for the Psalms and, like *The Missal for the use of the laity*, it probably remained in use till the end of the century.[53] Another prominent author was John Lingard. Today, his reputation mainly rests on his work as a historian, but in 1833 he produced a *Manual of Common Prayer*. It is divided into four parts:

1. Prayers before Mass;
2. The Ordinary of the Mass, together with a complete translation of the canon;
3. Prayers after Mass; and
4. The *Te Deum*.

In addition some translations of the epistle and gospel readings are provided.[54]

Lingard's *Manual*, in the first instance, was produced for his congregation at Hornby, near Lancaster; in other words, it was intended to meet a specific local need. This was by no means untypical. The Catholic Relief and Emancipation Acts allowed Catholics to worship more openly, and consequently this impelled many clergy to produce publications that would make the liturgy more accessible to

---

50 Ibid., pp. 66–79.

51 Ibid., pp. 76–7.

52 Ibid., p. 73.

53 Ibid., pp. 74–5, 83–4.

54 Ibid., pp. 98–100. For a more detailed discussion see Emma Riley, 'John Lingard and the liturgy', in Peter Phillips (ed.) *Lingard Remembered: Essays to mark the sesquicentenary of John Lingard's death* (CRS, 2004): 151–69.

their congregations.[55] On the other hand such activity fell foul of the centralising Ultramontane tendencies promoted by Wiseman. Worse, by this stage, vernacular liturgies of this type were associated with the Cisalpine movement.[56] Lingard himself was sympathetic towards such viewpoints. He argued that not only would a vernacular liturgy make Catholicism seem more acceptable to the Protestant establishment, it would also promote conversions.[57] Vernacular liturgies also conjured up Gallican associations which, as has been seen, in the wake of the French Revolution were viewed with great suspicion by many Catholics. Lingard himself had been trained at Douai, where he had imbibed Gallican ideas from Claude Fleury.[58] It is tempting, then, to see the reversal of such tendencies in the late nineteenth century as the inevitable consequence of Ultramontane dominance in the episcopal hierarchy. Certainly there seems to be a parallel with what was happening in France where, under the influence of Guéranger, local Gallican varieties of the liturgy, many of which had been developed in the eighteenth century, were abandoned by every diocese in favour of the Roman usage.[59]

Yet such divisions between Cisalpines and Ultramontanes over the liturgy must not be over-emphasised. For example, modified versions of Thomas Billing's *Missal* were published in 1815 and 1833 by Brown and Keating, who were Ultramontanes. The same firm also published *Vespers or Evening Service in Latin and English according to the Roman Breviary* in 1822 and *Tenebrae or the Evening Service of Holy Week according to the Roman Breviary in Latin and English* in 1837. As late as 1850 Burns and Lambert, another Ultramontane firm, produced a *Vesper Book* of their own, which was also in Latin and English. This was reprinted in 1859. Copies of these, and other similar volumes, can still be found in the Everingham collection stored in the Bar Convent at York. Yet the Constable-Maxwells of Everingham were committed Ultramontanes and personal friends of Robert Cornthwaite, the Ultramontane bishop of Beverley.[60] This means that old practices dating back to the

---

55 Riley, pp. 146–51, citing Nicholas Morgan, Joseph and William Dunn, *Prayers to be said before and after Mass and in the afternoon* (Manchester, 1805) for churches in Blackburn and Preston. All the authors were ex-Jesuits. See also the anonymous publication *Instructions and Prayers before, at and after Mass for Sundays and Holy days, as used in the Northern District* (Manchester, 1830). Similar publications, relating to Wardour Castle (1820) and the chapel at Worcester (1822) are cited by Crichton, *Worship in a Hidden Church*, pp. 97–116. These are also Jesuit publications.

56 Crichton, *Worship in a Hidden Church*, p. 98. Riley, pp. 160–62, Geoffrey Scott, *Gothic Rage Undone: English Monks in the Age of Enlightenment* (Downside, 1992) pp. 140–41 supplies details of work by Michael Benedict Pembridge and Gregory Gregson. The latter was chaplain to John Throckmorton, a leading Cisalpine.

57 Riley, pp. 151–2.

58 Ibid., pp. 160–62. Crichton, *Worship in a Hidden Church*, p. 98.

59 Baudot, p. 66. For a simple description of these Neo-Gallican liturgies – all permitted because French dioceses had liturgical traditions more than 200 years old in 1570 – see Sheppard, pp. 86–99. See also Reid, pp. 40–44 and 46–50.

60 Other early nineteenth-century volumes of the same type from Everingham are: *Morning Prayers: The Litanies and other Evening Prayers which are usually said in Catholic families with the daily examination of Conscience* (Sold by C. Crowshaw of the Stonegate,

eighteenth century did not die out quickly, and in some cases, most notably with Challoner's *Garden of the Soul*, they survived into the twentieth century.

It is at this point that we encounter *The Crown of Jesus: A complete Catholic manual of devotion, doctrine and instruction*, first published in 1862. This was the work of Thomas Alban Groom (1840–71), Charles Raymund Palmer (1819–1900) and Robert Rudolph Suffield (1821–91). All of them were Dominicans; yet, although the manual was largely compiled at the Dominican Priory of Woodchester, Stroud, in Gloucestershire, Suffield's background as a well-known preacher and missioner in Newcastle suggests that it was aimed at an urban Catholic audience.[61] Despite its 880 pages its relatively small size and cheap price helped ensure it was purchased in large quantities by laity as well as clergy. Indeed, within four years the publishers were claiming that over 98,000 copies had been sold. As the title implies it is a complete compendium of everything the average Catholic might be expected to need; and there is a clear overarching unity between Catholic devotion expected in the home, public worship in church and catechetical belief underpinning the whole. In this sense the manual is defensive in character, the object being to confirm religious belief and practice within the Catholic family. Yet the materials are at once devotional and participatory. Prayers, paraphrases and explanations are provided for every service and devotion. In addition the full text of the Mass, Vespers and Compline in English as well as Latin is provided. However, as noted earlier, there is little expectation of vocal lay participation at such functions; their role is simply to follow and meditate upon what is happening. Yet within every section hymns – almost all of them in English – are provided; and these formed the basis for the *Crown of Jesus Music*, the first English Catholic hymnal aimed at a national constituency.[62] The *Crown of Jesus* manual, then, combines defensive Ultramontane attitudes with the outward-looking populist vernacular approaches noted earlier. As such it constitutes an essential link between them and the liturgical scene of the early twentieth century.

The other major development during the nineteenth century concerned the changing balance between Office services and extra-liturgical devotions. As has been seen, in monasteries, thanks to the efforts of Guéranger, there was a greater emphasis on the Office, with inevitable effects on the promotion of plainchant and eventually the production of separate monastic Antiphoners, Graduals and other liturgical books.[63] On the other hand the rise of devotions such as public Rosaries and Benediction accelerated its decline elsewhere; a decline, it should be noticed, that had already begun in the late sixteenth century. In the late nineteenth century figures for the rise of these two particular devotions are quite startling (see Tables 2.12 and 2.13). Growth though was somewhat uneven. For example, while with Stations of

---

York, n.d.), *The Vesper Book for the use of the laity*. (London, Dublin and Derby, 1848 and 1863 (copies of both editions are survive here); and the *Missal of the Laity*, incorporating English scripture readings (London, n.d).

61   Tony Cross, 'Robert Rudolph Suffield's Dominican Decade (1860–70)', *RH*, 28/1(May 2006): 102–128.

62   [Henri Hemy (ed.)], *Crown of Jesus Music, Parts I–III* (London, Dublin and Derby, 1864).

63   See chapter 10.

the Cross there was a similar expansion, Expositions of the Blessed Sacrament and the Forty Hours Devotion proved to be less popular.[64]

Table 2.12   Churches offering Benediction services in the dioceses of Westminster and Hexham*

Year	Westminster	Hexham and Newcastle
1851	15 out of 47 churches	None
1875	69 out of 101 churches	15 out of 94 churches
1900	100 out of 153 churches	112 out of 148 churches

*   Adapted from figures in Heimann, pp. 178–82, which themselves are culled from data in annual issues of the *Catholic Directory.*

Table 2.13   Churches offering public Rosary services in the dioceses of Westminster and Hexham

Year	Westminster	Hexham and Newcastle
1851	3 out of 47 churches	None
1875	28 out of 101 churches	4 out of 94 churches
1900	41 out of 153 churches	24 out of 123 churches
1914	54 out of 192 churches	29 out of 148 churches

Turning to the early twentieth century, some of the changes advocated by *TLS* have already been noted. There were other principal features. First, there was the admonition under the bull *Sacra Tridentina Synodus* in 1905 for more frequent Holy Communion. This can be read as an attempt to encourage people to take more interest in the public aspect of the Mass as a rite instead of treating it as an occasion for private prayer and personal devotions. Second, under the decree *Divini Afflatu* of 1911, the Roman Breviary was revised. This, as Harper noted, was occasioned by the proliferation of Double and Semi-Double Feasts that had taken place since the early seventeenth century (Table 2.14).

Table 2.14   The number of Double and Semi-Double Feasts, 1568–1882*

1568: 149	1631: 176
1602: 164	1882: 275

*   Harper, p. 157.

The response was twofold. First, the Breviary was reorganised to enable the entire Psalter to be chanted during the Office in one week. Second, there was a determined bid to restore the Temporale by combining the Ferial Psalter with the Office of Saints and by ensuring that the usual Sunday Office generally took precedence over the

---

64 Mary Heimann, *Catholic Devotion in Victorian England* (Oxford, 1995), p. 42.

Office of a Saint.[65] These changes coincided with the work of the Pontifical Biblical Commission. A new Latin translation of the Vulgate was issued in 1907, followed by a new translation of the Psalter in 1913.[66] At the same time Missals with English translations alongside the Latin text were published by, among others, Adrian Fortescue and Fernand Cabrol in 1912 and 1920 respectively. However, it should be noted that Fortescue's Missal was really a revision of Husenbeth's *The Missal for the use of the laity*, which had been reprinted in 1898. Thus, in one sense, a tradition stretching back to Recusant times was being revived.[67] Clearly the intention was to encourage laity to take more of an interest in the public aspect of the Mass.

Such developments reflected changes in philosophy. As has been seen, in the nineteenth century the prime concern had been with rubrics. Following Guéranger, people argued that the liturgy was specially divine, and therefore it should possess a static timeless quality. It was thus essential to get the ceremonies right. Yet such concerns could also justify a historical scholarly approach to the study of ancient documentation.[68] Similar developments were already taking place in other related disciplines: notably straight historical research as advocated by Lord Acton, in theology by fellow Modernists like George Tyrrell and Anatole Von Hugel, with the revision of the Vulgate in 1907 by Gasquet and in plainchant by Pothier and Mocquereau. Indeed, Gasquet was well aware of the similarity between his methods and those used for plainchant by Solesmes.[69] The effect of such scholarship was rather different from what many bargained for. First, it revealed some rather unpalatable truths. Edmund Bishop, in his *The Genius of the Roman Rite* of 1899, argued that the early Christian liturgy had many non-Roman elements in it. He also demonstrated that the Office and the Mass were partly the result of Frankish modifications in the eighth and ninth centuries. Moreover, further significant changes – notably the development of the Curial Office and Mass – were shown to have taken place at Rome in the thirteenth century and then exported to the rest of Catholic Europe by the Franciscans. Contrary to fond Ultramontane imaginings, then, the liturgy was not entirely Roman at all.[70] Worse still, it was the product of accretions, as revelations of the widely differing periods for the introduction and subsequent modifications

---

65 See the introduction to *Daily Prayer from the Divine Office: The Liturgy of the Hours according to the Roman Rite as renewed by decrees of the Second Vatican Council and promulgated by authority of Pope Paul VI* (London and Glasgow, 1974), pp. x–xiii.

66 See, for example, Edwin Barton and Edward Myers, *The New Psalter and its use* (London, New York, Bombay, 1913), pp. 2–49. For work on the Vulgate see Aidan Gasquet (the chairman of the commission), 'The Revision of the Vulgate' *DubR*, 143 (July–October 1908): 64–73.

67 Crichton, *Worship in a Hidden Church*, pp. 74, 88–9. Heimann, p. 71. Reid, pp. 68–99. Crichton states that Fortescue's Missal was first published in 1915; but the 1928 edition states that the first edition was produced in 1912.

68 Reid, p. 59.

69 Gasquet, 'Revising the Vulgate', pp. 267, 270–72. Like Solesmes with plainchant he also knew about the effects of Papal revisions of the Vulgate in 1590 and 1592. For further details, especially the relevant Papal bulls *Cum Sanctissima* and *Si Quid Es*, see O'Connell, p. 8.

70 Baudot, pp. 21–35. Sheppard, 20. Hiley, pp. 302–303.

to different parts of the Mass showed.[71] These, for instance, are the periods when, according to Cabrol, different parts of the Ordinary were introduced to the Mass (Table 2.15).

Table 2.15   Periods when selected parts of the Ordinary of the Mass were introduced, according to Cabrol

Item	Period of introduction to the Mass	Page reference in Cabrol*
Kyrie	Fourth century as Litanies. Later it was cut back to its present form.	53
Confiteor	Tenth century	49
Gloria	Fifth century	54
Credo	Eleventh century (but introduced earlier in Spain, Gaul and Germany).	55
Sanctus	Third century	66
Agnus Dei	Late Seventh century	70

*   Fernand Cabrol, trans. C.M. Anthony, *The Holy Sacrifice: A simple explanation of the Mass* (London, 1937).

Various consequences followed. A tension between the claims of historical authenticity and legitimate change – or at any rate a value put on more recent developments – emerged, and it is significant that exactly the same discussion occurred over the introduction of the Vatican plainchant editions at that time.[72] The Church would also have to admit that it had made errors; again, something that no Ultramontane could willingly contemplate. Worst of all, the nature of historical research, far from achieving absolute certainty, produced exactly the opposite – a state of permanent revolution as scholars made further discoveries or argued about what had already been found.[73] Once again, there is a parallel with Solesmes plainchant, as Katherine Bergeron's discussion of the implications of Mocquereau's work reveals.[74] In short, a shift in authority was taking place. Liturgy was no longer simply what prelates in high authority declared it to be; willy-nilly they were dependent on advice given by scholars who were usually their clerical inferiors and might even be laymen. Liturgy had become an academic and semi-independent discipline.

71 O'Shea, pp. 311–15 (Introit), 352–5 (Gradual), 365 (Offertory), 416–17 (Communion), 323–5 (*Kyrie*), 326 (*Gloria*), 385–6 (*Sanctus*), 413 (*Agnus Dei*). For the Frankish contribution see p. 469. See also Fortescue's discussion of developments to the Proper, *The Ceremonies of the Roman Rite Described*, pp. 215–18, 267, 269, 271–2, 303–304, 385–7.

72 Henry Bewerunge, 'The Vatican Edition of Plainchant, Parts I and II' attacks the Vatican *Kyriale* and *Graduale* of 1905 and 1907 on the grounds that many of the melodies used were not in the most 'authentic' form as established by Mocquereau's research team at Solesmes and Appuldurcombe. *IER*, 19 (4th series) (1906): 44–63, and 20 (1906): 414–28.

73 For example Fortescue in his *The Mass: A study of the Roman Liturgy* (London, 1912), pp. vii–viii and 138–41 felt compelled to list the numerous different theses advocated by various scholars about the origins of the Mass without coming to any firm overall conclusion.

74 Bergeron, pp. 151–61.

PART II
Catholic Music in the
Late Eighteenth and
Early Nineteenth Centuries

Chapter 3

Plainchant in the Late Eighteenth and Early Nineteenth Centuries

Catholic perspectives on plainchant

> Gregorian Chant has always been regarded
> as the supreme model for sacred music.
>
> *TLS*, clause 3

Plainchant forms the bedrock of Catholic church music. Not only does it constitute its oldest surviving stratum, it provides a fairly complete coverage of most liturgical texts – more complete, in fact than any other genre of church music. In addition, since *TLS* in official quarters it has enjoyed pre-eminence over all other styles. Indeed, many argue that, at least by implication, it held this status before 1903.

Plainchant is surrounded by a vast corpus of literature, contributions to which have been made in all periods. However, it is here that ambiguities emerge. Much plainchant literature is apologetic or polemical, so it is not objective. Nonetheless, such writings reflect and inform us about the level of understanding in different periods. For instance, as shall be seen, nineteenth-century understandings depend on the fact that most plainchant at that time was the 'measured chant' developed from the late Middle Ages onwards. A different sort of example concerns its changing official status *vis-à-vis* other styles. Analysis of documents in Hayburn's *Papal Legislation on Church Music 95AD to 1977 AD* shows that, contrary to what Pius X asserted, Papal recognition of its pre-eminence over other styles was comparatively recent. Prior to *TLS* it surfaces in Leo XIII's *Musica Sacra* (1894) and Pius IX's *Multos et commovendos annos* (1870), the latter recognising the formation of the Society of St Cecilia. In Medieval times, in terms of purely *musical* quality, plainchant was not elevated above other styles. The latter were only attacked because of their profane elements, as John XXII's *Docta Sanctorum Patrum* (1324–25) illustrates. Provided these were purged, no distinctions between styles needed to be made.

It is true that, during the Council of Trent, moves were made to ban all music other than plainchant from church. Yet what is significant is that these were defeated, although the Council did require all seminaries to teach plainchant. This policy was endorsed by Benedict XIV's *Apostolicum Mysterium* (1753), and Hayburn cites several eighteenth-century Papal rulings requiring various religious orders to sing an all plainchant repertoire in their Office. Nevertheless in *Annus Qui*, Benedict, citing John XXII, continued to recognise the equality of other styles provided they were purged of profane elements. Bishop Ullathorne's claim in the 1880s that *Annus Qui* gave plainchant pre-eminence is not borne out by the actual text. Rather, it throws light on what he wanted to believe. As shall be seen, such formal, rather than implicit, recognition only emerged in the late nineteenth century, partly as a result of Ultramontane agitation.

A particular difficulty with plainchant concerns its origins. Ideologically this is important because its claims to precedence partly depend on the idea that it enjoyed a continuous existence from the earliest Christian era. Indeed, without it, Solesmes's claim that it is of divine origin carries little conviction. Moreover, its association with Gregory I made it a useful instrument for promoting Papal supremacy. The idea had special resonance in England because St Augustine was reputed to have brought plainchant with him to Canterbury direct from Gregory's Rome. In such guise it became part of wider nineteenth-century ambitions to convert England. For instance, bishop Ambrose Burton (1852–1931), in his hymn 'Lover of Christ's immortal Bride', dedicated to Bede, states.

> Now stand our altars unprofaned;
> Again our Victim lies thereon; [a reference to the sacrifice of the Mass]
> Thence rises up that orison [plainchant]
> By Gregory of old ordained.[1]

Unfortunately, no plainchant manuscripts survive from Gregory's time or earlier. The earliest samples date from the late eighth, ninth and tenth centuries, and most are of *north European* – not Papal – origin. Attempts to bridge the gap have been ingenious and scholarly, but are conceptually unsound. For example the idea that simpler plainchant *must* be older ignores the *a priori* possibility that it could have been as complicated as later versions. If, as shall be seen, many plainchant melodies were actually simplified in the sixteenth century, theoretically there is no reason why something similar did not happen at other points during the Dark Ages. Another approach has been to study liturgical texts, relying on the idea that plainchant was a development from Classical methods of oratory. The difficulty, as Crocker noted, is that liturgists and liturgical musicians look at texts in different ways. Worse, such texts could have been altered during the Carolingian Renaissance.[2] A third technique, deployed by Solesmes, is to focus on the close similarity between plainchant melodies in different documents. As Pothier put it 'tous les morçeaux du répertoire grégorien ont été conservés intégralement, très souvent note pour note, et groupe par groupe, dans les manuscrits antérerieurs au dix-seizième siécle'.[3] The trouble is that such documents are based on only a few ninth- and tenth-century exemplars copied in a limited number of centres, all of them subject to tight control from the Carolingian regime. There could have been other plainchant or the same plainchant in significantly different versions that was discarded. Indeed, this seems inherently likely, given the sheer variety of chant in later centuries. Solesmes ignored

1   *WH*, no. 249, verse 6.

2   Richard Crocker, 'Gregorian studies in the twentieth century', *PMM*, 4/1 (April 1995): 35–42.

3   'Every part of the Gregorian repertoire has been integrally preserved, often note for note, and group by group, in pre-sixteenth-century manuscripts', Joseph Pothier, *Les Mélodies grégoriennes d'après la tradition* (Tournai, 1880), pp. 22–3 and iv.

this because of its obsession with recovering *one* allegedly authentic version of a given melody. As Guéranger put it 'Lorsque des manuscrits différents d'époque et de pays, s'accordent sur une version, on peut affirmer qu'on a retrouvé la phrase grégorienne.'[4] This is an Ultramontane concept, born of Guéranger's ambition to impose Roman uniformity on a diverse Gallican church. Ultimately the motivation is ideological, not scholarly, in character.

A moment's consideration shows that oral transmission is inherently inaccurate. As Crocker suggests, the act of writing is a *confession* that inaccuracies have arisen.[5] Even Pothier admitted that plainchant notation must originally have been developed as an *aide-mémoire*. In such circumstances deviations from an original are inherently probable, especially if, due to the paucity of liturgical books, only key singers had access to written parts. Peter Jeffreys, using ethnographical techniques adapted from literary studies by Leo Treitler and Helmut Huckle, shows what might have happened.[6] The incipits and other motifs in a given chant are cues; the passages in between are versions of material that must have originally been semi-improvised. This fits with Eugene Cardine's concept of Gregorian semiology, resting on the proposition that the earliest staveless neums do not give very exact pitches, but are more precise indicators of performance interpretation.[7] Conversely, later plainchant notation, especially after the development of the four-line stave, provides fairly accurate pitches, but at the expense of interpretative detail, especially with rhythm.

The difficulties do not end there. Any attempt, for ideological reasons, to connect plainchant with the earliest days of Christian Rome sets up a choice between two approaches to repertoire. An 'archaeological' approach, as it was sometimes described in the 1900s, asserts that the earliest plainchant is the finest, because it is the most authentic. By definition, later plainchant reveals progressive decay.[8] The alternative is to view plainchant as a *tradition* to which additions of varying quality have been made at different times. Later plainchant therefore has the potential to be aesthetically 'as good' or 'better' than earlier samples. Yet this weakens the proposition that plainchant is divinely associated with a liturgy allegedly presented by God to Gregory and his predecessors. In addition many protagonists of this approach, while willing to accept late medieval accretions, drew the line at subsequent compositions.

To sum up, as Crocker has shown, despite the vast literature, understandings of Medieval plainchant are inherently deficient. This also applies to performance. As Alphege Shebbeare (1851–1958), a Downside supporter of Solesmes, admitted: 'In the last resort we simply do not know what the chant sounded like in its golden

---

4   'When manuscripts from different periods and countries agree on a version, you can be sure you have re-discovered the Gregorian phrase'. Quoted by Pothier, pp. ii and 15.

5   Crocker, p. 56.

6   Peter Jeffrey, *Re-envisioning Past Musical Cultures: Ethnomusicology in the study of Gregorian chant* (London and Chicago, 1992).

7   Eugene Cardine, trans. Herbert M. Fowells, *Gregorian Semiology* (Solesmes, 1982), pp. 7–8.

8   For an example of this approach see Henry Bewerunge, 'The Vatican Edition of Plainchant' (Parts 1 and 2), *IER*, 20 (1906): 44–63 and 414–28.

days'.[9] Yet paradoxically, despite the paucity of studies, it *is* possible to know much more about post-Medieval plainchant, especially its measured variety, and this was the chant with which most people were familiar during the nineteenth century.

Measured chant in the late Middle Ages and Renaissance

According to Mary Berry, the measured system of plainchant had its roots in late fifteenth- and early sixteenth-century developments. Key aspects were the development of mensural notation, the slowing down of tempi, and a simplification of melodies. Berry argues that, in the thirteenth century, the type of symbol employed usually signified a change of pitch, rather than duration. Thus the virga was used for higher notes, the punctum for lower ones. This, clearly, was a hangover from the days of stave-less notation. Moreover, it implied that Solesmes's theory that all notes were of the same length was correct, at least at that time.[10] However, influenced by the Renaissance, things then began to change. Humanists were concerned with the correct pronunciation and accentuation of the text according to Classical, rather than Medieval, models. Given the Classical emphasis on quantity this meant that notes had to be of unequal length. As a result, note symbols began in some cases to be used to denote duration rather than pitch. In any case, the latter could be determined by their position on the four-line stave. As one would expect, the technique was first applied to Latin hymnody. This, after all, was a late antique variety of Classical poetry. It was then extended to *Credo* settings and other parts of the plainchant repertory. In England, the effects can be observed in publications printed under the aegis of such noted scholars as Dr John Sampson and Bishop Fox of Winchester.[11] A Continental example is the 1525 hymnal prepared by Zacharias Ferreri, bishop of Guardi Alfieri. A notorious early seventeenth-century instance is Pope Urban VIII's revision of the Roman Hymnal of 1629, which was incorporated within the 1631 Breviary.[12]

The idea is encapsulated in John Guidetti's *Directorum Chori*, first published in 1582.[13] There are three basic note lengths (see Table 3.1).In other words there is a proportion of 4:2:1. Moreover, as Guidetti himself admitted, this represented a simplification of the more complex array of symbols available to Medieval scribes. Guidetti's declared motive was to make the chant easier to learn, but there is a strong suspicion that such policies were conditioned by the limited capabilities of early musical type.[14]

---

9   Alphege Shebbeare, *The Music of the Liturgy* (Society of St Gregory publication, 1959), p. 20. The 'golden age' he refers to is the era of Pope Gregory I up till the eleventh century.

10   Mary Berry (otherwise referred to as Sr. Thomas More), *The Performance of Plainsong in the Late Middle Ages* (Cambridge PhD thesis, 1968), pp. 14–56.

11   Ibid., pp. 53–67, 76–9, 106–20, 144–71.

12   Bennett Zon, *Plainchant in the Eighteenth-Century Roman Catholic Church in England (1737–1834); an examination of surviving printed and manuscript sources with particular reference to the work of John F. Wade* (Oxford, DPhil thesis, 1993), pp. 1, 4–5.

13   John Guidetti, *Directorum Chori* (Rome, 1582).

14   David Hiley, *Western Plainchant: A handbook* (Oxford, 1995), pp. 391–7.

Table 3.1   Note lengths in Guidetti's *Directorum Chori*

The Long = ◖

The Breve (the basic pulse) = ■

The Semibreve = ◆

Simultaneously, there was a slowing down of tempi. Partly this was due to the Humanists' concern for clarity; but it also arose due to the development of polyphony. In particular, Berry noted the effects of the interpolation of faburden and interludes for organ between passages of unaccompanied chant. Faburden usually employed note-for-note harmonisations; but this left scope for elaborate vocal ornamentations, pulling back the tempo even more. Such devices also required the development of equivalencies between plainchant and 'modern' notation. Usually this was on the basis that two minims or one semibreve equalled a standard note of plainchant, while with organ parts one breve in 'modern' notation was the same as a single plainsong breve.[15]

The full effects became apparent at the end of the sixteenth century. Guidetti was a pupil of Palestrina. In 1577 Palestrina and Amabile Zoilo (c.1537–92) were commissioned by the Papacy to reform the plainchant books, and although the work was not completed this was the origin of the legend that the Medicean Gradual was really Palestrina's work. It was at this point, moreover, that the third feature of the new style became manifest. Many of the elaborate melismas characteristic of much Medieval plainchant were pruned away and, once again, this seems to have been motivated by a desire for textual clarity (see Example 3.1). Thus Gregory XIII noted that chant books 'since the publication of the Breviary and Missal ordered by the Council of Trent have been filled to overflowing with barbarisms, obscurities, contrarieties and superfluities as a result of the clumsiness or negligence and even wickedness of the *composers* [my italics], scribes and printers.' Thus Hayburn's claim, citing this very document, that Gregory only wanted Palestrina and Zoilo to modify the texts and ignore the music cannot be sustained. Indeed, following the Tridentine decrees, and despite Gregory's criticisms, this policy was already being pursued elsewhere, as Berry noted with the Roman Antiphoner published in 1572 by Plantin of Antwerp.[16] Such features, along with measured notation and the assumption of slower tempi, were incorporated in the Medicean Gradual of 1614–15 printed by Giovanni Raimondi under the supervision of a commission headed by Felice Anerio (1560–1630) and Francisco Soriano (1549–1621).[17]

---

15 Berry, pp. 173–81 followed by analytical tables on 184–245 for organ passages dating from the fourteenth century up to a Magnificat by Samuel Scheidt dating from 1602. See pp. 244–80 for her discussion of faburden.

16 Berry, pp. 55–8. Robert Hayburn, *Papal Legislation on Sacred Music 95AD to 1977AD* (Collegeville, MN, 1979), pp. 27 (Canon 8 of 10 September 1562), 37–8.

17 Hayburn , pp. 33–65. Other musicians on the commission were Giovanni B. Nanini (c.1560–1618), Mancini, Ruggiero Giovanelli (c.1560–1625) and Felini. John Rayburn, *Gregorian Chant: A history on the controversy concerning its rhythm* (Westport, CT, 1964), pp. 6–8 and Bennett Zon, *The English Plainchant Revival* (London, 1999), p. 22.

Example 3.1   Contrasting Medieval and Medicean versions of the Introit *Justus ut Palma* ('Commune Confessis non Pontificis') as presented in editions by Pustet and Solesmes. (The Pustet edition, vol. 2, [54] is a straight copy from the Medicean editions of the early seventeenth century. The 1925 Solesmes *Liber Usualis* (p. 1032) is based on medieval manuscripts.)

Pustet 1873

Solesmes 1925

Pustet 1873

Solesmes 1925

Pustet 1873

Solesmes 1925

Plainchant in late seventeenth- and eighteenth-century England and France

Although intended for use throughout the Roman Catholic Church, in practice general employment of the Medicean Gradual did not extend beyond the Italian peninsula;[18] and in the ensuing centuries there developed considerable variety of practice. In terms of notation, for convenience this can be broken down into three basic patterns:

1. a continued tradition of non-metrical chant loosely based on the accentuation of the text, the Fernyhalgh manuscript being a late example;
2. plainchant that used a partially proportional system; and
3. plainchant following rigid metrical patterns as in the Medicean Gradual.[19]

In some instances the metrical emphasis was tightened still further through changes to the layout and the development of a more complex array of symbols. The former is illustrated by Example 3.2.

Example 3.2   *Antiphonale Romanum*, copied in 1682 by Maria Joseph Lawson, a member of the English Benedictine nunnery in Ghent. Oulton Abbey archives MS 6, p. 1

Be – ne – dic – tus   Dó – mi – nus   De – us   me – us

Here, each phrase is delineated by a double barline; each word is separated by a single barline. This is due to the way the manuscript was copied. Lawson first wrote out the text, unfinished examples of which can be found at the back of the antiphoner. Next she marked off each word with bar lines. Finally, and sometimes with difficulty, she inserted music into the resulting spaces. Visually, the effect is to focus attention on each word of a phrase, thereby holding back the tempo and weakening the sense of musical-textual overview. On the other hand, care is taken to ensure coincidence between musical and textual accentuation, especially as regards the placing of melismatic groupings of notes. Indeed, as in some other manuscripts, slurs are added over these in interpolated passages. However, such note groupings were not taken faster, given the provision of diamonds in places to cover this eventuality.

The use of more complex symbols is most apparent with the development of figured chant in France. Francis Bourgeoing's *Directorum Chori* (1634), printed in Paris, is an early example.[20] The basic impetus seems to have been the practice of supplying continuo bass parts for organ below the melody, classic instances being the

---

18 Dominic Johner, trans. W.H. Hoffer, *A New Manual of Gregorian Chant* (Ratisbon, 1914), p. 197.

19 Zon, *Plainchant in the Eighteenth-Century Roman Catholic Church in England*, pp. 28–9.

20 Ibid., pp. 30–31.

substantial collections of manuscript music by the late eighteenth-century composer Faboullier at Downside, Stanbrook and Douai Abbeys. However, as shall be seen, such symbols spread to manuscripts with a melodic line only.

In the same period quantities of new plainchant were composed and existing versions rearranged. For example David Hiley noted that the *Miazga Catalogue* contained 700 new Credo settings and 500 variants of *Credo I* produced between the fifteenth and eighteenth centuries.[21] Henri Dumont's Masses, composed in the reign of Louis XIV, remained in use right into the twentieth century.[22] Nor should the influence of La Feillée's *Méthode normale*, published in 1782, be forgotten. Indeed two of his melodies surface in *The Westminster Hymnal* of 1912.[23] Much of the new chant was written for Gallican liturgies, and this could include polyphonic writing and improvisation.[24]

Inevitably, French activity affected English practice through the Continental seminaries and monasteries serving the English Mission. For example, in 1787 Constanio Hennon and Faboullier prepared an enormous *Vesperale* for the English Franciscan Recollect community in Douai. Correspondence between G. Sharrock, later Vicar Apostolic of the Western District, and a Fr Walsh, shows that in the same period Faboullier copied several manuscripts for the English Benedictine nuns at Cambrai.[25] Their successors at Stanbrook received another Faboullier manuscript formerly owned by Downside Abbey. This was probably brought over by Benedict Wassell, their chaplain between 1817 and 1820. Faboullier also remained a regular feature of Downside's repertoire into the early 1900s.[26]

What is more, the French-English plainchant nexus extended to Flanders. For example, Douai Abbey, near Reading, possesses an *Antiphonale Romanum Franciscorum* copied at Douai, France in 1762 for the English Franciscan Convent in Bruges.[27] Wade trained in the Dominican house at Bornhem, in Flanders and then had ties with Douai, in France.[28] Copies of a 'Missa Gallia' (really Dumont's *Missa Regia*) and a 'Missa Duacena' (Douai Mass) appear not just in his chant books but in a set of six manuscript chant books belonging to the Canonesses of the Holy Sepulchre, formerly based at Liège.[29] Indeed these hold not one, but two Douai Masses, two 'Dunkerque' Masses, two Masses by Van Hamm, two 'London' Masses, and Masses by a 'Mr Austin', a 'Mr Holden' and a 'Mr Gay'. In addition the nuns

---

21 Hiley, p. 171 citing Tadeusz Miazga: *Die Melodien des Einstimini gen Credo der romish-katholoschen lateluschen Kirche* (Graz, 1976).

22 See, for example, the Desclée publications, with Latin and French rubrics, No. 2285, No. 2285b, No. 2286, No. 2286b, No. 2281 and No. 2282.

23 *WH*, No. 57: 'O God of Loveliness' (text by Alphonsus Liguori trans. Edward Vaughan) and No. 220: 'Thou art left of God' (text by Henry Newman).

24 See for example the CD recording: *Plainchant: Cathédrale d'Auxerre XVIIIeme siècle* (Ensemble Organum, directed by Marcel Pérès, 1990, 901319).

25 Douai Abbey archives, Douai Ms 52 and Lille 18H56.

26 *SAA*, Antip 1. T. Leo Almond, 'The opening of the new choir', *DR*, 24 (1905): 262–4. Downside Abbey archives, nos. 443–9.

27 Zon, *Plainchant in the Eighteenth-Century Roman Catholic Church in England*, p. 141.

28 Zon, *The English Plainchant Revival*, p. 105.

29 Archives of the Canonesses of the Holy Sepulchre, Colchester. No number.

have a *Graduale Romanum*, published at Lyons in 1787, containing a 'Missa Nova in Solemnoribus'.

Nor is such cross-fertilisation surprising, given the fact that Douai was once part of Flanders. Table 3.2 shows that the Sepulchrine nuns owned chant books from a mixture of French and Flemish centres.

Table 3.2   Printed chant books owned by the Canonesses of the Holy Sepulchre, Liège

Title	Year of publication	Publisher/printer	Place of publication
Processionale	1628	Societatem Typographicam	Paris
Antiphonale Romanum	1648	Martin Hauteville	Paris
Antiphonale Romanum (3 copies)	1657	No details	Paris
Antiphonale Romanum	1662	Jean Baptiste Verdussen	Antwerp
Proprium Sanctorum (specially prepared for the nuns)	1674	William Henry Streel	Liège
Two mss copies of the same	1701	Thomas Herzens	Liège
Missa Defunctorum	1733	Plantin Press	Antwerp
Graduale Romanum (3 copies)	1787	No details	Lyons

Such crossover concerned not just new repertoire, but notation. Measured neums could be made compatible with modern noteheads. For example, the *Lulworth Organ Book* contains a transcription by Wade of Thomas Arne's *Mass in G Major* from modern to a modified form of La Feillée's neum notation. Table 3.3 illustrates the relationship between the two systems in a selection of manuscripts. Indeed, the Sepulchrine chant books use both modern and neum notation, occasionally even in a single piece.

Such practices forced copyists to borrow several 'modern' devices to eke out deficiencies in neum notation. Following Guidetti they sometimes substituted a breve with a pause mark over it for a 'long'; three-quarter lengths (or, for example, dotted crotchets) are indicated by placing a dot after the diamond (♦.); sharps, as well as flats, are used as accidentals; occasionally there are dynamic markings and even time signatures. In addition, following common eighteenth-century practice, they used five line staves.

This means that there is sometimes considerable doubt about whether a composition is really a piece of plainchant. Faboullier, for example, may have used neums and unequal bar lengths, but otherwise his music consists of one or two melody lines with what is, effectively, a basso continuo accompaniment. The Sepulchrine manuscripts have compositions in both modern and plainchant notation. Sometimes they are used interchangeably in the same piece. For example, the 'Kyrie' in the *Mass of the Resurrection* starts off as a two-part setting in thirds using

Table 3.3   Notational relationships in chant books copied by Faboullier and the
              Sepulchrine nuns, Liège

Modern symbols	Van Hamm's Mass (Sepulchrine chant book: 112–117)	Mass of the Resurrection (Sepulchrine chant book: 13–34)	Faboullier Antip Vol. 1 (Stanbrook Abbey archives)	Faboullier Vesperale (Douai Mss 52)
▯◖	Tailed Breve	No equivalent	▭	■■■■
o	No equivalent	No equivalent	▭	■■
♩	■	□	□	■
♪	◆	o	o	◆

breves and diamonds. There is then a space marked 'Org.' – presumably indicating an improvised passage for keyboard – followed by the 'Christe eleison' in 2/2 time using modern semibreves, minims, dotted minims, crotchets and quavers. The 'Kyrie eleison' then returns using plainchant symbols.

The classic example of music 'migrating' between plainchant and modern idioms is *Adeste Fideles*. In Wade's *Cantus Diversi* at Stonyhurst (1751) it appears as measured chant in something akin to triple time (Example 3.3).

Example 3.3   Wade's version of *Adeste Fideles*. (Transcribed from John Francis Wade, *Cantus Diversi Pro Dominicis et Festi per Annum* (1751). Manuscript volume held in the Stonyhurst Archives (Arundell Library), CVI:7. However, the 1761 *Cantus Diversi* at Douai has a setting that is closer rhythmically to Webbe's (p. 123).)

Next, Samuel Webbe the elder, in his *Motetts and Antiphons* of 1792 'translated' it into 'modern' notation using regular common time (Example 3.4). Like Faboullier, he realised the harmony with a continuo bass. In turn, this formed the basis for the four-part harmony versions known today. In addition, his pupil Vincent Novello produced an anthem version of the same.

Example 3.4   Samuel Webbe's version of *Adeste Fideles*. (Douai Abbey archives, Ms
                55. After Princethorpe the nuns took it with them to Fernham. When the
                community was dissolved in 2003 the manuscript came to Douai.)

Into the early nineteenth century

Adeste Fideles illustrates the importance of Wade for the transmission of plainchant
into England. Zon's researches show just how active he was as a copyist.[30] Moreover,
many of his volumes enjoyed long chequered histories in the confused migrations
of clergy caused by the French Revolution. For example, the title page of the
Stonyhurst *Cantus Diversi* (1751) refers to a Nicholas King. The book is signed by
James Thomas King SJ, who studied at Stonyhurst (1805–11) and then worked as a
priest at Lincoln (1818–23). In 1826 the volume was signed by Francis Muth, who
joined the Society of Jesus in 1815 and worked at the German Chapel, Old Hall
Green, Hertfordshire (1810–35). In 1836 he joined the seminary staff at Stonyhurst,
he died in 1841 and he is buried at St Ignatius church, Preston, which was served

---

30 Zon, *Plainchant in the Eighteenth-Century Roman Catholic Church in England*,
pp. 48–99.

by the Society. More interesting still is the *Graduale Romanum* (1765) at Douai Abbey, near Reading. This is signed 'Joseph Barrett, May 5th, 1789'. Barrett gave it to the Benedictine nuns exiled from Montargis during their stay in London in 1792. The nuns then moved to Bodley Hall, Norfolk and eventually to Princethorpe in Warwickshire.[31]

Such ties, especially with London, are confirmed by the contents of Wade's volumes. For instance, in addition to the 'Missa Duacena', there is a 'Missa Sardonica' and a 'Missa Hispanica', suggesting ties with the Sardinian and Spanish embassies there. Likewise, in some sources, *Adeste Fideles* is referred to as a Portuguese melody, implying connections with the Portuguese embassy in London, where Vincent Novello worked.[32]

Wade's influence was also indirect. For example, Zon shows his influence (sometimes limited) on the *Heptenstall Vesperal* (1767), now at St Edmund's, Ware and the *Ushaw Chant Book*. Ware and Ushaw were both founded by exiled clergy from the Douai seminary, where Wade had worked.[33] As has been seen, Wade influenced the *Lulworth Organ Book*. Lulworth was owned by Thomas Weld, who gave the house at Stonyhurst to the ex-Jesuit community from Liège. Wade's transcription of Arne's Mass also ties it directly with the London embassy chapel scene, where it was first performed.

Wade was perhaps most influential through *The Evening Office of the Church* in the 1790 edition published by James P. Coghlan (c.1732–1800) and *The Evening Office of Holy Week*, produced by the same author. Both publications enjoyed wide circulation. *The Evening Office* had first been published in 1688. So Coghlan built on work by its earlier publishers, notably Thomas Meighan (d. c.1771), author of *The Art of Singing* (1748) and James Marmaduke (d. 1788), who wrote *The True Method to learn the Church's Plainsong* (1748).[34] In this work Coghlan was assisted by Webbe (the elder), who is the real author of Coghlan's publication *An Essay on the Church's Plainchant* (1782/1799R), which included a version by Wade of *Adeste Fideles*.[35] Coghlan also published *Plainchant for the Chief Masses* (1788) and *Divers Church Chants* (1790). *Plainchant for the Chief Masses* was originally prepared for Wardour Castle, Wiltshire, which was served by Jesuits from Stonyhurst. Coghlan also consulted them about his plans to publish *The Gregorian Note*, which were frustrated by his inability to get suitable plainchant type.[36] Coghlan therefore illustrates the ties between London, where he lived, and provincial centres. These could be surprisingly obscure. For example, the manuscript *Abergavenny Gradual*

---

31 Douai Abbey archives, Ms 55. After Princethorpe the nuns took it with them to Fernham. When the community was dissolved in 2003 the manuscript came to Douai.

32 *CJM*, No. 201.

33 Zon, *Plainchant in the Eighteenth-Century Roman Catholic Church in England*, pp. 89–93. Zon, *The English Plainchant Revival*, pp. 157–8.

34 Zon, *The English Plainchant Revival*, pp. 76–87.

35 Frans Blom, Joseph Blom, Frans Korsten and Geoffrey Scott (eds), *The Correspondence of James Peter Coghlan (1731–1800)*. CRS, London, 2007: 103. Letter 59 'Coghlan to Hay', 14 January 1781.

36 Ibid., p 236. Letter 142 'Charles Plowden to Coghlan', 15 May 1794. Zon, *The English Plainchant Revival*, pp. 87–103.

(1794–95) is associated with a correspondence between Coghlan and James, or Janico Preston, who wanted to promote plainchant there. Before the French Revolution Preston had been educated at the Jesuit Seminary in Liège and had then been Canon Treasurer at the cathedral there. His activity therefore illustrates the transmission of plainchant between the Low Countries or France, exiled Continental English Religious communities, London and Abergavenny itself.[37]

Such threads were picked up by Embassy Chapel musicians in the early nineteenth century, notably Samuel Wesley and Vincent Novello. Novello's *Twelve Easy Masses* (1816) displays three striking features. First, it was dedicated to Lord Arundell of Wardour, underlining the association between embassy chapels, Wardour and Stonyhurst – where Arundell had been educated. Second, it demonstrates a continuing compatibility between plainchant and modern styles. Alongside works by Joano Baldi (1770–1816), Giovanni Casali (1715–92), Joachim de Natividad, Samuel Webbe the elder and Vincent Novello himself, there are five Gregorian Masses: the *Missa De Angelis*, the *Gregorian Mass for the Dead*, a Roman Mass, Dumont's *Messe Royale* and Samuel Wesley's *Mass with Gregorian Chants*. Wesley's correspondence also shows that he drew directly on work by Wade. Third, it contains important information about performance practice. Modern notation, fully harmonised diatonically on a note for note basis, is used. Moreover, unlike in Solesmes style chant, the dynamic levels are sharply differentiated into well-defined alternating sections, as the scheme in Table 3.4, derived from the Missa De Angelis, demonstrates.

In addition, in the preface Novello supplied a list of recommended organ registrations for all the compositions, plainchant or otherwise, corresponding to each dynamic level (Table 3.5). These show just how great and clear-cut the differences could be. Novello then adds that 'the Trumpet may be occasionally added at the termination of the fugues and full choruses which generally end the 'Gloria', 'Credo', and 'Domine'.

In short, Novello adapted and fully realised the hidden potential of measured chant to fit early nineteenth-century circumstances. Strongly differentiated dynamics combined with diatonic note-for-note block harmony and the use of different note lengths to give a sense of power: a power, moreover, that was accentuated by the very slow tempo he advocated. For example, in his *Convent Music* (1834), he recommended a basic metronome pulse of $\downarrow$ = 66.[38]

37 Blom, Blom, Korsten and Scott, (eds), *The Correspondence of James Peter Coghlan*, xx identifies James Coghlan as Janico Preston.
38 Zon, *The English Plainchant Revival*, p. 59.

Table 3.4   The musical dynamics in the Credo from Vincent Novello's version of
the *Missa De Angelis*

Dynamic level	Text
p	Credo in unum Deum … Deum verum de Deo vero
f	Genitum non factum … per quem omnia facta sunt
f	Qui propter nos homines, et propter nostram salutem descendit de coelo
f	Et incarnatus est de spiritu sancto ex Maria Virgine: et homo factus est
p	Crucifixus etiam pro nobis: sub Pontio Pilato passus, et sepultus est.
f	Et resurrexit terria die … cuius regni non erit finis
p	Et in Spiritum Sanctum … Filioque procedit
f	Qui cum Patre … Qui locutus est per Prophetas
p	Et exspecto resurrectionem mortuorum
ff	Et vitam venturi saeculi, Amen

Table 3.5   Vincent Novello's recommendations for organ registration in *Twelve Easy Masses*

Dynamic level	Recommended stops
pp	Stopped Diapason only on the Swell manual. For the bass line use the Stopped Diapason on the Choir manual
p (solo parts)	Stopped Diapason and Dulciana on the Choir manual; 2 Diapasons on the Swell manual
p (for whole choir)	2 Diapasons on the Great manual
mf	2 Diapasons and the Principal on the Great manual
f	2 Diapasons, Principal, 15th without the 12th
ff	2 Diapasons, Principal, 12th and 15th Mixture, Cornet Treble and Sesquialta Bass

Similar features are apparent with the plainchant items in Novello's Evening Service (c.1822). Here, in Example 3.5, the position of the breathing marks indicates just how slow Novello intended a performance to be.

Nonetheless, for all Novello's efforts, there is a suspicion that he was fighting a rearguard action. As Zon noted, already concern was being expressed about the future of plainchant.[39] Moreover, Novello put most of his energies into publishing contemporary or near-contemporary music. In this context Novello's use of modern notation and diatonic choral harmonies is clearly part of a strategy designed to make plainchant acceptable alongside more modern styles; he did not add to the repertoire in the way eighteenth-century musicians had done. Yet, at the same time, Novello was a shrewd businessman. He would not have published plainchant if there was no market for it. His object was to reach the widest circle of people within a relatively

---

39 Zon, *The English Plainchant Revival*, pp. 174–8.

Example 3.5   Novello's arrangement of the plainchant for the Miserere. (Taken
               from Vincent Novello, *The Evening Service Book* (London, n.d.) II,
               p. 22.)

'The marks* indicate where breath is to be taken' (Vincent Novello's editorial note)

restricted Catholic community, hence his eclectic range of tastes. In addition, he cannot have been unaware of the appeal of continuity for Catholics from the earliest times to the present. The introduction to The Evening Service is a concise summary of his credo.

> The editor trusts this publication will be found particularly useful in Catholic chapels, as he has endeavoured to combine almost every species of style, from the primitive but noble simplicity of the ancient Gregorian, to the more diversified and elaborate school of the modern Classical composers: – thus affording an opportunity to different choirs to select whatever mode of performing the service may be most acceptable to their taste.

Chapter 4

Music at the London Embassy Chapels and their Successors

The embassy musical scene

Reference has been made at various points to the Catholic music scene in London, and that of the embassy chapels in particular. This concerned not just plainchant, but music in a more contemporary idiom, which will be discussed here.

The London embassy chapels maintained by Catholic powers were the only places where Catholic worship could legitimately be carried on in Recusant times. To them resorted not just London Catholics, but casual non-Catholic strangers, and Catholic visitors from the provinces. The latter, by definition, tended to come from wealthier upper-class backgrounds. As shall be seen, they helped transmit the music they heard to rural household chapels whence, later on, it percolated to Catholic missions established after the passage of the Catholic Relief and Emancipation Acts.

Such chapels were centres of musical excellence and musical training. For example, in 1792 the Spanish Chapel stated that 'instruction is given *gratis* to those who offer to learn church music'.[1] Moreover, they constituted a crucial link with Catholic music on the Continent, especially since their choirs included professional singers from the London opera scene. For example, Giovanni Liverati (1772–1846), composer and conductor at the King's theatre, worked at the Bavarian embassy chapel, which came to be known as the 'Shilling opera'. Other professionals were its choirmaster Gesualdo Lanza (1779–1839), Begrez (1787–1803) and Manuel Garcia (1776–1832), who composed three masses for the chapel.[2] As a result, an operatic performance style became an established feature in many Catholic choirs before Vatican II.

Musically speaking, the most important chapels in the late eighteenth century were those maintained by the Portuguese, Bavarian, Sardinian and Spanish embassies. Between 1724 and 1747 the Portuguese chapel was at 23–4 Golden Square and then moved to 74 Audley Street. At the same time the Bavarian embassy took over the Portuguese chapel. The Sardinian Chapel was located at Duke Street, Lincoln's Inn Fields; whilst the Spanish Chapel was first at Ormond Street, then at Hartford House, Manchester Square. After the passage of the Catholic Relief Acts the embassies phased out these activities and the establishments acquired a largely independent existence on their own. The Bavarian chapel was shut down

---

1   'Chapels in or near London' in the *Directory* (London, 1792), p. 5.

2   Rosemarie Darby, *The Music of the Roman Catholic Embassy Chapels in London 1765–1835* (Manchester, MMus thesis, 1984), pp. 109–126, Appendix 2.

in 1788, and replaced by Our Lady of the Assumption, Warwick Street, opened in 1790, albeit under the patronage of the ducal authorities. The same thing happened to the Sardinian Chapel in 1798, where links were maintained with the Sardinian authorities till 1859. St James, Spanish Place developed from the Spanish embassy facilities in 1791; its official links were severed in 1827, but unofficial ties with the church built on the opposite side of the street in 1890 continue to this day. The Portuguese chapel endured till 1829.[3]

The contemporary music performed in these centres fell into two categories, namely Continental imports and compositions by native or domiciled composers working at the embassies. In the late eighteenth century much Continental music came from the Italian and Iberian peninsulas. For instance when, in 1811, Vincent Novello (1781–1861), choirmaster at the Portuguese Chapel, produced his first publication, *A Collection of Sacred Music*, it included music by Joanno Baldi (1770–1816), Giovanni Casali (1713–94), Claudio Casciolini (1697–1760), Joachim de Natividad (dates unknown), David Perez (1711–78), Francesco Ricci Pasquale (1732–1817) and Nicolo Zingarelli (1752–1837). Later, such music was supplemented by compositions from the Classical Viennese tradition, especially Mozart and Haydn. This had a limited presence in *A Collection of Sacred Music*, but was already being copied by hand at the Bavarian chapel, many of whose manuscripts still survive.[4] Likewise Novello began copying Haydn Masses from the collection of Charles Latrobe from 1806. Between 1819 and 1825 he published 15 Masses by Haydn and 18 by Mozart.

The native strain is represented by composers such as Thomas Arne (1710–78), John Danby (1757–78), Matthew King (1773–1823), Stephen Paxton (1735–87), Samuel Webbe the elder and younger (1740–1816 and 1770–1843), Samuel Wesley (1766–1837) and, of course, Vincent Novello himself. All except Arne figure in *A Collection of Sacred Music*.[5] Danby was organist at the Sardinian Chapel and sang in the Drury Lane theatre; Wesley was a colleague of Novello at the Portuguese chapel; Webbe the younger worked in Liverpool (1798–1817) and the Spanish Chapel (1817–35). Indeed, he dedicated a Mass to the Spanish ambassador.

The most influential composer was Samuel Webbe the elder, who trained under Charles Barbandt (1716–74 or later) at the Bavarian chapel before taking over the music at the Sardinian and Portuguese chapels, where he taught Novello. In 1785 he published his *Selection of Motetts in 1,2, 3 and 4 parts and chorus*. This contained 50 items. It was followed in 1792 by his *Collection of Sacred Music*, with 25 items. Both were published by 'J. Jones', who may be the same person as a John Jones who worked at the Warwick Street chapel between 1808 and 1843.[6] Alongside his own

---

3   Philip Olleson, 'The London Roman Catholic Embassy Chapels and their music in the eighteenth and early nineteenth centuries', in David Wynn Jones (ed.), *Music in Eighteenth-Century Britain* (Aldershot, 2000), pp. 103–104.

4   Darby, Appendix 2 for a list of surviving mss copies.

5   Performances of Arne's Masses are reported in William Mawhood's diary during 1767, 1770, 1771, 1778, 1780, 1781 and 1790. E.E. Reynolds (ed.), *The Mawhood Diary: Selections from the diary note-books of William Mawhood, woollen-draper of London for the years 1764–1790* (CRS, 50 (1956)): 27, 29, 34, 36, 45–6, 58, 60, 125, 149, 164, 215, 278, 280.

6   R.C. Fuller, *Warwick Street Church: A short history and guide* (London, 1973), pp. 36–7.

compositions these included selections of harmonised plainchant, including *Adeste Fideles* and the 'Tantum ergo' known as *St Thomas*. In addition that same year, Webbe published six of his Masses in *A Collection of Masses, with an accompaniment for Organ, particularly designed for the use of small choirs*.

Webbe's compositions are usually short, simple and straightforward. Consequently, many acquired enduring popularity. The extract in Example 4.1 is a typical example. Note the exclusive reliance on chords I, II IV and V.

More ambitious were works by Samuel Wesley. His *Dixit Dominus*, for instance, requires a double choir. His *Missa De Spiritu Sancto* for choir and orchestra lasts 90 minutes. This was presented to Pius VI, and was probably beyond the capacity of embassy establishments. Wesley was also important as a promoter of plainchant in Novello's publications, as well as works by J.S. Bach and William Byrd.[7]

The dissemination of embassy chapel music

Initially, as one might expect, most embassy music was copied by hand. But from the mid-eighteenth century onwards materials appeared in print. The first of these, *Sacred Hymns, Anthems and Versicles*, was produced in 1766 by Charles Barbandt, who had been a pupil of William De Fesch (1697–1758), choirmaster at the Bavarian chapel (1733–58). This was the first Catholic publication of music in England since Byrd's *Gradualia*.

Barbandt's example was followed, as has been seen, by Webbe and Novello. The latter was especially prolific. In addition to his *Collection of Sacred Music* and editions of Haydn and Mozart masses, Novello's publications included *Twelve Easy Masses* (1816), *The Evening Service* (c.1819), *Motetts for the Offertory and other pieces principally adapted for the Morning Service* (c.1822), *The Fitzwilliam Music* (1825–27), and *Convent Music* (1834). This last was a collection designed for the nuns at Hammersmith. The nature of the market is revealed by the list of 307 subscribers in *A Collection of Sacred Music*. These can be divided between 'the great and the good' – headed by members of the royal family, Catholic and non-Catholic members of the music establishment in England (for example Thomas Attwood, Charles Burney, Muzio Clementi, William Shield, Samuel Webbe the elder and younger), and representatives of the Catholic aristocracy (for example the Townley, Jerningham and Weld families). The Welds, in particular, expose a strong Jesuit connection, not least because Thomas Weld of Lulworth gave his house at Stonyhurst, in Lancashire, to the English ex-Jesuits from Liège. His son, John Weld, who was President (1813–16) there, subscribed for copy, as did the procurator,

---

7   Olleson, 'The London Roman Catholic Embassy Chapels', pp. 112–13. Phillip Olleson and Fiona Palmer: 'Publishing music from the Fitzwilliam Museum, Cambridge: The work of Vincent Novello and Samuel Wesley in the 1820s', *Journal of the Royal Musical Association* 130/1(2005): 53–60. Phillip Olleson, 'Samuel Wesley and the English Bach Awakening'; Yo Tomita, 'Samuel Wesley as analyst of Bach's Fugues'; Leo Kassler, 'The Horn/Wesley edition of Bach's "Trio" Sonatas', in Michael Kassler (ed.), *The English Bach Awakening: Knowledge of JS Bach and his music in England 1750–1830* (Aldershot, 2004), pp. 251–314, 379–402, 417–30.

Example 4.1   'Kyrie' from Webbe's *Mass in G Major*

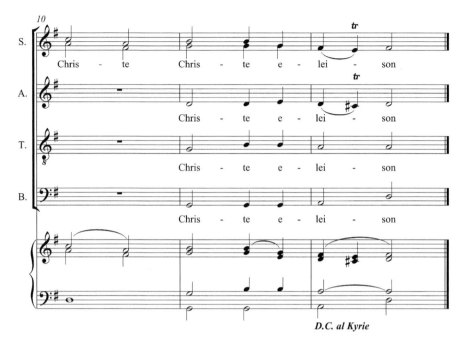

D.C. al Kyrie

Charles Wright, his brother Thomas Wright, who was Stonyhurst's London banker, Charles Brooke, the Prefect of Studies, and Marmaduke Stone (President 1790–1808). These names demonstrate the nexus between London embassy chapels, rural Catholic aristocrats, and the major seminaries and schools where most of them, especially at Stonyhurst, were educated.

The pattern is repeated with *Twelve Easy Masses*. This is dedicated to Lord Arundell of Wardour, a major centre of Jesuit-run Catholic worship in Wiltshire with a congregation in 1780 of over 540.[8] On his death Arundell left his library to Stonyhurst; and, during the nineteenth century, two of its organists – John Beresford and Joseph McArdle – came to work at that college.

Even so, by definition, such dissemination was relatively restricted, confined as it was to the wealthy and educated. Undoubtedly, one factor was the costs of production. Novello's publications, as was common practice, were engraved. This meant that, although they were of excellent quality, only limited print runs were possible. So, to recoup the costs, high prices had to be charged, placing them beyond the reach of a mass market.[9] Indeed, there was an unspoken expectation that they would be treated as 'master copies' from which individual parts would be written out by hand. This, in fact, was exactly what happened, for instance, in collections at Stonyhurst, Downside Abbey, St Cuthbert's, Durham and St Mary and St Everilda's

---

8 Philip Caraman, *Wardour: A short history* (Bristol, 1984), p. 17.

9 For further discussion of the publishing costs, along with Novello's editing and publishing philosophy, see Fiona Palmer, *Vincent Novello (1781–1861): Music for the Masses* (Aldershot, 2006), pp. 139–44.

chapel, Everingham, East Yorkshire, this last being built by the Constable Maxwell family, many of whom were educated at Stonyhurst.

However, in the 1820s and 1830s the situation was changing. First, thanks to the opening of new churches and chapels, the Catholic market was expanding, especially since many quickly set up volunteer choirs. As a result, in London, the centre of musical gravity moved from the embassy chapels to major establishments, such as St Patrick, Soho Square and St Mary, Moorfields. It is significant that Novello worked at the latter between 1840 and 1843. Second, there was the emergence of the Choral Society movement, which Novello sought to capitalise on by publishing editions of Haydn and Mozart Masses with piano accompaniments. In effect, music originally designed for the liturgy was transformed into concert oratorios appealing to religious and non-religious alike.

The full implications were grasped his son, Joseph Alfred Novello, who took over the publishing business in 1830. Joseph immediately cut the costs of engraving. Next, in 1849, he brought out the first of his *Cheap Musical Classics* series – Haydn's 'Mass No. 1' (Hob.XXII). The key feature was the re-introduction of improved moveable musical type, enabling far longer print runs to be undertaken for the same costs of setting up the edition as with engraving. This enabled Novello to cut his prices, opening up a wider market which in turn helped him cut them still further. The process was accelerated by the removal of advertisement and paper duties in 1851 and 1861. Such tactics enabled Novellos to become the largest music publishing business in the country, especially once it took over other companies and their stock (notably Ewer and Co. in 1867).[10] Consequently, their rivals were forced to follow suit or go under. In the Catholic field this was exemplified by such firms as Richard Butler of Holborn, Thomas Richardson, and Thomas Boosey, who used lithography to produce his substantial *Motets for the Year* series.

In the process significant adjustments were made in the style and presentation of music, originally designed for professional performers and wealthy listeners, so as to meet the needs of lower-middle and working-class Catholics. Early on, Vincent Novello recognised that the average Catholic organist could not realise a figured bass, so he provided full parts. Likewise, he expanded much of Webbe's music from two or three parts to a standard SATB choral combination of voices. In addition, Novello's provision of full organ parts in his editions of Haydn and Mozart masses extended the market range of such works, since they could now be performed with or without orchestral backing. For example, an orchestra and choir of 34 players and 39 singers respectively tackled a Haydn Mass at the opening of St Walburga, Preston, in 1854.[11] More characteristic, perhaps, was the 'orchestra' of 2 violins, bass, 2 flutes, euphonium, cornet and organ that accompanied the rendition of Haydn's 'Mass No. 1' by a choir of 15 singers at the 1899 Golden Jubilee of St Mary's, Burnley.[12] In the circumstances many mid-nineteenth-century Catholic organs had to be of only

---

10 Michael Hurd, *Vincent Novello and Co.* (London, 1981), pp. 29–43, 50–52, 68, 86.

11 Anon., 'Parochial History', *The Walburgian* (1923): 23–4, citing reports from the *Preston Guardian*, 5 August 1854.

12 Margaret Durkin, *A Short History of St Mary's, Burnley* (Burnley, n.d.), p. 30.

moderate size – that is sufficiently powerful to accompany a choir by itself, but not so large as to swamp any other instruments that might be added.[13]

Mass production made it possible to supply every choir member with full vocal scores, instead of relying on hand-copied voice parts. For this reason, starting with the *Cheap Musical Classics* series, such scores were produced in a handy octavo size. The result must have been a hidden, and un-remarked, revolution in singing technique. Singers no longer followed the music lineally from individual parts, relying on the ear to establish vertical connections with other lines; they could *visually* perceive those connections – and find their notes – by reference to elements in the vocal score.

Finally, it should be observed that cheap mass production for the first time really made it worthwhile for publishers to enforce and strengthen copyright law. This was because they could now supply the whole market over which copyright then gave them a monopoly of production. Thus, it was no accident that the Lytton-Bulmar Act was passed in 1844.

In the long run the combination of cheap mass production with copyright enforcement had three effects. First, Catholic music publishing became centred on London; second, local initiative in arranging music to suit particular circumstances was restricted, creating a greater degree of uniformity in performance; third, once firms had an established list of compositions, there was less incentive for them to publish new works. From that time onwards, and especially in the twentieth century, there would always be a danger that the English Catholic musical repertoire would become atrophied.

Further developments

Nonetheless, in the short and medium term Novellos and their rivals were not just content to publish Haydn and Mozart. Almost automatically they turned to works by their successors, for example Masses by Beethoven, Hummel, Weber, Gounod and Eduoard Silas (1827–1909). Nor did such developments lack an English dimension. Similar works were composed by Henry George Nixon (1791–1849), who first worked at the Sardinian and Bavarian chapels, then – after a spell in Glasgow – at St George's Cathedral, Southwark. Likewise, there was Henry Farmer (1849–1928), who trained at Stonyhurst and spent most of his life at Richmond, in Yorkshire. Above all, there is the output of Joseph Egbert Turner (1853–1897), much of it in a sub-Haydn style picked up during his monastic education at Ampleforth, in Yorkshire. Copies of his four Masses, dedicated to St John the Baptist, St Cecilia, St Mary Magdalene and the Good Shepherd, can still be found in most old Catholic music collections across the country. In addition, as with Vincent Novello, contributions by composers of foreign origin or ancestry working in England should not be forgotten, examples being Meyer Lutz, based at St George's Cathedral, Southwark and Joseph,

---

13 *NPOR* N14981, R00616 and D04513 for examples of such organs at St Mary and St Everilda, Everingham (18 stops), St Cuthbert, Durham (9 stops), and St Mary, Burnley (19 stops); all with two manuals and a pedal board. The Sardinian Chapel organ, built in 1808, had 15 stops on 3 manuals but no pedal board, as was standard English practice at that time.

Count Mazzinghi (1765–1844), whose Mass composed for the opening of Downside chapel in 1817 was quite widely circulated.

A particular aspect of such developments was the output of certain English composers at the end of the century, notably in work such as Edward Elgar's *Ave Verum,* or in pieces by Albert Edmonds Tozer and Francis M. de Zulueta, who despite his Spanish origins was educated by Jesuits at Beaumont College and spent virtually all his life working in England. In his *Adoro Te Devote,* the differences with compositions by Webbe are clearly felt, but difficult to pin down, as Example 4.2 shows. Like Webbe, he relies on melody, and just as with many antiphon settings by Webbe it is stated first by a solo voice and then by the full choir. However, aspects of the line, such as the falling f–c in bars 3–4, are expressive of the Victorian religious sentimentality that is such a hallmark of this style. This is reinforced by the carefully graded dynamics and the linking phrases at bars 4 and 8. The key difference, though, lies in the harmony. Built around chords I, IV and V, in many respects it as plain as Webbe could have wished. What establishes the distinction is the sustained pedal in bars 1–4, the inner part writing at bars 3 and 7 and the chromatic alto line in bar 5. In any case Zulueta, unlike Webbe, is not thinking in terms of a figured bass foundation.

Example 4.2   The opening solo from Zulueta's *Adoro Te Devote* (London, n.d.)

Such differences are writ large in William Sewell's (b. 1863) *Mass of St Philip Neri in A flat*.[14] Sewell was Organist and Choirmaster at the Birmingham Oratory, and it is clear that he wrote for a large and accomplished choir. However, unlike with a Classical Viennese Mass, there are no solos. The potential for operatic associations was thereby reduced. Another feature is that Sewell, like Turner, in the first instance planned for organ, rather than orchestral accompaniment. This was the logical consequence of writing a Mass for a large urban congregation, as opposed to an aristocratic clientele, which was Haydn's original audience. It also suggests that Sewell never intended his Mass to be performed in the concert hall like an oratorio, as indeed happened with many Classical Viennese Masses.

Next, it should be observed that the organ envisaged was much more powerful, with a wider range of stops, than the instruments known to Novello. Sewell specifies three manuals and a pedal board and, at the very least, he expected a 16ft stop to be available on the Great manual as well as the pedal board. This shaped the style of writing. The organ is pitted against the choir as an equal partner. In places, for example throughout the *Kyrie*, the organ dictates the entire musical framework. This may be one reason why Sewell eschews the use of vocal solos and often treats the voices as a single block of sound. Such facets, of course, were not unknown to the Classical Viennese tradition. Indeed, there was no theoretical reason why Sewell could not have used the sophisticated range of small stops available to accompany solos, as Zulueta did. The key difference lies in the way the organ, in conjunction with the choir, is used to accumulate 'washes' of at times highly sophisticated harmony, often over long pedal points (see Example 4.3). Elsewhere, and by contrast, the organ simply gives harmonic support to the choir. For instance, the sample given in Example 4.4 comes immediately before the passage in Example 4.3. This section reveals Sewell's skills in modulation. These enable him to plan the whole Mass around a fairly wide range of related keys, but fundamentally on a very simple tonic-dominant framework (see Table 4.1).

Another feature is that virtually all the material is motivic. For instance, large parts of the 'Kyrie', 'Gloria' and 'Sanctus-Benedictus' are assembled from the figures given in Examples 4.5, 4.6 and 4.7 respectively. This approach enables Sewell to use considerable amounts of counterpoint in various places. In the sample provided in Example 4.8 it will be noted that the main figure is derived from the 'Sanctus' motif. The contrast with other bold but simple textures elsewhere is striking (see Example 4.9).

Throughout, it should be observed that such technical-musical features are subservient to a wider extra-musical purpose, namely to enhance the religious effect of music used in the service. The emphasis varies according to the different movements. The 'Kyrie' and 'Agnus Dei' are designed to engender the mood associated with a petitionary prayer. It is significant, for instance, that the motif associated with 'Kyrie eleison' returns with the final 'Pacem' at the end of the 'Agnus Dei'. The use of A♭ *Major* in the 'Kyrie eleison' petition therefore is not as incongruous as might at first seem. There is an implied assurance that the prayer will be answered, an assurance that is justified in the 'Agnus Dei'. One function of the Mass – a gigantic prayer or sacrament fulfilling the doctrine of atonement – is thus fulfilled. On the other hand,

---

14 William Sewell, *Mass of St Philip Neri in A flat* (London, n.d.).

Example 4.3   'Descendit de coelis' from the 'Credo' of Sewell's *Mass of St Philip Neri*, showing the accumulation of harmony over an organ pedal point

Example 4.4   'Qui propter nos homines' from the 'Credo' of Sewell's *Mass of St Philip Neri*, showing Sewell's use of basic but sophisticated organ chords underpinning the choral melodic line

Table 4.1   Key relationships in Sewell's *Mass of St Philip Neri*

Movement	Section of movement	Keys
Kyrie	'Kyrie eleison' 'Christe eleison' 'Kyrie eleison'	A♭ F minor to A♭ A♭
Gloria	'Gloria … terra pax hominibus' 'Laudamus te … Pater omnipotens' 'Domini fili unigenite' onwards 'Qui tollis' onwards 'Quoniam tu solus' onwards 'Amen'	A♭ to E♭ E♭ C E♭ E♭ A♭
Credo	Credo … Descendit de coelis' 'Et incarnates … Homo factus est' 'Crucifixus … et sepultus est' 'Et resurrexit' onwards 'Et in Spiritum Sanctum' to end	E♭ (touching on C major and minor) G G minor C E♭
Sanctus-Benedictus	Whole movement	E♭
Agnus Dei	Whole movement	A♭

Example 4.5   Basic motif used in the 'Kyrie' of Sewell's *Mass of St Philip Neri*

Example 4.6   Basic motif used in large parts of the 'Gloria' of Sewell's *Mass of St Philip Neri*

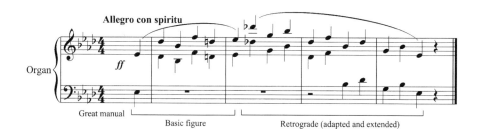

Example 4.7   Basic motif used in the 'Sanctus-Benedictus' of Sewell's *Mass of St Philip Neri*

as one might expect, the opening and concluding sections of the 'Credo' project doctrine, hence the use of unison singing or choral passages in block harmony. Pictorial drama is presented in the 'Gloria' and the 'Sanctus-Benedictus'. Note, for instance, the bell-like quality of the 'Gloria' motif in Example 4.6 or the repetitive alternation of organ statements of the 'Sanctus' motif with vigorously chanted choral 'Hosanna's in the 'Sanctus' movement (Example 4.9)

The central portion of the 'Credo' combines the statement of a doctrinal story with pictorial drama. The words 'ET HOMO FACTUS EST' are written in block capitals, underlining the importance of the idea of atonement achieved by the sacrifice of God made man. This is followed by the strikingly bold and simple statement of the crucifixion built on an appropriately twisting motif given by the organ (Example 4.10).

In many respects this part of the 'Credo' lies at the very heart of Sewell's conception of this Mass. It is at this point that you are furthest away from the tonic-dominant relationship of A♭ and E♭ major; and in the phrase 'Et homo factus est' Sewell – rather predictably – moves from G major to G minor on the word 'est'. Indeed, Sewell's sense of key underpins the whole extra-musical conception. A♭ major is the basic key of the 'Kyrie' and 'Agnus Dei'. It is therefore associated with man's prayer to God. E♭ is the predominant key in the other movements, which are all about God. The rather basic tonic-dominant relationships in the 'Sanctus-Benedictus' and 'Agnus Dei' therefore may not necessarily be symptomatic of weakening creative concentration on Sewell's part. The most important things have been described in the 'Credo'. What follows is the logical conclusions from these acts. The 'Sanctus-Benedictus' describes the heavenly glory and holy rejoicing consequent upon the resurrection; the 'Agnus Dei', as already mentioned, carries the assurance that man will be saved.

Sewell's Mass shows just how far English Catholic musical composition had developed from Classical Viennese roots put down in the embassy chapels at the beginning of the nineteenth century, and it appeared alongside the continued and widespread performance of that repertoire. As late as Easter 1900 the *Organist and Choirmaster* reported the performance of Haydn and Mozart masses at Our Lady of Victories Kensington, St Mary Chelsea, St Thomas of Canterbury Fulham, the Sacred Heart Hove, St Mary Monkwearmouth, St Peter Scarborough, St Mary Sunderland, and St Mary Morecombe.[15] Such success inevitably produced challenge. In particular there was the claim that such music was too secular and operatic, a claim lent substance by Example 4.11, taken from Turner's *Mass of St Cecilia*. Such reactions were already in train by the 1840s, and were to be associated with

---

15 *OC*, 8 (1900–1901): 617.

Example 4.8   Fugal counterpoint in the 'Benedictus' of Sewell's *Mass of St Philip Neri*

Example 4.9   'Hosanna in excelsis' from Sewell's *Mass of St Philip Neri*

the development of Ultramontane interest in plainchant and a revived Renaissance polyphony. It is significant that Sewell relies on motivic development rather than the juxtaposition of melodic material associated with the Classical Viennese style, for such dependence on motifs is a characteristic of Renaissance polyphony. Moreover, his Mass was dedicated to Fr Robert Eaton, who displayed a keen interest in Renaissance polyphony. Indeed, dyeline copies of works by Palestrina and Lassus edited by Sewell survive in the choir loft at Oscott. In addition, it may also be inferred that Sewell's introduction of strongly religious extra-musical meanings was, in effect, an attempt to counter suggestions that a contemporary dramatic idiom was irredeemably secular in character. Sewell's Mass, then, lies at the tipping point between the transition from 'modern' to Renaissance polyphonic styles at the end of the nineteenth century.

Example 4.10   Sewell's treatment of 'Crucifixus etiam pro nobis' in his *Mass of St Philip Neri*

Example 4.11   'Qui tollis peccata mundi' in Turner's *Mass of St Cecilia*

PART III
Ultramontane Influences on Catholic Church Music

Chapter 5

Plainchant Reinterpreted

Ultramontane associations with plainchant in the early nineteenth century

The rise of Ultramontanism was one of the most significant aspects of Catholic church music in nineteenth-century Catholic England. This was especially true with plainchant. The reasons for this phenomenon are not hard to identify. Plainchant was a reminder of the glory days of a Medieval Catholic church dominated by a powerful Papacy. This fitted in with the Victorian Romantic interest in things Medieval. Simultaneously the sixteenth-century reforms associated it with the Rome of the Counter-Reformation. Plainchant could therefore be a vehicle for the Ultramontane promotion of uniform 'Roman' ways of doing things in Catholic England. Moreover, in campaigns against secular musical influences plainchant offered an alternative style that was specifically religious and, once again, something that appealed to Romantics horrified by the spectacle of rampant urban industrialisation. However, as shall be seen, for this to be fully effective, the nature of plainchant had to be modified.

Ultramontane interest was apparent from the 1780s onwards. Coghlan, whose work has already been discussed, was an Ultramontane. At his death Coghlan's bookstock was passed to Richard Brown (1797–1837), his nephew by marriage. In 1820 Brown went into partnership with George and Patrick Keating, founding the firm Keating, Brown and Keating. All of them were Ultramontanes with some interest in plainchant, although George Keating (1762–1836) had probably been trained by Coghlan's business rival, James Marmaduke (d.1788). As a result plainchant publications by Coghlan and Marmaduke continued to appear in Keating, Brown and Keating book catalogues during the early nineteenth century. Between 1817 and 1818 these also refer to *Instructions for learning plainchant, including hymns etc set to the Gregorian note*.[1]

Another Ultramontane with plainchant interests was William Eusebius Andrews (1773–1837), publisher of the *Orthodox Journal*. Under his management this periodical included hardly any items on music; but at his funeral an all-plainchant programme, including Samuel Wesley's arrangement of the *Missa De Angelis*, was performed.[2]

---

1   Bennett Zon, *The English Plainchant Revival* (London, 1999), pp. 81–7. Joseph Gillow, *A Literary and Biographical History, or Bibliographical Dictionary of English Catholics* (5 vols, London, 1894), vol, 1, pp. 322–5, 526–7; vol. 2, pp. 673–6; vol. 4, pp. 426–34. Keating, Brown and Keating catalogues often appear as part of *The Laity's Directory*, which they published annually between 1801 and 1839.

2   Gillow, vol. 1, pp. 43–52. For details of his funeral see 'A Memoir' in *OJ*, 4 (January–June 1837): 244–6.

However, at this time it is important to note that plainchant had not yet become the exclusive preserve of Ultramontanes. As has been seen, eighteenth-century plainchant, including that mediated by Wade, had Gallican associations. Indeed, as Jean-Yves Hameline has shown, such plainchant was often intended for congregational singing.[3] So it had a popular streak, and therefore fitted in with eighteenth- and early nineteenth-century experiments with vernacular liturgies. For example, Husenbeth incorporated eight plainchant tones into his 1844 edition of *The Vesper Book*, and the 1850 *Catholic Directory* advertises John M. Beste's *Church Hymns in English, that may be sung to the old Church Music*.[4]

Even without this, we have already seen how plainchant at that time was designed to fit in with and be performed alongside the latest contemporary styles. The behaviour of the Jesuits at Stonyhurst illustrates just how complex such relationships could be. On paper the Jesuits, thanks to their special oath of obedience to the Pope, should all have been Ultramontanes with a strong Romanising bent. Yet the vernacular liturgical experiments by Dunn and Morgan show that this was not always entirely the case. As regards plainchant it is true that Stonyhurst obtained copies of manuals such as Alfieri's *Saggio Storico Pratico de Canto Gregoriano o Romano*, Benz's *Cantica Sacra*, and N.A. Jansen's *Les Vrais Principes du chant Grégorien*; but, at the same time, the College maintained a repertoire of modern and Classical Viennese music. For example, in 1836, for the opening of their new church, dedicated to St Peter, they commissioned a Classical Viennese-style Mass from Salvatore Meluzzi, director of the Papal choir at St Peter's, Rome. In this way they showed they could be both up-to-date and Roman, even though their church was built in a Perpendicular Gothic style.[5]

The Ultramontane appropriation of plainchant

Nonetheless, it was at about this time that plainchant began to acquire a new and special association with Ultramontanism. In 1837 Peter Paul Andrews took over the management of the *Orthodox Journal*. Immediately, he used it as a vehicle to promote plainchant. For example, that year he published a detailed account of the

---

3   Jean-Yves Hameline, 'L'Intérêt pour le chant des fidèles dans le catholicisme français d'Ancien Régime et le premier mouvement liturgique en France', *La Maison Dieu*, No. 241 (2005), pp. 32, 37–40, 48–51(for the Ultramontane takeover of the idea), 59–60 (for its spread to England class via Fernand Cabrol) and 74 (for its worldwide dissemination at the International Congress of Sacred Music, held at New York in 1920).

4   *Catholic Directory* (1850): 165.

5   Pietro Alfieri, *Saggio Storico Teorico Pratico del Canto Gregoriano o Romano per istruzione degli ecclesiastici*, (Rome, 1835). N.A. Jansen, *Les Vrais Principes du chant Grégorien* (Mechlin, 1845). Both are stored in the Arundell Library at Stonyhurst. This also holds a copy of Louis Lambilotte SJ (ed. P.J. Dufour), *Esthétique théorie et pratique du chant Grégorien restauré d'après la doctrine des anciens et les sources primitives* (Paris, 1855). Dufour presented this copy to Fr Clough, the rector at Stonyhurst. In 1858 Clough also obtained a folio-size *Graduale Juxta Missale Romanrum* (Lyons, 1816), which is stored in the room known as 'Cacus'. The *Cantica Sacra* is stored in the music basement.

consecration of Ambrose Phillips De Lisle's chapel at Grace Dieu and the abbey church at Mount St Bernard, in Leicestershire. In both cases the proceedings were dominated by plainchant.[6] This marked the beginning of a barrage of plainchant publications and articles in the 1840s and 1850s. Many of the latter were published by *The Dublin Review*, founded by Nicholas Wiseman, *The Tablet* and *The Rambler*. All of them were published by the Ultramontane firm Burns and Lambert.[7] In particular, as shall be seen, James Burns, John Lambert and John Moore Capes, editor of *The Rambler* from 1848, had strong musical interests.

Three years later Thomas Walsh, Vicar Apostolic of the Midland District, recruited Nicholas Wiseman to be President at Oscott College, near Birmingham. Wiseman was a fervent protagonist for plainchant; and, as Cardinal Archbishop of Westminster he was to be the prime mover in the declaration at the First Synod of Westminster, held in 1852, that plainchant was the ideal form of church music.[8] This met at Oscott, and it was at Oscott, during his time as President, that the choirmaster, Johann Benz (1807–1880), produced the *Cantica Sacra, or Gregorian Music*, in 1845. Three years later John Moore, Wiseman's successor at Oscott, imposed an exclusive diet of plainchant on the students there.[9] Wiseman also wrote the preface for J.A. Novello's *Cantica Vespera*, which was favourably reviewed by the *Orthodox Journal*. Immediately afterwards there is a letter by Wiseman attacking the employment of Protestant singers in Catholic choirs and blaming them for encouraging theatrically florid styles of singing and repertory. Wiseman also demanded uniformity in the performance of plainchant in the Catholic Church at Vespers. In particular he emphasised the importance of correct punctuation, especially the vowels, recommending Italian practices for this purpose. Here then plainchant was tied to an Ultramontane agenda, with its emphasis on Italianate uniformity, and it is contrasted favourably with modern musical styles tainted by their association with Protestants.[10]

At the same time Ultramontanes used plainchant to trump liberal Catholic experiments with vernacular elements in the liturgy as a means of obtaining lay participation. Moreover, as Pugin noted in *An earnest appeal for the revival of Ancient*

---

6 'Philalethes', 'Consecration of churches at Grace Dieu, Whitwick and Mount St Bernard', *OJ*, 5 (July–December 1837): 382–4. The reports were originally published in the *Staffordshire Examiner*. In the same volume see the account of 'a religious festival at Grace Dieu, Leicestershire' p. 30.

7 Zon, *The English Plainchant Revival*, pp. 217–46.

8 Sybille Mager, *The Debate over the Revival of Ancient Church Music in Victorian England* (Cambridge, PhD, 2000): 276–8.

9 Johann Benz, *Cantica Sacra, or Gregorian Music* (London, Dublin, Derby, 1845/ R1849). Zon says this was first published in 1846, but the anonymous preface is dated 1845. Zon, *The English Plainchant Revival*, pp. 192–3. For Moore's musical policies see Judith Champ, *Oscott College Chapel* (Oscott, 2002), p. 47.

10 J.A. Novello, *Cantica Vespera: The Psalms chanted at Vespers and Compline adapted to the Gregorian songs* (London, 1841). This was reviewed in the *OJ*, 13 (July–December 1841): 65–6. Wiseman's letter is on page 67. For further developments of such ideas, including the link between Plainchant and Renaissance Polyphony, see 'F.M.' (Francis Miller), 'Church Music', *OJ*, 19 (June–December 1844): 202.

Plainsong, mass printing of plainchant books made this more than a theoretical pipe dream.[11] For example the anonymous preface (possibly by Wiseman himself, since it was written at Oscott) in Benz's *Cantica Sacra* argues that plainchant is easy to learn and therefore suitable for congregational singing in small churches that have difficulty forming a choir. It also drew attention to the fact that Catholic choirs 'are but imperfectly provided with music for the secondary portions... of the service' (i.e. the Introit, Gradual, Offertory and the proper hymns for Vespers). *Cantica Sacra*, by remedying such deficiencies, was therefore extending the scope of congregational singing to more parts of the liturgy. The same ideal of congregational participation in singing plainchant is articulated in Ambrose Phillips De Lisle's *The Little Gradual, or Choralist's companion* of 1847 and in William Kelly's *The complete Gregorian Chant manual* of 1849.[12] However, there is a significant difference of emphasis. With Lisle the target was the rural working class. His *Little Gradual* expressed the congruence between the Romantic rural idyll and Medieval Catholicism. Kelly, on the other hand, was interested in the urban Catholic proletariat. His publication therefore fitted in with the Ultramontane concern to rescue such people from the perils of Protestantism and secularism in industrial cities.

The opening of St Chad's Cathedral, Birmingham, on 21 July 1841 was meant to be a showcase for the new Ultramontane plainchant order. However, as at Stonyhurst, it showed how much more needed to be done. This was a Gothic building designed by Pugin (see Figure 5.1). At its consecration by Walsh and Wiseman, twelve bishops served as canons. The music, performed by Catholic amateurs and students from Oscott under Benz's direction, consisted entirely of plainchant. So far so good; but at the Pontifical Mass celebrated two days later – the first in England since the Reformation – Benz and the Oscott choir performed a hitherto unpublished Mass by Haydn. In other words, Benz showed that he belonged to the older tradition represented by Samuel Wesley, the Webbes and Vincent Novello. He saw no incompatibility between plainchant and modern styles of music.[13] In his hands plainchant was not a device separating people from the contemporary world.

The search for and dissemination of an 'authentic' plainchant

In short, what Ultramontanes needed was a change in plainchant scholarship. They had to show that authentic Gregorian chant was different from and incompatible with modern styles of music. This implied a move towards modality, especially in plainchant accompaniments. It was also necessary to purge the plainchant repertory of post-Medieval compositions, especially if they were Gallican. This had the added advantage of producing an exclusively Latinate repertoire with no hint of vernacular adaptation. Plainchant of this sort, when sung by congregations, associated them with the Roman liturgy favoured by Ultramontanes.

---

11 Augustus Welby Pugin, *An Earnest Appeal for the Revival of the Ancient Plainchant* (London, Dolman, 1850), p. 10.

12 Anon. 'Preface', in Benz, n.p. Zon, *The English Plainchant Revival*, pp. 193–8.

13 Anon., 'St Chad's Cathedral, Birmingham: Consecration and dedication', *OJ*, 13 (July–December 1841): 400–402.

THE LONDON AND DUBLIN

ORTHODOX JOURNAL

OF USEFUL KNOWLEDGE;

AND

CATHOLIC INTELLIGENCER.

Careful to preserve the Unity of the Spirit in the Bond of Peace.—EPH. iv. 3.

VOL. XII.   SATURDAY, JUNE 26, 1841.   No. 313.—2*d*.

ST. CHAD'S CATHOLIC CATHEDRAL, BIRMINGHAM.

P. & M. Andrews, Catholic Printers, 3, Duke-street, Little Britain, London.

Figure 5.1   Contemporary print of the interior of St Chad's Cathedral at the time of its opening

The impetus was supplied by the 'discovery of a complete and authentic copy of the original antiphonary of St Gregory'. This was none other than the Montpellier Antiphoner, or Tonary of St Bénigne de Dijon, copied in the eleventh century and recovered by J.-L.-F. Danjou in 1846.[14] Shortly afterwards Louis Lambillotte SJ produced a facsimile edition of the St Gall MSS 359 in 1851. In turn, this formed the basis of a *Graduale Romanum* published from Paris in 1857.

In the short and medium term, however, the Montpellier Antiphoner proved more significant. For the first time it enabled scholars to decipher the staveless neums of the ninth and tenth centuries. Lisle used elements from it in *The Little Gradual*. His example was followed with the publication of the great Mechlin series of plainchant books, beginning with the Vesperal of 1848, as well as the Rheims-Cambrai Gradual of 1851 produced in Paris under the auspices of Cardinal Sterkx. The Mechlin books were published by H. Dessain and P.J. Hanicq, again with support from Cardinal Sterckx. However the editors, Pierre Duval and P.F. De Voght, also drew on the Medicean Gradual of 1614–15 and the 1599 Plantin Gradual from Antwerp. So the connection between plainchant and the Papacy – an essential point for Ultramontanes – was retained, although diluted by Flemish regional associations. Moreover, the Medieval elements are overshadowed by the Renaissance style. For example, as regards measured notation, Medicean principles are faithfully reproduced:

> Nota quadrata (■) signum est semibrevis seu communis. Nota caudata, id est quadrata cui a dextris vel a sinistris, sursum vel deorsum linea verticalis seu cauda appingitur (◗), sonum longum designat. Semi-breven denique exprimit nota rhombi figuram referens (♦).[15]

Mechlin books were widely used in England, especially by monasteries. Indeed they were the first more or less complete plainchant series to be available in sufficient quantities for use, not just by cantors and other key officials, but by monastic and other choirs. In other words, a significant step had been taken towards the ideal of congregations singing plainchant. As a result, the nature of plainchant performance was fundamentally altered. The problem was no longer how to train a body of singers to execute a large corpus of work orally by rote from individual master copies; now everyone in the choir could *read* their part, opening the way for a much greater degree of accuracy and uniformity of performance. This was music to Ultramontane ears. In addition, it meant that the measured style of plainchant encapsulated in the Mechlin notation acquired a far greater dominance than had been achieved in earlier periods.

Mechlin books, and the scholarship behind them, also exerted a significant indirect influence through the work of Sir John Lambert (1815–92). In 1848

---

14 'ALP', 'Discovery of a complete and authentic copy of the original antiphonary of St Gregory', *The Rambler*, 3/11 (November 1848): 174–80. This quotes substantial extracts from Danjou's report. David Hiley, *Western Plainchant: A Handbook* (Oxford, 1993), pp. 622–3.

15 'The square sign is commonly referred to as a semibreve. The tailed note, that is a square sign with a vertical tail attached to the right or left hand side, designates a Long. The semi-breve likewise is referred to by a rhomboid symbol'. *Tractatus de Cantu Ecclesiastico ad usum seminarii Mechliniensis* (Mechlin, 1864): 7.

Lambert, in partnership with the Ultramontane James Burns, established the firm Burns and Lambert, which eventually developed into Burns and Oates. Lambert lived in Salisbury and had close contacts with the chapel at Wardour Castle nearby. An Old Gregorian, he helped reorganise the music at Downside. Later, between 1854 and 1856, in collaboration with Henry Formby, John Hardman, and John Moore, he did the same thing at St Chad's Cathedral, Birmingham, where William Ullathorne, a monk of Downside, was bishop. Here, an exclusive diet of plainchant and Renaissance polyphony was prescribed. In this way the 'modern' musical deficiencies of Benz's regime were eliminated.[16] Next, as a friend of Francis Weg Prosser, the donor of Belmont Abbey, he was brought in to advise on chant at that foundation, which was consecrated in 1860. For this purpose, the future bishop and English Benedictine President Austin O'Neill (1841–1911) was recruited by him from St Edmund's Priory, Douai as organist.

Lambert therefore represents a bridge between the world of aristocratic household chapels, Wiseman-style Ultramontanism and the Gothic monastic revival. His plainchant publications are extensive, providing a more or less complete range of liturgical musical books with organ accompaniments.[17] These reveal the cross-fertilisation of Medieval and Renaissance source material used in the Mechlin books. For instance his *Grammar of Ritual Music* uses exercises in the eight modes found in Guidetti's *Directorum Chori* as well as material from N. Jansen's *Les Vrais Principes du chant Grégorien*, published from Mechlin in 1845, the year before the discovery of the Montpellier Antiphoner.[18] However, in his *Organ accompaniments for the hymns, antiphons, litany chants and other pieces appropriate to the rite of Benediction* his notes indicate a partial shift from the rigid measured system towards that being developed at about the same time by Guéranger and Gontier at Solesmes (see also Example 5.1). It is significant that this was published in 1850, four years *after* the discovery of the Montpellier Antiphoner.

The sign ∧ is used to mark the musical accent, and it will be found to be a most useful guide to the rhythm of the music. It requires an emphasis of voice, which singers must be careful to observe. The single crotchet indicates a very short syllable. The notes which resemble the minim have no positive relative value as to time, nor are they to be intended to be of equal length one with the other; but they must be sung quicker or slower, according to the prosody and musical account of the verse. The accented notes are to be held on longer than the unaccented notes; and the latter, when there are two or more to a syllable should be executed more rapidly than a single note to a syllable.[19]

16 'Cathedral Clergy' (compilers), *A History of St Chad's Cathedral, Birmingham. 1841–1904* (Birmingham, 1904), pp. 123–9.

17 Zon, *The English Plainchant Revival*, pp. 202–211 lists his plainchant publications available in 1851. These and additional items are advertised in the Burns and Lambert catalogue (p. 18) at the back of the *Catholic Directory* (1855). For his work at St Chad's Cathedral see *A History of St Chad's Cathedral, Birmingham*, pp.126–8. Basil Whelan, *The History of Belmont Abbey* (London, 1956), pp. 28–9. Newlyn Smith, Mss History of Belmont Abbey (Belmont Abbey Archives MS 754), p. 128. Geoffrey Scott, 'Bishop Austin O'Neill OSB 1841–1911: An Edmundian Enduring *Diu Quidem*' (EBC History Conference, 1999): 32.

18 Zon, *The English Plainchant Revival*, p. 208.

19 John Lambert, *Organ Accompaniments* (London, 1850), p. 1.

Example 5.1   Extract from J. Lambert: *Organ accompaniments to the hymns ... appropriate to the rite of Benediction*

Example 5.2, taken from the *Easy Music For Church Choirs*, published in 1853 shows that Lambert, like Solesmes (though perhaps not to the same degree) also advocated a faster tempo. Lambert's directions state that 'the chants are to be sung spiritedly in moderate time, breathing *not at all* at the bars, but *only* at the commas'. Since this implies that choirs at that time commonly breathed on the bar lines, the tempo must have been somewhat faster than that recommended by Novello. If 'commas' are supposed to include the colons at the second double bar then a comfortable metronome speed for breathing in this way would probably be at about ♩ = 80.

Lambert was not unique in this respect. The anonymous preface in Benz's *Cantica Sacra* requires singers to 'avoid a drawling, heavy and slow manner of performing' plainchant.[20] In this way it would be made more palatable for congregations to sing. However, the preface then goes on to say that in monastic communities the slower speed is acceptable because it increases the opportunities for meditating on each syllable of the text during the Office. There is no means of knowing whether Lambert accepted this reasoning for Belmont; but if he did not, then his preference for faster tempi may again be the result of Medieval influences. On the other hand, Lambert states that 'the mark ⌃ shows accented notes, and the syllables under them are to have a swell of the voice, and to be held on longer than the others'. He then remarks that 'the syllable before the bar[line] must be made short... and the one after it... long: and no pause whatever must be made between them, as the bar[line] merely indicates the end of the recitation note'.[21] This produces a measured effect in 3/2 time at the words 'Domino' and 'Dextris'. Here, then, is the consequence of synchronising the musical rhythm with the syllabic pattern of a text organised according to Classical rules of quantity – even when chanted on a reciting note – as Note 2 and Direction III demonstrate. In addition, although Lambert used modal harmonies elsewhere, here, as with Novello, the four-part setting is strictly diatonic and organised on a note-for-note basis. Lambert also follows Novello in prescribing the use of loud and soft organ passages on alternate verses. In some respects, then, *Easy Music for Church Choirs* represents a partial retreat from the position taken up in the *Organ accompaniments*.

---

20 See Zon, *The English Plainchant Revival*, pp. 211–15, for other examples of this phenomenon.

21 Lambert 1853: 3 directions II and III.

Example 5.2   Psalm Tone 1 from *Easy Music for Church Choirs* (London, Burns and Lambert, 1853), p. 3

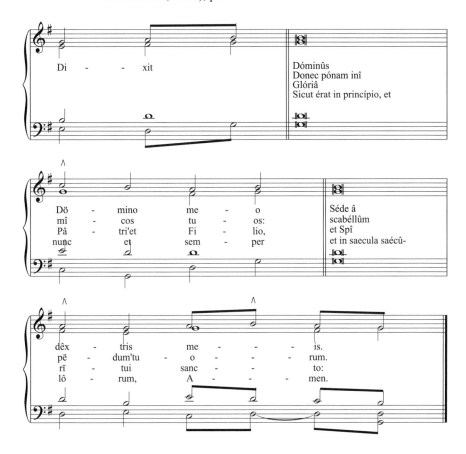

Plainchant developments in the English Benedictine Congregation (EBC)

During the consecration ceremonies at Belmont, the Pontifical Mass was celebrated by none other than Abbot Guéranger, and it is known that he met Lambert on that occasion. The coup was engineered by Laurence Shepherd (1825–85), an Ampleforth monk who visited Solesmes every year between 1855 and his death thirty years later. As novice master Shepherd had already introduced Guéranger's ideas to Ampleforth.[22] These were of direct relevance to English Benedictines. As noted before, hitherto the EBC had been centrally organised to serve missions, where monks lived relatively isolated lives after training in what were, in effect,

---

22 Whelan, p. 32. Eanswythe Edwards and Margaret Truran, 'The influence of the EBC on Guéranger's revival', *EBC History Symposium* (1985): 41. See also Shepherd's Mss, ' My Personal Souvenir of the Abbot of Solesmes: Dom Guéranger. A Chapter of an autobiography', SAA, Box: 'D. Laurence Shepherd and Guéranger', pp. 9–11 and 16 (describing Guéranger's meeting with Lambert).

monastic seminaries. Monks such as Shepherd wanted to move away from this and, like Guéranger at Solesmes, establish fully fledged autonomous communities headed by abbots. Belmont was a compromise between these two approaches. On the one hand, it was established as a central noviciate for the whole EBC; on the other, it was a place where a full monastic life could be celebrated around the Office. This aspect was reinforced by the fact that it provided a monastic chapter, since Belmont also served as the Cathedral for the diocese of Menevia. Plainchant, then, was central to its existence as a monastic community. Accordingly, Shepherd was designated as novice master. Yet, due to ill health, he did not take up the appointment, and perhaps conservative monks might have been afraid of what he might do. Instead, he became chaplain for the nuns at Stanbrook Abbey, near Worcester in 1863. Stanbrook then became the powerhouse for subsequent EBC reform.[23]

The Stanbrook community had been founded at Cambrai in 1623. During the French Revolution, the nuns migrated to England and eventually settled at Stanbrook in 1838.[24] Up until Shepherd's arrival, they had subsisted on a musical diet of Webbe, Novello and representatives of the Viennese Classical tradition.[25] Shepherd changed all that. Daily conferences with the nuns were instituted, using Guéranger's *L'Année liturgique*, which Shepherd translated and had printed on the press he installed at the abbey. In 1869 the house adopted, for a five-year trial period, the rule Guéranger had written for the nuns at St Cecile de Solesmes. The Cambrai custom of having two daily Masses was re-instituted in 1870; a new Gothic church designed by Edward Pugin was opened in 1871; and, following the completion of a new monastery wing, full monastic enclosure was adopted in 1880. In 1914, daily Conventual Mass was instituted. Stanbrook, in short, became a clone of Solesmes.[26]

Inevitably this affected the music. The new rule stated that only plainchant could be used in the Office.[27] It also seems that the failure to recruit new postulants between 1852 and 1862 made it almost impossible to perform the existing repertoire. Plainchant monody was thus a solution for a pressing musical problem. Accordingly Placcid Burchill, President of the EBC, gave £5 for the purchase of new chant books.[28] Mechlin and Lambert's publications were used. For example there survives at Stanbrook a copy, signed by Shepherd, of Lambert's *Ordinarium Missae e Graduale Romano*.[29] However, Shepherd's instructions, derived from the Mechlin Vesperal, show that, unlike Lambert, he stuck to a rigidly measured form of chant.

---

23 Edwards and Truran, pp. 32 and 45.

24 [Kathleen Felicitas Corrigan], *In a Great Tradition: A Tribute to Dame Laurentia McLachlan by the Benedictines of Stanbrook* (London, 1956), pp. 5, 32 and 41.

25 Ibid., p. 54 where Corrigan reports the purchase in 1833 of two copies of Novello's *Collection of Sacred Music*. The abbey also still holds a 1792 edition of Webbe's *Motets and Antiphons*.

26 Ibid., pp. 56–7 and 103.

27 *The Holy Rule of our most Holy Father Saint Benedict with declaration of the same approved by the Holy See of Our Lady of Consolation, Stanbrook OSB* (Worcester, 1874 and 1876), pp. 50–51. See also the 1897 *Rule*, p. 118.

28 [Corrigan], pp. 55 and 140.

29 John Lambert, *Ordinarium Missae e Graduale Romano: A Complete Organ Accompaniment for the Ordinary of the Mass from the Roman Gradual* (London, 1850).

For him, 'The notes of duration... are the Long, the Breve and the Semibreve, and as their names imply, express the longer or shorter continuance of the sounds. What is principally needed in the execution of this style is vigour, concentrated power, and massiveness of effect.'[30]

Needless to say, these changes were not made without opposition. Shepherd was excluded from the EBC chapter in 1883; and in 1886, one year after his death, there was an EBC visitation, prompted by Stanbrook's attempt to elect Gertrude Dubois as abbess in perpetuity. Dubois was deposed and, along with her supporters – including Laurentia McLachlan, the principal protagonist for Solesmes style plainchant in the next generation – she was made to do penance. However, a fortnight later, at the instigation of Cardinal Manning, the verdict was reversed. In 1886, O'Neill, the ex-organist at Belmont recruited by Lambert and a supporter of Stanbrook, was elected President of the EBC, and in 1897 Guéranger's Constitutions were accepted by Rome. Dubois was then re-elected Abbess at a chapter presided over by Manning.[31] Such changes prepared the way for, and overlapped with, the transformation of the EBC into a more authentically Medieval form associated with the Downside movement noted in chapter 1. As a result the stage was set for a new phase in the history of English Catholic plainchant, one that would be dominated by Solesmes.

Late nineteenth-century attempts to consolidate the performance of measured plainchant

Meanwhile, the predominance of the measured system of plainchant was further reinforced as a result of the formation, in 1867, of the Society of St Cecilia in Germany by Franz Xavier Witt (1834–88). Irish, Italian and American societies soon followed, whilst in England Ullathorne, following up the reforms at St Chad's cathedral, founded a branch at the Birmingham diocesan seminary at Olton. Witt's prime objective was to promote plainchant and Renaissance polyphony, and in 1868 he was helped by Friederich Pustet of Ratisbon's offer to produce for the Papacy a complete set of new chant books. These were edited by Franz Xavier Haberl. An octavo Gradual was produced in 1871 and a complete Gradual appeared in 1873. Haberl was a specialist in Renaissance polyphony, so the Pustet books were directly based on the Medicean Gradual. Indeed, it seems that Haberl had little choice. Every sheet was inspected by the Sacred Congregation of Rites. Astonishingly, in view of what had been happening in France, they believed that the Medieval stave-less neumes could not be interpreted, and anyway they could not agree on what sort of plainchant to use. Since Ultramontane uniformity was the watchword, the Congregation therefore fell back on the Medicean books. As a reward for the financial risk he was undertaking, Pustet was granted a monopoly over plainchant publications

---

Its dedication to the Nuns at Handsworth reveals Lambert's Birmingham connections with Ullathorne.

30 Quoted by [Corrigan], p. 144.

31 [Corrigan], p. 164. Edwards and Truran, 49. Geoffrey Scott, 'Bishop Austin O'Neill OSB 1841–1911. President of the EBC 1888–96, Teacher, Benedictine President and Bishop', *Douai Magazine*, No. 163 (2000): 4–5.

in 1868. Two years later, the Sacred Congregation of Rites recommended them to all the bishops. Some dioceses in Britain – notably Dublin, Salford and Beverley – tried to make their use compulsory. In the next two decades Pustet successfully lobbied the Papacy for further endorsements of his publications culminating in the 1894 decree *Quod Sanctus Augustinus*.[32]

The imposition of strictly measured chant was not achieved without difficulty, especially when taken at very slow speeds. These are illustrated by the following extracts from the diary of John Gerard at Stonyhurst.[33]

> Jan 17th, 1869
>
> Vespers tonight celebrated in a new and prodigious fashion – another move of the high and mighty party which at present controls our musical state. Ye choir in ye sanctuary in surplices – singing such tones; pure Gregorian I believe but to the uninitiated very awful. Fr Splaine remarks that it will deprive the office of ye dead of its unique solemnity. Fr Kingdom [the Prefect of Studies] that he wonders how the singers know what note to put next, as one would do quite as well as another: "Its [sic] full of surprises".

> Sept 26th, 1869
>
> Ye last appearance, as I believe of ye real original Gregorian Vespers. Their demise I do not regret, agreeing with Tom the gardener that the method of singing therein is "too much bowlin, and never comes to nought."

Yet, despite this setback, the very next year a completely new set of plainchant accompaniments for Vespers was prepared in manuscript by the organist, Edwin Sircom; and the College also obtained a full Pustet 1871–73 octavo Gradual.[34] Even so, it is significant that Stonyhurst then fell back on Lambert publications, purchasing several copies of *The Choir Manual* for its 'Congregational Choir' as late as the 1890s.

Elsewhere, a similar ambivalence, especially regarding tempi, can be found in Louis Hall's publication *Evening Services for Sundays and Festivals*, compiled for Portsmouth Catholic Cathedral in the 1890s. Here the psalms are laid out in modern notation using note-for-note diatonic harmony and, unusually for that time, an English text is used. The tempi can be deduced from the metronome markings given for the matching antiphons, although these are original compositions. They range from a basic minim pulse of ♩ = 66 (the same as with Novello), through ♩ = 88 (as with Lambert) to ♩ = 144 for the Easter period! At about the same time Heinrich Oberhoffer confessed that when the Ratisbon editions were first published he had at Pustet's request made numerous corrections, but that only some, mainly concerning clefs, had been accepted. The rest had been blocked by persons unknown. Moreover he was acutely aware of the challenge represented by Solesmes scholarship based on

---

32 Hiley, p. 616. Robert Hayburn, *Papal Legislation on Sacred Music 95AD to 1977AD* (Collegeville, MN, 1979), pp. 145–67. 'Sacerdos', 'Article IX – Plainchant', *DubR.*, 1874 (2): 172–204.

33 [Diary of John Gerard. 1868–69]. 'Log of Ye Corpus Doctum of ye doings thereof with some notice of contemporary history'. Stonyhurst Archives, Arundell Library, E/III/2.

34 These can be found in the Music Basement Library and Arundell Library respectively at Stonyhurst. No catalogue numbers.

Medieval manuscripts. As he himself stated: 'looking at these books so beautifully printed, a feeling of great sorrow steals over me, for their introduction, I fear, is equivalent to the loss of true Gregorian plainsong.'[35]

This, then, was the scene as 1900 approached. Plainchant, by and large, had been harnessed to the Ultramontane cause. Partly because of this, the Renaissance tradition of measured chant purged of more modern features held the field. Given that the Pustet editions, and to a lesser extent those from Mechlin, were based on Roman books this seemed appropriate. Moreover, as shall be seen in the next chapter, such chant was linked, via Palestrina especially, with the revival of Renaissance polyphony that was occurring at the same time. In addition the mass printing of such volumes had made plainchant available in more uniform form at least to monastic choirs, the clergy, seminary students and even the more prestigious Catholic schools such as Stonyhurst. Yet the very attempt to impose such policies had thrown up problems, not just in practical performance practice, but in scholarship. The problem was exactly the same as that encountered with liturgy. In their search for an authentic plainchant Ultramontanes wanted a 'once and for all solution'. Plainchant would be rediscovered and restored in a permanent form for all time. The trouble was that in practice real research often did the opposite. Lambert's developing work shows the beginnings of this. As shall be seen the Solesmes revolutions in plainchant from the 1880s onwards demonstrated it on a grand scale. Some recognised the issue quite early. Belmont Abbey archives contains a correspondence dating from 1856–57 between Weg-Prosser and Burchall. Prosser demanded, as a condition of his support for the Abbey, that only unaccompanied plainchant 'according to the best models' should be sung. By this he meant the Mechlin editions. Failure to comply at any time would lead to the revocation of the gift. In reply Burchill noted that, due to scholarly research, plainchant could easily change, and with it, Papal regulations. Thus, 'as all do not understand the words Gregorian Music in the same way, may not the day arrive when difficulties and misunderstandings may arise from this circumstance?'[36]

---

35 Heinrich Oberhoffer, 'Desiderata; In connection with the official Ratisbon edition of the Choral Books: Parts I and II', *AJ*, 2 (December 1896): 195–202 and 318–37, esp. 200, 326 and 336–7.

36 Belmont Abbey archives. Envelope MS 39–73. Weg Prosser 15/8/1857; Burchill 21/1/1856, 17/2/1856, 6/3/1857 (from which the quotation, including the underlinings, is taken) and 22/7/1857.

Chapter 6

The Revival of Renaissance Polyphony

The revival of Renaissance polyphony and the burgeoning output of imitations thereof was one of the most important musical developments in the nineteenth-century Catholic Church. As such it had considerable implications for the English Catholic community. From small beginnings, officially at least, by 1900 it was poised to become the most important form of church music after plainchant. However, as with plainchant, that did not necessarily mean that this status was automatically accepted at grass-roots level. The unspoken tension between official policy and local willingness or ability to comply is one of the more revealing themes of the early twentieth century.

Crucial to such developments was the relationship between Renaissance polyphony and plainchant. The widespread use of plainchant *cantus firmus* in such compositions was clearly understood. Indeed, the slow tempo at which measured chant was taken in the nineteenth century made the connection between the two styles easier to grasp. Even when it was not used plainchant often still acted as an inspiration for new imitative compositions as well as in the real thing. Moreover, the reform of plainchant in Renaissance times was firmly associated with Palestrina and other late sixteenth-century Roman polyphonists.

It was this 'Roman' character that made the style so attractive to Ultramontanes. At times there is even a sense that, because it was ideologically appropriate, the music *had* to be excellent. In other words, there may have been a partial suspension of aesthetic judgement. This is signalled by practical considerations. Unlike with more modern music, the prevailing belief that it was performed *a cappella* meant that it was especially suitable for performance during Advent and Lent, when the use, not just of organs, but of string, woodwind, brass and percussion instruments – with all their secular operatic associations – was increasingly discouraged. Thus Renaissance polyphony, especially that composed by Palestrina and his school after the Council of Trent, had fewer secular overtones than the Classical Viennese style. As such it offered a credible alternative for choirs reared on more modern fare. This was important because Renaissance polyphony, by definition, has an exclusively choral repertoire, whereas some plainchant can be sung by congregations. Thus, the abolition of modern styles and reduction to an all-plainchant repertoire advocated by some had the potential to destroy the *raison d'être* of choirs as distinctly separate entities. The substitution of Renaissance polyphony was therefore important in campaigns to persuade choirs, as well as congregations, to accept plainchant and do away with more modern and allegedly secular music.

Plainchant and Renaissance polyphony thus enjoyed a symbiotic relationship. It was no accident that the principal developments in both styles occurred in tandem. In the early nineteenth century Vincent Novello produced editions of plainchant and Renaissance polyphony; Lambert and Burns did the same in the 1840s and 1850s; and in the latter half of the century the Cecilian movement again coupled the two together. In addition there was a parallel revival of interest within the Anglican Church, as well as among scholars and secular musicians generally. One symptom was the foundation of the Plainsong and Medieval Music Society in 1888; another was the production of early editions of Byrd's masses.[1] For instance, E.F. Rimbault and W.S. Rockstro edited an edition of his *Five Part Mass* for the Musical Antiquarian Society in 1847–48; in 1890 Rockstro and William Barclay Squire produced his *Four Part Mass*; and between 1889 and 1902 G.E.P. Arkwright's *Old English* edition of Tudor music appeared.[2] In this context the conversion of High Anglican musicians such as Capes and Terry was significant. For example, in 1899 Terry and Rockstro collaborated in the production of a new edition of Byrd's *Five Part Mass*. What is more, convert musicians with Renaissance polyphonic interests tended to be Ultramontanes, as the careers of Capes and Terry illustrate.

Attempts to promote Renaissance polyphony in the early nineteenth century

The first major English Catholic musicians to take a serious interest in Renaissance polyphony were Samuel Wesley and Vincent Novello.[3] In 1826–27 and 1830 Wesley projected a publication of 21 motets drawn from an eighteenth-century manuscript copy of Byrd's *Gradualia* in the Fitzwilliam Collection, Cambridge.[4] At about the same time Novello was at work on his *Fitzwilliam Music*, published in five volumes between 1825 and 1827, drawing on music from the same collection. He also produced *A Periodical Collection of Sacred Music Selected from the best Masters*, containing works by Allegri, Palestrina and Guiseppe Baini, the current master of music in the Sistine Chapel. In addition he revised Capes's *Selection from the Works of Palestrina, "Prince of Music"*.[5] Such activity grew from a more general English interest in such music during the eighteenth century with the foundation of such organisations as The Academy of Ancient Music (1726), the Catch Club (1761), the Concerts of Ancient Music (1776) and the Glee Club (1788), in which many Catholics, including Webbe and Wesley, participated. However, the nature of such interest needs to be clearly understood. 'Ancient' music meant music by composers who had been dead for as little as twenty years, so it encompassed people such as Purcell or Handel, as well as Byrd and Palestrina. Novello's *Fitzwilliam Music* reflects this. Only 4 out of its 58 items were written by 'classic' late sixteenth-

---

1 Mager, *The Debate over the Revival of Ancient Church Music*, pp. 88–203.

2 Hilda Andrews, *Westminster Retrospect: A memoir of Sir Richard Terry* (London, 1948), pp. 46–7 and 171.

3 Philip Olleson and Fiona Palmer, 'Publishing the Fitzwilliam Music: Vincent Novello, Samuel Wesley, and the music collections of the Fitzwilliam Museum, Cambridge', *Journal of the Royal Musical Association*, 130/1 (2005): 38–73.

4 In fact one item, a setting of 'Super Flumina Babylonis', was composed by Victoria.

5 Mager, *The Debate over the Revival of Ancient Church Music*, p. 49. Michael Hurd, *Vincent Novello and Company* (London, 1981), p. 3. Both were re-published by his son J.A. Novello in the 1840s.

century Renaissance polyphonic composers.[6] All the others date from the mid–late seventeenth and eighteenth centuries. In any case Novello's activities in this area pale into insignificance alongside the scale of his other activities.

More important perhaps were later publications by Burns and Lambert. James Burns converted from Scottish Presbyterianism in 1847, and in association with Lambert he produced a range of plainchant and Renaissance polyphonic publications. With the latter he employed John Moore Capes, John Crookall, Charles Newsham and John Richardson as editors.[7] The most important of these publications were *The Choir: Collection of Church Music Original and Select* and *The Ecclesiastical Choir Book: Selections from the Great Masters of the Sixteenth Century.*[8] *The Choir* contains a mixture of Renaissance polyphonic and compatible modern music, some of which could be performed unaccompanied. Many items were composed by John Richardson (1816–79), choirmaster at Liverpool Pro-Cathedral. Richardson thus represents a bridge with the earlier practical straightforward traditions of Webbe at the former London embassy chapels. With *The Ecclesiastical Choir Book* there is a sharper focus on the period 1551–1650 as the great era of Renaissance polyphony. All 42 items, including 29 by Palestrina and 6 by Victoria, date from this period. All are by Italians, or composers who worked in Italy, most of whom had close associations with Rome. None are by Englishmen.[9] It is significant that the volume was dedicated to Wiseman, at that time Rector at Oscott College and shortly to be appointed Cardinal Archbishop of Westminster. As Rector of the English College in Rome, Wiseman had become well acquainted with the music directed by Guiseppe Baini (1775–1844) in the Sistine Chapel. For example, in 1833 he sent transcripts of its Holy Week music to his friend Charles Newsham (1791–1863), President of Ushaw College. In 1839 he published a collection of four lectures describing the Holy Week ceremonies there. Lecture 2 in particular contains a detailed account of the music.[10] Thus, for someone like Wiseman, Renaissance polyphony was a useful adjunct in the Ultramontane campaign to 'Romanise' the Catholic Church in England. Yet, like many English visitors before, he appears to have been blind to deficiencies in Roman performance standards in his own time and during the Renaissance period. In 1832 Berlioz noted that, although the Sistine Chapel had maintained its standards, 'the

---

6   These are Lassus, Lupo, Palestrina and Victoria.

7   For a list of these see the Burns and Lambert catalogues at the back of issues of the *Catholic Directory* from 1855 onwards and throughout the 1860s.

8   *The Ecclesiastical Choir Book: Selections from the Great Masters of the Sixteenth Century* (London, 1848). *The Choir: Collection of Church Music, original and select* (2 vols, London). Vol. 1 is undated; vol. 2 appeared in various parts from 1852 and 1853 onwards. Some were edited by John Richardson. This contains works by the following composers: Allegri, Casali, Casciolini, Croce, Farrant, Lotti, Palestrina, Soriano, Terziani and Tye (Renaissance polyphonists), Baini, Ett, Richardson (modern composers). Mager also refers to their 1868 publication *Masses and Motets of the Great Vocal Schools of Italy.* Mager, *The Debate over the Revival of Ancient Church Music*, pp. 281–3.

9   The other composers are Anerio and Nanini (2 works each), Marenzio, Morales and Waert (1 work each).

10   Nicholas Wiseman, *Four Lectures on the Office and Ceremonies of Holy Week as performed in the Papal Chapel delivered in Rome in the Lent of* 1837 (London, 1839).

other churches in Rome… have lapsed into an incredible state of decay, some might even say degradation.'[11] Berlioz, in fact, illustrates the divide between a modern professional nineteenth-century composer and an amateur ideologue like Wiseman who accepted unquestioningly the alleged supremacy of a composer like Palestrina. Thus, commenting on some psalm settings, Berlioz remarked that 'although these psalmodies in four parts contain neither melody nor rhythm, and the harmony is confined to common chords interspersed with a few suspensions, one may concede taste and a certain skill to the musician who wrote them. But genius! They must be joking.'[12]

Wiseman's arrival at Oscott (1840) coincided with and boosted its role as a centre for the promotion of Renaissance polyphony. For example, the library possesses a copy of Pietro Alfieri's *Raccolta di musica sacra*, published in seven volumes between 1841 and 1848, with numerous works by Palestrina.[13] Benz, organist and choirmaster between 1838 and 1841, had been trained by Baini in Rome, and his compositions, like Richardson's, were sufficiently restrained to fit in with a repertoire of sixteenth-century polyphony.[14] Benz became the first choirmaster at St Chad's Cathedral, Birmingham. Yet, as has been seen, at the consecration ceremonies in 1841 a Gregorian repertoire was balanced by the performance of a Haydn Mass. Benz thus inherited some of the attitudes of Novello. He saw no incompatibility between plainchant, Renaissance polyphony and the Viennese Classical style. It was not till 1854 that revised choral regulations drafted by Henry Formby, John Lambert and John Hardman prescribed an exclusive diet of Renaissance polyphony and plainchant.[15]

Given this background it was entirely understandable that as Cardinal Archbishop of Westminster, Wiseman and his successor Manning promoted Renaissance polyphony and plainchant across the English Catholic church, albeit with a greater emphasis on the latter in official decrees. Thus, at the First and Fourth Synods of Westminster (1852 and 1873) plainchant was endorsed as the highest form of church music. As regards more modern styles, the 1873 synod declared that 'it is not for us to condemn the use of harmony or figured music', but later it stated that 'harmonised singing should be clear and simple; that the words be intelligible; that there be no frequent repetition; that there be no addition, omission or change in the sacred liturgy' and 'that, as far as practicable, the laws as to the use and non-use of the organ in the "Ceremonial of Bishops", which is binding everywhere, should be kept.'[16]

---

11 Trevor Cairns (ed. and trans.), *The Memoirs of Hector Berlioz* (London, 1969), p. 184. For details of the state of affairs in the sixteenth century see Richard Sherr, 'Competence and incompetence in the Papal choir in the age of Palestrina', *EM*, 22 (November 1994): 607–29. This draws a sharp contrast between impressions reported by visitors and the reality as recorded in official investigations of the Sistine Chapel choir.

12 Cairns (ed.), *The Memoirs of Hector Berlioz*, pp. 183–4.

13 Pietro Alfieri, *Raccolta di musica sacra* (7 vols, Rome, 1841–47).

14 Zon, *The English Plainchant Revival*, pp. 192–3. Mager, *The Debate over the Revival of Ancient Music*, p. 32.

15 Cathedral Clergy (compilers), *History of St Chad's, Birmingham* (Birmingham, 1904), pp. 15–16, 124–6.

16 Robert Guy (arranged by), *The Synods in English being the text of the four synods in English translated into English* (Stratford on Avon, 1896), pp. 185–95. Mager, *The Debate*

Thus, although no distinction was drawn between different kinds of more modern music, the basic thrust of the decrees favoured the Renaissance style, especially given the belief that many vocal compositions from that period were meant to be sung *a cappella*.

The Cecilian movement

These developments overlapped with the burgeoning influence of the Cecilian movement. The original German Society of St Cecilia was founded by Franz Xavier Witt in 1867, and affiliated societies were soon established in other countries, notably Holland, the USA, Italy and Ireland. In 1870 it acquired official Papal recognition through the brief *Multos ad commovendos annos*, cited in an appendix to the translated decrees of the Fourth Synod of Westminster. The brief was issued shortly after the conclusion of the First Vatican Council, where the doctrine of Papal Infallibility was defined; so there is an unmistakable association with the Ultramontane temper of that Council. The chief centre of activity was at Ratisbon Cathedral; but from 1880, with the establishment of the Schola Gregoriana, the Cecilian movement also acquired a presence in Rome.[17]

Its principal activities concerned the promotion of plainchant; the recovery, publication and performance of Renaissance polyphonic music; and the composition of modern works in the same style. In the recovery and publication of Renaissance polyphonic works the most important figure was Haberl, President of the German society after Witt's death, and founder of the Ratisbon School of Sacred Music in 1874.[18] Haberl's work on the Pustet editions of plainchant has already been discussed. However, between 1874 and 1907 he also produced a complete edition of Palestrina's known output, in the process identifying and publishing many virtually unknown manuscript works.[19] At the same time he produced a complete edition of the motets of Orlando Lassus.[20] Lassus's Flemish background, his work in the Sistine Chapel, and above all his activity at the ducal court of Bavaria have significant connotations. Lassus was representative of a Catholic musical culture that was Roman, Bavarian and international, neatly resolving the inherent tension

---

over the Revival of Ancient Music, pp. 278–9 and 286–300.

17 Alec Robertson, *Music of the Catholic Church* (London, 1961), p. 139. Hayburn, pp. 128–9.

18 For a useful outline survey of such late nineteenth-century editorial work as perceived in the early 1930s see Henry B. Collins, 'Ecclesiastical Polyphony', *ML*, 2/2 (December 1931): 28–31.

19 Franz Xavier Haberl (ed. and others), *Palestrina's Werke* (15 vols, Leipzig, 1874–88, with supplements in 1891, 1892 and 1907). The most commonly known mass recovered by Haberl was Palestrina's *Missa 'Assumpta Est Maria'*. Credit for this has sometimes been ascribed to Karl Proske, but it does not appear in his *Musica Divina* collection which Haberl helped complete.

20 Franz Xavier Haberl (ed.), *Orlando di Lasso's Werke. Magnum Opus Musicum Von Orlando de Lasso* (10 vols, Leipzig, 1894–1908). Haberl acknowledges that some of the initial preparation had been done earlier by Karl Proske. By 1931, according to Collins (p. 28) Haberl's work had been supplemented raising the total in this series to 20 volumes.

between nineteenth-century nationalism and Roman Ultramontane claims. For instance, a parallel edition of Lassus's settings of non-Latin texts (including Luther) in sacred works and madrigals was prepared at the same time by Adolf Sandberger of Munich. It should also be noted that the first volume of Haberl's edition of Lassus's works was published in 1894, when the tercentenary of Palestrina's and Lassus's deaths was celebrated at a summer festival of music in Ratisbon.[21] As will be shown in chapter 11, this approach was imitated by Richard Terry in England.

Such achievements built on earlier work undertaken by Caspar Ett (1788–1847) and Karl Proske (1794–1847). Ett was commissioned by Duke Ludwig II of Bavaria to reform church music in Munich, and as part of this enterprise he published his *Cantica Sacra*, which was later revised by Witt.[22] This contains 42 works, most of them plainchant, but also some original compositions by Ett and Witt themselves. Ett's setting of *Haec Dies* was published and performed in England right up to the early 1960s.[23]

Proske meanwhile published a massive collection of Renaissance polyphony in his *Musica Divina Sive Concentuum Selectissima*. The series was completed by Haberl and recommended to English Catholic musicians in diocesan lists of approved music produced by Salford and Westminster early in the twentieth century.[24]

In addition to promoting a genuine Renaissance polyphonic repertoire Cecilians also composed many works inspired by the same style. Such compositions have often been dismissed, to quote Alec Robertson, as 'a dreary and turgid stream of mainly unoriginal and imitative music'.[25] However, their sheer quantity demands closer inspection, if only to distinguish their leading features. Two works will be discussed here. The first, Johann B. Molitor's *Missa 'Rorate Coeli' Opus XIV*, is a characteristic product of the German Cecilians. It is rooted in Medicean style plainchant, as the basic melody in Example 6.1, taken from the opening Introit, shows. Since the chant does not appear in the Pustet editions of plainchant it may in fact have been composed by Molitor himself. His note-for-note block harmonisation of this, coupled with the fact that his music is influenced by Medicean style plainchant,

---

21 See for example Adolf Sandberger (ed.), *Orlando Di Lasso's Werke. Kompositionen mit Deutschen Tert. Kompositionen mit Franzoscichen Tert* (Leipzig, n.d.) The madrigals series begins in 1895. The first item in the German collection is Lassus's setting of Luther's translation 'Vater Censer Im Himelreich' (The Lord's Prayer). Robert Eaton, 'At Ratisbon in 1894', *ML*, 3/3 (July 1932): 60–61.

22 J. Michael Hauber and Caspar Ett (eds), *Cantica Sacra in usum studiosae juventatis* (Monachii, 1855). The revision by Witt was published by Pustet (Ratisbon, New York and Cincinnati) in 1869. See also Arthur Hutchings, *Church Music in the Nineteenth Century* (London, 1967), p. 60.

23 For an example of a later edition of Ett's *Haec Dies* see the version published by Cary and Co. in their *Motets Ancient and Modern* Series No. 26.

24 Karl Proske (ed.), *Musica Divina Sive Concentuum Selectissima* (4 vols, with several subsections. Ratisbon, 1854, 1855, 1859, and 1863). Diocese of Salford Episcopal Commission on Ecclesiastical Music, *List of Church Music* (Salford, 1904). Archdiocese of Westminster Episcopal Commission on Ecclesiastical Music, *List of Church Music* (London, 1906), Section B: 'Volumes of Polyphonic Masses', p. 16.

25 Robertson, *Music of the Catholic Church*, p. 139.

suggests a very slow speed of performance, although he provides no instructions about this. Where a chant is not used, as in the Agnus Dei, this gives a hymn like character to the music (see Example 6.2). Diatonic use of major and minor scales – in this case A major and D minor – is employed throughout.

Some attempts are made at integrating the musical material across the Mass in the settings of the 'Kyrie' and the 'Sanctus' using the basic material given in the Introit. The opening of the 'Kyrie' shows how it has been adapted (see Examples 6.3a–c). In the 'Sanctus' Molitor then presents the material in inverted skeletal form (Example 6.3d).

Example 6.1   'Introit' from Molitor: *Missa 'Rorate Coeli,' Opus XIV*

Example 6.2   Opening of the 'Agnus Dei' from Molitor: *Missa 'Rorate Coeli', Opus XIV*

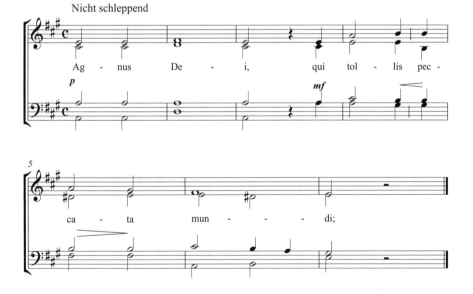

Example 6.3   Opening of the 'Kyrie' from Molitor: *Missa 'Rorate Coeli', Opus XIV*

(a) Skeleton phrase from the opening of the 'Introit'

(b) Variation on the descending phrase taken from the 'Introit'

(c) Combination of phrases (a) and (b) from the 'Introit'

(d) The opening phrase of the 'Sanctus'

Molitor's developmental analysis of a chant is pitch based. Indeed, the note lengths are usually of equal value, despite occasional signs of measured notation. However, Molitor's groups of notes are quite large, so his approach is not governed by Medieval-style neumes. On the other hand, the concept of adding or subtracting notes to adapt a chant phrase to different texts has been clearly grasped.

The second example is quite different. Seymour's *Mass in A♭* is a product of the Irish Cecilian movement. Indeed, it won second prize in a competition sponsored by the Archbishop of Dublin in 1889 that was adjudicated by Haberl. It also seems to have been quite widely performed in England.[26] The approach is more flexible and less academic, with some features taken from more modern music. Technically it is also more accomplished. Moreover, since the alto and bass parts divide, this indicates that a large choir is assumed. In addition, the fact that the alto part rises to e″ suggests that female upper voices were envisaged, contrary to the Cecilian preference for all male choirs with boys' voices. The dynamic range is much greater too, moving from *pp* to *ff*. As for the organ, much of the time it doubles the voice parts in the approved Cecilian *a cappella* style. Indeed, the 'Kyrie' is supposed to be unaccompanied. Elsewhere, though, the organ definitely has an independent role. Moreover at various points the instructions indicate that a pedal board and up to three manuals constitute the ideal. In other words Seymour compromised Cecilian values against the practical needs and preferences of typical parish choirs.

Table 6.1 shows that the work is more coherent than Molitor's Mass. In terms of length, each movement corresponds directly to the size of the text set. Thus the 'Credo', with 280 bars, is the most important part of the Mass. There is a recognisable key cycle. The 'Kyrie' and 'Gloria' are set in A♭; the 'Credo' is set in F (with excursions into B♭ and D major); the 'Sanctus' and 'Benedictus' are in A♭ and its relative F minor; while the 'Agnus Dei' is cast in three sections moving from F minor to A♭ major, to D♭ major, and back to F minor. There is also an alternation between movements dominated by counterpoint (the 'Kyrie' and the 'Sanctus') and those where unison singing or block harmony predominate (the 'Gloria', 'Credo', 'Benedictus' and 'Agnus Dei').

In addition, Seymour achieves much greater thematic unity. Examples 6.4 and 6.5 from the 'Kyrie' display two basic sets of material [a] and [b]. Note how the [b] material is offered in embryo form by the altos in bar 9 of Example 6.4. Their full import only becomes clear with the 'Gloria' and 'Credo'. Example 6.6 shows the relationship [a] has with key elements in the plainchant intonation offered by the celebrant. In the 'Credo' the statement is fairly direct; in the 'Gloria' it is reversed. The main ingredients are the combination of the rising fourth and third to or from the tonic. The plainchant intonation itself is of interest since it is Seymour's 'translation' of the measured plainchant notation current at the time. Meanwhile, Example 6.7 shows how the organ part at the start of the 'Gloria' delivers a 'walking bass' version of the [b] material against a unison vocal figure that is plainly derived from the [a] motif. These features are then picked up in the other movements. The opening of the 'Sanctus' is built out of the 'Kyrie' [b] material (Example 6.8). The 'Agnus Dei' is in many respects a mirror of the 'Kyrie' (see Example 6.9). The opening bass line

---

26 Joseph Seymour, *Mass in A♭* (London, n.d).

Table 6.1   Structural features of Seymour's *Mass in A♭*

Movement	Tempi	Character	Dynamics	Key	No. of bars
Kyrie	Andante ♩ = 84. 4/4	Contrapuntal	*p*	A♭	63
	Alla Breve 𝅗𝅥 = 60. 2/2		*mf*	(A♭ to E♭)	
	Andante ♩ = 84. 4/4		*p/f/p*	(E♭ to A♭)	
Gloria	Allegro Maestoso ♩ = 108. 4/4	Unison or block harmony	*mf* ('et in terra' onwards)	A♭–E♭	98
			pp ('Miserere nobis' section. 4 bars only)	G minor–E♭	
			f ('Quoniam tu solus' to end)	A♭	
Credo	(a) Con moto 𝅗𝅥 = 66. 4/4 ('Patrem omnipotens' onwards)	Unison or block harmony	*f/ff*	F major	280
	(b) Andante ♩ = 76. 3/4 ('Qui propter nos homines')		*p* *f* (from 'Crucifixus pro nobis')	F major D minor into major at 'sepultus est'	
	(c) Andante ♩ =104. 4/4 ('Et resurrexit' onwards)		*f*	B♭ major	
	(d) Con moto 𝅗𝅥 = 66. 4/4 ('Et in spiritum sanctum' onwards)		*f* *ff* on the final 'Amen'	F major	
Sanctus	Lento ♩ = 88. 4/4 time	Counterpoint & block harmony	pp/mf/p/pp	A♭	64 (22 bars)
	3 Vivo /4 time		*f*		

Movement	Tempi	Character	Dynamics	Key	No. of bars
(Benedictus)	Lento ♩ = 88. 4/4 time	Block harmony	**pp/p**	A♭	(42 bars)
	Vivo 4/4 time	Block harmony	**f/ff**		
Agnus Dei	Andante ♩ = 96 4/4 time	Unison or solo vs. block harmony	mf/pp/mf/p	(a) F minor to A♭ major	56
			mf/p/mf/p	(b) A♭ major	
			f/p/ppp	(c) D♭ major to F major	

Example 6.4   Extract from the 'Kyrie' of Seymour's *Mass in A♭* (the organ part has been left out here)

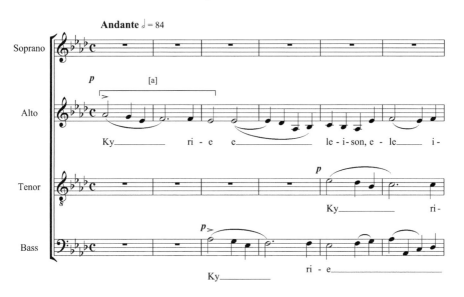

continued

Example 6.4 *concluded*

has the same [a] material, albeit in F minor; the 'miserere' phrase presents the [b] material on a C major pedal.

Throughout, the approach is essentially motivic and ultimately derived from plainchant. In this sense, Seymour conforms to Renaissance polyphonic ideals as understood by the Cecilian movement. On the other hand this is balanced by his willingness to use up-to-date harmonic methods. The 'Benedictus' provides a striking instance of this with a shift from A♭ to G♯ major preparing the way for a temporary modulation into E major! (Example 6.10)

Example 6.5   Second extract from the 'Kyrie' of Seymour's *Mass in A♭*

Example 6.6   Seymour's *Mass in A♭*

(a) The celebrant's opening intonation for the 'Gloria'

(b) The opening intonation of the 'Credo'

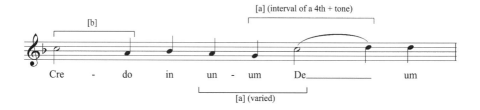

(c) The opening motif from the 'Credo'

(d) The basic (a) motif from the 'Kyrie'

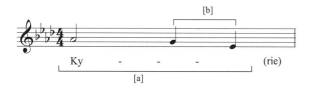

Example 6.7   The 'walking bass' accompaniment at the start of the 'Gloria' in Seymour's *Mass in A♭*

Example 6.8   Opening of the 'Sanctus' from Seymour's *Mass in A♭*

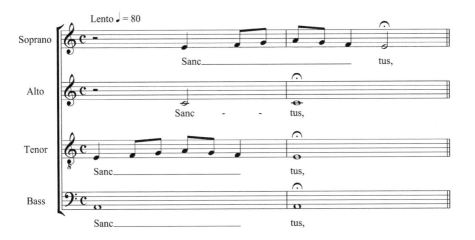

Example 6.9   The opening section of the 'Agnus Dei' from Seymour's *Mass in A♭*

continued

Example 6.9   *concluded*

These elements reveal the congruity between some Cecilians and 'modern' composers, such as Sewell, Tozer and Zulueta. For instance, Tozer, like Sewell, edited motets by Soriano in Cary's *Antiphons of the Blessed Virgin Mary* series alongside works by himself, Webbe and Cecilians such as Joseph Smith. The exact dividing line between the two sides can be ascertained by discussion of a work such as Zulueta's *Mass of the English Martyrs*.[27] The title is suggestive; for Zulueta, as a member of the Society of Jesus, would have been thinking not just of Thomas More and John Fisher, but of such Jesuit Elizabethan and Jacobean figures as Edmund Campion, Robert Southwall and Thomas Garnet. Not surprisingly, then, he moved further in a Renaissance polyphonic direction than is apparent in *Adoro Te Devote*.

For a start, the Mass was intended 'for voices alone for use in Lent and Advent'. It therefore conforms to Ultramontane liturgical preferences and the accepted idea that Renaissance polyphony should be sung *a cappella*. However a 'Gloria' with an organ part was 'added for Feasts and Festivals'. The fact that this is set in G major, as opposed to the predominant key of F, suggests that it was composed as an afterthought.

---

27 Francis M. de Zulueta, *Mass of the English Martyrs* (London, n.d.).

Example 6.10   The enharmonic modulation in the 'Benedictus' from Seymour's
                Mass in A♭

Next, although the harmony has modern chromatic inflections, the effect is much simpler than in Sewell's *Mass of St Philip Neri*, as Example 6.11 shows. Here, at bar 8, there is even a sixteenth-century style suspension and cadence. What is more, although there is a recognisable melody, there are clear motivic elements within it. There is even an opening solo 'incipit'. Nevertheless, the fact remains that this is not a fragment from plainchant, such as Seymour might have used; and, except at 'Qui sedes ad dexteram patris' in the 'Gloria', Zulueta's reliance on melodies precludes the development of elaborate counterpoint such as can be found in Sewell's *Mass of St Philip Neri*.

In addition Zulueta, like Sewell, cannot resist word painting for Romantic pictorial effect. For instance the material for 'Quoniam tu solus' in the 'Gloria' is first given by a soprano soloist, then presented by all. Immediately before this, at 'miserere nobis', Zulueta suggests a sense of abasement by the muddying effect of splitting the choir into an SSAATTBB formation singing first *p*, then repeating the passage *pp*. Here too, and in a manner reminiscent of what has been noted in Sewell's *Mass of St Philip Neri*, the alternation between the two basic chords of D minor and its tonic A major mirrors the conflicting emotions of fear and reassurance that Zulueta hopes to create. Similarly, in the 'Credo' Zulueta resorts to what can only be described as theatrical drama with the sudden change to *ff* at 'est' in the phrase 'sub Pontio Pilato passus et sepultus est' (see Example 6.12). This Mass, then, demonstrates

Example 6.11   Opening passage from Zulueta's *Mass of the English Martyrs*

Example 6.12   Zulueta's treatment of 'Passus et sepultus est' in his *Mass of the English Martyrs*

that, although Zulueta was not unaffected by the Cecilian movement, he remained a 'modernist' at heart.

Cecilian influence in late nineteenth-century England

Cecilian influences penetrated England both directly and indirectly. Many Cecilian works were published by Friedrich Pustet of Ratisbon; usually these were sold in England via Breitkopf and Härtel. Several attempts were made to found Cecilian societies. Archbishop Ullathorne's at Olton, created in 1888, has already been mentioned; but earlier, in 1875, one was set up by Fr Victor Schobel at Oscott, which at that time was just a school, following the temporary departure of the seminarians to Olton in 1873. However, in 1889 the seminarians returned and the two organisations amalgamated.[28] Meanwhile, in 1876, a national Society of St Gregory and St Cecilia had been attempted. In 1888 this was repeated with the formation of an English Society of St Cecilia; and in 1906 the London Society of St Cecilia was founded.[29] Indirectly, influence was exerted through societies formed in the USA and Ireland. In the USA there were societies in New York, Newport (Rhode Island) and Cincinnati (Ohio). Of these the most active was that at Cincinnati, founded by Joseph Singenberger, who had studied at Ratisbon. Friedrich Pustet also set up a branch of his publishing business there, and references to its magazine – *Caecilia* – occur in part books belonging to St Cuthbert's Church, Durham, indicating that copies circulated in England.[30] The Irish Cecilian Society was founded in 1878 by Nicholas Donnelly, who also played a key role in setting up the Gregorian School in Rome. Within a year its membership peaked at 730. Donnelly had been a pupil at the Irish College in Rome and visited Ratisbon in 1873. In 1879 he founded the journal *Lyra Ecclesiastica*. Among other things this published the decrees of the National Synod held at Maynooth in 1879 along with its official list (and supplements) of approved church music. From 1883, additional editorial assistance was provided by Joseph Seymour, an organist from Cork who came to Dublin in 1882 and had been trained at Mechlin and Ratisbon. Seymour's compositions circulated quite widely in England and later appeared on diocesan lists of approved church music published there after 1904.[31] Another key figure was Henry Bewerunge, who managed *Lyra Ecclesiastica* from 1891 till the collapse of the Irish Cecilian society in 1903. As of

---

28 Judith Champ, *Oscott College Chapel: A temple of living stones* (Birmingham, 2002), pp. 47–8.

29 Kieran Daly, *Catholic Church Music in Ireland 1878–1903: The Cecilian Reform Movement* (Dublin, 1995), p. 107. Mager, *The Debate over the Revival of Ancient Church Music*, pp. 329, 331, 334–5.

30 Daly, pp. 15–16, 107. Hayburn, p. 115. For manuscript items copied from *Caecilia* at St Cuthbert's Church, Durham see the reference to two anonymous Litanies in the Organ Book and matching part books there. F.X. Witt's *Mass of St Caecilia* and a 'Two Part Mass' by Simon Schter were also copied into the same volumes. The latter was sung at the 1910 consecration ceremonies.

31 Daly, pp. 22–35, 44–5.

1902 he was also editor of the *Irish Musical Monthly*.[32] In addition, while professor of music at Maynooth seminary, he arranged a considerable quantity of Renaissance polyphony for male voices, some of which was published and made available in England.[33]

Cecilian policies were actively promoted by several English bishops. Like Wiseman, Robert Cornthwaite had been Rector at the English College in Rome, and as bishop of Beverley he produced the first list in England of officially approved music, drawing almost exclusively on the Vereinskatalog of the German Cecilian Society. He also recruited Robert W. Oberhoffer to direct the music at the projected pro-Cathedral of St Wilfrid's, York. Elsewhere, Meyer Lutz's professional orchestra and choir at Southwark Cathedral, with their Viennese Classical repertoire, were abolished by John Butt shortly after his consecration there in 1885; while in Manchester Herbert Vaughan, a protégé of Manning, appointed G.A. Oesch, a pupil of Haberl, to run the choir at St Wilfrid's church, in 1878. His successor Louis Casartelli vigorously continued his policies, as has been seen.[34]

However, the chief conduits for Cecilian influence were the seminaries. Naturally Oscott was among the most receptive, and here Wiseman's policies were continued by Monsignor Henry Parkinson. In 1889, following the return of the seminarians, he put together a special choir for the performance of more complex music; and in 1904 the *Tablet* published details of the annual St Cecilia festival held there. In addition to plainchant from the *Liber Usualis*, works by Lassus, Nanini, Palestrina, Richert, Soriano and Victoria were performed, alongside more modern imitative works by Benz, Engel, Haller, Hamma, Mitterer, Perosi, Piel and Singenberger. At Upholland College in Lancashire, F. Ambrose Turner introduced works by Cecilian composers such as Johann Molitor and Oreste Ravanello, works that were still being performed there in the late 1920s.[35] A spectacular collection of Cecilian music survives at Ushaw, where there are several bound volumes of works stamped in gold with the signature of Edwin Bonney, choirmaster between 1899 and 1917.[36] They include music by at least forty Cecilian composers, including Michael Haller, Ignatius Mitterer, Johann Molitor, Singenberger, Seymour and Witt alongside works by Anerio, Byrd, Casciolini and Victoria.

Bonney also possessed three bound volumes containing more than 100 publications edited by Charles Bordes. In 1891 Bordes was appointed music director of the church of St Gervais in Paris. The following year he founded the Chanteurs de St Gervais, specifically to perform recently re-discovered Renaissance polyphonic

---

32 Ibid., pp. 117–18 and 164.

33 See, for example, the reference to his arrangement of six motets by Palestrina of 1898 in the *List of Church Music* (Salford), p. 164.

34 Mager, *The Debate over the Revival of Ancient Church Music*, pp. 308–11, 320, 337 and 338.

35 See the letter by his nephew Canon J.F. Turner to Laurentia McLachlan of 28/9/1928 in SAA, Box D.L. McL. to Allen/Holland, Edeson, Turner. For the year 1928 works by Ravanello (*Veritas Mea*), Molitor (*Mass Opus XIII*), Witt (*Salve Regina*), Terry (*Mass: 'Veni Sancte Spiritus'*), Palestrina (*O Filii et Filiae*) and Victoria (the *Turbae* for Good Friday and Holy Saturday) are mentioned.

36 C.G. Clifford, 'The Choir', *UM*, 45 (July 1935): 112–16.

works, many of which were then published in his *Anthologies* series. In conjunction with Vincent D'Indy he also founded the Schola Cantorum, Paris, where musicians were taught plainchant and Renaissance polyphony.[37]

Beyond the seminaries, Cecilian influence was variable. For example, several Pustet publications survive from St Augustine's church, Preston.[38] More unusual perhaps is the survival of 31 compositions by identifiable Cecilian composers in the household chapel of the Tempest family at Broughton, near Skipton. Twelve of these can be found in a copy of Michael Haller's *Cantica Sacra Vol. III* of 1893; 10 more appear in Haller's *Maier-Grusse I Samlung Zehn Gesange zur sebigsten Jungfrau und Gottermutter Maria für vierstimmijen Gemischterchor* of 1903. Both were published by Pustet of Ratisbon. In addition there are separate copies of works by Koenen, Koethe, Molitor, Singenberger and Witt. Alongside them though are works by Webbe, Schulthes and Reger, the latter two of whom were not Cecilians.

Elsewhere, Cecilian and Renaissance polyphonic works had only limited impact. The examples from Lancashire given in Table 6.2 show this clearly.

Table 6.2   Number of works composed before 1650 and Cecilian imitations in selected collections of music

Collection	Proportion of compositions written before 1650 (excluding Plainchant)	Proportion of pre-1650 compositions published before 1914 (excluding editions by Terry after 1904)	Number of Cecilian compositions (excluding works by Terry)
St Mary of the Angels, Bolton Le Sands	3/50	0/3	7/50
St Mary, Burnley	17/96	2/17	5/96
St Mary, Chipping	3/126	3/3	3/126
St Michael, Alston Lane, nr Longridge	14/342	6/14	2/342
Our Lady of Mt Carmel, Liverpool	3/66	2/3	2/66

37 Harry Haskell, *The Early Music Revival: A History* (London, 1988), pp. 45–50.

38 These are currently stored in the Talbot Library, Preston. They include works by Bill, Joanne, Ebner, Gruber, E. Gruberski, Haller, Singenberger, Stehle and Witt as well as three parts of *The Choir*. In addition there are works by Palestrina (*Missa Papae Marcelli* (London, 1881)) and Victoria (*Missa 'O Quam Gloriosam'*, published by James Burns (London, 1848)). However, there are also Masses by non-Cecilians such as Kalliwoda and J.E. Turner.

The reasons for such phenomena are hard to establish, and beyond a certain point you are dependent on informed conjecture. This is because there are no surviving statements by choirmasters and local priests about the motivation behind their selection of repertoire. Clearly, the persistence of Viennese Classical music and its successors up till the end of the century has some bearing on the issue since, automatically, it made it hard for other styles to gain a foothold. This, though, is not necessarily proof of its popularity. Force of habit could just as easily explain a choir's reluctance to abandon a hard-learned repertoire; and here it should be noted that most of these missions had been established *before* 1870. However, this cannot apply to Bolton Le Sands and Mount Carmel, whose choral establishments were set up after that date. Cecilian failure, then, may have something to do with the allegations of poor aesthetic quality referred to earlier. If this was so, it might explain why no amount of official promotion could overcome the aesthetic sensibilities of local choirmasters. However, this begs several questions. Leaving aside questions of technical competence, which can be measured, purely aesthetic music judgements are ultimately a matter of personal opinion. Note that it was not just Cecilian imitations, but the genuine Renaissance polyphonic article that was not being performed, which few dared openly to condemn on aesthetic grounds. Moreover, if we accept that there is an absolute musical aesthetic, then we must ask why local choirmasters, many of them amateurs, should necessarily have superior judgement than Cecilian 'experts'. An obvious answer might be that the latter were biased in favour of their own cause. Nonetheless, differences in emphasis amongst them cannot be concealed, as the comparison between the Molitor and Seymour Masses shows. Terry, in particular, was excoriating about Cecilian music, describing it as 'invariably dull, barren and uninspired; and the bulk of it amateurish to the last degree'. Yet, as shall be seen later, he himself was a Cecilian imitator![39] Besides, in church music, aesthetic considerations to some extent have to be subordinated to functional liturgical requirements. By the official standards of the day, Cecilian compositions were appropriate, Viennese Classical ones were not. Even Terry acknowledged this.[40] Yet, in this context, any claim that the promotion of Cecilian compositions was a triumph of Ultramontane ideology over aesthetic taste seems over-simplistic. The issue was whether such works were thought to work effectively *in the given liturgical context* at a *local* level.

It is also obvious that, regardless of whether such music is aesthetically 'bad' or 'good', it will not be performed if it is not readily available. Here the behaviour of the music publishing industry is particularly relevant. As noted earlier, most Cecilian compositions were published and imported from abroad. This reduced their level of availability. It also shows that in the late nineteenth-century English publishers do not appear to have paid much attention to the genre, despite the promising beginnings made by Vincent Novello and James Burns. Except with hymnody, Burns and Oates after the 1860s gradually pulled out of music publishing. At the same time Butler and Thomas Richardson disappeared from the scene. No interest in Renaissance

---

39 Richard Terry, 'Why is Church Music so bad?', in *A Forgotten Psalter and other Essays* (London, 1929), p. 109.

40 Ibid., pp. 106–107.

polyphony was displayed by Boosey, whilst Novellos invested only a modest amount of effort in the genre. It is significant that between 1856 and 1866 J.A. Novello was handing over the business to Henry Littleton, who was not a Catholic. Novellos anyway preferred to concentrate on the more lucrative choral society market and broaden their market base through takeovers of other firms with their existing stock. In addition, the strengthening of copyright enforcement, coupled with the changes in production methods described earlier, meant that they had every incentive to continue marketing the embassy chapel repertoire they had already published to a secure block of customers rather than risk expensive outlays on the uncertain Renaissance polyphonic and Cecilian markets.

Conclusions

Thus, by the mid-1890s, Cecilian attempts to promote Renaissance polyphony and imitations thereof had only achieved a modest degree of success. What was needed was a new impetus. This would be provided by renewed official endorsement, especially in *Tra Le Sollectudini*, and through the vigorous promotion with a new 'English' dimension added by Terry, coupled with the arrival of a new company – Cary and Co – willing to publish a wide selection of such works in significant quantities.

This means that the implications of the Cecilian movement only really became manifest in the early twentieth century. Nonetheless, their importance cannot be underrated. First, the movement reoriented the international dimension of Catholic music in England from a Classical Viennese to a Renaissance polyphonic base. At first, as Ultramontanes hoped, it seemed to strengthen the 'Roman' aspect of this phenomenon; but, as the association of Lassus with Bavaria and French examples had already showed, this could be tempered by the rediscovery of national strains. This, as shall be seen, was what Terry undertook.

Second, partly due to its association with Ultramontanism, the revival had a strongly authoritarian streak. This was revealed by a strident insistence by some on a plainchant and Renaissance polyphonic repertoire only, by the production of lists of officially approved music and by the conscious *imitation* of older styles in new works. Not only would this have tended to stultify creativity; it reduced the links between the latest developments in music and what was performed in church, links that composers such as Sewell wished to maintain. In short the Catholic Church was abdicating from the position it had hitherto held at the forefront of musical innovation, and as illustrated by its adoption of the Classical Viennese style in the late eighteenth century. This is symptomatic of its wider rejection of a modern secular world and its conscious appeal to a Christian past.

PART IV
Music for Extra-Liturgical Services

Chapter 7

Catholic Vernacular Hymnody
c.1842–1913

Origins and development

The late nineteenth century witnessed the development of a considerable body of Catholic vernacular hymnody, evidence for which lies in the growing number and size of Catholic hymnals. For convenience these can be divided between those produced by religious orders, sometimes to meet particular local circumstances, and those aiming at a national Catholic constituency. Table 7.1 lists some of them.

This development occurred despite some apparently paralysing obstacles. In Recusant times the need to keep a low profile, in theory at least, restricted opportunities for the emergence of a Catholic congregational hymn-singing tradition. Even after Emancipation there was a persistent reluctance among many Catholic congregations to sing. Moreover, during the late nineteenth century there seemed to be little place for vernacular hymnody in a predominantly Latin liturgy, especially in the face of increasingly stringent ecclesiastical legislation. However, several factors conspired to overcome such difficulties. First, throughout Recusant times numerous translations of Latin hymns were incorporated into the *Primer* and other liturgical or devotional books intended for use by the laity. For example, Blom's catalogue of translations in various editions of the *Primer* between 1599 and 1800 lists 206 English versions of 114 Latin texts.[1] In addition Tessa Watt has pointed to evidence for carol singing in publications produced between 1562 and 1638.[2] Second, in Britain generally, the nineteenth century was an age of hymn singing, as shown by the production of *Hymns Ancient and Modern* in numerous editions after 1861 and the preparation of the *English Hymnal*.[3] Catholics, envious of the vigour of Protestant hymn singing, could not remain uninfluenced by this. Third, there was the impact of Anglican converts: Richard Terry, the principal musical editor of

---

1   Joannes Maria Blom, *The Post-Tridentine Primer* (n.p., 1979), pp. 80–103, 138–53, 158–61, 197–238.

2   Tessa Watt, *Cheap Print and Popular Piety 1550–1640* (Cambridge, 1991), pp. 86–7. Note, in particular, the registration of several carol books with the London Stationers Company between 1562 and 1638. This, of course, suggests that carol singing was not confined to Catholics, although Watt also draws attention to Protestant literature attacking such practices.

3   William H. Monk (ed.), *Hymns Ancient and Modern* (London, 1861 and in subsequent revised edns). William Birkbeck, Percy Dreamer and others (eds), *The English Hymnal* (London, 1906).

Table 7.1   A selection of Catholic hymnals c.1842–1913

(a) Hymnals produced by religious orders

Editor	Title	Place of publication	Publisher	Date of publication
Anon.	*St Winifrid Hymn Book* (Jesuit)	London	R. Butler	n.d.
Frederick Faber (text only)	*The Oratory Hymn Book* (Oratory)	London	Thomas Richardson and Son	1854
Anon.	*St Dominic's Hymn Book* (Dominican)	London	R. and T. Washbourne	1881
Anon.	*Convent Hymns and Music used by the Sisters of Notre Dame*	Liverpool	Printed by Rockcliff Bros. Ltd.	1891
Franck Birtchnell and Moir Brown	*The Notre Dame Hymn Tune Book* (Ladies of Notre Dame, Liverpool)	Liverpool	Printed by Rockcliff Bros. Ltd.	1905

(b) Hymnals intended for national circulation

Editor	Title	Place of publication	Publisher	Date of publication
Frederick Faber (text only)	*Hymns by Frederick William Faber*	London	Burns and Oates Ltd.	1861/1890R
Henri Hemy	*Crown of Jesus Music. Parts I–III.* Part IV was added in subsequent editions	London	Thomas Richardson and Son. Later by Burns and Oates Ltd.	1864
William Maher and Francis Trappes	*Liturgical Hymns*	London	R. Butler	n.d. (pre-1877, when Maher died)
No name supplied, but actually F. Police	*The Parochial Hymn Book*	London	Burns and Oates Ltd.	1883

Editor	Title	Place of Publication	Publisher	Date of Publication
Albert Edmonds Tozer	*Catholic Hymns, Original and Translated*	London	Novello, Ewer and Co/Boosey/ Cary and Co.	1898
John Storer	*The Catholic Tune Book*[a]	London	Alphonse Cary/R. and T. Washbourne Ltd.	1892
Anon.	*Hymns for the Ecclesiastical Year*	London	Art and Book Co.	1895
Charles Gatty and Henry Howard, Duke of Norfolk	*Arundel Hymns*	London	Boosey/R. and T. Washbourne Ltd.	1898/1901/ R1905
Richard Terry et al.	*The Westminster Hymnal*	London	R. and T. Washbourne Ltd.	1912 and several times afterwards[b]
Samuel Ould and William Sewell	*The Book of Hymns with tunes*[c]	London	Cary and Co.	1913/R1933

[a]   The full title reads *The Catholic Tune Book containing a complete collection of tunes in every metre to all English Hymns in general use.*
[b]   *The Westminster Hymnal. New and Revised Edition* (London, 1940) in terms of texts, choice of melodies and harmonisations, is substantially different. All subsequent references in this chapter relate to *The Westminster Hymnal* of 1912.
[c]   This was the Scottish equivalent of *The Westminster Hymnal.*

The Westminster Hymnal (1912 edition), is a classic example, but there were others. In particular the work of three Oratorians – Edward Caswall, Frederick William Faber and Cardinal Henry Newman – cannot be ignored. Table 7.2 show how great a contribution the first two made to the stock of texts in a selection of hymnals.[4]

Fourth, there was the impact of mass production and distribution in a printing and publishing industry that was increasingly centred on London. The *St Winifrid Hymnal* shows the scene before this really took off. Produced by students from the Jesuit seminary of St Bueno's in North Wales, its 12 hymns were designed originally to meet purely local needs. Yet it was published in London by Richard Butler. Faber's hymn collection shows how variants of such a hymnal could break out of a local straitjacket, and simultaneously bridge the divide separating publications for religious orders from those aiming at a national market. An early hymn, 'Hail, Holy Joseph, Hail!' first appeared in *The Catholic Instructor* in 1847. The following year

---

4   Newman's influence is more meagre, for example accounting for eight texts in *The Westminster Hymnal.*

Table 7.2   Texts contributed by Caswall and Faber to some Catholic hymnals

Name of hymnal	Number of texts	Texts contributed by Caswall	Texts contributed by Faber
Crown of Jesus Music (1864)	214	17	16
The Parochial Hymn Book (1883)	633	53	41
The Catholic Hymnal (1898)	186	23	32
Arundel Hymns (1905)	306	21	27
The Westminster Hymnal (1912)	263	86	46

a limited selection was published in Derby by Thomas Richardson. In 1849 Richardson printed a further 1,000 copies under the title *Jesus and Mary, or Catholic Hymns for Singing and Reading*. At this stage, then, Faber had a very restricted circulation. The breakthrough came with the production in 1852 of 10,000 copies of *Jesus and Mary*, an enlarged version of the original, while the 1861 and 1890 editions of *Hymns by Frederick William Faber* held 149 items.[5] A parallel publication was *The Oratory Hymnal*, produced in 1854. This contained 79 hymn texts, of which about a quarter were by Faber. However, its musical companion, *Oratory Hymn Tunes*, edited by William Pitts, organist at the London Oratory, had 93 tunes set to 95 texts, and was still being printed in the early 1900s, as the reference to 'Novello and Co.' shows.[6] *The Catholic Choralist* and *Crown of Jesus Music* show the same broadening of horizons in slightly different ways. *The Catholic Choralist* was originally produced in Dublin for the Irish Catholic market. It therefore came over to England to serve the needs of Irish migrants, and spread from there to the rest of the Catholic community. *The Crown of Jesus Music* is more complex. As noted before it was produced as a musical companion to *The Crown of Jesus* manual, which had urban, North Eastern and Dominican connotations. These are mirrored in the hymnal. Its editor, Henri Hemy, taught music at Ushaw College, near Durham; so the music includes several items by Charles Newsham, President of Ushaw, as well as items by J.D. Aylward, subprior at Woodchester, in Gloucestershire.[7] However, the manual was backed by a battery of Episcopal endorsements, including recommendations by Cardinal Wiseman and Cardinal Cullen in Dublin. *The Crown of Jesus Music* therefore targeted a national constituency that included Ireland. Indeed, like Faber's hymnals, it was published by Thomas Richardson, who by this time had offices in

---

    5   These details have been derived from Faber's own statements in *Hymns by Frederick Faber DD* (London, 1861), pp. vii–xi.

    6   William Pitts (ed.), *Oratory Hymn Tunes* (London, n.d. but post-1902, when the publisher's trade name – 'Novello and Co' – was adopted).

    7   See for example Newsham's *Missa De Sancto Cuthberto.*

London and Dublin, as well as Derby. The initial 1864 edition had three parts, which could be bought separately as well as in a single collection. However, by 1864, a fourth part, containing Masses by Webbe and Newhsam, as well as the plainchant *Missa Pro Defunctis*, was available by 1873; and it was in this form that it continued to be published by Burns Oates and Washbourne into the 1890s.

The changing character and function of Catholic hymns c.1842–1913

Traditional usage

The most fundamental cause – and effect – of the explosion in Catholic vernacular hymnody was the transformation in the function of a Catholic hymn. The Catholic Church inherited from medieval times a stock of Latin hymns, many of which, as has been seen, were translated into English during Recusant times. In their Latin guise especially these were closely associated with the liturgy, whether in the form of Sequences or in the use of particular hymns at certain times of the year. For example, 'Pange Lingua' was always sung on Palm Sunday, while 'Crux Fidelis' and 'Vexilla Regis' were associated with Good Friday.[8] The same is true for the Office, with certain hymns assigned to particular services, feasts or seasons. Such hymns, then, were often incorporated into the relevant liturgical books, as well as appearing in separate 'Hymnale', and there was a tendency to regard them as part of the liturgical cycle in the manner espoused by Guéranger. This aspect was further reinforced by the fact that they were usually sung to plainchant melodies. As Blom has noted, this applied even to English translations. As a result, in early Recusant times especially, these were often fairly literal versions of the Latin originals.[9] However, with plainchant settings of Latin hymns, a variation was for the choir to sing every alternate verse as a faburden, settings of which continued to be composed during the nineteenth century. For example, the choir at Stonyhurst College, Lancashire between 1905 and 1938 is frequently reported to have sung such settings of 'Pange Lingua' and 'Vexilla Regis' by William Maher (1823–77) and Wilhelm Bernard Molique (1802–69) during Holy Week.[10]

Another approach, dating back to the sixteenth century, was to treat the hymn as a choral anthem. Palestrina made several settings of this type. Later Vincent Novello made a widely performed anthem setting of 'Adeste Fideles'. Evidence of a different sort survives in the collection of nineteenth-century music at St Cuthbert's church, Durham. Here the surviving copy of the *Crown of Jesus Music* is marked 'IV' and 'for the use of the choir'. Moreover, only 11 items in its copy of *The Parochial Hymn Book* are marked up, indicating that this hymnal was also used in the same way.

---

8   Note though that the 'Stabat Mater' was also used at Stations of the Cross.
9   Blom, pp. 79–80.
10 For details, see the 'Choir notes' published in most issues of the *SM* during this period. Thus, Maher's setting of 'Pange Lingua' was performed annually between 1905 and 1914, in 1926, 1933, 1936 and 1937. Molique's setting of 'Vexilla Regis' appeared every year between 1905 and 1912, and between 1934 and 1938, and in 1914, 1923, 1926 and 1945.

Such practices discouraged congregational hymn singing. The assignment of particular hymns to particular times in the liturgy militated against the regular performance needed to familiarise people with the music, there were difficulties singing the plainchant, and their use as anthems or in faburden settings worked in favour of choirs at the expense of the general public.

Translations

It was thus essential to decouple hymns from their liturgical associations. This was achieved in two stages. First, from the late Middle Ages the Office was often recited in private, hence the value of the Breviary. The emergence of missionary religious orders, such as the Jesuits, who obviously could not recite the Office in a community, further encouraged this tendency, especially in countries such as Britain where Catholics were persecuted and therefore had to keep a low profile. Second, English hymn translations appeared not just in the *Primer*, but in other vernacular and semi-vernacular publications intended for use by the laity. From the late seventeenth century onwards this encouraged the use of freer translations and even the writing of original vernacular hymn texts. In the long run this loosened the ties between texts and plainchant, especially if they were *spoken* or meditated upon in private. A notable example of this tendency was *Devotions in the ancient way of Offices* (Paris, 1668), by John Austin (1610–69). This has 40 hymns, most of which are free paraphrases of Latin texts; but some are original compositions.[11] These traditions continued into the nineteenth century. *The Catholic Choralist* is a notable example. An even later specimen is *The Roman Breviary translated into English*, by John, the Marquis of Bute (Edinburgh, 1879); and some of these texts appear in twentieth-century Catholic hymnals, including *The Westminster Hymnal*.[12]

Third, such developments were picked up by Anglican converts. However, it should be noted that their activity sprang from the early nineteenth-century interest in religious poetry and hymn writing shown by many High Churchmen, as Nancy de Flon has demonstrated.[13] Nevertheless, they had similar motivations. Such work

---

11 Blom, pp. 146–9. For details of the insertion of translations into other publications see pp. 150–51 (*Office of Holy Week* (1670)), with translations by Sir George and Sir Walter Blount), 151–3 (*The Evening Office of the Church*, published in numerous editions from c.1688 onwards, including seven by Thomas Meighan and five by James Marmaduke), 158–61 (*The Garden of the Soul* (1740)).

12 Ibid., pp. 158–61. For examples of such hymns in the *WH*, see nos. 47 and 57 (by John Dryden), and no. 48 (by John Austin). More can be found in the revised edition of 1940, viz. nos. 63, and 147 (by John Dryden), 73 and 92 (by Richard Crashaw revised by John Austin), 165 (an original text by John Austin), 18 (by Richard Verstegan), and 109 (by Bute). Strictly speaking, Lingard's 'Hail Queen of Heaven, the Ocean Star' does not belong to this tradition, although clearly it was inspired by the texts 'Ave Maris Stella' and 'Salve Regina'. It was originally written for the Gillow family at Leighton Hall, near Lancaster and first published in *The Catholic Magazine* during 1834 (vol. 6: 607). John Trappes-Lomax (ed.), *The Lingard-Lomax Letters*, CRS, 77 (2000): 30.

13 Nancy Marie de Flon, *Edward Caswall: Newman's brother and friend* (Leominster, 2005), pp. 149–50, citing publications by John Chandler, William J. Copeland, John Keble,

was regarded as part of their pastoral ministry. In particular, they wanted to make not just the liturgy, but the truths and tenets of Christianity part of the daily lives of the laity, whether through services, schools or personal devotions.[14] Undoubtedly, it was also seen as a means to re-connect with a medieval past. For nineteenth-century Catholics, three such works are outstanding: John Henry Newman's *Hymni Ecclesiae* (1838), Edward Caswall's *Lyra Catholica* (1849) (the most influential of the trio), and Frederick Oakeley's *Lyra Liturgica* (1865).[15] Newman's collection was assembled while he was an Anglican; Caswall's was published two years after his conversion, but many of the texts and some original poetry and hymns that he published later were drafted while he was still an Anglican.[16] High Anglican attitudes are therefore present, in particular a wish to 'Anglicise' Roman Catholic elements. Newman, for example, drew on medieval breviaries from Salisbury and York, as well as ones from Paris and Rome.

Translations rarely produce an exact reproduction of the original. To be effective there usually has to be some modification, sometimes even transformation. Caswall's translation of 'Stabat Mater' shows one way that this could happen. In the Breviary and the Missal it is organised into three-line stanzas.[17] However, Caswall in his translation uses six-line verses, and these are grouped into three separate hymns corresponding to Vespers, Matins and Lauds in the Office of the Feast of the Seven Douleurs.[18] In *The Westminster Hymnal*, although the text is still appears in six-line verses, it is presented as one entity, presumably because here it is associated primarily with 'Passiontide'.

A second effect follows from the fact that different people may produce radically different translations of the same text. In effect, translation can create a proliferation in the stock of hymns, which then have to be assigned different tunes. This happens four times in the *Westminster Hymnal*.[19] For example, Table 7.3 shows what happens to 'Ave Maris Stella'.

The effect on the choice of melody is obvious, even though both have the same 6666 metre. No. 109 has 7 four-line verses; No. 110 has 3½ eight-line verses.

Richard Mant and, of course, John Henry Newman.

14 Ibid., pp. 151–3, 158–60. See also her article: 'A work to do': Edward Caswall and Pastoral ministry at the Birmingham Oratory during the 1850s and 1860s', *RH*, 27/1 (2004): 103–123. This gives a detailed account of Caswall's educational work at Stratford (during his Anglian days), Edgbaston and Smethick.

15 John Henry Newman (ed.), *Hymni Ecclesiae* (London, 1838/1865R). Edward Caswall (trans.), *Lyra Catholica, containing all the Breviary and Missal hymns with others from various sources* (London, 1849). Frederick Oakeley (ed.), *Lyra Liturgica: Reflections in verse for Holy Days and Seasons* (London, 1865).

16 Flon, *Edward Caswall*, p. 153.

17 *Breviarum Romanum* (Mechlin, 1913/1920R/1932R), pp. 689–90 and 701.

18 Edward Caswall (ed.), *Hymns and Poems* (London, 1873), no. 76. Verses 1–5 are sung at Vespers, verses 6–7 at Matins, and verses 8–10 at Lauds.

19 These, apart from 'Ave Maris Stella' concern 'Adoro Te Devote', where translations are supplied by Caswall and J.D. Aylward (nos. 76 and 81); 'Jesu Dulcis Memoria', again with two translations by Caswall and one by Aylward (nos. 19, 45 and 67); and 'Lux Alma, Jesu Mentium', using translations by Newman and Caswall (nos. 60 and 242).

Table 7.3   Two translations of 'Ave Maris Stella' in *The Westminster Hymnal*

No. 109: from an anonymously edited *Selection of Catholic Hymns.* Glasgow, 1867.	No. 110: by Edward Caswall
Hail, thou resplendent star, Which shinest o'er the main; Best Mother of Our God, And ever Virgin Queen.	Hail, thou Star of Ocean! Portal of the sky! Ever Virgin Mother Of the Lord most High!
Hail happy gate of bliss, Greeted by Gabriel's tongue; Negotiate our peace, And cancel Eva's wrong	Oh! By Gabriel's Ave, Utter'd long ago. Eva's name reversing, 'Stablish peace below'

Accordingly, Terry composed two separate hymn tunes, each treating the hymn as seven four-line verses; but with No. 110 he also supplied another melody by John Richardson which kept to the eight-line verse structure by stopping half way through the music on the final verse.

New devotional texts

Parallel with the production of translated texts, many new hymns were composed as devotional poems, supplementing the stock inherited from Recusant times. Here, once again, important work was done by Caswall. For example, his collection *Hymns and Poems, Original and Translated* contains 242 texts of his own alongside the 238 translations abstracted from his *Lyra Catholica*. Even more significant was Frederick Faber's *Jesus and Mary, or Catholic hymns for singing and reading*. Faber's object, as the title suggests, was 'first, to furnish some simple and original hymns for singing; secondly to provide English Catholics with a hymn book *for reading*'.[20] As an Oratorian, Faber was interested in developing devotional literature for Jesuit-style spiritual exercises or examinations of conscience on occasions such as retreats. However, taking their cue from *The Catholic Choralist*, both Caswall (another Oratorian) and Oakeley recognised that there could be a connection between this and private study of translations from the Breviary. The full title of Oakeley's collection is *Lyra Liturgica: Reflections in verse for Holy Days and Seasons*. Similarly, Caswall states in *Lyra Catholica* that 'the laity are not bound, like the clergy, to its [the Breviary's] recital, yet that portion of it that includes Hymns and Canticles might be frequently, if not daily, recited by them with great spiritual benefit and truth'. This, it should be noted, is an almost exact paraphrase of William Young's ideas in *The Catholic Choralist*.[21] The effect, once again, was to separate hymn texts from music.

---

20 Faber, *Jesus and Mary*, Preface, n.p.

21 Caswall, *Lyra Catholica*, p. v. *The Catholic Choralist* states 'although, by reason of their secular avocations, the laity are not bound, like the clergy, to its recital; yet that portion

Hymns for schools

However, a third development worked powerfully to reconnect hymn texts with music, but not, it should be noted, with plainchant. Hymns came to be seen as useful adjuncts in children's religious education. Thus, Faber's 11 original hymn texts were intended for his St Wilfrid's schools, on the site of what became Cotton College, in Staffordshire. Similarly, the *Crown of Jesus Music* has 60 children's hymn settings, 38 of which are in a specially designated children's section (Part 1: 'Hymns chiefly for children'). Hemy's educational psychology is simple yet sophisticated, and it is derived directly from the principles underpinning the *Crown of Jesus* manual. In addition, the link with private devotions should be noted.

> In every instance ... an alliance between sense and sound is secured: the people become familiarised with the music, and can use it in their domestic devotions; the melody becomes associated and intertwined in the mind with the Hymn, the tune suggests the Hymn; the Hymn calls to memory the tune.

Hemy practised what he preached. For example, the text 'I am a faithful Catholic' is set to Papageno's aria 'Ein mädchen oder weibchen wünscht Papageno sich' from Mozart's opera *The Magic Flute*.[22] The effect was to encourage two types of text: texts with a didactic or doctrinal purpose, and texts with a devotional function. Didactic texts can be subdivided as follows: texts designed to propagate doctrine, for example Newman's 'Firmly I Believe and Truly'; texts that were intended to inculcate loyalty, such as 'I am a Faithful Catholic' or Wiseman's 'Full in the Panting Heart of Rome'; and texts reminding people of past endeavours and sacrifices, such as 'Faith of Our Fathers' or Sister Mary Xavier's 'Martyrs of England!'[23] Similar subdivisions can be applied to devotional hymns. Of these the most important concern the cult of the Virgin Mary. Out of the 263 texts in *The Westminster Hymnal*, 34 fall into this category.[24] Similarly, the *Notre Dame Hymn Tune Book* devoted 58 out of 137 texts to the subject. In this context the underlying thinking, as set out by the *Crown of Jesus* manual, is worth noting.

> All the hymns in this book are intended to be used either as prayers or meditations. Many of them are addressed to God through his servants, his martyrs, or his Mother. It must be remembered that every prayer to a saint is in reality a prayer to God, for in addressing a saint you are certain it is passed on to God, who was in your intention the ultimate object of your prayer.[25]

---

of it which includes hymns and canticles ... might, without interfering with their ordinary business, be frequently, if not daily, recited by them with great spiritual benefit and fruit'. Young, *The Catholic Choralist*, p. i.

22 *CJM*, no. 62.

23 All these except 'I am a faithful Catholic' are provided in the *WH*, nos. 245, 139, 138 and 196.

24 See, for example Faber's 'Mother Mary, at thine altar' in the children's section (no. 155).

25 Alban Groom, Raymund Palmer, Robert Suffield (eds), *The Crown of Jesus, a complete Catholic Manual of devotion, doctrine and instruction* (London, Dublin, Derby, 1862), p. 16.

The spread of Catholic vernacular hymnody

In addition, many Catholic schools, especially Jesuit establishments, had sodalities, or prayer groups holding regular services of a devotional nature. Senior sodalities were dedicated to the Virgin Mary, junior groups to the Guardian Angels. *The Westminster Hymnal* devotes nine hymns to the latter theme. There were also May devotions, again dedicated to the cult of Mary. It was only a step to extend the use of hymns from these activities to those promoted by the proliferating numbers of guilds and confraternities. The *Crown of Jesus Music* has hymns specifically devoted to the Temperance Guild, the Confraternity of the Holy Family, the Confraternity of the Bona Mors and the Sanctuary Guild.[26] Similar groupings can be found in the *Parochial Hymn Book* and the *Catholic Hymnal* of 1898.[27] *The Westminster Hymnal* only has sections for the Sacred Heart, the Precious Blood, the Rosary and the Holy Family, but many of the hymns devoted to particular saints could be adapted for this purpose. St Joseph, for instance, for whom nine hymns are provided, was the patron saint of guilds for young men.[28] Hymns, then, came to be seen as instruments for instilling social and moral discipline in a chain extending from the church, through the guilds or schools, and into the home. Thus, *The Catholic Choralist* was intended 'for the use of the choir, drawing room, cloister and cottage'. It was meant to 'serve the cause of temperance and religion, by supplying innocent, edifying, and agreeable occupation for hours of recreation which an indulgent Providence allows to a weak and exhausted nature'.[29]

Guilds frequently took part in outdoor processions, not just on civic occasions, but at events such as Corpus Christi and Palm Sunday. Almost invariably hymns were sung on such occasions, usually accompanied by a band. This is precisely what the Catholic Guild at Hurst Green, Stonyhurst, the oldest in the country, still does every year on St Peter's Day. This explains why early editions of *The Westminster Hymnal* advertise the availability of band parts from Terry, its musical editor. Note also a set of six 'Litanies of BVM for processions' in the *Crown of Jesus Music*, indicating that this form of music was also sung at such events.[30]

All this fitted in with a general shift in the use of hymns from the Mass and the Office to extra-liturgical devotions, in which guilds and confraternities played an active part. As suggested earlier, these enjoyed an enormous growth in popularity at the expense of Office services in Catholic parish life during the nineteenth century. Benediction was the most important of these services, and hymns tended to be sung before or after this devotion, linking it up with other services – such as Rosary devotions, Compline, Vespers or Stations of the Cross – that commonly took place on Sunday afternoons and evenings. Thus, as Albert Tozer explains in the 1898

26 *CJM*, nos. 9, 56 and 57, 67 and 104 respectively.

27 [F. Police (ed.)], *The Parochial Hymn Book*, nos. 633–701. Tozer (ed.), *The Catholic Hymnal*, nos. 613–45.

28 *WH*, nos. 173–9.

29 Young (ed.), *The Catholic Choralist*, in the dedication to Rev. Theobald Matthew, n.p.

30 *CJM*, nos. 272–7. The possible use of a band is also specified on the title page of Young, *The Catholic Choralist*, n.p.

edition of *The Catholic Hymnal*, 'the common practice among Catholics, hitherto, has been to look upon an English hymn as something of no great importance – a kind of 'stop-gap' in the interval between Vespers and the sermon, or while the Altar is being prepared for the rite of Benediction'.[31]

Little wonder that the principal Benediction texts appear at the back of every edition of *The Westminster Hymnal*.[32] Indeed, some hymns were specifically written for the service, the most obvious example being Francis Stanfield's 'Sweet Sacrament Divine'.[33] Likewise Part III of the *Crown of Jesus Music* is organised into 20 'Benediction Services', along with 13 'Hymns to the Blessed Sacrament' in Part II, underlining this hymnal's usage as a Benediction book. There are also three other sub-sections in Part II – the 'Crown of Jesus Rosary', the 'Holy Rosary of B.V. Mary' and 'Stations of the Cross' indicating the use of hymns in these services as well.[34] The contrast with the contents of *The Catholic Choralist*, produced some 20 years before, is striking. Here only ten hymn texts were provided for Benediction, as opposed to 170 for Prime and Vespers over the liturgical year; and, in addition, 17 hymn texts were assigned for singing after Holy Communion at Mass.

Redesigning the Catholic hymnal c.1842–1913

Hymns thus acquired new roles in the Catholic church, and this meant that not only had new texts to be provided, but also the hymnal had to be redesigned, since in many respects it had ceased to be used as a liturgical book. Three basic patterns were available, and it was from mixtures of these that different varieties of Catholic hymnals were developed. The first pattern was that offered by Caswall in *Lyra Liturgica*. Its four sections are entitled 'Hymns for the Week', 'Antiphons of the Blessed Virgin', 'Hymns of the moveable feasts', 'Hymns belonging to the Common of the Saints'. This provides a liturgical framework based on the Office; indeed, hymns are specifically assigned to particular services. Faber's approach, however, is completely different. The seven sections of the hymnal *Jesus and Mary* are entitled (1) 'Hymns to God, his attributes and the three persons of the adorable Trinity', (2) [The] 'Sacred humanity of Jesus and the mysteries of the thirty-three years', (3) 'The Blessed Virgin Mary and the Holy Family', (4) 'Angels and Saints', (5) 'Sacraments, Faith and Spiritual Life', (6) 'Miscellaneous: The World, Poor and Nature', and (7) 'Last Things'. The whole thrust is thematic, devotional and meditational.

The third model is exemplified by analysis of the *Notre Dame Hymn Tune Book*, a volume designed for use in schools (Table 7.4).

Inevitably there were attempts to combine different approaches. For example, in Caswall's *Hymns and Poems: Original and Translated* (1873) the first four sections

---

31 Tozer, *The Catholic Hymnal*, Preface, n.p.

32 *WH*, pp. 399–400.

33 Ibid., no. 78.

34 *CJM*, nos. 206–271. In addition there are the Litanies for processions mentioned above. The 'Hymns to the Blessed Sacrament' are nos. 170–82. The 'Crown of Jesus Rosary', the 'Holy Rosary of Mary' and the 'Stations of the Cross' sections are nos. 118–20, 121–31 and 132–7 respectively.

Table 7.4   Analysis of the *Notre Dame Hymn Tune Book* (1905)

Subject		Hymn numbers
I: God, the Holy Ghost and Jesus (the most heavily emphasised of the three)		1–39
(The Holy Child)		(20–7)
(The Sacred Heart)		(31–9)
II: The Blessed Virgin Mary		40–79
III: Angels and Saints		100–15
(St Patrick)		(130)
(The hymn: 'Martyrs of England')		(124)
IV: Miscellaneous		
(i) The Church:	'Faith of Our Fathers'	118
	'I am a faithful Catholic'	134
(ii) Heaven and purgatory		124
(iii) Human dependence on God and Jesus		125–9, 131–13 & 136
(iv) Hymn 'Angel of Schools at the bidding of Peter'		137

are lifted straight from *Lyra Liturgica*. There then follows a pot-pourri from later publications entitled 'Hymns and Sequences from the Roman Missal', 'Hymns from the various Offices and other sources', and 'Original texts: Hymns and meditative pieces', the last of which is clearly driven by Faberesque devotional principles.[35] *Arundel Hymns* is more sophisticated, for here a Faber-type framework encapsulates liturgical features (Table 7.5).[36]

The general tendency with hymnals designed for national circulation was to have a threefold or fourfold division between (i) hymns for the liturgical year, (ii) hymns for feast days, (iii) hymns for children, guilds, morning and evening services, along with other miscellaneous purposes, and sometimes (iv) a small selection of Latin hymns. Table 7.6 shows the evolution in this direction by analysis of four selected hymnals

---

35 These include: 'The "Masque of Angels" before Our Lady of the Temple', 'The "Minister of Eld"', 'Odes' and 'Poems'.

36 Faber's influence is explained by the fact that the Duke of Norfolk, one of its two editors, had been a pupil at the London Oratory. Moreover, the 1861 edition of Faber's hymnal had been dedicated to him.

Table 7.5   The structure of *Arundel Hymns* (1905)

Section	Hymn number
I. Almighty God and the most Holy Trinity	1–52
Sacred Humanity of Jesus Hymns for the period from Advent to Christmas	
II. Lent and the Passion of Our Lord	53–204
Easter, Ascension, the Eucharist and Corpus Christi The Blessed Sacrament, the Holy Name, 'Our Blessed Lord', St Francis Xavier Miscellaneous items, including 'God the Holy Ghost' and hymns for the Blessed Virgin Mary	
III. Saints and Guardian Angels	205–52
St Joseph, Martyrs and Confessors, the 'Crown of Jesus', Guardian Angels, 'the Dead', and 'Judgement'	
IV. Heaven	253–61
V. The Church and the Faith	262–7 & 308
Missions	275–6
Penance and confession	268–74
Miscellaneous	277–8 & 300–307
Morning and evening hymns	279–95
Various hymns on the Christian life	296–8
The 'Flower Garden of Jesus'	299

Towards a new orthodoxy. Attempts to regulate and standardise hymn texts and music c.1842–1913

The compatibility of interests between publishers and Ultramontanes

A drift towards a standard approach is thus apparent, and this was reinforced by positive attempts to regulate, and sometimes restrict, the proliferating output of hymns and hymnals. This was partly due to the attitude of publishers, who wished to establish monopolies; and in this they were helped by the growing respect for copyright. Most publishers, then, tried to get the highest possible ecclesiastical endorsement for their products. The *Parochial Hymn Book*, for example, contains a battery of eulogistic statements by senior figures, headed by Cardinal Manning,

Table 7.6　　The contents and organisation of four selected hymnals c.1877–1912*

Section	Maher (d. 1877) and Trappes. *Liturgical Hymns* (n.d.) (70 items)	Tozer. *Catholic Hymns* (1886) (79 items)	Tozer. *Catholic Hymns* (1898) (150 items)	Terry et al. *The Westminster Hymnal* (1912) (263 items)
[1] Hymns for particular parts of the liturgical year	Nos 1–48. Advent to Trinity Sunday (Nos 1–6: Hymns throughout the year). Nos 49–55. Festival of 'Holy Housel or Eucharist'; nos 56–7	Nos 1–31. Advent to Corpus Christi	Advent to Corpus Christi	Advent to All Saints Day
[2] Hymns for feast days associated with the Virgin Mary, Saints, Confessors etc.	Transfiguration; Nos 58–70. Festivals of the Virgin Mary, Saints, Confessors etc.	Sacred Heart; Precious Blood; the Virgin Mary; Festivals of Saints up to All Souls Day	Sacred Heart; Precious Blood; the Virgin Mary; Festivals of Saints up to All Saints Day	The 'Holy Name'; 'The Blessed Sacrament'; 'The Sacred Heart'; the Precious Blood and Sacred Wounds; 'The Blessed Virgin'; followed by 'The Church', 'Holy Angels', 'Heaven', 'The Rosary', 'The Holy Family', Saints, Apostles and Martyrs etc.
[3] Hymns for children, retreats, morning and evening prayer, sacraments, confraternities and other miscellaneous occasions	Nos 68–9. The 'Children's Mass'	Missions and Retreats; 'Occasional'; and 'Evening'	Missions and Retreats; General Hymns; 'Evening'; 'Confirmation'; Confraternities; Stations of the Cross and the 'Children's Mass'	Confirmation; Missions; Children; the Seas; General Hymns; 'Morning' and 'Evening'
[4] Latin hymns				Latin hymns

*　I have imposed the main sub-divisions here. Terry and Tozer's hymnals, while in general following a numerical order, scatter some items across the book. The contents page is therefore, as the 1916 edition of *The Westminster Hymnal* puts it, an 'Index of subjects' (p. xiii).

archbishop of Westminster.[37] *Arundel Hymns* goes one better, incorporating a letter from Pope Leo XIII.[38] *The Westminster Hymnal* ripostes by declaring that it is 'the only collection authorised by the Hierarchy of England and Wales'. However, this statement occasioned some surprise. James Britten, in a letter to *The Tablet*, claimed that one bishop had said that he never saw the collection till it appeared in print. Britten therefore argued that the phrase 'authorised by the hierarchy' 'I have good reason to believe was an unauthorised statement, or rather it was allowed by one of the five bishops who formed the committee'.[39] However, neither Britten nor anyone else should have been surprised at all. *The Westminster Hymnal* is a musical version of *The New (Complete) Catholic Hymn Book* published by the Hierarchy in 1910; and the relevant committee had been formed in 1905 in reaction to a proposal by the Catholic Truth Society to prepare a new national hymnal.[40] Moreover, Terry circulated a memorandum to all the bishops stating that an unnamed publishing company had agreed to publish the new hymnal at its own expense, provided that they gave it their imprimatur as the authorised version of the tunes and that diocesan inspectors enforced correct performances at inspections of Catholic schools.[41]

The drive to remove non-Catholic texts and music

It is clear, therefore, that publishers' interests meshed with the centralising tendencies of Ultramontane bishops, concerned at the apparently uncontrolled proliferation of texts and music. For instance, there was a drive to eliminate Protestant texts, and this is clearly enunciated in the preface to *Arundel Hymns*.[42] The Bishops' Acta of 1907 declare the same policy, which is repeated by Terry in his preface to *The Westminster Hymnal*.[43] Indeed, he goes on to state that 'it has been deemed advisable that the tunes, like the hymns, should be by Catholic authors, or from Catholic sources'.

This extension was Terry's own idea, since the bulk of his preface is a straight copy of the original memorandum he sent to the bishops. However, he must have known that such a statement was just what Ultramonatanes would have wanted. Nevertheless, the malleability of his personal convictions is shown by the fact that immediately afterwards he concedes that 'in the case of Continental tunes the

---

37 These include endorsements by the archbishop of Cashel, along with the bishops of Edinburgh, Aberdeen, Dumfries, Dunkeld, Oban, Leeds, Middlesbrough, Shrewsbury and Emmaeus (an auxiliary bishop at Westminster).

38 Howard and Gatty, *Arundel Hymns*, p. v.

39 James Britten, 'Letter to the Editor' in *Tablet*, 88 (July–December 1912): 222. The bishop who authorised the statement may have been Cuthbert Hedley, who chaired the commission responsible for collecting and editing the texts.

40 The full title is *The New (Complete) Catholic Hymn Book containing the hymns prescribed and arranged by the Catholic Hierarchy: with Latin hymns and Benediction service* (London, 1910). For details of the decision-making process see the Westminster Diocesan Archives, 'Bishops Meetings 1888–1909': 366 and 'Low Week Acta' (1905) No. 6.

41 Westminster Diocesan Archives, Bourne Papers Bo1/33 'Church Music 1904–1910'.

42 Howard and Gatty, *Arundel Hymns*, p. iv.

43 Westminster Diocesan Archives, 'Bishops Acta 1907' 10/10/1907, 'Bishops Meetings 1864–1974' in the folder marked 'Bourne 1903–1908'. *WH*, p. ix.

authorship is sometimes difficult to fix, since many were sung by Catholics and Protestants alike. The presence of such tunes in Catholic Chorale books and their constant use among Catholic congregations has been deemed sufficient warrant for their inclusion here'. Note, however, that he also included two tunes by Claude Goudimel, the author of *Les Psaumes mis en rime française*, produced in collaboration with Theodore Beza, Calvin's successor at Geneva.[44]

Patterns in the development of a consolidated repertoire of texts and melodies

Despite these problems, such policies produced a consolidation of texts and melodies, albeit with significant differences between the two. With texts, what is striking is the large number of hymns used in earlier collections that reappear in *The Westminster Hymnal*, one reason for this being the fact that so many were contributed by Caswall, Faber and Newman (see Table 7.7).

In addition, a sense of continuity with the past was sometimes enunciated. Thus, in the preface to *Arundel Hymns* it was stated that 'the editors … have gathered together the most representative anthology they could collect of popularly used Latin hymns, together with a large selection of English hymns by Catholic writers … to illustrate the great truths of the Catholic faith'.[45] Yet the contents of *The Westminster Hymnal* show that this could be very unbalanced. Most of the texts are by nineteenth-century authors or, due to the liturgical emphasis, are derived from the medieval sources. Only eleven texts can clearly be placed in the period 1500–1800.[46]

With melodies, however, there is a different pattern of consolidation. The key factors were as follows. First, as has been suggested, the provision of vernacular translations decoupled Latin hymns from their plainchant melodies, although a few attempts were made in *The Catholic Choralist* to adapt these to English texts. In any case, most later Catholic hymnals had few Latin texts. Tozer's *Catholic Hymns* of 1898 has only six; *The Westminster Hymnal* has 13, of which 12 use plainchant settings; the *Notre Dame Hymn Tune Book* contains none at all. On the other hand *The Catholic Choralist* has 30 Latin items, but 11 are supplied with parallel English translations and only 3 have plainchant settings. The *Crown of Jesus Music* of 1864 has a respectable total of 39 plainchant items, one of which contains 12 Vesper chants. These, though, are early exceptions that prove the rule, since Young and

---

44 *WH*, nos. 15 and 134. Paul André Galliard and Richard Freedman, 'Goudimel, Claude' in Stanley Sadie and John Tyrell (eds), *The New Grove Dictionary of Music and Musicians* (London, 2001 (2nd edition)), vol. 10, pp. 209–11.

45 Howard and Gatty, *Arundel Hymns*, p. v.

46 These are nos. 26, 33, 57, 65, 73, 90, 103, 104, 108, 231 and possibly 251 ('Adeste Fideles'). In addition to Faber and Newman original nineteenth-century texts include contributions by Francis Stanfield (six texts), Edmund Vaughan (four texts), M. Bridges (six texts), Louis Hall (two texts), Frederick Oakeley (two texts), the Sisters of Notre Dame, Aubrey De Vere, M. Russell, Canon Scannell, and Fr Wyse (one each).

Table 7.7   Hymn texts from selected collections in *The Westminster Hymnal*

Author or editor	Collection title	Total number of texts in the collection	Number of texts from the collection in *The Westminster Hymnal*
H. Hemy (ed.)	*Crown of Jesus Music* (1864)	214[a]	64
F. Faber	*Hymns* (1861/R1890)	150	34[b]
Trans. and composed by E. Caswall	*Hymns and Poems* (1849/R1873)[c]	480 pp.	86pp.
[F. Police (ed.)]	*The Parochial Hymn Book* (R1883)	633[d]	160
Anon.	*Convent Hymns and Music* (1891)	45	15
J. Storer (ed.)	*The Catholic Tune Book* (1892)	319	134
A.E. Tozer (ed.)	*Catholic Hymns* (1898)	186	91
H. Howard and C. Gatty (eds)	*Arundel Hymns* (1898/1901/R1905)	306	88
F. Birtchnell and M. Brown (eds)	*Notre Dame Hymn Tune Book* (1905)	137	46

[a]   This total excludes Benediction and Mass settings.
[b]   This total excludes Benediction and Mass settings.
[c]   First published as *Lyra Catholica* in 1849. This is the title for the revised expanded edition of 1873.
[d]   This excludes 79 other prayers and texts not intended for singing.

Hemy still felt it necessary at that time to incorporate several items for use at Mass or the Office.[47]

Second, the increasingly hostile official attitudes towards the allegedly secular characteristics of much Viennese Classical music and its successors have to be taken into account. Yet, initially this style seems to be have been very popular. For example, Young, in *The Catholic Choralist*, states that '...to render these hymns still more worthy of the dignity of divine worship ... they have been adapted, and arranged with considerable care, to the most exquisite airs – the compositions of

---

47   Note also that in *The Catholic Choralist* only 11 of the Latin texts occur in the section giving texts; the remainder appear in B. Walsh's music section.

the first masters'; and by this he and Walsh meant works by Beethoven, Guynemer, Haydn, Mozart, Pleyel and Spohr. In addition, Walsh drew on music from the London embassy chapel tradition, with settings adapted from works by Novello and the two Samuel Webbes.[48] Similarly, 175 out of 377 melodies in Parts I–III of Hemy's hymnal belong to the Viennese Classical school, its offshoots and immediate forebears.[49] Indeed, as late as 1905, the preface of *Arundel Hymns* asserts that 'the tunes represent, roughly speaking, the plainchant period … the polyphonic epoch; and the modern age, including Haydn, Mozart and the musicians of today'.[50] However, such a division is also testimony to the effects of the revival, by that time, of interest in plainchant and Renaissance polyphony; and the reference to more modern compositions may also explain why, despite Papal endorsement, this publication, even though at first adopted for use at Westminster Cathedral, failed to become the official hymnal of the English Catholic church. By that time in most major Catholic hymnals music by great eighteenth- and nineteenth-century Classical composers, along with representatives from the London embassy chapel tradition, had been virtually eliminated. There are only three such works in the 1886 edition of *Catholic Hymns*, eleven in the edition of 1898, eight in *The Catholic Tune Book*, and four in the *Notre Dame Hymn Tune Book*.[51]

On the other hand, at the same time the great Renaissance composers exerted relatively little influence either, perhaps because the main surge associated with Terry in the revival of such music had not really taken place before the end of the nineteenth century. No such works appear in the 1886 edition of *Catholic Hymns* and the *Notre Dame Hymn Tune Book*, only one in the 1898 edition of *Catholic Hymns*, and four in *The Catholic Tune Book*.[52] Instead, in addition to items by the editors themselves, many hymnals incorporated tunes by contemporary English musicians. For example, Tozer's 1898 edition of *Catholic Hymns* contains 177 melodies by 56 such composers.[53]

---

48 Young, *The Catholic Choralist*, p. viii. Walsh, the musical editor, also included an adaptation of a melody by J.S. Bach.

49 47 tunes are by Haydn, 43 by Beethoven, 37 by Mozart, 14 by Handel, 11 by Mendelssohn, 4 by Pleyel, 3 by Gluck, and 1 each by J.S. Bach, Cherubini, Cimarosa, Clementi, Michael Haydn, Himmel, Purcell, Romberg, Rossini, Spohr and Weber. There are also two melodies by Farrant and Tallis.

50 Howard and Gatty, *Arundel Hymns*, p. iv.

51 The details are as follows: *Catholic Hymns* (1886): three works by Mendelssohn; *Catholic Hymns* (1898): four works by Nixon, two each by Novello and Webbe (the elder), one each by Haydn, Mendelssohn and Stainer. *The Catholic Tune Book*: three melodies each by Bach and Mendelssohn, one each by Haydn and Webbe (the elder). *The Notre Dame Hymn Tune Book*: three melodies by Mendelssohn, one each by Haydn and Webbe (the elder).

52 The composers are as follows: *Catholic Hymns* (1898): one work by Palestrina; *The Catholic Tune Book*: one work each by Farnaby, Goudimel and Palestrina, two by Orlando Gibbons.

53 The number of compositions contributed is as follows: Tozer: 36, Terry: 15, Richardson: 8, C.E. Miller: 9, H. Whitehead: 6, S.P. Waddington, J. Smith and A.H. Mann: 4 each; J. Barnett, F. Birtchnell, G. Bruche, L. Hall, J. Hallett Sheppard, C. Lloyd, B. Louard Selby, W. Maher and R.B. Sankey: 3 each.

However, many of these new melodies were not incorporated in *The Westminster Hymnal*. According to Terry this was due to 'the refusal of two proprietors of large collections of tunes to use their copyrights'.[54] Perforce, he was compelled to draw upon the contents of 32 old Continental chorale and hymnbooks, most of them dating from the seventeenth and eighteenth centuries.[55] This strategy was not entirely new. No such sources, it is true, are cited in Tozer's *Catholic Hymns* of 1898, apart from two that he describes as 'German'.[56] On the other hand, Storer in 1892 included 80 that are classified by the same epithet, as well as citing an *Aachen Gesangbuch*, a *Trier Gesangbuch*, and a hymnal from Lausanne.

The result was a greater weighting among hymn tune sources towards the Early-Modern period, in contrast to the predominantly Medieval and nineteenth-century bias of the texts. A Germanic emphasis is also evident, which is in sharp contrast to Gatty's research work for *Arundel Hymns*. His papers, now held at Downside, reveal detailed study of Italian sources, especially Laudi Spirituali. This is what one might expect from a hymnal impregnated with Oratorian values, and it fits with the prevailing Ultramontane emphasis on all things 'Roman'.[57] *The Westminster Hymnal*, curiously enough, evades this, perhaps because shortage of time prevented Terry from doing in-depth research like Gatty. In effect, then, German Early-Modern hymnbook sources were substituted for the despised Viennese-Classical repertoire favoured by Young and Hemy.

Thus, whereas in terms of texts *The Westminster Hymnal* represented a fairly natural development from earlier hymnals, with melodies it constituted a significant break with the past, as the details given in Table 7.8 reveal. Such differences, moreover, were accentuated by Terry's response to the deadweight of existing tradition:

> The collection includes all the popular tunes in common use amongst English-speaking Catholics. Some of these tunes are good, some indifferent; and some are bad. But it has

---

54 *WH*, p. xi. James Britten identified one of these as one of the publishers of *Arundel Hymns*. These were R. and T. Washbourne and Boosey and Co. Since R. and T. Washbourne also published *The Westminster Hymnal* it seems that Booseys were the culprits. 'Letter to the editor' in *The Tablet*, 120 (July–December 1912): 222–3.

55 These are: Vehle's *Gesangbuchlein* (1537), *Leisentritt's Gesangbuch* (1567), the *Catholicum Hymnologium Germanicum* (1587), the *Speier Gesangbuch* (1589), the *Andernach Gesangbuch* (1608), M. Praetorius *Musae Sionae* (1609), *Catholische Geistliche Gesange* (1608 and 1698), the *Koln Gesangbuch* (1631), the *Psalteriolum Harmonicum* (1642), J. Cruger's *Psalmodia Sacra* (1658), the *Mainz Gesangbuch* (1661 and 1725), the *Nurnburg Gesangbuch* (1676), *La Santa Scala* (1681), the *Strassbourg Gesangbuch* (1697), *Tochter Sion* (1741), *Katholisches Geistlichte Gesangbuch* (Vienna 1744), the *Paderborn Gesangbuch* (1765), the *Landshut Gesangbuch* (1777), La Feillée's *Méthode du plainchant* (1782), Hartig's *Siona* (1832), the Limburg *Gesangbuch* (1838), Ett's *Cantica Sacra* (1840), the *Rottenberg Gesangbuch* (1865) the *Trier Gesangbuch* (1872), the *Cantiarium S. Galli* (undated), the Miltenburg Processionale (undated), and a 'Tours Breviary' (undated).

56 These are nos. 125 and 185.

57 Downside Abbey archives: Gatty Papers, boxes 1267–9, 1275–6, especially in 1267 and 1268. Among other things these show that Gatty had access to A. Feist's 'Zeitschift fur Romanische Philogia' of 1889, xiii band, containing 1381 Laudi Spirituali.

been felt that since some of these last- named class have been – for one generation at least
– bound up with the pious aspirations of so many holy lives, this is hardly the occasion
for their suppression. They have therefore been retained ... Alternative tunes have been
provided for most of them.

The crucial words come in the final sentence. Terry provided alternative tunes for
melodies that, in his opinion, were 'bad'; and in 8 out of the 21 cases composed
the music himself. Moreover, the index shows that he composed 40 other tunes.
Thus, although Terry may have been only one among the team of people constituting
the musical editorial committee chaired by his former employer Abbot Ford of
Downside, in effect he imposed his taste on the hymnal. His attitude was not unique.
The editors of the *Crown of Jesus Music*, *The Catholic Tune Book*, Tozer's *Catholic
Hymns* and *The Notre Dame Hymn Book* all did the same.[58] The differences were that
first, as has been suggested, the copyright situation excluded other new melodies to
an extent that had not happened before; second, *The Westminster Hymnal* enjoyed
a peculiar status as the officially recognised hymnal of the Catholic Church in
England. In effect, it was an attempt to freeze the available repertoires of melodies
at an arbitrarily chosen time.

Table 7.8   The number of hymn tunes found in *The Westminster Hymnal* and in
             earlier Catholic collections

Date of publication	Title of hymnal	Total quantity of numbered items in the hymnal	Number of tunes that also appear in *The Westminster Hymnal*
1864	*Crown of Jesus Music Parts I–III*	377	9
1883	*The Parochial Hymn Book*	633	23[a]
1886	*Catholic Hymns*	79	14
1891	*Convent Hymns and Music*	45	0
1892	*The Catholic Tune Book*	319	21[b]
1898	*Catholic Hymns*	186	29
1905	*The Notre Dame Hymn Tune Book*	168	11

[a]   18 with significant variations to the tune.
[b]   217 with English texts, 4 with Latin texts.

Terry's attempts to impose uniform versions of each hymn melody

The campaign for uniformity was not confined to repertoire. In his preface, Terry laid
considerable stress on the need for accurate performance of a uniformly accepted

---

58 The relevant statistics are: *CJM Parts I–III*: 33 compositions by Hemy; *The Catholic
Tune Book*: 56 compositions by Storer; *Catholic Hymns*: 36 compositions by Tozer; *The Notre
Dame Hymn Book*: 26 tunes each by Birtchnell and Brown.

melody. Eleven examples are cited to illustrate his belief that at the time 'each congregation is a law unto itself'.[59] In turn this depended on *The Westminster Hymnal* being recognised as the sole authorised version by an Ultramontane-orientated Hierarchy. The parallel with similar developments in plainchant at that time is inescapable. In both cases the object was to discover the one allegedly authentic version of a given melody. There was no conception that variants might be legitimate, despite the fact that many hymns underwent considerable modification during their history. This applied not just to old tunes such as 'Adeste Fideles' but even to more recent ones such as 'Sweet Sacrament Divine'. In this case the differences between the versions given in *The Parochial Hymn Book* and *The Westminster Hymnal* are startling. First, the different choice of key places *The Parochial Hymn Book*'s version beyond the scope of the congregation (Example 7.1a). Second, the visual effect of using a crotchet pulse encourages singers to emphasise the 'three-in-a-bar' rhythm. This, along with the employment of semi-quavers every alternate bar, gives it a more jagged feel that corresponds more closely to the syllabic rhythm. It also makes it more varied, as there are six, rather than four, different note lengths.[60] Here, then, the hymn is clearly meant to be sung by a choir, rather than a congregation; whereas, with *The Westminster Hymnal*, the opposite is more likely to be the case (Example 7.1b).

Inevitably, this drive to establish the existence of an authentic melody placed a premium on scholarship. Many claimed that *The Westminster Hymnal* was an improvement in this respect. Thus, Hedley in his preface stated that 'the musical setting is, on the whole, far more scientific and satisfying than anything that has hitherto appeared', and he goes on to state that 'it often happens... that a hymn or a setting, in the course of use, has undergone slight variations in different localities, and it is useful to have an authentic version both in text and music'.[61] The use of the word 'scientific' is itself significant, as it denotes the 'scientific' method of comparative study of original sources espoused by Solesmes with plainchant at that time. On the other hand, Hedley also interpolates the phrase 'on the whole'. As chairman of the commission and a composer himself Hedley was in a position to identify possible shortcomings. Moreover, the limited period of preparation time meant that Terry could not compete scholastically with Gatty's achievement in *Arundel Hymns*; and if, later on, he was found to be careless as chief editor for the *Tudor Church Music* series, it is likely that he was equally careless with *The Westminster Hymnal*. Certainly his work did not escape criticism in *The Tablet*. Francis Gladstone remarked on 'the inattention to the rules of prosody shown (not infrequently) by the musical editor', citing nos. 110, 180 and 229 as examples. Mary Simpson, the daughter of the composer George Herbert, complained that, as in other hymnals, a G♯ had been incorrectly inserted in the fourth bar of his tune 'Sunset' (set to the text 'Sweet Saviour bless us ere we go'; no. 215). In this case, moreover, Terry had failed to reply to her letter warning him of this possible danger before publication.[62]

---

59 Terry in *WH*, p. v–ix.

60 Excepting the dotted crotchet and quaver used in bar 10.

61 Cuthbert Hedley in *WH*, p. iii.

62 *Tablet*, 88: 104 (20 July 1912) for Gladstone; 146 (27 August 1912) for Simpson. See also 'P.L.'s attack on the 'mangling' of Burge's hymns, (3 August 1912): 184–6, James

Example 7.1   Stanfield's melody for 'Sweet Sacrament Divine'

(a) Version in *The Parochial Hymn Book* (no. 285)

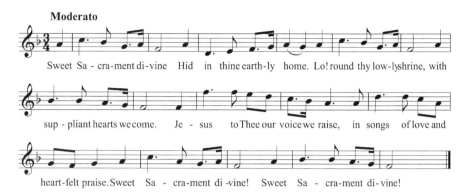

(b) Version in *The Westminster Hymnal* (no. 78)

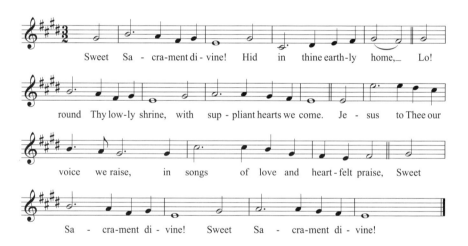

In his defence, as with Renaissance polyphony, Terry could argue that 'this book is intended for immediate practical use; and while a reversion to the original form of ancient tunes is possible in a country with an unbroken Catholic tradition, it is *at present* [Terry's italics] in England ... rather a council of perfection than a practicable idea'.[63] Yet, if this was so, then, as with the choice or repertoire, it undermined the claim that *The Westminster Hymnal* should be the only authorised collection of hymnody as far as English Catholics were concerned.

Britten; Anon. review (10 August 1912): 222–3. With *Sunset* it should be noted that the issue is confused by the fact that Terry had transposed it into E♭ major. This error was not made in Ould and Sewell's *Book of Hymns with Tunes*.

    63 *WH*, p. x.

Changes in musical layout and performance practice c.1842–1913

Procedures in selected mid- and late nineteenth-century hymnals

Nonetheless, despite all these deficiencies, *The Westminster Hymnal*, because it was official, became the standard English Catholic hymnal in the early twentieth century. This is demonstrated by numerous reprints – for example those of 1913, 1916 and 1919. In doing so it marked a culmination in a series of changes affecting the relationship between choirs and congregations in the performance of Catholic hymnody. As the different versions of 'Sweet Sacrament Divine' show, such changes can be illustrated by comparing the layout and notation of music in various hymnals.

As already noted, in the mid-nineteenth century the emphasis was on choirs. Indeed, if hymns were regarded as prayers, as the *Crown of Jesus* manual asserted, this would have come quite naturally. However, there were gestures towards congregational participation. For instance, Young in *The Catholic Choralist* assumes that local priests will train choirs from scratch ' … which will inspire emulation among their flocks'.[64] The promotion of hymn singing in schools might also be construed as a long-term strategy for developing congregational participation, as seems to be the case with many of the unison settings in the *Crown of Jesus Music* and *Convent Hymns with Music*. Yet, in all three collections, the layout of the music often implies a bias towards choirs at the expense of congregations. In *The Catholic Choralist* the most common pattern is the provision of the melody and a bass line in full-sized type, whilst the remaining notes of each chord are smaller in size (Example 7.2). This suggests that a choir providing the melody and bass with keyboard accompaniment was expected to be the norm, although obviously congregational singing with keyboard accompaniment was possible too.

In the *Crown of Jesus Music* and *Convent Hymns and Music* a similar approach is often used, but frequently with an extra treble or alto line added (see Example 7.3). Indeed, with the latter there are separate sections for chorus and solo voices; and sometimes, as in Example 7.4, the chorus part is divided. In these cases girl pupils were being taught to sing as choirs, not as congregations. The same sort of thing happens in parts of *The Parochial Hymn Book*. Here, there are 74 arrangements for solo voice and chorus, 7 for duet and chorus, 12 in three parts, 37 in four parts and 1 in six parts.

Next, it should be observed that, in many cases, the basic melody rises above an e' for male voices, placing it beyond the reach of a congregation. The version of 'Sweet Sacrament Divine' cited above is one of 53 such cases in *The Parochial Hymn Book*. The same thing happens on 29 occasions in *The Catholic Choralist*, 34 in Parts I–III of the *Crown of Jesus Music*, and 14 (out of 45 melodies) in *Convent Hymns and Music*.

Such features explain why Tozer, in his preface to *Catholic Hymns* (1898), distinguished between two sorts of hymn:

---

64 Young, *The Catholic Choralist*, p. xii.

Some hymns are essentially suited for singing in unison with the whole body of worshippers … Other hymns, by their very structure, are utterly ruined and put out of place by such a mode of treatment: these should be sung by the choir alone with every attention to light and shade which the words will naturally inspire in a truly artistic mind; they may become veritable 'Sermons in music'.[65]

Example 7.2   *The Catholic Choralist*. Air 20, by 'a C. priest of Meath'

* denotes a breathing mark, indicating just how slowly this hymn was meant to be sung.

Example 7.3   Hemy's setting of a Mozart theme to the text 'Sweet Angel of Mercy', *Crown of Jesus Music* (no. 7)

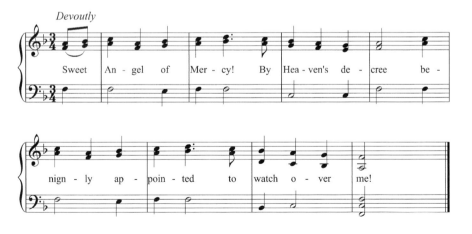

65 Tozer, *Catholic Hymns*, n.p.

Example 7.4   'Star of the Sea'. *Convent Hymns and Music* (1891), p. 19

continued

Example 7.4   *concluded*

thee,   Thine   are the   gra - ces   unclaimed[sic]   by   a   mo - ther,

Sin - less and beau - ti - ful   Star   of   the   Sea!

The general adoption of block four-part harmony by Tozer and Terry.
Its implications for the singing of Catholic hymnody by choirs and congregations

Nevertheless, despite this Tozer is important because he helped diffuse the use of block four-part harmony settings in the English Catholic world. This signalled a new relationship between choirs and congregations. Unlike with many of the earlier hymn settings that have so far been examined, all such arrangements have a multiple purpose. They can be sung in unison, by choirs alone, or by choirs and congregation together, with or without keyboard accompaniment. As noted earlier, steps in this direction had already been taken with diatonically harmonised arrangements of plainchant. Occasionally, there are even cases in the *Crown of Jesus Music* where Hemy gets very close to providing block four-part harmony settings of more modern melodies that can be sung by an SATB choir; although here the arbitrary way the tenor line moves between the top and bottom staves suggests that he was thinking more in terms of providing a keyboard accompaniment.[66] Tozer, on the other hand, extended the technique to virtually every item in his hymn collections; and the same policy was largely adopted by Charles Gatty in *Arundel Hymns*. In *The Westminster Hymnal*, with the exception of Solesmes-style plainchant settings, Terry did the same. This was hardly surprising. Terry had assisted Tozer in the preparation of *Catholic Hymns* (1898); as an ex-Anglican, he was familiar with this style of hymn setting, and his study of Early-Modern Continental chorale books pushed him further in that direction.

Now, on the surface, it appears that Terry was well aware of, and fully endorsed, the implications of this change for congregational singing. Thus, in his preface to

---

66 See, for example, *CJM*, nos 6 and 12.

The Westminster Hymnal, he states that 'since vernacular hymns are essentially intended for the congregation rather than the choir, the first requisite is a strong and well-defined melody which lends itself easily to unison singing'.[67] His setting of 'Sweet Sacrament Divine', cited above, illustrates how he tried to achieve this. Yet, on closer examination, there is some ambivalence in his thinking. For a start, his background as a choirmaster with a considerable interest in Renaissance polyphony may well have militated against the congregational ideal. Only five years before, in *Catholic Church Music*, he had stated that he did 'not think it desirable that the people should sing in Mass where a really good choir is in existence'; and, since he thought this was more likely to occur in large churches, this implied that congregational singing was likely only to flourish in parishes with small populations.[68] In other words he was repeating the strategy for promoting plainchant outlined in Benz's *Cantica Sacra* some 60 years before. It is therefore significant that *The Westminster Hymnal* was published in two formats: a cheap 'words only' copy for congregational use, and a more expensive choral version equipped with the music.[69] Moreover, Terry, as in earlier hymnals, occasionally allowed his melodies to rise above e' for male voices. This he attempted to explain away by arguing that 'experience has shown that the difficult tunes for a congregation are those in which the melody lies at a high pitch throughout, and not those which contain an occasional high note'.[70]

To conclude, as in so much else, Terry's attitude towards congregational singing meant that *The Westminster Hymnal* imposed a freeze on developments that were still unfolding. The uneasy compromise this left between the rival claims of choirs and congregations meant that, by Protestant standards, English Catholic congregational singing in the early twentieth century was often unsatisfactory. For example, in 1928 'Cantate Domino', writing to *The Tablet*, lamented that ' … for a long time it has been a reproach against Catholics that they lag horridly behind Protestants in congregational song'.[71] However, perhaps this did not really matter. If, by that time, hymns were primarily being used in the devotional atmosphere of Benediction or other extra-liturgical services, then a quiet, mood-setting rendition of a suitable text that most people heard, rather than sang, might have been considered more appropriate.

---

67 *WH*, p. ix.

68 Richard Terry, *Catholic Church Music* (London, 1907), p. 122.

69 The prices in 1912 were between 2d and 1s for the 'words only' version and between 3s 6d and 7s for the full music version. The variations within each price range were dictated by the quality of the covers, paper and binding.

70 *WH*, p. ix. For an example of this see bar 13 of no. 87, 'O Sacred Heart, all blissful light of heaven', which rises to f'. This is Terry's own tune. Such special pleading did not fool T.H. Knuckley in his 'Letter to the Editor' in *Tablet*, 87 (January–June 1912): 1022.

71 'Cantate Domino', *Tablet*, 151 (January–June 1928): 549.

Chapter 8

Music for Benediction

The growth of Benediction music

One of the most significant aspects of nineteenth-century Catholic music in England was the emergence of a substantial repertoire of works for the rite of Benediction. Typically this focused on settings of *O Salutaris*, the Litany, and *Tantum Ergo*; and sometimes these were grouped together to form what was known as a 'Benediction Service'. Benediction music could also include settings of *Adoremus in Aeternum* and other Latin hymns, including *Stabat Mater*. For example, at Our Lady of Mount Carmel, Liverpool, there are 14 hand-bound copies of Marian antiphon settings by Franz Abt, Arthur O'Leary, Joseph Egbert Turner, Vincent Novello and Samuel Webbe the elder. Given the absence of Office services there, these must have been associated with Benediction. Yet, even if these are ignored, the sheer quantity of output is impressive, as shall be illustrated from the contents of Benediction manuals such as Newsham's *Selection of Music suitable for the rite of Benediction*, Tozer's *New and Complete Manual for Benediction*, or the contents of the *Crown of Jesus Hymnal*.[1]

Individual nineteenth-century collections often paint the same picture. There is nothing at Mount Carmel, and the proportion at St Michael, Alston, with only 39 out of 343 pieces, is disappointing – however, both could draw on the contents of the *Crown of Jesus Music* – whilst at St Cuthbert, Durham Litanies, *O Salutaris* and *Tantum Ergo* settings account for 233 out of 1,053 pieces. At St Mary Chipping, SS Mary and Everilda Everingham, St Augustine Preston and amongst the nineteenth-century publications at Stonyhurst the figures are 63 out of 124, 387 out of 1,204, 41 out of 239 and 188 out of 860. The enduring impact of such nineteenth-century repertoire can be seen in the Benediction manuals edited by Robert Hasberry and Terry in 1931 and 1937.[2]

Furthermore, a high proportion of Benediction music was composed by British composers during the nineteenth century. The balance at Alston, St Augustine, Chipping, Everingham, and St Cuthbert is 18 out of 39, 24 out of 41, 43 out of 63, 129 out of 385 and 105 out of 233; but at Stonyhurst it is only 37 out of 188. Likewise, it is significant that most Benediction music was composed during the nineteenth century. This, then, was a contemporary repertoire. Works composed before 1750

---

1   Charles Newsham (ed.), John Richardson (revised), *Selection of music suitable for the Rite of Benediction* (London, n.d.). Albert Edmonds Tozer (ed.), *New and Complete Manual for Benediction* (London, 1898).

2   Albert E. Tozer (ed.), Robert Hasberry (revised), *New and Complete Benediction Manual* (London, 1931). Richard Terry (ed.), *The Benediction Choir Book* (London, 1937).

account for only 8 out of 39 works at Alston, 4 out of 24 at St Augustine, 6 out of 43 at Chipping, 34 out of 105 at St Cuthbert, 20 out of 129 at Everingham, but 17 out of 37 at Stonyhurst. This means that nineteenth-century Benediction music was relatively uninfluenced by plainchant. No plainchant for Benediction can be found at Chipping or Everingham, whilst at Alston, St Cuthbert and Stonyhurst the figures are 3, 7 and 10. On the other hand, as shall be seen later, there is a marked fall-off in production during the twentieth century when, as with hymnody, the keynote appears to be consolidation rather than expansion. For example, at Alston only two items were composed after 1914, whilst at Chipping there is nothing.[3] Stonyhurst is a little different, thanks to the presence of John Driscoll's *Cantionale: Hymns Latin and English*, specially produced for the College in 1918. Here 94 of its 340 items of music are intended for Benediction, but only 15 of these were composed in the period 1851–1914.[4] The same applies with the Benediction items in Driscoll's *Stonyhurst Cantionale* of 1936. Once again very few items were composed in the twentieth century. Such patterns help explain the enduring influence of nineteenth-century repertoire.

Factors behind the growth in Benediction music during the nineteenth century

An obvious reason for the nineteenth-century growth in Benediction music was the rising popularity of the rite, along with other extra-liturgical devotions, noted in chapter 2. This implies that much of the running was made by secular priests, members of missionary orders such as the Society of Jesus or the Oratory, and laity. Conversely, it might be supposed that monks living in coenobitic institutions with a life revolving around the Office were, by definition, less likely to be active in the field, especially once the Downside Movement got under way within the EBC. Yet, in fact, this was not so; and in any case monastic communities often ran schools, where Benediction might be fostered to encourage religious devotion. Many monks also continued to work in parish missions, where the demands for Benediction were likely to be greater. This helps explain the activity of a monk such as J.E. Turner, seven of whose highly elaborate Litany settings can be found in the 1931 *Complete Benediction Manual*.[5]

The growing popularity of the Benediction service was not the only factor. Just as important perhaps was the need to have settings in every likely key. Indeed, the contents page of the 1931 *Complete Benediction Manual* is mainly organised in a cycle of fifths and fourths for each type of text. This shows that performers wanted

---

3   The St Cuthbert, St Augustine and Everingham collections are almost exclusively nineteenth century in content and so cannot be analysed in this way.

4   These figures are not included in the statistics relating to nineteenth-century publications at Stonyhurst cited earlier.

5   Tozer/Hasberry, *New and Complete Benediction Manual*, Litanies nos. 93–100. There are also two settings of the *Tantum Ergo* (nos. 30 and 47). See also Turner's *Five Motets to the Blessed Sacrament* (London, n.d.), one of which is an arrangement of plainchant rather than an original work.

to create musical unity in the service by selecting works with the same, or at any rate musically compatible, keys, even if they did not pick a given 'Benediction Service'.

Another factor was the brevity of the service, and in particular of the *O Salutaris* and *Tantum Ergo* texts. This, and the simple structure of the Litany, gave scope to composers with a penchant for writing short works, either because they were amateurs with limited skills or because of shortage of time due to other major commitments. This could be especially true for clergymen such as Charles Newsham, Henry Farmer or William Maher. In addition the often isolated nature of nineteenth-century life on the mission encouraged local talent. For example, some Litanies by Alexander Peckett of Scarborough can be found at St Cuthbert's, Durham and at Everingham. At Durham twelve items by him were copied by hand into the organ and part books; but at Everingham six settings survive in editions by Burns and Lambert. These are also advertised in 1860s editions of *The Catholic Directory*.[6] Everingham also holds the manuscript of a *Litany of the Incarnation* specially commissioned by the Constable-Maxwell family there from S. Eloorat of Bath, and a printed edition of two Litanies by Sidney Sykes, organist at St Wilfrid's pro-Cathedral nearby in York.[7] Similarly, at Alston, in central Lancashire, there are copies of Benediction service settings by G.B. Chamberlain and John Richardson.[8] Here it is significant that Chamberlain worked at Wigan and Richardson was, by birth, a Preston man. Yet, in both cases, the music was bought by Alston from London-based publishers. This illustrates how, as with hymnody, locally composed Benediction music could nonetheless find a national audience.

Such factors help explain the high proportion of contemporary or near-contemporary works found in nineteenth-century collections, as well as the weak influence exerted by plainchant in this genre at the time. On the other hand this did not preclude the adaptation of other music for Benediction, especially hymn tunes or, in the case of Litanies, Anglican-style psalm chants. There also seems to have been little hesitation about raiding non-Catholic sources. For example, arrangements of J.S. Bach's original works, as well as his chorale harmonisations, regularly appear in collections. Similarly at St Cuthbert's, Durham there are three Litanies adapted from Anglican psalm chants by Frederick Lingard (1811–47), a lay clerk at the Cathedral.

Crucial to all these developments was the shift from plainchant to four-part diatonic settings, enabling both choirs and congregations to participate in the music. In this respect Benediction music was similar to Catholic vernacular hymnody. Indeed, the process seems to have occurred earlier and more rapidly with the Benediction repertoire. This was because the Latin texts were retained, so there was no hiatus created by the de-coupling of text from melody caused by translation, as happened with the Latin Office hymns. *Tantum Ergo*, with its straightforward 878787 metre, was a hymn text anyway, and it proved easy to treat *O Salutaris* in similar fashion. Likewise, as noted above, the Litany lent itself readily to Anglican-style chanting.

---

6   'Burns and Lambert catalogue of music', *The Catholic Directory* (1866): 16.

7   Sidney Sykes, *Two Litanies of the Blessed Virgin Mary* (London, n.d).

8   G.B. Chamberlain, *Benediction Service No. 1* (London, n.d.). John Richardson, *Benediction Service No. 1* (London, n.d.)

The process can be illustrated by examining the transformation of a *Tantum Ergo* setting to be found in Wade's *Graduale Romanum* of 1765 at Stonyhurst. Example 8.1 gives Wade's plainchant version; Example 8.2 shows how Webbe then presented this in modern harmonised notation, smoothing out Wade's rhythmic irregularities. Here the occasional independence in the part-writing (especially for the altos) and the fact that, as with Wade, the melody rises to an F suggests this was primarily designed for a choir rather than congregational singing. Nonetheless, this formed the basis for all subsequent versions, notably those given in Charles Newsham's *A Collection of Music Suitable for the Rite of Benediction*[9] and the 1931 edition of Albert Edmond Tozer's *Complete Benediction Manual*. In both cases it was set not in F, but E♭ major, enabling it to be performed by both choir and congregation.[10] In turn, this formed the basis for its mid-twentieth-century adaptation by Sister M. Teresine to the hymn text 'Lord Accept The Gifts We Offer'.

Example 8.1   Wade's setting of *Tantum Ergo*, in *Graduale Romanum* (1765), p. 142, ' Hymnus Ad Benedictionem'

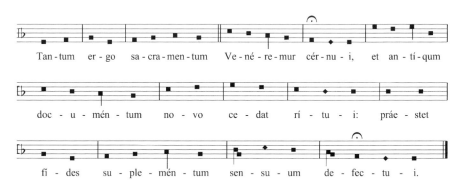

Benediction music in the London embassy chapels and their successor churches

The earliest evidence for the emergence of Benediction music comes from the London embassy chapel repertoire of the late eighteenth and early nineteenth centuries. For example, all of Samuel Webbe the elder's masses, whether published by himself, Vincent Novello or by Thomas Boosey, have a *Tantum Ergo* and sometimes an *O Salutaris* setting added at the end.[11] Vincent Novello does the same with his own Masses, as settings in his publication *Twelve Easy Masses* (1816) show.[12] Such

---

9   Newsham/Richardson, *A Collection of Music*, 'Tantum Ergo No. 6'.

10 Tozer/Hasberry, *New and Complete Benediction Manual*, 'Tantum Ergo No. 31'.

11 Samuel Webbe the elder, *A Collection of Sacred Music* (London, 1792). Samuel Webbe the elder, ed. Vincent Novello, reprinted by J.A. Novello in his *Cheap Musical Classics* series (London, n.d.). Boosey, *Short Masses for Small Choirs* series (London, n.d.)

12 Vincent Novello (ed.), *Twelve Easy Masses* (London, 1816). Vincent Novello, 'Convent Mass' (No. 2) in *Masses for Four Voices* (London, n.d).

Example 8.2   Webbe's setting of the *Tantum Ergo* in Wade's *Graduale Romanum,*
               A Collection of Motetts or Antiphons for 1,2,3 and 4 voices or chorus
               calculated for the more solemn parts of Divine Worship by S. Webbe
               (London, 1785), pp. 88–9

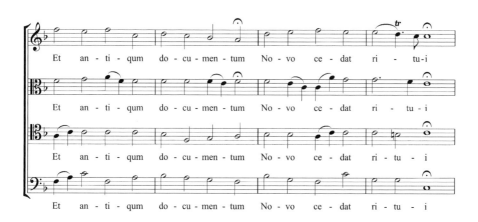

practices point to a custom of holding Benediction immediately after High Mass. Indeed the layout of Wade's 1765 *Graduale Romanum* at Stonyhurst may reflect this; since the 'Hymnus ad Benedictionem' section comes straight after a set of Mass Ordinaries and is followed by a 'Missa Pro Defunctis' and two other Ordinary Mass settings.[13]

At this time, then, the Benediction service, and the music that went with it, still had some liturgical associations with the Mass. Indeed, the occasional practice of holding Benediction after Mass survived into the twentieth century. Yet there is no reference to the service as such at the embassies in the Directories of the time.[14] However, a tantalising glimpse of the spread of Benediction music to the provinces is given in the file of letters written between 1797 and 1799 by James Preston of Abergavenny to James Coghlan, the Catholic London bookseller and publisher. As noted earlier, these show Preston's active promotion of plainchant in Abergavenny, and such promotion applied not just to Mass and Vespers but to Benediction as well.[15] Moreover, many Benediction compositions composed during that era had a long life, and some survived into the twentieth century. For example, the 1931 *New and Complete Benediction Manual*, in addition to the Wade *Tantum Ergo* mentioned earlier, contains two settings of the *O Salutaris* and *Tantum Ergo* to a 'Melody XVIII century'. There is also a *Tantum Ergo* setting in E♭ by Henry Nixon and two others in A and G adapted to a 'Spanish Chorale' and an 'Italian Chorale'. These probably came from the Spanish and Sardinian chapels respectively.[16]

Much of this evidence suggests that the growth in Benediction music at this time needs to be kept in perspective. In many sources it constitutes a very small part of the total repertoire. For example only 8 out of 66 and 5 out of 245 pieces in Wade's *Cantus Diversi* (1751) and *Graduale Romanum* (1765) at Stonyhurst are for Benediction. Similarly, in Webbe's *A Collection of Motetts and Antiphons* (1785) and *A Collection of Sacred Music* (1792) the proportions are 4 out of 50 and 4 out of 26; whilst in Part II (Books 7–12) of Vincent Novello's *Evening Service* (1822) the figure is 8 out of 71. Yet all these are collections of music intended primarily for

13 John F. Wade (ed.), *Graduale Romanum* (1765, Stonyhurst copy), pp. 139–42. The Mass Ordinaries start on p. 107. The same phenomenon can be observed in Wade's *Cantus Diversi* of 1761 and *Graduale Romanum* of 1765 now held in the Douai Abbey archives, MSS 6 and MSS 5.

14 For example the *Laity's Directory* of 1819 lists High Masses at the Sardinian, Bavarian, Spanish and Portuguese chapels at 11.00 with Vespers at 3.00 or 3.30 followed by catechism with no reference to Benediction (London, Appendix n.p.), and this remains true in its equivalent for 1843 (London) pp. 8–9 even though by that time afternoon or evening Benediction is being advertised elsewhere. However, Webbe, in his *Motetts or Antiphons* (1785), specifies that the two *Tantum Ergo* settings he provides were intended for use 'At Benediction', suggesting that already the service had a distinct free-standing identity of its own, pp. 88–9 and 112–13.

15 Bennett Zon, 'Plainchant in the Eighteenth-Century English Catholic Church', *RH*, 21/3 (May 1993): 373–9. The letters cited are stored in the Lancashire Record Office, RCBu 14/66, 14/93, 14/115 and 14/142.

16 Tozer/Hasberry, *New Complete Benediction Manual*, *O Salutaris* settings nos. 17 and 32; *Tantum Ergo* settings nos. 4, 5, 9, 18 and 45. See also Webbe's *O Salutaris* setting, no. 29.

Mass or the Office, not an extra-liturgical devotion such as Benediction. The true scale of the growth that was already taking place is revealed by Vincent Novello's *A Complete Collection of Tantum Ergos for every Sunday of the Year*. At present, the exact date of publication is problematical, given that the sole reference known to the author survives as a later offprint by Novello Ewer and Co. at Alston, but it must belong to the early or mid-nineteenth century, and not later than Novello's death in 1861. It contains 51 settings of *Tantum Ergo*, 13 of *O Salutaris*, and 9 other works, but no Litanies; so at this stage integrated musical settings of the primary Benediction texts have not yet become a priority. This, then, provides crucial evidence of the first real surge of interest in Benediction music during the nineteenth century.

Nineteenth-century Benediction music at Ushaw College

The next stage is closely associated with Ushaw College, near Durham. Here, the key figure was Charles Newsham, President of the College between 1837 and 1863, though there are earlier signs of interest in compositions by his predecessor Charles Youens (1798–1848) and by Richard Gillow (1811–67), professor of theology. The manuscript evidence at the college, though, is meagre. Among 423 works in nineteenth-century manuscripts and printed copies there are only four *O Salutaris*, four *Tantum Ergo* and eight Litany settings. Hence the importance of Newsham's *A Collection of Music Suitable for the Rite of Benediction* as revised by John Richardson (copies of the original edition, advertised in the Burns and Lambert catalogue at the end of the 1855 *Catholic Directory*, do not appear to survive). There are also several manuscript copies of other works by Ushaw composers in several collections.

The book contains 32 Litanies, 1 *Adoremus*, 15 *O Salutaris* and 19 *Tantum Ergo* settings – 67 pieces in all. Here the key components of Benediction music have been defined – namely settings of *O Salutaris*, the Litany and *Tantum Ergo* – but they are not grouped together into 'Benediction Service' settings, although, as shall be observed in the *Crown of Jesus Music*, there were trends in this direction. The vast majority use four-part harmony. However, because each voice is assigned to a single stave with an organ realisation below each system, it is clear the settings were intended to be sung by a choir.[17]

The balance of sources is interesting. Apart from Allegri's *Adoremus* only three *Tantum Ergo* settings date from the period 1551–1650.[18] There is also a *Tantum Ergo* by Caspar Ett in the Appendix. On the other hand, at least ten pieces are associated with the London embassy chapels.[19] However, the largest single contribution – 23

---

17 The exceptions occur with five settings of the *Tantum Ergo*. Nos. 3 and 11 by Richardson and De Weigl are in four parts but with a partially independent organ setting; no. 5, by Rowland Davies, opens for SAB voices before reverting to the SATB combination; no. 7, by Newsham, has an opening for two soloists and organ before an SATB chorus section; no. 18, by Richardson, has a second verse for double choir.

18 These are by Anerio, Palestrina and Perti respectively.

19 These are works by Rowland Davies (1740–97), Nicolo Pascoli (or Pasquale) (1718–57), Samuel Webbe (the elder), T. White (1764–1826), an 'Italian Chorale', a 'Spanish Chorale', a 'Maltese Litany', and a 'Roman Litany'.

pieces – comes from Ushaw itself, 18 of which were composed by Newsham himself.[20] In addition there are ten other pieces by Richardson. Richardson is probably also responsible for the Appendix at the end.

Richardson's role was pivotal. For 20 years he was organist and choirmaster at St Nicholas' Pro-Cathedral, Liverpool; then, between 1860 and 1864, he worked at St Alban's, Warrington before retiring to his native Preston. He was therefore responsible for adapting a repertory intended for seminary students to suit the needs of urban churches. Yet, at first sight, his involvement is somewhat surprising. The collection includes settings by Richard Gillow, who was at loggerheads with Newsham. At Ushaw Gillow had slated Newsham's pupils in *viva voce* examinations, opposed Newsham's appointment in 1837 as President and even accused him of heresy. The upshot was that he left Ushaw and eventually became a canon at St Nicholas. From there, he and his brother played a leading part in efforts by bishops George Brown and Alexander Goss to establish St Edmund's College, which some suspected would become an independent seminary siphoning off Lancashire students from Ushaw. How, then, did Richardson become involved? An answer may lie in the fact that he and Newsham shared an interest in Renaissance polyphony. More tellingly, for Ushaw's Jubilee celebrations in 1858 Richardson set the new College Ode that had been specially composed by Wiseman.[21] The following year Newsham was incapacitated by a stroke, so it must have been at this point that Richardson took over the editorial work. In this context it may also be significant that in 1860 Richardson left St Nicholas for Warrington, tactfully distancing himself from the centre of conflict.

Nevertheless, there is clear evidence of Liverpudlian influence. This is most evident in Richardson's compositions. His *O Salutaris No. 12*, *Tantum Ergo No. 10* and *Tantum Ergo No. 17* are set for double choir and soloists. They therefore must reflect the substantial choral resources available at St Nicholas. Moreover, in all his compositions and in his arrangement of Allegri's *Adoremus In Aeternum* Richardson adds crescendo and diminuendo markings. Such instructions are not found with the other settings. This suggests that the choir at St Nicholas had greater vocal proficiency and dynamic control. The edition also states that Richardson was responsible for all the organ parts. This means that many items were originally meant to be sung *a cappella*. Clearly, this was a key step in rendering the collection more suitable for use outside a seminary. Moreover, the different arrangements highlight changes in organ playing. The Embassy chapel compositions have accompaniments designed for manuals only, as can be seen from the agile and wide-ranging Baroque-style left-hand line in the *O Salutaris No. 5* and *No. 11* settings by Rowland Davies and De Weigl. On the other hand, Richardson's *Tantum Ergo No. 17* cannot be performed without a pedal board. What is more, as in the vocal parts, he provides crescendo and diminuendo markings. This is very different from the terraced dynamics that were such a hallmark of Vincent Novello's organ arrangements.

---

20 The other composers are Charles Youens, Richard Gillow and his brother Robert Gillow (1812–47).

21 David Milburn, *A History of Ushaw College* (Ushaw, 1964), pp. 160–62, 198–214, 230–58.

Given its dual Ushaw–Liverpudlian origins it is almost certain that the Newsham–Richardson manual was fairly widely circulated. After all, Ushaw was a major seminary for the English Catholic church in its northern heartland, whilst Liverpool was a focal point for Irish Catholic immigration. Indeed, the distribution of some copies throws interesting light on the way the music was disseminated. St Cuthbert, Durham, naturally enough, has a copy, as it is only three miles away from Ushaw. So does the Everingham collection – in this case because Matthew Newsham, brother of Charles, worked there. Similarly Richard, Gillow's work at Fernyhalgh and St Mary, Mount Pleasant, Chorley, explains the existence of copies there. Note that the copy from Mount Pleasant was published by Burns and Oates and therefore is a second edition produced after 1866.[22] More interesting is an organ book belonging to Roger Taylor, from St Augustine's, Preston. This contains manuscript copies of compositions taken from the Newsham–Richardson manual *and* otherwise unknown works by Newsham, Youens and Gillow. There are also other works by embassy chapel composers who appear in the Newsham–Richardson collection. Taylor was an Ushaw man, and worked at St Augustine's between 1857 and 1862. This suggests that he had access either to the original Newsham edition or to manuscripts from Ushaw, but that the revised Richardson edition became available sometime during or just before 1862. It may also be significant that he was succeeded in 1864 by a Thomas Newsham (1809–68), who had been a canon at St Nicholas from 1853.

In addition there are Jesuit links. As has been noted the Constable-Maxwell family at Everingham all went to Stonyhurst. Indeed the rector, Richard Norris, presided at the opening of the chapel there with Matthew Newsham. Likewise, there are copies at Chipping and from St Ignatius Preston. The latter is signed by a 'Miss Oldfield', whose parish priest – Henry Walmesley (1811–78) – came from Stonyhurst. Miss Oldfield also had a manuscript organ book into which items from the Newsham–Richardson collection were copied. This was later owned by a Miss Lizzie Buckley, who played at St Gregory's, Weld Bank, Chorley, near where Gillow had worked.

A most interesting item concerns a *Tantum Ergo* by Palestrina (see Example 8.3). In the Newsham–Richardson collection it is set for four voices, but in Taylor the requirement is doubled. Here it is marked 'Tantum Ergo commonly sung by the Coro Papale'. The Taylor arrangement also appears in *The Ecclesiastical Choir Book* published by James Burns in 1848, as well as in an untitled manuscript of 1888 at Stonyhurst, some 20 miles away. These facts, taken together, suggest three possibilities. First, that Stonyhurst and St Augustine's had access to a copy of Alfieri's *Raccolta di Musica Sacra* of 1841–46. In this context the presence of a Litany by Alfieri in both their manuscripts may be significant. Second, that Stonyhurst and St Augustine's used copies of *The Ecclesiastical Choir Book* that have since been lost. Third, that the version was circulating in a manuscript original brought over by Cardinal Wiseman, a personal friend of Newsham, who also presented to Stonyhurst a signed copy of his *Four Lectures on the Office and Ceremonies of Holy Week*. In this context Burns's dedication to Wiseman in *The Ecclesiastical Choir Book* may

---

22 This copy is now held at the Presbytery, English Martyrs Church, Whalley. It is signed 'T. Mulvey. Clifford St'. Clifford St is in Chorley, near the Mount Pleasant and St Gregory's churches there.

Example 8.3   Newsham's arrangement of Palestrina's *Tantum Ergo*

be significant, especially since he was the publisher of the Newsham–Richardson manual.

The basic picture, then, seems to be that Benediction music from or obtained by Ushaw was circulating in manuscript and printed form across northern England. The pattern was reinforced by the publication in 1864 of *The Crown of Jesus Music*, edited by Hemy, who worked at Ushaw, as has been seen. Part III has 20 Benediction Services and 6 Processional Litanies. These were drawn from four major sources: plainchant (12 pieces), music from the embassy chapels (5 pieces), music by Ushaw composers (11 pieces, including one by Gillow), and 32 of arrangements from works by established Classical composers.[23]

The grouping of items into 'Benediction Services' is in itself significant, and marks the further development of the genre as an integrated musical form. However, in most instances such integration is only partial, given that the constituent parts are often in different keys and by different composers. In several cases the title is defined by the same name being applied to the litany. For example, 'St Benedict's service' has an original litany by Hemy bracketed by an *O Salutaris* and a *Tantum Ergo* set to an 'Old English Air' and music by Cimarosa. Likewise, Newsham composed the Litany for 'St Andrew's Service' preceded and followed by an *O Salutaris* by J. Aylward and a *Tantum Ergo* set to a 'Russian Air'. Aylward himself lived at Woodchester, in Gloucestershire; but Suffield, an editor of the *Crown of Jesus* manual, had been an Ushaw seminarian, and worked at St Andrew's Church, Newcastle between 1858 and 1860. So this service may well be associated with that church whilst Suffield was based there. Likewise, the different parts of the 'St Cuthbert's service', although entirely composed by Newsham, are all in different keys, and therefore composed at different times. However, the 'St Cuthbert's Litany' was in all probability written in 1837, the first year of Newsham's presidency, when St Cuthbert was adopted as Ushaw's patron saint. These deductions suggest that Hemy assembled music that had been written or collected at Ushaw over at least 30 years.

The Jesuit contribution

It should be apparent from the above that there was some overlap between Benediction music associated with Ushaw and Jesuit activity at the same time. Indeed, the latter were just as prominent in the field. For example, the Everingham collection contains the publication *Litany Chants as used at the Church of the Immaculate Conception, Farm St*, the London headquarters of the English Jesuits. This, along with other Jesuit collections, was published by Burns and Oates, and must have been purchased by the Constable-Maxwells on one of their trips to London.[24] There is

---

23 The embassy chapels are represented by one piece each by Samuel Wesley, Webbe (the elder), and Peter Von Winter, along with a 'Venetian Chorale' and a 'Spanish Chorale'. The Ushaw composers are Newsham (five pieces), Hemy (two pieces) Richard Gillow and Youens (one piece each). There are ten arrangements from Beethoven, four from Mozart, three each from Gluck and Mendelssohn, and one each from Cherubini, Handel, J. Haydn, Neukomm, Rinck, Romberg, Spohr and Weber.

24 No publication date is supplied, but it probably was first produced in the 1850s.

also a manuscript book containing eight settings of the *O Salutaris*, one of which is by the French Jesuit Louis Lambillotte (1796–1855). This French Jesuit connection is confirmed by the presence of Lambillotte's publication *Salut du St Sacrement* marked with the stamp of a Paris shop where it must have been purchased.[25] In addition, the Everingham collection holds a copy of *Fourteen Benediction Services* by Henry Farmer SJ (1849–1928). Two other Jesuit publications are listed in the Burns and Lambert catalogue at the back of *The Catholic Directory* in the 1860s – *Easy Litanies, Hymns etc for Vespers, Benediction and other occasions, including the original Farm St Litanies*, and *Thirteen Litanies, New Series, as used at the Church of the Immaculate Conception, Farm St*. Moreover, as might be expected, Jesuit influence extended beyond their immediate circle. For example, St Cuthbert's church, Durham, possesses a copy of Farmer's *Fourteen Benediction Services*.

Farmer was not the only Jesuit interested in Benediction music. In the late nineteenth century there are two outstanding figures. The first is William Maher (1823–77), translator and composer of the words and music of the hymn *Soul of My Saviour*. At Stonyhurst there are numerous copies of his *Nineteen Benediction Services*, for double choir, organ and soloists.[26] This was dedicated to Salvatore Meluzzi, choirmaster at the Vatican Basilica, St Maria Maggiore and the Gesu in Rome, who had composed a *Mass in D* for the opening of St Peter's Church, Stonyhurst in 1836. The collection is important because, unlike with the *Crown of Jesus Music*, each 'Benediction Service' is planned as a complete whole. His example was followed by other Jesuits, notably Henry Famer.

Another major Jesuit figure was Zulueta. He was responsible for the publication *Benediction Services for Choir and Congregation with music for the 'Via Crucis'*.[27] It contains 26 and 21 settings of *O Salutaris* and *Tantum Ergo*, 22 Litanies, 3 motets and 1 other work – 73 items in all. In every case four-part harmony is used except for four items set for SATB choir, congregation and organ. There are 33 compositions by Zulueta, and 32 others by British composers, including 5 by Newsham, 1 by Richard Gillow, 13 by J.E. Moore SJ, 3 by Maher, 5 by Charles Raymond Barker SJ, and 3 by George Herbert, who worked at Farm St. There are also 5 other items that are anonymous in origin. The publication therefore has a contemporary 'feel' about it. Only one identifiable item – by J.S. Bach – was composed before 1800, and anyway it appears in the appendix of Newsham and Richardson's manual. Thus, once again the overlap between Ushaw and the Jesuits is apparent.

Zulueta and Maher's output was to some extent amalgamated in *Catholic Evening Services*, originally published in 1891 and then reprinted in 1919.[28] It combines four originally separate publications: A 'Bona Mors Choral Service' by Maher produced by the Jesuit press at Roehampton, a 'Rosary of the B.V.M.', 'Vespers of the Blessed Virgin, Compline, Benediction etc.' and 'Antiphon chants for Vespers and

---

25 No other publication details can be seen on the copy of this work at Everingham.

26 William Maher, *Nineteen Benediction Services* (London, n.d.).

27 Francis M. de Zulueta, *Benediction Services for Choir and Congregation with music for the 'Via Crucis'* (London, n.d.).

28 Francis M. De Zulueta and others (eds), *Catholic Evening Services* (Roehampton, 1891/R1919).

Compline'. Elements also appear to have come from Zulueta's *Choral Devotions for the League of the Sacred Heart*, published privately by the Church of the Holy Name, Manchester, in 1890, where Zulueta briefly worked. The whole volume is a hybrid between the Benediction rite, other extra-liturgical devotions and Office services. In all there are 24 items: 3 of them by Maher, the rest by Zulueta. Seventeen are set in four-part harmony, the rest for various combinations of a Cantor, SATB choir, congregation and organ. As with the Newsham–Richardson manual Jesuit Benediction composers wrote for a *combination* of the congregation, choir, solo cantors and organ.

Benediction music from the London Oratory

No study of English nineteenth-century Benediction music is complete without reference to the London Oratory. As has been seen, under Faber it was a major engine in the development of Catholic vernacular hymnody, but from its foundation in 1849 it also made daily use of its *Oratory Evening Service Book*, containing many elements of the Benediction rite. Not surprisingly Oratory musicians were active in the composition of Benediction music. Two publications, copies of which survive in the Everingham collection, are outstanding. The first is William Schulthes's *Benediction Service and a Collection of 36 Litanies with Organ accompaniment.*[29] Schulthes was choirmaster at the Oratory. All the settings except six Litanies (which are for two upper voices and organ) are for an SATB choir and organ. The second is William Pitts's *One Hundred and Thirteen Litany Oratories*, the composers of which can be identified in 83 cases.[30] Once again, the pattern is familiar: 65 settings are by British composers, 15 by Germans (including 10 by Schulthes), 2 by Italians and 1 by a Frenchman. There are 75 pieces by composers active in the period 1801–1900, 1 in the period 1801–50, 2 each in the periods 1701–1800 and 1751–1800, and 3 in the years 1751–1850. These figures show that most of the compositions in Pitts's publication are by British-born composers active during the nineteenth century. Indeed, 58 are by people directly connected to the London Oratory.[31] There are also a few non-Catholic items, but no plainchant.[32]

---

29 William Schulthes, *Benediction service and a collection of 36 Litanies with organ accompaniment* (London, 1861). There are, in fact, only 34 Litanies along with a setting of *O Salutaris* and *Tantum Ergo*.

30 William Pitts (ed.), *One Hundred and Thirteen Litany Oratories* (London, n.d.). A second copy can be found in the choir loft at Arundel Cathedral, where his son worked as parish priest for 40 years.

31 Apart from Schulthes they are Edmund Bagshawe (1829–1915): 2 works; Charles Bowden (1836–1906), who received Richard Terry into the Catholic Church: 17 works; Edmund Garnet (1848–96): 15 works; Archibald McCall (1852–1926): 2 works; Pitts (1829–93): 12 works.

32 There is one work each by Boyce, Mendelssohn, Arthur Sullivan and Charles Wesley.

A.E. Tozer's *New and Complete Benediction Manual* (1898)

So far most Benediction music appears to have been of Northern or London origin, a feature that reflects the demographic balance within the Catholic community for most of the nineteenth century. However, towards its end the first signs of the shift to the south and east noted in chapter 1 became apparent. This is reflected in A.E. Tozer's *New and Complete Benediction Manual*, published in 1898 by Alphonse Cary. This began life as a revision of an earlier publication, copies of which no longer appear to exist. The title betrays its 'national' ambition, but most of its contents are of southern origin. Tozer worked at Hove, in Sussex, whilst Alphonse Cary began his career as a composer and publisher in Newbury.

The manual contains 48 Litanies, 14 *O Salutaris*, 11 *Tantum Ergo* and 7 *Adoremus* settings – 80 pieces in all. Of these, 13 items were composed by Tozer, 6 by Cary, 8 by G.L. Stutfield, 7 by Frank Birtchnell and 3 by Cyril Vaughan. Stutfield, Birtchnell and Vaughan knew Tozer and Cary through their work on hymnody. In addition, there are three other contributions by Elgar, who came from Worcester. On the other hand there are no compositions by Newsham, Richardson, Pitts, Schulthes, Pitts and Zulueta. In other words northern, Jesuit and Oratorian contributions to the Benediction repertoire have been ignored. There is also virtually no sign of embassy chapel repertoire. Nevertheless, the strong nineteenth-century weighting and the virtual absence of continental input are typical of the time. Indeed, apart from plainchant, there are just two adaptations for the *Adoremus* text from Mendelssohn's oratorios *Elijah* and *St Paul*, which were well known to British audiences.

Plainchant, in fact, is used in nine instances, and again this distinguishes Tozer's manual from Oratorian and Jesuit practice. However, as one might expect in the period immediately before *TLS*, there is some confusion about the sort of plainchant that was used. One item comes from Guidetti's *Directorum Chori*, two from the Ratisbon editions of plainchant, and another is simply marked 'Roman Canon'. The rest, presumably, are associated with Solesmes.

The exclusion of existing repertoire has two possible explanations. Either Tozer was consciously developing a separate Southern tradition of Benediction music, or he assumed that Catholics already had adequate access to existing repertoire. Either way, the title may be significant. It implies that Tozer sought to reorientate Benediction music across the country. However, apart from providing new music from Southern sources and more plainchant, it is difficult to see whether this amounted to very much. Indeed, the division of the material by liturgical text – that is *O Salutaris*, the litany, *Tantum Ergo* and *Adoremus* – marks a retreat from the concept of an integrated 'Benediction Service' explored by Jesuits. Nevertheless, as shall be seen, Tozer's manual was important because it formed the basis of one of the two Benediction collections that came to dominate English Catholic musical repertoire in the first half of the twentieth century. This itself suggests that the original book was popular and widely used.

The early twentieth century: an era of consolidation and adjustment

By 1900, then, English Catholics had accumulated a vastly expanded repertoire of Benediction music from several different but overlapping traditions. In the prevailing Ultramontane atmosphere of the time it seemed natural to look for some consolidation and adjustment, and in the process take account the official promotion of plainchant and Renaissance polyphony. The issues raised surface clearly in the paper 'Music at Mass and at Benediction' read by Henry Bewerunge at the Nineteenth Eucharistic Congress held at Westminster Cathedral on 9–13 September, 1908.[33] Its critique encompasses both liturgy and music.

> If we consider the wonderful musical organisation of the Mass, the variety of liturgical forms and texts, its superabundant supply of musical compositions, the music of the Benediction service must strike us as poor.[34]

Liturgically Benediction failed because its inherent flexibility had not been exploited. According to Bewerunge 'the general law of the Church' specified only the last two stanzas of *Pange Lingua*, a versicle and a prayer, leaving maximum scope for creative initiative. In practice, as has been seen, a standardised service built around the *O Salutaris*, Litany and *Tantum Ergo* texts had become the norm. Yet the nature of such texts inhibited musical development, particularly once the limited plainchant and Renaissance polyphonic repertoires had been exhausted. Benediction music therefore depended on modern compositions; but 'taking these in bulk, we cannot, I am afraid, say we have much reason to be proud of them. What is worse, however, is that the form of the pieces does not lend itself to much variety of treatment.' Bewerunge was especially critical of the Litany, which he described as 'essentially a responsorial chant' for which only 'very simple melodies' could be provided. He therefore suggested that 'hymns, antiphons, responsories, motets or any other variety of form' be substituted.

It should be recognised, though, that Bewerunge represents a particular standpoint. As has been seen he was a plainchant and Renaissance polyphonic specialist, so he was unlikely to have much time for a modern Benediction repertoire. His approach also shows the effects of emerging liturgical study as an academic discipline. Indeed, the Westminster Eucharistic Congress was a landmark in this respect. Like Bewerunge, liturgists emphasised the rich complexity of form and meaning in the Mass, and the nature of such study pushed them in the direction of greater congregational participation. Benediction, by contrast, seemed to be not just over-simple, it was a rival to the Mass and, despite opportunities for congregational participation, its atmosphere reeked of private devotion. Bewerunge's strategy of importing forms from the Mass was, in effect, an attempt to reconnect Benediction to that service, preferably as a subordinate – rather than as an independent – element. Indeed, from the mid-nineteenth century onwards attempts were being made to import Marian antiphons and other motets, hitherto used in the Office and the Mass, into

---

33 *Report of the Nineteenth Eucharistic Congress, held at Westminster from 9th to 13th September, 1908* (London, 1909), pp. 95–103.

34 Ibid., pp. 102–103.

the Benediction service, hence the significance of the collection of Marian antiphons at Mount Carmel referred to earlier. The same phenomenon can also be found in Burns and Lambert catalogues at the back of issues of the *Catholic Directory* in the 1860s. Here, collections of Marian antiphons, for example E. Fagan's *The Four Antiphons of the Blessed Virgin Mary usually sung after Vespers* are listed under the Benediction heading.

Yet such Cecilian attitudes ignored other possibilities. As suggested earlier, the very simplicity and standardised character of Benediction may have been what made it attractive, otherwise it would not have evolved in that direction. Bewerunge cut against this. He wanted more complex and varied forms, which in turn required more sophisticated music, tilting the participatory balance away from the congregation towards the choir. Moreover, the importation of forms from the Mass and the Office would produce a higher proportion of Latin, as opposed to vernacular texts. There was thus a strong, but unspoken, case for leaving Benediction service as it was.

Such tensions shaped the contents of the two main Benediction books produced in the 1930s. In 1931 Cary and Co published *The Complete Benediction Manual*, edited by Robert Hasberry. This was a revised version of Tozer's *New and Complete Benediction Manual*. Six years later Burns and Oates produced Richard Terry's *Benediction Choir Book*, an abridgement of an earlier much larger and at present apparently unobtainable volume. In different ways both represent a response to the issues articulated by Bewerunge, and it was in this form that the nineteenth-century repertoire was handed on to subsequent generations.

In many respects Hasberry's volume seems more conservative. He himself was choirmaster at St James's, Spanish Place, London; so, in a sense, the wheel had come full circle with a return to the descendant of one of the embassy chapels. His collection holds 213 items, of which only 41 came from Tozer's edition of 1898.[35] In the process Hasberry restored some music from the embassy chapel and Ushaw repertoires (nine and eight pieces respectively). However, there are only two pieces by Jesuits and none from Oratory sources.[36] On the other hand, he was not averse to works by major continental Classical composers, nine of which appear in the collection.[37] Hasberry also added 23 works that had become available after 1898. However, since 12 of these were by J.E. Turner, who had died in 1897, there is virtually no twentieth-century input.[38] At the other end of the spectrum, following

---

35 Tozer's 1898 edition includes 8 out of Hasberry's 48 settings of the *O Salutaris*, 20 out of his 100 Litanies, 7 out of his 47 settings of the *Tantum Ergo* and 6 out of his 13 settings of *Adoremus*.

36 Embassy chapel music consists of two *O Salutaris* set to a 'Melody XVIII century', the 'Spanish Chorale', the 'Italian Chorale', two works by Webbe (the elder) and three by Nixon. The Ushaw contribution consists of one work by Richard Gillow, three by Newsham and four by Richardson. There is one work each by Maher and Zulueta.

37 There are two works by J.S. Bach, two by Mendelssohn (taken from Tozer's 1898 edition), and one each by Beethoven, Joseph Haydn, Michael Haydn and Padre Martini. Two other items are simply described as 'German'; and there is an *O Salutaris* setting by Ett (the same as in Newsham's manual).

38 The other composers are C.E. Miller: six works; F.J. Stone: four works; and Terry: one work.

the trend started by Tozer, there are 18 plainchant settings. This, though, is still a small proportion of the whole. Moreover, because he retained some of Tozer's original selections, some of the ambivalence in 1898 about what was the appropriate plainchant style remains. For instance, there is the setting from Guidetti's *Directorum Chori*, another from the Mechlin and a third from the Pustet editions.[39]

Despite all this, Hasberry's edition has a solidly British and nineteenth-century orientation. Yet, by 1931, the latter had a different meaning. The nineteenth century had ended 31 years before, so music from that era no longer had a contemporary feel. It had become an established repertoire. Unlike Tozer and his predecessors Hasberry was not really attempting to break new ground. He provided what congregations expected – hence his restoration of embassy chapel and Ushaw music. It is symptomatic that 20 Litanies and one *Tantum Ergo* setting are simply marked 'Traditional'.

Terry's collection is rather different. It contains 189 pieces: that is, 30 Litanies (together with 4 separate 'Kyrie' and 'Agnus Dei' settings), 32 settings of *O Salutaris*, 44 settings of *Tantum Ergo*, 15 settings of *Adoremus* (to which 7 separate 'Laudate Dominum' settings can be added), 34 hymns and motets and 4 Marian antiphons. It should be observed straight away that it was published at the same time as the revision of *The Westminster Hymnal* was commenced. Indeed, Dom Gregory Murray assisted Terry with many of the preparations in both works. A novel feature was the incorporation of several motets, hymns and antiphons, 32 of which were in Latin. Moreover, 41 of the 189 pieces use plainchant, a higher proportion than in Hasberry's manual, but in keeping with what was happening with the revision of *The Westminster Hymnal*. In other words, Terry was more responsive to the concerns expressed by Bewerunge. Note, though, that instead of introducing recent compositions, he preferred to expand the limited stock of plainchant and Renaissance polyphonic settings. This meant that he had to follow an already well-established practice of adapting plainchant melodies associated with other texts.

Another feature, again echoing his work on *The Westminster Hymnal*, was the inclusion of 20 adaptations from Continental hymnals.[40] He also included compositions by numerous named Continental composers, some of which had appeared in Newsham and Richardson's publication.[41] However, unlike in Hasberry,

---

39 Three other items are described as 'Roman', 'Dominican Processionale' and 'XIII century'.

40 These are taken from the *Andernacht Gesangbuch*, *As Hymnodus Sacer*, (Leipzig 1625), *Cant. S. Galli*, *the Koln Gesangbuch*, Leisentritt's Gesangbuch, *Leve Le Coeur* (1547), the *Miltenburg Processionale*, and La Feillée's *Méthode de plainchant* (1782). Terry also refers to a 'Dresden Chorale', a 'French Melody', a 'German Chorale', 'Traditional German', 'Traditional German 1741', 'Traditional German 1755', 'Traditional Parisian', 'Unknown Tours', 'Wolfenbuttel', an 'Italian Melody', a 'Spanish Melody', a fourteenth-century Laudi Spirituali, and a J.S. Bach harmonisation of a piece by Joseph Klug.

41 See for example Ett's *O Salutaris*, Palestrina's *Tantum Ergo*, and adaptation of a Bach chorale for the same purpose and Allegri's *Adoremus*. Other named Continental composers are C.P.E. Bach, Louis Bourgeois, Casciolini, Alexander Choron, N. Choron, Croce, F. Filitz, Gounod, Adam Gumpeltzheimer (c.1560–1625), Michael Haydn, Nanini, Schein, J. Schop, Schutz, and Johann Stiastny (1746–1820).

apart from one item by Michael Haydn, Viennese Classical eighteenth- and early nineteenth-century compositions were excluded. Yet, despite Terry's strictures on the subject, there was some non-Catholic material (Louis Bourgeois and J.S. Bach). Indeed, Terry even added adaptations from John Goss's setting of the hymn *Praise my Soul the King of Heaven*, a melody by Jeremiah Clarke that had been harmonised by Vincent Novello, and Thomas Helmore's plainchant arrangement of *Veni Emmanuel*.

Like Tozer, Terry did not hesitate to incorporate 20 works of his own, together with 9 others by his friends Anselm Burge (under the pseudonym 'Laurence Ampleforth') and Murray. Yet, apart from Murray's compositions, most dated from before the Great War. Moreover, to a greater extent than Hasberry, he restored several items from the embassy chapel and Ushaw repertoires. Eleven works are associated with the former, 26 with the latter, including 13 drawn directly from the Newsham–Richardson manual.[42] Jesuit contributions were limited to one work each by George Herbert, William Maher and Charles Raymond- Barker.

The key differences between Terry and the Hasberry–Tozer edition are twofold: namely, the influence exerted on Terry by hymnody and the fact that, according to the title, his collection is a book for choirs. Only 16 works appear in both collections, and just as striking is the absence from Terry's collection of compositions by Frank Birtchnell, Alphonse Cary, Edward Elgar, G.L. Stutfield, A.E. Tozer and J.E. Turner. Another difference is the fact that in 42 cases Terry avoided the usual four-part harmonisations, though these still predominate. Partly this is due to the adoption of a wider variety of forms, as advocated by Bewerunge. Yet in 27 cases Terry preferred unison plainchant settings, so the effect is more apparent than real. On the other hand, the British nineteenth-century weighting was still retained, although the proportions from other countries and periods are somewhat greater. Out of 189 items, 81 are by British composers and 33 by Germans; 48 were composed between 1801 and 1900, and 29 between 1900 and 1937, as opposed to 21, 10 and 13 dating from the eighteenth, seventeenth and sixteenth centuries respectively.[43] Terry's publication therefore is not as radical as it seems. It represents no more than a modification of the Benediction repertoire inherited from the nineteenth century and retained by the English Catholic community after the Great War.

---

42 The embassy chapel material consists of the 'Spanish Chorale', and works by J. Clarke (arr. V. Novello), V. Novello, Webbe (the elder and younger), S. Wesley and T. White. Ushaw composers are represented by Newsham and Richard Gillow. There are also three pieces by John Richardson.

43 There are only nine works by French composers, along with one each by identifiable Italian, Polish and Spanish composers.

PART V
The Iron Frame:
Catholic Music during the
Early Twentieth Century

Chapter 9

The New Legislative Framework

In the early 1900s a conjunction of factors led to an official attempt to impose a tighter degree of regulation and control by the Catholic Church over its music than had ever been seen before. Inevitably, this had significant effects on Catholic church music in England. Central to the process was the promulgation of *Tra Le Sollectudini* by Pius X on 23 November 1903. This chapter, then, examines the content, context and implications of this document. Subsequent chapters discuss its practical effects, especially as regards plainchant and Renaissance polyphony.

The contents of *Tra Le Sollectudini*

For convenience the provisions of *TLS* can be divided into four main areas: (1) the preferred style of music, (2) the relationship between music and liturgy, (3) methods of musical performance, and (4) regulations for enforcement.

As regards style Pius started from three basic principles: first, that church music 'must be holy'; second, that it 'must be true art'; third, that it be universally available across the whole Catholic Church. He concluded that

> on these grounds Gregorian chant has always been regarded as the supreme model for sacred music, so that it is fully legitimate to lay down the following rule: the more closely a composition for church approaches in its movement, its inspiration, and savour the Gregorian form, the more sacred and liturgical it becomes. [1]

Plainchant, then, was the touchstone by which all other church music would be judged. Moreover, Pius demanded that 'special efforts are to be made to restore the use of Gregorian chant by the people, so that the faithful may again take a more active part in the ecclesiastical offices, as was the case in ancient times'.[2]

Next in value was Renaissance polyphony. Pius stated that 'the above mentioned qualities are also possessed in an excellent degree by the classical polyphony, especially of the Roman school, which reached its greatest perfection in the sixteenth century, owing to the works of Pierluigi da Palestrina'. This was because 'the classical polyphony agrees admirably with Gregorian chant, the supreme model of all sacred music'.[3] In other words the high status of Renaissance polyphony was directly due to its perceived association with the plainchant, especially the measured

---

1   *TLS*, clause 2.
2   *TLS*, clause 3.
3   *TLS*, clause 4.

style of plainchant developed in Renaissance times and in general use throughout the nineteenth century.

More modern music could also be acceptable. Pius accepted that 'the Church has always recognised and favoured the progress of the arts ... consequently modern music is also admitted to the Church'. However, 'since modern music has risen mainly to serve profane uses greater care must be taken with regard to it, in order that the musical compositions of modern style which are admitted in the Church may contain nothing profane, be free from reminiscences of motifs, adopted in the theatre, and be not fashioned even in their external forms after the manner of profane pieces'.[4]

Central to Pius's thinking was the relationship between music and liturgy. In particular, Pius demanded the sole use of Latin at 'solemn liturgical functions', as well as strict fidelity to the text and the rubrics governing it. Thus, 'as the texts that may be rendered into music, and the order in which they are to be rendered, are determined for every liturgical function, it is not lawful to confuse this order at will, or to omit them entirely or even in part'. Consequently there could be no 'alteration or inversion of the words', no 'undue repetition' and no 'breaking [of] syllables'. Indeed, a musical setting had to render the text 'in a manner intelligible to the faithful who listen'. Moreover, since the integrity of a liturgical text had to be respected, it could not be split up into separate musical movements.[5] Pius was also concerned to ensure the supremacy of liturgy over music. For example, he stated that the priest should not be kept waiting at the altar while music was performed, and 'in general it must be considered to be a very grave abuse when the liturgy in ecclesiastical functions is made to appear secondary to, and in a manner, at the service of the music, for music is merely a part of the liturgy and its humble handmaid'.[6]

In addition liturgy informed Pius's perception of the role played by the choir. Clause 12 states that ' ... with the exception of the celebrant at the altar and the ministers ... all the rest of the liturgical chant belongs to the choir of Levites, and therefore singers in church, even when they are laymen, are really taking the place of the ecclesiastical choir'. This has a twofold interest. First, the emphasis on the choir contradicts Pius's hope that congregations might sing plainchant; second, it shows that he thought that a choir of laymen, as substitutes for ecclesiastics, had a liturgical office. In turn this explains why vocal solos, while not forbidden, were downplayed, and why women had to be excluded from choirs.[7] Indeed, the delivery of liturgical text was a factor behind the proscription not just of secular repertoire, but of musical instruments with secular connotations. Apart from the organ no other instruments could be used without special permission from the local bishop, whilst pianos and other percussion instruments were banned outright. Even the organ was only expected to sustain and accompany the choir; vocal pieces could not be preceded

---

4   *TLS*, clause 5.
5   *TLS*, clauses 7–11.
6   *TLS*, clauses 22–3.
7   *TLS*, clause 13.

by an instrumental prelude, nor could the singing be interrupted by instrumental intermezzi.[8]

The liturgical emphasis also lies at the back of regulations to enforce *TLS*. Every seminary was expected not just to establish a Schola Cantorum for the singing of plainchant, but to provide training in 'liturgical figured music', as well as lectures and academic theoretical grounding in the 'principles and laws of sacred music'.[9] In this way the clergy would acquire the necessary liturgical *and* musical expertise to dictate the form church music would take in the Church at large. Control of church music would therefore be wrested back from the laity with their suspect secular proclivities. Meanwhile, out in the field Pius required every cathedral to re-establish Schola Cantorum for the singing of plainchant and encouraged parish churches to do likewise.[10] Commissions 'composed of persons really competent in sacred music' were to be set up in every diocese. 'Nor are they to see merely that the music is good in itself, but also that it is adapted to the powers of the singers and is always well executed.'[11] So, here again, the emphasis on conveying liturgical text was paramount.

The implications of *Tra Le Sollectudini*

TLS, then, was a liturgy-driven document. Clause 1, for instance, opens by stating that 'Sacred music, being a complementary part of the solemn liturgy, participates in the general scope of liturgy; which is the glory of God, and the sanctification and edification of the faithful. Moreover, since its principal office is to clothe with suitable melody the liturgical text proposed for the understanding of the faithful, its proper aim is to add greater efficacy to the text'. Such emphasis was a consequence of the development of liturgy in the mid-late nineteenth century as an academic discipline noted earlier. It was also a reaction against irreverent and secular influences. As such it denied the proposition that secular methods could be used for the promotion of Catholicism, and the emphasis on the 'sanctification and edification of the faithful' marked a preference for insulating an existing constituency from outside corruption at the expense of missionary outreach. Not surprisingly, it was backward-looking in ethos. Thus, as already noted, 'Ancient' musical forms were promoted, especially plainchant and Renaissance polyphony, whilst the allegedly secular aspects of more modern styles were viewed with suspicion. Sometimes past tradition was deployed as an argument *per se* to support a given policy. For instance, plainchant was justified on the grounds that it is 'the only chant she [the Church] has inherited from the ancient fathers, which she has jealously guarded for centuries in her liturgical codices'.[12] Likewise clause 8 stated that 'it is permissible, according to the custom of the Roman Church, to sing a motet to the Blessed Sacrament after the *Benedictus* at solemn Mass'.

---

8   *TLS*, clauses 15, 17 and 20.
9   *TLS*, clauses 25–6.
10 *TLS*, clause 27.
11 *TLS*, clause 24.
12 *TLS*, clause 3.

Such features are the hallmarks of musical policies previously adumbrated by people such as Wiseman, Manning, Cornthwaite, Ullathorne and Herbert Vaughan in England (see Tables 9.1 and 9.2). Particularly noteworthy are the measures designed to assert clerical control in the name of liturgical purity. In other words, *TLS* underpinned clerical authority by its application of the principle of Papal supremacy to music. It is this that makes it a thoroughly Ultramontane document. It was meant to apply 'Roman' ways of doing things across the whole Church. As such, it demonstrates that, as in so much else, Ultramontane attitudes had become predominant in the Vatican's thinking about music.

Table 9.1   Musical decisions made at Diocesan and Provincial Synods in England*

Date	Synod (and convenor)	Musical decisions
1852	First Synod of Westminster (Cardinal Wiseman)	[1] General promotion of plainchant as the ideal form of church music [2] All seminarians to be taught plainchant [3] Boy singers to be trained to replace women in choirs
1873	Fourth Synod of Westminster (Cardinal Manning)	[1] Primacy of plainchant in church music upheld (clause 4) [2] Congregations to be encouraged to sing plainchant (clause 4) [3] Plainchant editions published by Pustet recommended (clause 3) [4] Seminarians to be taught chant and music (clause 1) [5] Boys to replace women in choirs (clause 2) [6] Musical items in church services not to be advertised in advance (clause 4) [7] In all music the text should come across clearly and the harmonisation should be simple (clause 4)
1880	Salford Diocesan Synod (Herbert Vaughan)	[1] The Pustet editions of plainchant to be made compulsory. [2] The employment of women in choirs should cease

*   Mager, *The debate over the revival of Ancient Church Music in Victorian England*, pp. 276–8. Robert Guy (arranger), *The Synods in English being the text of the Four Synods in English translated into English* (Stratford on Avon, 1886), pp. 185–91.

TLS, then, was not a neutral document, and such bias, once appreciated, exposes the dangers of accepting its ideas at face value. According to Robert Hayburn, *TLS* marked the peak of a crescendo of growing Papal interest in music from its first

Table 9.2   The musical contents of a selection of bishops' pastorals in England*

Date	Author (and diocese)	Musical provisions
1852	Cardinal Nicholas Wiseman (Westminster)	Clergy in the Westminster archdiocese to use the Roman chant books
1869	Cardinal Henry Manning (Westminster)	[1] Music performed in services should not be advertised
		[2] Light theatrical music to be excluded
		[3] No solos at Benediction
		[4] The clergy should make the musical decisions
1875	Robert Cornthwaite (Beverley)	[1] Plainchant upheld as the highest form of church music
		[2] The Pustet editions of plainchant to be compulsory
		[3] A list of approved music based on the German Cecilian Society's *Vereinscatalog* was published, the first of its kind in England
1876	Cardinal Henry Manning (Westminster)	[1] The Pustet editions of plainchant to be compulsory
		[2] There should be no organ playing at Requiems or during the seasons of Advent and Lent
		[3] There should be no secular music in organ voluntaries
1896	Cuthbert Hedley (Newport and Minevia)	[1] Plainchant promoted as the highest form of church music
		[2] The priest should approve all the music performed in his church

*   Mager, *The debate over the revival of Ancient Church Music*, pp. 279, 293–4, 300, 309, 313.

origins under Clement I in 95AD.[13] As such it justifies the implication that Pius's document was the realisation of ideas that have always been held by the Church and are therefore universally and forever valid. Hayburn's selection, layout and commentary on relevant documents suggest that the same ideas keep coming up and being developed over and over again. For example, the promotion of plainchant and the suspicion of secular influences in music runs like a leitmotif across the centuries. Likewise, the emphasis on clarity of text and musical training for seminary students can be found in decrees by the Council of Trent in 1562 and 1563.[14]

13 Robert Hayburn, *Papal Legislation on Sacred Music 95AD to 1977AD* (Collegeville, MN, 1979) p. xi.
14 Ibid., p. 27.

Yet such perspectives are misleading, not least because they largely ignore the changing historical contexts in which the different documents were drafted. For example, the relationship of plainchant to other musical styles was very different in the Middle Ages compared with that in the early twentieth century, not least because the array of other musical styles was so very different. Note too that *TLS* was the first occasion since the promulgation of *Annus Qui* in 1749 when a Pope had attempted to impose a standard musical approach across the whole Catholic Church. Between 1749 and 1903 the documents Hayburn cites are much more localised in scope. These mainly relate either to Rome itself, or to particular dioceses, or certain religious orders, or, more rarely, to whole countries or regions. The large number of regulations for Rome reflect the fact that the Pope had temporal jurisdiction there up till 1870. Indeed, the bulk of late Classical and early Medieval rulings concern just that city. By contrast, directives to religious orders and dioceses were usually a response to questions or appeals from certain groups. In other words the Pope intervened when invited to do so.[15]

What is more, *TLS* was a different sort of pronouncement compared with *Annus Qui*. The latter, to quote Hayburn, 'was a fine summary of the legislation which had preceded it as well as a practical exposition of the problems of Church music during the time of Pope Benedict XIV'; throughout, that Pope was careful to cite past authorities.[16] Apart from generalised appeals to past tradition *TLS* does not do this. It purports to be a personal statement, a 'Motu Proprio', by Pius X. In certain areas it breaks new ground, and occasionally it even reverses past policy. For example, whereas Benedict permitted certain orchestral instruments in church, Pius X only allowed them to be used on special occasions and then only with the permission of the local bishop. Pius also differed from Benedict in the special status he accorded to Renaissance polyphony. Even with plainchant, he does not simply reiterate past ideas, he extends its influence by making it the touchstone against which all other church music should be judged.

Such differences show the effects of the changing relationship between Church and State during the nineteenth century, especially in hitherto Catholic countries. In Italy the Risorgimento had by 1870 deprived the Pope of all temporal authority. In France the Third Republic during the 1880s and 1900s broke the Church's domination of the education system, drove numerous religious orders into exile and finally, in 1904, formally severed all remaining ties between Church and State. In Germany Catholic states were absorbed into Second Reich, formally promulgated at Versailles in 1870. This was followed by the Kulturkampf movement against the Catholic Church there.[17] As a result, in all these areas the situation became much more analogous to that pertaining in the USA and England, where the Catholic Church

---

15 Ibid., pp. 121–7, 132–7 (Rome), 110–13 (dioceses, religious orders and regions), 428–79 (directives by the Sacred Congregation of Rites).

16 Ibid., p. 108.

17 Frank Coppa, *The Modern Papacy since 1789* (London and New York, 1998), pp. 74, 78–85. Friedrich Heyer (D. Shaw (trans.)), *The Catholic Church from 1648 to 1870* (London, 1969R/1963), pp. 151–2. J.D. Holmes, *The Triumph of the Holy See. A short history of the Papacy in the nineteenth century* (London, 1978), pp. 224–57.

was one among many religious groupings operating within a secular or at any rate a non-Catholic polity. In short, the State was no longer a friend but a potential enemy. Consequently it no longer acted as a bulwark of particularist Catholic practice against the Papacy, as had been the case with Gallicanism under the French monarchy. In such circumstances many French, German and Italian Catholics, like their British counterparts, looked to Rome for guidance and support.

TLS, then, was as much a product of Ultramontanism from below as from above. Indeed, key aspects – such as the promotion of plainchant, Renaissance polyphony and lists of approved music prepared by diocesan music commissions – were ringing endorsements of policies adumbrated by the Cecilian movement. The German, Irish and Italian Cecilian Societies all received official Papal recognition as a result of direct solicitation by their leaders. The Cecilian School of Music in Rome was created as a result of collaboration between the Cincinnati, Irish and German Cecilian branches with the Papal authorities in 1880. As such, it served as a base for propagating Cecilian ideas there. In particular, Italian Cecilians – following earlier leads given by Gaspare Spontini (1774–1851) – played a leading role attempting to shape the music performed in Rome.[18]

Not surprisingly, Cecilians appealed to Papal documents originally designed for Rome as exemplars to be followed elsewhere. Terry, for instance, printed the text of Pius X's letter of 1903 to Cardinal Resphigi, Vicar General of Rome and Resphigi's own regulations of 1912.[19] Not only did these promote plainchant, musical training for Seminarians, the exclusion of women from choirs, and the establishment of a Roman music commission packed with Cecilians, they stated that no new choir could be formed and no choir master appointed without approval by the *Sacri Visita Apostolica*, or Papal Visitor. What is more, the qualifications of choirmasters had to be approved by the Roman Music Commission and all choir members had to make a sworn signed declaration of loyalty to the liturgical rubrics, the rulings laid down in *TLS*, and Resphigi's own regulations. As shall be seen, some at least of Resphigi's rules provided a template for the sort of policies Terry and his friends were already promoting in England.

Yet, such an appeal could be a double-edged weapon. It opened the way to the idea that *TLS* was a response to specifically Roman or Italian conditions that might not be applicable elsewhere. Resphigi's authoritarianism looks like a reaction against the consistent neglect of repeated Papal regulations displayed by Roman musicians throughout the previous century.[20] It has to be asked, as Spontini did, whether the Classical Viennese styles current in Britain, Germany and Austria were *as* secular and theatrical as the equivalent traditions in Rome; and, besides, the musical culture of the predominantly peasant society of Southern and Central Italy was very different from that of urban Catholic England.[21] Worse, if *TLS* was the product of pressure-

---

18 Kieran Daly, *Catholic Church Music in Ireland 1878–1903: The Cecilian Reform Movement* (Dublin, 1995), pp. 36, 43. Hayburn, pp. 121–9.

19 Richard Terry, *Music of the Roman Rite: A manual for choirmasters in English speaking countries* (London, 1931), pp. 264–82.

20 Hayburn, pp. 115–27.

21 Ibid., p. 123.

group activity, then its credibility was undermined. As Terry noted, some argued that what one Pope could enact, another could repeal. Others claimed that Pius had been misled; if this were so, then his 'Motu Proprio' might not be a divinely inspired document expressing the true mind of the Church.[22]

Such issues relate directly to the legal status of *TLS*. This has two aspects: the first concerning the doctrine of Infallibility, the second dealing with its official classification as a Papal document. As regards the former, Terry asserted that 'The Holy Father has spoken, and matters which were regarded as subjects for discussion have been removed from the region of controversy to the region of obedience'.[23] This is unsatisfactory. As Cuthbert Butler has shown, before 1870 there were many different definitions of Infallibility. For instance, Wilfrid Ward in the mid-nineteenth century regarded every Papal pronouncement as infallible; whilst the great Jesuit theologian Cardinal Bellarmine in the early seventeenth century asserted the Pope's supremacy in decisions concerning faith and morals but argued that if he became a heretic, that very fact would mean that he had ceased to be Pope and he could be judged and deposed by the Church. Then again, 'moderate' Gallicans in eighteenth-century France recognised the primacy of the Pope over the Church, but tempered it by arguing that he had to act within the legislation of the Church and by claiming that other bishops also derived their authority directly from Christ. In that sense, then, they were equal to him.[24] However, at the First Vatican Council held in 1870, a more precise legalistic definition was adopted. For a judgement to be infallible, first it had to be an *ex cathedra* statement representing the divinely inspired mind of the Pope, and second it had to be concerned with faith and morals and be in line with Church teaching on such matters. According to Butler, between 1870 and 1930, strictly speaking, only two Papal decrees fulfilled the required conditions – namely *Lamentabile* and *Pascendi* in 1907, both of which condemned Modernism.[25] The question, then, was whether *TLS* fell within this remit. True, its thinking is liturgical, and liturgy deals with matters of doctrine and morals. Moreover, if one accepts Guéranger's thinking, then it is something received from God and therefore divine. In addition, after his death Pius was declared to be a saint, and, if one accepts Hayburn's presentation of the evidence, his Motu Proprio was in keeping with past rulings about music. On the other hand, there is the view that while some parts of the liturgy might be regarded as divine, others could be fallible. This was the line taken by Pius XII in clause 50 of *Mediator Dei* in 1947, and it is a consequence of the development of acadamic study of liturgies past and present. Worse, Hayburn's own evidence shows that Pius X developed his musical ideas *before* he became Pope. As a child he was introduced to plainchant by the local parish priest, Fr Pietro Jacuzzi; at the seminary in Padua his taste for this style was developed, and most of the ideas in *TLS* – sometimes even the wording – can be found in his synodal decrees of 1888 as bishop of Mantua, in the *votum* he sent to the Sacred Congregation of Rites

---

22 Ibid., p. 235–6. Terry, *Music of the Roman Rite*, pp. 188–9.

23 Richard Terry, *Catholic Church Music* (London, 1907), pp. 39–40.

24 Cuthbert Butler, *The Vatican Council 1869–1870* (London, 1930/1962R), pp. 27–43, 50, 57–62, 458–65.

25 Ibid., pp. 385–472.

in 1893 and in his Pastoral Letter of 1894 as Patriarch of Venice.[26] What is more, in all these documents he was influenced by Angelo De Santi (b. 1846), who also drafted the basic text of *TLS*, which Pius then modified in his own hand. So, even if *TLS* was in keeping with past rulings, as Hayburn infers, ultimately it was a piece of 'ordinary' legislation which Catholics were expected to obey but which, unlike infallible judgements, was not irreformable.

It is at this point that the precise legal classification of *TLS* becomes significant. The emergence of a uniform system of categories is surprisingly recent, dating from 1878, the first year in the pontificate of Leo XIII. Even then, the exact binding force of any document was not properly defined until 1917, when Benedict XV issued the code of Canon Law.[27] Moreover, as with liturgy, such developments were the product of academic study undertaken by scholars such as Louis Duchesne and J.P. Migne. In order of importance the principal categories are (1) Papal Constitutions, (2) Motu Proprio decrees, (3) Apostolic Constitutions, (4) Encyclical Letters, (5) Chirographs or personal autograph letters written by the Pope, and (6) Decrees, rulings or instructions issued by Roman Congregations.[28] *TLS*, as a Motu Proprio document, is near the top of the list, rivalled – but not necessarily superseded – in importance only by decisions made at general councils. Its key characteristic is that it is a decision made by the Pope on his own accord; that is what 'Motu Proprio' means. Its high status derives from ideas of Infallibility. If the Pope is guided by God, then a decree of this sort carries greater weight than a ruling by a Papal bureaucracy, whose function is to implement the wishes of the Pope. For this reason *TLS* has shaped all subsequent Papal legislation on music, as the classifications listed in Table 9.3 show. The only major divergence has occurred with *Sacrosanctum Consilium*, jointly issued by the Second Vatican Council and Paul VI, which, amongst other things, permitted the use of the vernacular in the liturgy (clause 101), a wider range of instruments (clause 120) and respect for local variations and customs in the liturgy (clauses 37–40).

Nevertheless, *TLS* is not airtight. It has been observed that it was a consequence of pressure-group activity from below. In other words, Pius X picked up ideas current at the time and we know that others, notably De Santi, helped draft the document. Indeed, in the preamble he refers to 'the great number of complaints that have reached us' since becoming Pope. This does not necessarily disqualify it as a Motu Proprio document, because some authorities allow that a Motu Proprio can be issued in response to a petition.[29] However, this in itself does not resolve the difficulty. No matter how much Pius insisted in the preamble that 'We do publish, *motu proprio* and with our certain knowledge, Our present instruction' it still leaves open the possibility that Pius might have been misled and that what he proposed could be reversed or modified as a result of a counter petition.

---

26 Hayburn, pp. 195–231.

27 Ibid., pp. 513–14.

28 Ibid., pp. 506–11.

29 Hayburn, p. 507, citing Ameleto Cardinal Cicognani, *Canon Law* (Westminster, MD, 1949), p. 81.

Table 9.3   Major Papal legislation about music classified by document type,
             1928–2003

Date	Document	Legal classification
1928	*Divini Cultus*	Apostolic Constitution
1947	*Mediator Dei*	Encyclical Letter
1955	*Musicae Sacrae Disciplina*	Encyclical Letter
1958	*De Musica Sacra et Sacra Disciplina ad mentem litterarum Pio XII 'Musicae Sacrae Disciplina' et 'Mediator Dei'*	Instruction by the Sacred Congregation of Rites
1963	*Sacrosanctum Consilium*	Constitution jointly issued by the Second Vatican Council and Pope Paul VI
2001	*Liturgiam Authenticam*	Decree by the Congregation for Divine Worship and the Sacraments
2003	*Chirograph of the Supreme Pontiff John Paul II for the centenary of the Motu Proprio 'Tra Le Sollectudini' on sacred music*	Chirograph or autograph letter

*   Relevant translated texts can be found in Terry, *Music of the Roman Rite*, pp. 285–93.
Encyclical Letter of Pope Pius XII: The sacred liturgy: Mediator Dei (London, n.d.). Hayburn,
pp. 345–56. Clifford Howell (trans.), *An Instruction by the Sacred Congregation of Rites on
sacred music and liturgy in the spirit of the encyclical letters 'Musicae Sacrae Disciplina' and
'Mediator Dei' of Pope Pius XII* (London, 1959). Joseph Gallager (trans.), 'Sacrosanctum
Consilium', in Walter M. Abbott (ed.), *The Message and Meaning of the Ecumenical Council*
(London and Dublin, 1966), pp. 137–8. For references to *Liturgiam Authenticam* and the
Chirograph of John Paul II see chapter 1.

This means that there was still legal scope for Catholics to evade *TLS* should
they wish to do so. The key question, then, was how far English Catholics in the
early twentieth century accepted its rulings in practice, as well as in theory. Here, the
principal battlegrounds would be plainchant and Renaissance polyphony.

Chapter 10

Plainchant from Solesmes

When Pius X defined plainchant as the touchstone against which all other forms of church music should be measured, he meant a chant 'which the most recent studies have so happily restored to its integrity and purity'.[1] Such studies, the work of the abbey of Solesmes, transformed the predominantly 'measured' form of plainchant that Pius and his English contemporaries had known in the nineteenth century, and they produced a style that, in its aesthetic ambiance, still dominates perceptions of the genre today.

The implications of Pius's pronouncement then were profound, and perhaps greater than he realised. First, the Solesmes style is so different from what was performed before that it is difficult to believe that Pius and his Ultramontane allies really believed that, on *musical* grounds alone, plainchant in both its 'measured' and Solesmes forms deserved to stand at the pinnacle of church music excellence. To some extent – perhaps only subconsciously – the motivation must have been liturgical. Second, Pius does not seem to have appreciated that, if the Solesmes chant was so different, then the connection between plainchant and Renaissance polyphony that was so obvious with 'measured' chant would be weakened. Yet, as has been seen, *TLS* took it for granted that plainchant underwrote the high status accorded to Renaissance polyphony. Third, the emphasis on *restoration* in the Solesmes work shows how extreme the backward-looking character of official Catholic attitudes towards music had become. In theory at least, there was little question about adapting plainchant to suit modern conditions, a trademark of plainchant in the eighteenth and early nineteenth centuries. The object was to recover a lost 'integrity and purity'. So, musically speaking, Catholics and potential converts were presented with a 'take it or leave it' option. Fourth, it will be noted that the credibility of Solesmes version of plainchant was underpinned by a more rigorous and detailed scholarship than had ever been seen before, making full use of – and pioneering – the latest techniques of palaeographical research. Now Pius and many other Ultramontanes, including the monks at Solesmes, believed that this would produce an authentic uniformity, and this was because they assumed that there was one master version of any given plainchant melody. All they had to do was to discover it by comparing and ironing out the differences between different original manuscripts. Yet, in practice, such hopes proved illusory, and not simply because of the contradictions and problems inherent in the nature of the evidence noted earlier. As any academic knows, there are strong centripetal tendencies in all arts subject research. Solesmes produced not one, but two rival varieties of plainchant. Worse, the depth of specialised research made the

---

1   *TLS*, clause 3.

clergy dependent on academics for their understandings of plainchant. Indeed, some of these academics might not even be Catholics.

Thus, at the very moment when Pius tried to assert clerical authority over church music, in effect he undermined it by recognising the validity of Solesmes's techniques. Within two years Pius discovered that his assertion of the supremacy of plainchant produced controversy rather than unanimity. The issue was not simply whether in practice plainchant would be accepted by Catholics as the supreme form of church music, nor was it just about the transition from 'measured' to Solesmes chant; it was about *what sort of Solesmes chant* would be adopted. What is more, because of the temporary exile of the Solesmes community on the Isle of Wight between 1901 and 1923, some of the key events took place in England. The result was that, here at least, there emerged a divide between two performance traditions, and the confusion of messages this produced must have been a factor, albeit unquantifiable, on efforts to promote plainchant within the English Catholic community at large.

The Solesmes revolutions

Solesmes abbey was founded by Guéranger in 1831–32, on the site of a minor religious house abandoned during the French Revolution. His object was to reconnect with a Pre-Revolutionary and, above all, Medieval past. In effect he wanted to recreate an idealised, but *living*, monastic life centred around the Office.[2] As a result, Guéranger was perhaps the first person to engage in liturgical research as an academic discipline.

The liturgical Office is expressed through chant, a connection recognised by Guéranger in Volume 1 of his *Institutions Liturgiques* of 1840.[3] The moment of truth, though, came in 1846, when a full monastic rite was introduced. At that point Solesmes discovered that the chant books at its disposal, especially antiphoners, were inadequate for the job. Perforce Guéranger paid considerable attention to plainchant. Two factors shaped his approach: first, the practical experience of singing the Office; second, theoretical understandings evolved on predominantly *a priori* principles in consultation with Augustin Mathuson Gontier, author of a *Méthode raisonée de plainchant* published from Paris in 1859 and a frequent visitor to Solesmes. The key features are as follows: (1) plainchant rhythm should follow the 'natural' speech patterns of the text; (2) such 'natural' patterns are best achieved if the principle of a single indivisible note length is substituted for the 'measured' system of chant notation; (3) the adoption of faster tempi, which suited a monastic regime dominated by numerous Offices, since services would thereby be shortened; (4) a shift from a martellato style of singing, initially favoured by Guéranger, to lower, more nuanced dynamic levels. These fitted in with the ideals of self-abnegation characteristic of Benedictine monastic life as understood at Solesmes.[4]

---

2   Katherine Bergeron, *Decadent Enchantments: The revival of Gregorian Chant at Solesmes* (Berkeley, Los Angeles, London, 1998), pp. 2–15.

3   Pierre-Marie Combe, 'La réforme du chant et des livres de chant Grégorien à L'Abbaye de Solesmes 1833–1893', *EG*, 6 (1963): 186.

4   Combe, 'La Réforme du chant', pp. 188, 195–7.

The evidence assembled by Pierre Combe, especially the correspondence between Guéranger and Gontier, shows that these ideas were developed in the 1840s and 1850s *before* Solesmes began a real palaeographical study of original sources. This is a potential weakness in its case, because there will always be a suspicion that its theoretical thinking skewed the conclusions it drew from its practical research. Solesmes's approach was inductive rather than deductive. The theory was worked out first; the historical proofs came later. On the other hand, Combe suspected that differences between the Guéranger–Gontier theory and the results produced by palaeographical research conducted by Pothier and Paul Jaussons (d. 1870) were one reason why the preparation of new chant books was delayed. In particular Gontier, unlike Pothier, conceded that musical aspects could sometimes override textual rhythms. This was a theme that would resurface later in the work of Mocquereau.[5]

The work of Joseph Pothier

Pothier and Jaussons are important because they provided the first block of research that gave so much credibility to the Solesmes method. Serious work began in 1860 with the establishment of a scriptorium.[6] Crucially, Medieval rather than Renaissance sources were studied. Guéranger's visit to England that year proved to be more than coincidental, for he was shown English manuscripts by Lambert. Indeed, the very first manuscript studied was a thirteenth-century Processional of St Edith of Wilton brought over by Laurence Shepherd in 1859.[7] The first major results appeared in 1880 and 1883 with the publication of *Les Mélodies grégoriennes* and a *Gradual*. Other publications followed, notably another *Gradual* and a *Liber Responsorialis* in 1895, followed by a *Liber Usualis* in 1896.[8] A notable feature was the use of new musical type developed by Desclée, enabling a wider variety of more nuanced symbols to be used. This fitted in with Guéranger's preferred performance practice, and was in sharp contrast with the boldly marked neumes hitherto used in the Mechlin and Pustet editions, which must have encouraged a martellato style of execution.[9]

These differences are clearly illustrated by comparison between the first page of Pustet's and Pothier's Graduals (Figures 10.1–2 and Example 10.1). In both cases the textual and musical accentuation coincide, the notes are grouped together at melismas, and the bar divisions are the same. However, the effects are very different, although both adhere to the 'sing as you speak' principle. With Pustet the chant moves more slowly, the melody has been simplified and, above all, the notes are 'measured'. Note, though, that Pothier has not entirely abandoned the 'measured'

5   Ibid., pp. 203–10.

6   Bergeron, p. 16.

7   Combe, 'La Réforme du chant', p. 194. However, in the Stanbrook Archives there is a letter by J.B.L.Tolhurst to Anne Field dated 20 May 1958 stating that Solesmes was enquiring about this manuscript which had been produced by Lambert. Box, 'Stanbrook Hymnale'.

8   Other examples are the *Variae Preces ad Benedictionem* and the *Processionale Monasticon* of 1888. Pierre-Marie Combe: 'Préliminaires de la réforme Grégorienne de S. Pie X.' (Part I). *EG*, 7 (1967): 79–80.

9   Bergeron, pp. 56–8.

Figure 10.1   The first page of Pustet's 1871 edition of the *Graduale Romanum*

principle. For instance, at the first and second syllables of 'animam' and 'Deus' respectively he adds an extra punctum on the same pitch. This encourages the singer either to double the note length or repeat it 'repercussively'.

Reproduction of a hand-copied script in identical printed copies had certain implications. A particular script had to be chosen, and once this had been selected a standardised version based on numerous individual manuscript examples had to be adopted. As Bergeron noted, Pothier created a supposedly authentic ideal that

Figure 10.2   The first page of Pothier's *Liber Gradualis* (Tournai, 1883)

had never existed in Medieval practice.[10] Note too that up to this time there had still been occasional cases of English monks performing direct from original Medieval manuscripts, as John Harper found at Mount St Bernard Abbey in Leicestershire. Under the impact of printed plainchant books this last direct practical performance link with authentic Medieval manuscripts now came to an end.[11]

---

10 Bergeron, pp. 25–60.

11 John Harper, 'Gothic Revivals: Issues of Influence, Ethos and Idiom in late Nineteenth-Century English monasteries', in Jeremy Dibble and Bennett Zon (eds), *Nineteenth-Century*

Example 10.1   The Pustet and Solesmes versions of 'Ad te levavi' compared, using
                modern notation

Pothier's work moreover contains some rather curious features. First, he opted for
a thirteenth- and fourteenth-century style of script. This had the practical advantage of
being known to nineteenth-century plainchant musicians. Yet the manuscripts he used
dated primarily from the ninth and tenth centuries, raising questions of authenticity;
hence the tables in *Les Mélodies Grégoriennes* tracing the evolution of the neum
from that period. These demonstrated the historical pedigree of the notation that
Pothier presented. Second, as was mentioned earlier, Pothier followed past tradition
by inserting plainchant melodies of his own, without attribution. Usually this was
to fill gaps created by liturgical developments since the Middle Ages.[12] The trouble
was that it undermined confidence in the atmosphere of Medieval authenticity he
was trying to create, as several commentators later remarked in connection with his
work for the Vatican editions.[13] Of greater significance, however, was the fact that,
by aiming to produce an authentic Medieval product, Solesmes in effect completed
the process begun earlier whereby plainchant was reduced from a living tradition, to
which modern composers could contribute, to a dead antique.

The work of André Mocquereau

Inevitably, Pothier's work constituted a challenge to the Pustet editions, and this
became clear at the Congress of Arrezzo, held in 1882, where Solesmes's case was
publicly presented. Personally, Pope Leo XIII gave his support, but the Sacred

---

British Music Studies. Vol. 2 (Aldershot, 2002), p. 19. Recently, fragments of Rhineland
manuscripts, including some eleventh-century ones from St Gall that were used at eighteenth-
century Dieulouard and bound into the backs of books during the nineteenth century, have been
found at Ampleforth. Joan Malcolm, 'The Ampleforth Fragments: A Preliminary Survey',
PMM, 7/2 (1998): 129–140.

12 For a collection of Pothier's own chants see *Le Livre de Saluts* (Paris n.d., c.1930).

13 See, for example, McLachlan's letter to Bewerunge dated 2 October 1905, SAA
W1219. See also the 'Letter to the Editor' by 'A Student' from Downside (probably Alphege
Shebbeare) in *Tablet*, 73 (15 January 1905), pp. 57–8.

Congregation of Rites was opposed. Accordingly, the 1883 Gradual was issued for use by Solesmes and its daughter houses, backed by a testament from Leo XIII. Pustet, however, fearful of the implications of this for his monopoly, persuaded the Pope to send a second letter saying that it should be regarded as a work of historical scholarship.

Such rebuffs led to a new phase, led by Mocquereau. The principal device was the publication of *Paléographie Musicale*, a series of volumes containing photographs of complete medieval documents, backed by critical essays.[14] In this way the deficiencies of scholarship based on a standardised printed reproduction of a mass of different hand-copied manuscripts would be overcome.[15] Volume 1 was issued in 1889. Volumes 2 and 3 compared versions of the *Justus ut Palma* chant from 219 manuscripts ranging from the ninth to the seventeenth centuries. This was the Solesmes research methodology writ large, the object being to show that the version given in Pothier's 1883 Gradual was authentic. Against Pustet's claims that this was just a single example Mocquereau then proceeded to extend the technique to the rest of the plainchant repertory.

Paléographie Musicale, though, could also have a corroding effect on clerical authority, for by making images of medieval documents generally available it enabled scholars to study the evidence for themselves and come to their own conclusions. Likewise, the comparative techniques used in Mocquereau's 'Paleographic Workshop' established in 1889 reinforced the effect because they removed the analysis on which judgements could be made about plainchant into the hands of specialists. Nevertheless, in the short run *Paléographie Musicale* proved to be a key weapon in promoting Solesmes's cause in Rome against Pustet. For example, De Santi, having been charged by Leo XIII to defend the Pustet editions in *Catolica Civilita*, the official organ of the Papacy, became a protagonist for Solesmes. In 1894, Pius X, then Patriarch of Venice, despatched Lorenzo Perosi (1872–1956), a Cecilian composer and a future director of the Sistine Chapel Choir, to study at Solesmes. Similarly, Baron Rudolph Kanzler, another Sistine Chapel Choir director and later secretary of the Pontifical Commission of Sacred Archaeology (Paleographical musical research), became a supporter.[16]

Gradually, however, it became apparent that Mocquereau's approach to plainchant was significantly different from Pothier's. As early as 1883, following Gontier, he was willing to accept that in plainchant musical aspects could outweigh textual considerations. However, it was with the development of his rhythmical theory that the full implications of this became manifest.[17] Pothier, guided by his regard for

---

14 Hayburn, pp. 173–9. For an account of Mocquereau's early life see Combe, 'Préliminaires de la réforme Grégorienne': 62–95.

15 Bergeron , pp. 65–89.

16 For details of Solesmes's campaign in Rome see Pierre-Marie Combe, 'Preliminaires de la Réforme Grégorienne de S. Pie X. Part II: Le P. De Santi and Mgr. Carlo Respighi', *EG*, 7 (1967): 99–139.

17 Combe, 'Préliminaires de la réforme Grégorienne', 67.

the rhythm of the text, preferred to rely on innate artistic judgement.[18] Mocquereau wanted something more exact and prescriptive.

His starting point was psalmody. In his article 'L'Influence de l'accent tonique et la psalmodie', drafted in 1892, he argued that Latin texts had a natural rhythm of impulse and relaxation – or 'Arsis' and 'Thesis'. [19] However, he then proceeded to apply it to the music itself. The process can be traced in his correspondence with McLachlan, which began in 1895. In 1896 he was working on an 'Essai de rythmique'; then there is discussion of his *Petit Traité de Psalmodie*, which McLachlan translated and later incorporated in her *Grammar of Plainsong*. On 12 March 1901, he triumphantly announced 'Je crois vraiment que je tiens la verité'; which he then followed by discussion of McLachlan's project to write an 'ABC of Gregorian Rhythm'.[20] The fullest expression of his ideas, however, was not realised until the publication of his *Le Nombre Musical Grégorien*. The first part appeared in 1908, the second in 1927.[21]

Mocquereau's approach depended on his concept of what was signified by 'accent'. It did not just mean how a note was 'struck'; just as important was the manner by which rhythm could be conveyed through changes of pitch, note durations, and dynamics. To guide singers Mocquereau added 'rhythmical signs' to the music (Example 10.2). These became standardised as an episema (or horizontal line), a vertical episema (to denote the arsic points in the music), and a dot to slightly lengthen a neume. Mocquereau claimed that these symbols were of Medieval derivation.[22]

Example 10.2   An instance of Mocquereau's rhythmic signs

Gló- ri- a in ex-cél- sis Dé-o.   Et in tér- ra pax ho-mi- ni- bus

bó-nae vo- lun- tá- tis.   Lau- dá- mus te,   Be- ne- di-ci- mus te.

Mocquereau did not regard arsis-thesis rhythms as merely local phenomena. They produced waves of sound – or chironomy – across the whole of a piece of plainchant. This is the origin of the chironomic method of conducting, whereby the

---

18 Bergeron, pp. 101–111.

19 This was published in 1895 at the diocesan Congress of Rodez and reappeared in *PM*, vol. 7. Combe, 'Preliminaires de la Réforme Grégorienne', 102.

20 SAA, Letters from Mocquereau to McLachlan, esp. 5 March 1896, 20 March 1896, 11 October 1896, 8 July 1900, 13 March 1901, 18 July 1901 and 22 March 1902.

21 Bergeron, pp. 111–18.

22 Ibid., pp. 122–4 for a summary of Mocquereau's earlier experimentation with various rhythmic symbols between 1899 and 1905.

choirmaster directs the choir by raising or lowering his hands in a kind of horizontal wave in line with the arsis-thesis rhythms of the music. In turn this produced a Schenkerian kind of rhythmic analysis, again derived from psalmody. In his *Petit Traité de Psalmodie*, Mocquéreau followed the standardised structuring of psalm tones presented in earlier manuals like Haberl's *Directorum Chori* (Example 10.3a). However, as his follower McLachlan shows in *The Grammar of Plainsong*, he then proceeded to regard other sorts of plainchant in the same way (Example 10.3b). Arsis-thesis rhythms could be applied to sections, and indeed the whole piece, producing a rhythmic 'middle ground' and 'background' to the local 'foreground' events (Examples 10.3c and 10.3d).

The whole thrust of Mocquereau's thinking was thus largely musical, creating a tension between linguistic and notated rhythms. Paradoxically, Mocquereau had to concede that it did not apply to psalmody – where obviously the demands of the text were paramount, if only because it was chanted. In most other respects Mocquereau's rhythmic approach was at odds with Pothier's, and it was the publication of the Vatican edition of plainchant that brought these differences to a head.

Example 10.3   Analyses of plainchant

(a)   Haberl's analysis of a Psalm Tone and its application to a portion of text (Franz Xavier Haberl (N. Donnelly, trans.), *Magister Choralis: A theoretical and practical manual of Gregorian Chant* (Ratisbon, 1877), pp. 120–121)

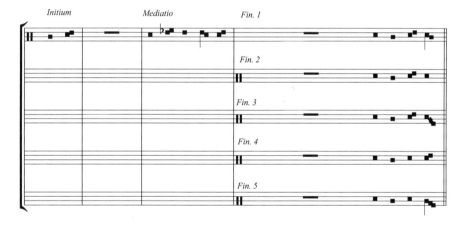

(b)   Mocquereau's analysis of Psalm Tone No. 1 (adapted from [L. McLachlan],
        Grammar Grammar of Plainsong (London,Worcester, New York, Cincinatti,
        1905), p. 105)

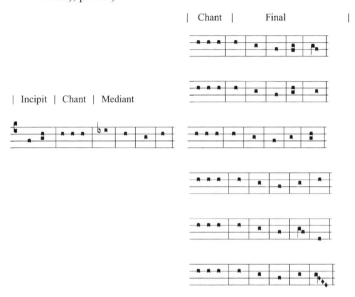

(c)   Schematic plan of the arsic-thetic structuring of a piece of plainchant
        ([McLachlan], *Grammar of Plainsong,* p. 106)

Period							
Section				Section			
2 bar group		2 bar group		2 bar group		2 bar group	
Bar		Bar		Bar		Bar	
A1	T1	A2	T2	A3	T3	A4	T4	A5	T5	A6	T6	A7	T7	A8	T8

(d)   Its practical application by Laurentia McLachlan to the antiphon 'Tu es Petrus'
        (The numbers correspond to the arsis-thesis (AT) units in the schematic layout;
        transcribed from [McLachlan] *Grammar of Plainsong*, p. 106)

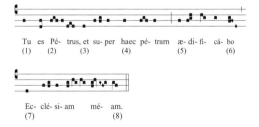

The Vatican Edition of plainchant

In 1901 the 30-year monopoly granted to Pustet expired and was not renewed. Moreover, that same year Raphael Molitor, pursuing researches conducted by Guiseppe Baini 60 years before, revealed that Palestrina was not directly responsible for the Medicean Gradual on which Pustet's books had been substantially based.[23] The question then was what to replace them with. In the authoritarian Ultramontane atmosphere of the time it was inconceivable that a definitive edition for use across the whole Roman Catholic Church should not be produced. Accordingly, Pius X on 25 April 1904 issued the Motu Proprio decree *Col Nostro*. A new series of plainchant books would be prepared by the monks of Solesmes vetted at every stage by a Papal Commission. Solesmes agreed to give up its copyrights, and the whole was to be published by the Vatican Press. However, this 'typical' edition could be freely reproduced by any other publisher.[24] In some respects Solesmes's willingness to give up its copyrights is surprising, even when allowance is made for the tradition of Ultramontane obedience inculcated there by Guéranger. However, the community were in a weak position following its expulsion from France because the French government had seized all its assets, including the book stock and printing press.[25] Nonetheless, *Col Nostro* vindicated its position against Pustet after two decades of lobbying. The occasion was celebrated at the Gregorian Congress held that year in Rome, where a special series of recordings was produced by *The Gramophone* company and sold in Britain. These were not merely commemorative; they provided exemplars for choirs to copy. In other words they were another means to promote a uniform performance style. Yet these very recordings show the differences that arise from performances by different choirs and choir directors. This is most evident with the plainchant items for the Mass in honour of Gregory the Great directed by Antonio Rella, Laurent Janssens and Mocquereau. In addition, no one seems to have appreciated how much the final product in any recording reflects the musical taste and judgement, as well as technical skills, of the recording engineer.[26]

In the ensuing months the Papal commission got to work. A visit was paid to Appuldurcombe, on the Isle of Wight, where the Solesmes community had temporarily settled, and there they saw Mocquereau's 'paleographic workshop' in action. In addition to H.G. Worth from Liverpool, who was a member of the commission, the visitors included Wilfrid Corney from Downside, Michael Maloney (d. 1905) from Westminster Cathedral, M.A. Booth – another Liverpudlian – and Augustus Gatard from Farnborough. The optimism of the time is reflected in the booklet *Plainchant and Solesmes*, written by Paul Cagin and Mocquereau and published by

---

23 [Felicitas Corrigan], *In a Great Tradition: Tribute to Dame Laurentia McLachlan* (London, 1956), p. 118.

24 Robert Hayburn, *Papal Legislation on Sacred Music 79AD to 1977AD* (Collegeville, MN, 1979), pp. 251–7. Combe, 'La restauration du Chant Grégorien': 148–54.

25 SAA, letter from Mocquereau to McLachlan dated 31 May 1907.

26 Bergeron, pp. 130–31 and 133 figures 26a and 26b. The recordings themselves have been reproduced on two LPs by Discant under the title *The Gregorian Congress of 1904. Plainchant and Speeches recorded in Rome by the Gramophone Company* (1982).

Burns and Oates.[27] However, the meetings soon exposed the differences between the Pothier and Mocquereau approaches. The focal points were the use of rhythmic signs and the balance between those who wanted to rely on the earliest possible sources and those who paid heed to the artistic validity of later traditions and the practical requirements of the early twentieth-century liturgy. Here *Col Nostro* was ambiguous, stating that 'Church melodies, called Gregorian, will be re-established in their integrity and in their purity, not only in conformity with ancient manuscripts, but also taking particular account of legitimate tradition, contained in manuscripts across the centuries, *and also of practical use in the liturgy*'. In this context it is significant that the italicised phrase had been interpolated by Pothier.[28]

The Papal response was articulated by Cardinal Merry Del Val, an ex-student from Ushaw, nephew of Zulueta, and Pius X's secretary. He ordained that the new edition should be based on the Solesmes Gradual of 1895; and he made Pothier responsible for correcting the melodies.[29] The Vatican *Kyriale*, *Graduale* and *Antiphonale* of 1905, 1908 and 1913 therefore reflected Pothier's approach. In particular they did not include rhythmic signs, and substantially ignored the most recent results produced by Mocquereau's Paleographic Workshop, as Bewerunge noted.[30]

Thus, on the surface, Mocquereau had been defeated, and his distress is reflected in his correspondence with McLachlan. For example, when the decision to rely on the 1895 Solesmes Gradual was announced he declared 'C'est la ruine matérielle et morale de Solesmes'. Similarly, in response to a report in *The Universe* that Merry Del Val, following Desclée's publication of Mocquereau's own *Kyriale*, had banned the use of the rhythmic signs deployed there, he wrote 'nous sommes sous la terreur Grégorienne'.[31] Yet here the Papacy was in a difficult position because Solesmes had not surrendered its copyright over the rhythmic signs. In January 1906 the Sacred Congregation of Rites therefore ruled that they could be 'tolerated', provided that they did not interfere with the notes as laid out in the Vatican edition.[32]

During the course of the controversy, as in the campaign against Pustet, Mocquereau did not hesitate to use *Paléographie Musicale* as a weapon in his support. This is particularly apparent in volumes 10 and 11, published in 1909–12 and 1912–21 respectively. In the former there are two chapters, complete with detailed rhythmic analyses, dealing with the Vatican edition's version of the Introit *In medio* and a *Credo*. Moreover, the photographic facsimiles of the accompanying medieval *Antiphonale Missarum* (Laon Codex 239) are deployed to support Mocquereau's

27 Although no publication date is given internal evidence in the text shows that it was produced in 1904.

28 Quoted in Combe, 'La Restauration du Chant Grégorien III L'Oevre de Saint Pie X', *EG*, 7 (1967): 165 and translated by myself from the French. See also Hayburn, pp. 260–63.

29 Bergeron, pp. 147–54.

30 Henry Bewerunge, 'The Vatican Edition of Plainchant' (Parts I and II), *IER* 19 (1906): 44–63, and 20: 414–28.

31 Mocquereau to McLachlan 26 June 1905 ('It is the material and moral ruin of Solesmes') and 24 January 1906 ('We are living in a Gregorian terror'), SAA.

32 Bergeron, p. 158. Mocquereau to McLachlan 14 October 1906, SAA.

case.[33] As will be seen, the same idea occurred to McLachlan in connection with the plan to publish a facsimile edition of the *Worcester Antiphoner* in the same series, and this was part of a strategy to outflank the Vatican edition by producing plainchant books, particularly a monastic antiphoner, based on hitherto unused manuscript sources.[34] In this context Mocquereau's English connections proved to be exceptionally important.

The competition between rival forms of plainchant in England

The publication of the Vatican editions produced a flurry of controversy in England, as the vigorous exchange of letters in *The Tablet* reveals. For example, Mocquereau was supported by Bewerunge, A. Eudine, 'a student from Downside' – probably Alphege Shebbeare – and Michael Malony, a canon of Westminster Cathedral and director of a well-known plainchant choir at Holy Trinity church, Dockhead. Opposed to him were the ex-prior of Ampleforth Thomas Anselm Burge (1846–1929), S.H. Sole and the anonymous reviewer of McLachlan's *Grammar of Plainsong*.[35] In practice at first the balance was fairly even between the two sides. Pothier's approach was adopted by F. Clement Egerton in his *A Handbook of Church Music*, with a preface by H.G. Worth.[36] Curiously, though, the ecclesiastical censor was Gatard of Farnborough, a supporter of Mocquereau. In their centrally produced editions of plainchant both the Cistercians and Dominicans did the same.[37] Terry at Westminster Cathedral also supported the Vatican edition, as his pupil Dom Gregory Murray admitted.[38] Here, things might have been different if the Solesmes community at Farnborough had taken up an invitation from Cardinal Vaughan to form the Cathedral chapter.[39] Moreover, Terry had connections with Burge, who under the pseudonym 'Laurence Ampleforth' contributed several tunes to the *Westminster Hymnal*, for which Terry was chief musical editor. Burge was so contentious that he was forbidden by his

---

33 'Les signes rythmiques sangalliens et solesmiens'; 'Edition Vaticane. L'Introit de la Messe "In Medio". Notes théoriques et pratiques'; 'Le Chant "authentique" du Credo selon l'edition Vaticane'; 'Aperçu sur la notation du manuscrit 239 de Laon. Sa concordance avec les "codices" rythmiques sangalliens', *PM,* 10: 41–66, 66–89, 90–176, 177–211. In vol. 11 see the preface, pp. 9–13.

34 See, for example, Mocquereau's confidential letter to McLachlan, 23 October 1909, SAA.

35 See especially the contents of vol. 73 (January–June 1905): 20–22, 57–8, 125–6, 176, 824 (Obituary of Michael Malony) and vol. 75 (January–June 1906): 21, 60, 92–3, 100, 139–41.

36 Clement F. Egerton, *A Handbook of Church Music* (London, 1909), esp. pp. 29–33.

37 See, for example, *Hymnarium Cisterciensis* (1909), *Laudes Vespertinae* (1926 and 1956), *Graduale Cisterciense* (1934 and 1960), *Antiphonarium Cisterciensis* (1947), all published from Westmallen, Belgium. For the Dominicans see *Graduale Juxta Ritum Sacri Ordinis Praedicatorum* (1928) and *Antiphonarium Sacri Ordinis Praedicatorum Pro Durnis Horis* (1933), all published from Rome.

38 Anthony Gregory Murray, 'Gregorian Rhythm: A Pilgrim's Progress', *DR*, 52 (1934): 15–17.

39 See, for example, the discussion of these proposals in letters by Cecilia Heywood (Abbess of Stanbrook) to Austin O'Neill. 9 March 1899, 22 October 1899, 22 July 1900, 23 November 1900 and 23 January 1901, Douai Abbey archives, File A. O'Neill.

abbot to make further contributions on the subject to the *Ampleforth Journal*.[40] Nevertheless, from his parish in Grassendale, he steered the Liverpool archdiocese firmly into the Pothier camp. As a result in 1905 the archbishop banned the use of Mocquereau's books and in 1908 he presented 50 copies of the Vatican Graduale to the diocesan seminary at Upholland College.[41]

Despite appearances, however, the balance began swinging Mocquereau's way. As early as 1905 W.H. Mitchell noted in the *Tablet* that 80 per cent of all chant book sales used the rhythmic signs.[42] Clearly Desclée's effective marketing policies, including the production of English rubrical editions, had something to do with this. The two most decisive factors, however, appear to have been the presence of the Solesmes community in England and the influence exerted by the Abbey of Stanbrook on the EBC and, through them, the wider English Catholic world. Solesmes's influence has already been noted with the visit of the Vatican Commission to Appuldurcombe. From there some of the leading figures, including De Santi, went on to visit Stanbrook. In August 1904 Maloney began the first of a series of summer schools at Appuldurcombe. In addition there was a constant succession of visitors to the community. The impact this could exert is well illustrated by a letter to 'Dear Buzzy Bee' from Gregory Ould (1865–1939), chaplain to the Canonesses of the Holy Sepulchre at New Hall in Essex and later at Stanbrook: 'I wish I could send you a gramophone record of these monks: they are splendid. They make you feel the rhythms – not jerkily or 'gaspingly', but smoothly as oil!'[43] Solesmes contacts with Farnborough were also important. In the long run, however, its most significant links were with Stanbrook Abbey.

Solesmes and Stanbrook Abbey

At Stanbrook the key figure was Laurentia McLachlan. A Scot, born in 1861, she came to the abbey as a schoolgirl in 1877. In 1883, in company with her schoolteacher Miss Anna Bossward and Laurence Shepherd, she visited Solesmes for the first time. The following year she joined the Stanbrook community and, once professed as a nun, she was appointed Precentress. Eventually, after holding various other offices, she was elected Abbess in 1931, a post she held till her death in 1953.[44]

McLachlan began as a supporter of Pothier. This is hardly surprising, given that in the mid-1880s the only Solesmes publications Stanbrook possessed were

---

40 This is described in McLachlan's letters to Bewerunge dated 11 November 1905 and 10 April 1906. SAA, W1219.

41 McLachlan to Bewerunge dated 5 January 1905 and 13 October 1905. Canon J.F. Turner to McLachlan dated 26 February 1930 and 12 March 1930. SAA, W1219 and Box marked 'D.L. McL to Allen/Holland, Edeson, and J.F. Turner'.

42 W.H. Mitchell, 'First fruits of the Gregorian Commission', *Tablet*, 74 (2 October 1905): 900.

43 Uncatalogued letter, dated 6 February 1909, found by myself inside one of several massive volumes of manuscript plainchant accompaniments prepared by Ould in the archives of the Canonesses of the Holy Sepulchre at Colchester.

44 [Corrigan], pp. 79–80, 83, 90–94, 98.

Les Mélodies Grégoriènnes and the 1883 Gradual.[45] The first signs of a shift in McLachlan's thinking appear in her *Gregorian Music: An Outline of Musical Paleography*, published in 1897. Here, the significant feature is not so much that she still subscribed to Pothier's idea that plainchant grew from and had to follow the pattern of the text; what is important is the title, with its echo of Mocquereau's *Paléographie Musicale*. The next step came the following year with her translation of his *Petit traité de psalmodie*. A revised version was then produced in 1904 and incorporated in her *Grammar of Plainsong*.[46]

The *Grammar of Plainsong* was produced at the request of archbishop Edward Ilsley for the Archdiocese of Birmingham, and it proved to be the most influential plainchant manual in the English-speaking world before the introduction of *Plainsong for Schools* in 1929. It was prepared in close collaboration with Mocquereau, who helped produce the French translation.[47] McLachlan reciprocated by helping with the English translation of his *Le Nombre Musical Grégorien*.[48] Not surprisingly, then, the *Grammar of Plainsong* adopted most of his ideas.[49]

The work was also closely vetted by Bewerunge, who visited Stanbrook every Christmas from 1902 onwards, and prepared the German translation.[50] The correspondence shows how McLachlan won him over to Mocquereau's way of thinking.[51] Bewerunge was an important ally. As has been seen, he was a useful protagonist in the press and had been president of the Irish Society of St Cecilia. Through his German contacts he arranged for the publication by Schwann of an edition of plainchant books with modified rhythmic signs, for which McLachlan provided an English translation of the rubrics. In addition he nearly succeeded in persuading the German Cecilians at their 1911 Innsbruck congress to support Mocquereau, in the teeth of opposition from Peter Wagner, another member of the Vatican Commission.[52] His correspondence with McLachlan also reveals the speed

---

45 Ibid., pp. 90–91 and 140.

46 [McLachlan], *Grammar of Plainsong* , pp. 46–58.

47 See, for example, Mocquereau's letters to McLachlan dated 16 July 1904, 29 July 1904, 5 August 1904, 5 January 1905, 5 June 1905. SAA.

48 Ibid. 8 October 1905. See also McLachlan's letters to Bewerunge dated 17 September 1922 and 3 December 1922. SAA, file W1219.

49 See especially the chapter on rhythm. [McLachlan], *Grammar of Plainsong* , pp. 46–58.

50 An Italian translation was also made by Giulio Bas and published by Capra of Turin. McLachlan to Bewerunge, 15 December 1906. SAA, W1219.

51 McLachlan to Bewerunge dated 5 October 1905, 10 December 1905, 11 November 1905, 13 December 1905, 24 March 1906 and 13 December 1906 for details of the translation. For general discussion of the *Grammar* and Mocquereau's ideas see 25 October 1904, 29 October 1904 and a long sequence of letters covering most of 1905 followed by further material in letters dated 19 February 1907, 15 October 1909 and 24 June 1911. SAA, W1219. For Bewerunge's visits to Stanbrook see Corrigan, 126.

52 McLachlan to Bewerunge, 23 June 1911. For the translation of the rubrics, Bewerunge to McLachlan, 6 November 1908, 2 December 1908, 8 January 1909, 15 January 1909, 19 January 1909, 22 January 1909, 23 January 1909, 1 February 1909, 5 February 1909, 7 February 1909, 12 February 1909, 20 February 1909, 27 February 1909, 28 February 1909, 5 March 1909, 8 March 1909, 18 March 1909, 28 March 1909, 3 April 1909, 8 April 1909, 23 April 1909, 2 May 1909, 10 May 1909, 14 June 1909, 29 June 1909, 13 August 1909 and 20

at which other religious replaced the Mechlin or Pustet books with Mocquereau's chant. For instance Ould, chaplain at Stanbrook from 1912, taught at Ampleforth, Fort Augustus (his own house) and the Sisters of Mercy in Glasgow. Aided by Dom Gatard of Farnborough he also persuaded the nuns at Teignmouth to abandon the Vatican editions.[53] Another important figure was Shebbeare, an Anglican former Cowley father who brought over the monks at Downside. As a joint collaborator with Walter H. Frere and John Stainer in *A Manual of Plainchant*, Shebbeare was a plainchant specialist in his own right.[54] In 1904, he produced the English Benedictine *Hymnale*, for which McLachlan contributed melodies from the Worcester Antiphoner and Bosworth Psalter. His principal source, however, was Frere's edition of *Plainsong Hymn Melodies and Sequences*, published by the Plainsong and Medieval Music Society in 1896.[55] Shebbeare therefore illustrates the crossover between Anglican and Catholic plainchant scholarship and performance. He was also behind the use of Sarum Chant at the three-day celebrations marking the opening of the chancel of Downside's abbey church in 1905. Yet, at the same time, late eighteenth-century plainchant compositions by Faboullier were still part of Downside's repertoire. Moreover, given that the basic dimensions of the building were laid down in the late 1870s, it is obvious that the acoustic with its long echo was designed to accommodate the heavier, slower moving measured Mechlin chant. The celebrations therefore mark a pivotal point in the switch at Downside from one tradition of plainchant to another; and it is significant that the keynote sermons preached by Francis Gasquet (President of the EBC), Cuthbert Hedley OSB (Bishop of Newport) and Ambrose Burton (Bishop of Clifton) emphasised the continuity with and restoration of past Medieval monastic glories in a manner that Guéranger would have approved. Hedley's sermon, in particular, is a straight summary of the basic philosophy underpinning *L'Année liturgique*.[56]

Such changes were not made without opposition. The London Oratory, for example, used Mechlin books till 1935; Douai Abbey did not abandon the Mechlin *Vesperal* till 1922; and there was considerable resistance at the Abbey of Belmont. During the 1906 EBC Triduum held at Stanbrook, Mechlin books were used by the monks on one side, and Solesmes volumes by the nuns on the other. McLachlan therefore had to change her organ accompaniments as required. However, by 1910

August 1909. The Innsbruck congress is described in his letters of 7 June 1911 and 2 August 1911. SAA, W1219.

53 McLachlan to Bewerunge, 11 May 1912 (describing his impact at Stanbrook), 8 May 1909 and 16 August 1909 (describing his work at Ampleforth and Fort Augustus) and 24 February 1907 (describing his activity in Glasgow). SAA, W1219. His role at Teignmouth is described in *A History of the Benedictine Nuns at Dunkirk now at St Scholastica's Abbey, Teignmouth, Devon edited by the community under the direction of Dom Adrian Hamilton OSB* (London, n.d. (1950s publication)), pp. 126–7.

54 London, 1902.

55 See, for example McLachlan to Bewerunge: 20 May 1905. SAA, W1219. Felicitas Corrigan to Abbot Byrne of Ampleforth dated 3 August 1959. SAA, 'Stanbrook Hymnale 1963'.

56 Thomas Muir, 'Vision and reality: Edward Hansom's work at Stonyhurst and Downside', *EBC History Symposium* (1996): 36–53. *Tablet*, 74 (July–December 1905): 485–95, 502–507. T. Leo Almond, 'The opening of the new Choir', *DR*, 24 (1905): 254–65.

Dunstan Sibley (1862–1938), helped by Ould, had brought Belmont over to Solesmes chant, albeit with the Vatican editions.[57]

As has been seen, McLachlan shared Shebbeare's interest in English Medieval plainchant, and this was further encouraged by visits from Anglican specialists and collectors, notably Sir Sydney Cockerell, Dyson Perrins (the inventor of Worcester Sauce) and Dr G.H. Palmer.[58] In 1909 and 1910 she discussed plans for a Hymnale with Mocquereau using English sources. Her *magnum opus*, however, was the publication, again with Mocquereau's assistance, of a facsimile edition of the Worcester Antiphoner in *Paléographie Musicale*.[59] Help was also given by Edmund Bishop. The project lasted from 1899 to 1925, and a key feature running through the negotiations was its potential as a weapon against the Vatican edition.[60] As already mentioned, such a source could be used to compile a monastic antiphoner according to Mocquereau's principles. The establishment of an Anglo-Saxon plainchant tradition going back to Rome was therefore important. So was the link with manuscripts from Corbie – because these were already being used by Solesmes. For instance, on 9 March 1913 McLachlan reported to Bewerunge that:

> Fr Gregory [Ould] tells me that the division of two vowels in laies and moyses is typically Roman. Wig. [The Worcester Antiphoner] is most careful in this respect and in the matter of liquescence – always, I think, by addition of a note. Fr G. [Gregory] likes to think that our MS [The Worcester Antiphoner] represents a tradition established at Wearmouth and Jarrow by John the Roman Cantor in the 8th century. Northern Mss may help to make this evident, but at any rate we get a very direct current from Rome if we trace our text to the 10th century revival in England. The chant at that time was got from Corbie in Picardy, the monastery to which Amalarius [of Metz] belonged and which gloried in possessing an Antiphoner straight from Rome.[61]

---

57 Henry Washington, 'The Oratory musical tradition', in Michael Napier and Alistair Laing (eds), *The London Oratory Centenary 1884–1984* (London, 1984), p. 153. McLachlan to Bewerunge: 5 November 1922 (for Douai), 20 July 1906 (for the EBC Triduum), 30 April 1905, 11 April 1905, 11 August 1905, 25 March 1910, 30 September 1910, and 20 May 1911. SAA, W1219.

58 [Corrigan], pp. 168–9. See also McLachlan to Bewerunge: 30 January 1906, 9 February 1907 and 24 February 1907. SAA, W1219.

59 'Antiphonaire Monastique XIIIeme Siècle Codex F.160 de la Bibliotheque de la Cathédrale de Worcester' *PM*, 12 (1922–25). Corrigan, p. 12. Mocquereau to McLachlan, esp. 20 January 1899, 9 March 1899, 16 March 1899, 28 June 1899, 8 July 1899. See also McLachlan's letters to Bewerunge, especially 20 May 1905, 29 May 1905, 26 January 1912, 14 June 1914 and 3 July 1914. SAA, W1219.

60 The idea first surfaces in embryo in McLachlan's letters to Bewerunge of 2 October 1905 and 5 October 1905 when comparisons are drawn between the Worcester Antiphoner and the Vatican *Kyriale*. SAA, W1219. It is possible that in 1899 the Worcester Antiphoner may have been seen as a useful weapon against the Pustet editions. However, since it was a thirteenth-century source it was less useful in this respect than ninth- and tenth-century Continental materials.

61 McLachlan to Bewerunge, 9 March 1913 and 28 February 1914. SAA, W1219.

Accordingly a plan was made in 1907 for Downside to produce a Kyriale based on
that in the Worcester Antiphoner, and which would then be followed by the production
of a Vesperale. Both plans proved abortive. Another scheme was the preparation
of an English Proper. In 1908 a commission, headed by Bewerunge, Mocquereau,
Worth, Corney and Terry was set up by Cardinal Bourne, Archbishop of Westminster.
However, this seems to have been blocked in 1913, although negotiations with
Pustet continued up till October 1914. The driving-force behind plans for a monastic
antiphoner appears to have been Cardinal Gasquet. It is significant that the facsimile
edition of the Worcester Antiphoner in *Paléographie Musicale* is dedicated to him.
McLachlan reported to Bewerunge that he had lobbied in Rome against Pothier in
1908; in 1912 he proposed a modified version of the Roman Breviary for approval
by the Sacred Congregation of Rites; and in August 1913 he presented a memorial
to the Pope recommending a new monastic antiphoner. Immediately afterwards he
visited the Solesmes community at Quarr Abbey on the Isle of Wight to put the idea
to them. Mocquereau was at first cautious. He pointed out that such a project needed
permission from the Sacred Congregation of Rites, and that an English plainchant
Hymnale would be easier to get past them. His real motive though seems to have
been that he was planning a monastic antiphoner of his own based on Hartker's St
Gall Manuscript Codex 390/391. Indeed, as early as 1901, he had shelved production
of the Worcester Antiphoner in *Paléographie Musicale* in favour of this source.
Nevertheless, in 1913 Mocquereau did collaborate with McLachlan by arranging
for the photography of several English manuscripts. However, in 1920, 1925 and
1931 three international Congresses of Benedictine Abbots approved Mocquereau's
scheme, which was eventually brought to a successful conclusion by his pupil Joseph
Gajard in 1934.[62]

The spread of Mocquereau's variety of plainchant in England before and after the First World War

The adoption of Mocquereau's style of plainchant by the EBC was of considerable
importance, because it was often through the Benedictines that it spread to the rest
of the English Catholic community. Here Stanbrook's role, though significant, was
somewhat restricted. The principal difficulty arose from the fact that it was an
enclosed community, so the nuns found it difficult to travel. For example, between

62 McLachlan to Bewerunge, 2 May 1905, 15 May 1907 and 13 August 1907 (for the
Downside Kyriale); 24 May 1907 (for the Downside Vesperal); 2 June 1908, 2 November
1913 and 14 October 1914 (for the English Proper); 10 May 1908, 11 July 1912, 5 August
1913, 20 August 1913, and 13 October 1913 (for Gasquet's activities). SAA, W1219. For
Mocquereau's views see his letter to McLachlan dated 23 October 1909. For his photography
of English manuscripts see letters dated 10 April 1910, 16 July 1910, 5 August 1913, 24
August 1913, 10 October 1913 and 23 October 1913. The manuscripts included a thirteenth-
century antiphoner at Hereford, identified by Ould, the Douce manuscript in the Bodleian
Library, Oxford; a Peterborough antiphoner and CCC339 and CCC391 at Cambridge. For
details of the production of the 1934 Monastic Antiphoner see *Antiphonale Monasticum Pro
Durnis Horis* (Tournai, Paris, Rome, 1934), pp. vi–viii.

1890 and 1913 McLachlan made only two outside visits: one to Princethorpe (in Warwickshire), the other to Milford Haven (in South Wales). In the 1920s such expeditions were a little more frequent. For example, in 1923 she visited the nunneries of East Bergholt (Sussex) and Oulton (Staffs). In any case, as has been seen, people could come to Stanbrook.[63] In addition to Mocquereau, Bewerunge, De Santi, Gasquet, Oswald Smith (Abbot of Ampleforth), Shebbeare and Sibley, visitors included Cardinal Bourne, Archbishop Ilsley (of Birmingham), Bishop Peter Amigo (of Southwark) and Bishop Cuthbert Hedley (of Menevia and Newport). It is clear, however, that monks had an advantage over nuns. They could travel more easily, as Ould's activities show. Dom Gregory Murray was also very active in this respect, so his conversion to Mocquereau's methods was especially important.[64] Moreover, despite the effects of the Downside movement, many monks still worked as parish priests. Anselm Burge's hostile activities at Grassendale, near Liverpool, show what could be done by just such a monk. Moreover, if this was the case for some Benedictines, it was even more applicable for members of a Mendicant Order such as the Dominicans. Their partial adhesion to Mocquereau's style then was important. It is revealed in two manuals: Fr James Harrison's *How to Sing Plainchant. Chiefly for the use of Dominican Choirs*, published in 1920; and Justin Field's *The Simplicity of Plainsong*, produced in 1931. Both cited the *Grammar of Plainsong*. Field's manual, although originally produced for Ontario, Canada, was used in England; and in his chapter on rhythm he follows Mocquereau closely.[65]

Work by laity also proved to be increasingly important. Vilma Little is an interesting example, because although she never became a nun she had close connections with many religious houses, especially those at Teignmouth and the Augustinian Nuns at Boarbank Hall, near Grange-over-Sands, in Cumbria, where she is buried. Her publications show this link too. For example, *Laudate Dominum: A Benediction Manual compiled chiefly from English Mss* has an introduction by McLachlan and used material supplied from Stanbrook and Farnborough.[66] The music is equipped with rhythmic signs and, as the title implies, Little followed McLachlan in her use of English sources, including those from Sarum, Worcester, York, Barking and Cambridge. More interesting perhaps is *The Chant: A simple and complete method for teachers and students by V.G.L.*[67] This employed a numerical system of notation, rather like the system of numbers used to denote pitches in Javanese Gamelan. Thus numbers 1–7 are equivalent to the notes in the C major scale, laid out according to

63 [Corrigan] , pp. 142–4. McLachlan to Bewerunge: 13 June 1913, 22 March 1923 and 23 April 1923. SAA, W1219.

64 See his article 'Gregorian Rhythm: A Pilgrim's Progress', *DR*, 52 (1934): 13–47.

65 James Harrison, *How to Sing Plainchant. Chiefly for the use of Dominican Choirs* (Ditchley, 1920). Justin Field, *The Simplicity of Plainsong* (New York, 1931), esp. pp. 29–32 (discussion of rhythm). The *Grammar of Plainsong* is cited by Field on p. ix; and by Harrison on pp. 86–7.

66 [Vilma Little (ed.)], *Laudate Dominum: A Benediction Manual compiled chiefly from English MSS*, (Liverpool, 1936 /1947R). Stanbrook sources are used for nos. 22, 23 and 47. Farnborough sources are used for nos. 3, 5 and 19.

67 [Vilma Little], *The Chant: A simple and complete method for teachers and students by V.G.L.* (London and Tournai, 1938).

the Sol-Fa system, with dots above or below the digits denoting higher or lower octaves. For example, number 1 with a dot over it denotes 'c' (or 'DO') one octave above middle C.

Little also recognised that 'to the great mass of the faithful plainsong was, and to a great extent still is, a sealed book'.[68] This was where the Society of St Gregory (or SSG) came in. The SSG was founded by Fr Bernard McElligott (1890–1971), a former choirmaster at Ampleforth. The publication of *Divini Cultus*, with its call for greater congregational participation in plainchant, prompted him to write a letter to *The Universe* on 2 November 1928, calling for action. By September 1929 the SSG had 343 members and 30 parish affiliates, and later its presidents included Cardinal Hinsley and Cardinal Griffin, successive archbishops of Westminster.[69] Its 'Four Aims', set out in its journal *Music and Liturgy*, were:

[1] To maintain the dignity of the Sacred Liturgy as the supreme instrument of congregational worship.
[2] To carry out the wishes of the Church with regard to church music: that is, to put into practice the instructions given by Pope Pius X in his 'Motu Proprio' of Nov 23rd, 1903 as Church Music [*TLS*], and confirmed by Pope Pius XI in his 'Apostolic Constitution' of Dec 28th, 1928 [*Divini Cultus*] on the same subject.
[3] To provide each year a course of instruction in Plainsong and Polyphony for Catholic choirmasters, teachers and others practically interested.
[4] To attempt, by mutual help, to find a solution for the practical problems of members.[70]

In essence, then, the SSG was a recrudescence of Cecilian ideals and methods. Its work can be divided into the following related areas. Annual summer schools held in Oxford, the first at Blackfriars, the others at Worcester College. Then there were the large plainchant festivals and competitions, a typical example being 'The Pope's Mass for World Peace' held at Westminster Cathedral on 13 April 1936. Here a choir of 100 priests, other ecclesiastics and laity rendered the Mass Proper, while the congregation sang the Mass Ordinary, including an unaccompanied rendition of the Creed, and the Mass Responses.[71] More lasting perhaps was the publication in two parts of *Plainsong for Schools*, in 1930 and 1934 respectively.[72] This was prepared by Dominic Willson, another Ampleforth monk, with a preface by McLachlan and equipped with rhythmic signs. McLachlan's and the SSG's involvement is revealed in a sequence of letters to her surviving at Stanbrook.[73] In the first instance it was

68 [Vilma Little (ed.)], *Cantate Domino: A collection of supplementary hymns* (Liverpool, 1932/1941R), Forward. n.p.

69 Alberic Stacpoole, 'Fr Bernard McElligott. I: The Ampleforth Years 1890–1927. II: The Liturgical Years'. *AJ*, 77/2 (1972) 102–109; 77/3: 86–97. A full list of members is supplied in *ML*, 1/1 (October 1929): 39–42. The reference to *The Universe* letter comes on page 88.

70 'The Four Aims', *ML*, 1/1(October 1929): 1.

71 Stacpoole, 'The Liturgical Years', p. 92.

72 [Dominic Willson (ed.)], *Plainsong for Schools* (2 parts, Liverpool, 1930 and 1934).

73 For the planning see especially Willson's letters of 31 March 1930, 9 April 1930, 15 May 1930 and 12 July 1930. SAA, Box 'D.L. McL. To Allen/Holland/Edeson and J.F. Turner.'

intended for use in the archdiocese of Liverpool, where from 1931 Willson was director of its school of music.[74] However, its use soon spread across the whole country. As the title implies the books were aimed at schools. In turn this required the training of plainchant teachers. As the Liverpool Archdiocesan Commission stated: 'No one should be allowed to teach plainsong to children who has not been properly grounded in the art. In [the] course of time it is to be hoped that many will qualify by taking the various examinations arranged by the Society of St Gregory in conjunction with the Benedictine Dames of Stanbrook Abbey'.[75] The link between *Plainsong for Schools*, examinations set by Stanbrook and the Society of St Gregory is therefore clear. So is the prescriptive character of the campaign, which is strongly reminiscent of earlier activities by the Society of St Cecilia. It is no accident then to find that Herbert P. Allen, Casartelli's former ally, was active in both in the North West. Preparation for such examinations took place at local training sessions and inspections as well as at the SSG's summer schools.[76] The programme for 11–18 August 1930 at the latter is given below:

> Advanced (taught by J.H.Desrocquettes): Rhythm, modality, psalmody, palaeography, analysis, chironomy, transcription, liturgical practice.
> Elementary and Intermediate (taught by J.F. Turner and H.P. Allen): Notation, modality, general principles of execution, palaeography, transcription, liturgical practice, rhythm.[77]

Plainsong for Schools was supported by two volumes of accompaniments prepared by Herbert P. Allen.[78] Contrary to what many suppose, such accompaniments were not simply an extra frill supplied to support singers too incompetent to manage plainchant in its 'pure' unaccompanied form. Its very character shaped – and reflected – the method of performance. It could therefore be used as a weapon in support of particular styles. As shown earlier, in the nineteenth century, such accompaniments were often diatonic and organised on a note-for-note basis. This reinforced the slow, massive martellato performances so often preferred at that time. Solesmes-style chant, whether that of Pothier or Mocquereau, required a completely different approach. The accompaniment had to be modal, it had to be understated, and it had to be suggestive of the required smoothly undulating melodic line. The number of chords was therefore reduced. In turn this meant that there was no longer a note-for-note accompaniment and that therefore several elements in the melody had to

---

74 Before that Willson worked at St Anne's church, Edgehill.

75 Quoted by Willson in a letter, dated 14 July 1930, to McLachlan. SAA, Box 'D.L. McL. to Allen/Holland, Edeson and J.F. Turner'.

76 Sample copies of *Examination Questions Grades I and II* published by Stanbrook Abbey in 1935 can still be found in SAA. Their detailed planning and execution is discussed in letters by Canon J.F. Turner to McLachlan, 3 April 1930, 15 August 1930, 2 May 1930, 1 June 1930, 30 November 1930, 11 January 1931 and 31 March 1931. SAA, Box 'D.L. McL. to Allen/Holland, Edeson and J.F.Turner.

77 The programme is enclosed in Willson's letter to McLachlan of 30 November 1930. SAA, Box 'D.L. McL. to Allen/Holland, Edeson and J.F. Turner'.

78 Herbert P. Allen, *Accompaniments to "Plainsong for Schools"* (2 Parts, Liverpool, 1930 and 1934).

be treated as passing notes. These features are illustrated in Example 10.4 which is taken from a pre-1914 anonymous manuscript organ book at Stanbrook Abbey. Note the assumption that the organist has access to a pedal board.

Example 10.4   Anonymous accompaniment for the *Commune Confessoris Pontificis In Simplicibus*: 1[79]

There are though several features in accompaniments of this sort that undermine the atmosphere of Medieval authenticity that plainchant was supposed to generate. It bears little resemblance to genuine Medieval methods of accompaniment or polyphony. For instance, there are no drones, and determined efforts are made to avoid the parallel fifths and octaves characteristic of Medieval organum. Thus the presence of two examples here (highlighted by asterisks), along with the prevalence of chords in root position, are indications of lack of skill on the part of the arranger. Instead the basic principles of conventional Classical harmonisation are resorted to. Chords always have thirds and contrary (as opposed to medieval parallel) motion in the part writing is preferred.

Plainchant accompaniments ruthlessly exposed the differences over rhythm between Pothier and Mocquereau. This was because the positioning of the chords under certain notes showed where the accent should be. Other parts of the melody, treated as passing notes, were therefore subordinate to them. Mocquereau's adherents therefore sought to place the chords according to his arsis-thesis principles.[80] Compare,

---

79 The volume from which this is taken (p. 40) is kept in the organ loft at Stanbrook Abbey.

80 For discussion of the issue see McLachlan to Austin O'Neill of 4 September 1907. Douai Abbey archives, File 'A. O'Neill1'. See also Henri Potiron, 'The aesthetics of Gregorian accompaniment' *ML*, 1/4 (July 1930): 97–100 (The article originally appeared in *Revue Pratique de Liturgie et de Musique* (March–April 1928).

for example, the following extracts from Terry's and Allen's accompaniments for the Gloria in the *Missa 'Cum Jubilo'* (Examples 10.5a and 10.5b). Notice how Allen, unlike Terry, starts 'Laudamus te' and 'Benedicimus te' on the off-beat, and how he inserts an extra chord (of E minor) on the 'ho' syllable of 'hominibus' in the second bar.

Differences of this sort explain the considerable amount of energy expended by McLachlan and Bewerunge at Stanbrook on the subject. As early as 1909 McLachlan was dissatisfied with the accompaniments for the Vatican Edition prepared by F.X. Mathias, and by 1913 they understood that with an accompaniment arranged according to arsis-thesis principles a choir, even if it was equipped with Vatican chant books inspired by Pothier, could be made to sing in Mocquereau's way.[81]

At the same time, though, accompaniments revealed differences between individual interpretations about what the arsis-thesis rhythm actually was. McLachlan, for instance, was particularly scathing about Gregory Ould's approach, declaring on one occasion that 'I don't think he will ever see beyond his rule of thumb on rhythm, any more than Dom Mocquereau will'.[82] The samples from accompaniments to the hymn *Pange Lingua* (Example 10.6) illustrate the sort of differences that can occur.

Despite this, by 1939, thanks to the efforts of the SSG and his adherents Mocquereau's approach to plainchant had made considerable impact in England. It is difficult though to be precise about this, as nothing less than a comprehensive survey of every ecclesiastical establishment and priest ordained before 1962 would be required to give the necessary statistical proof. Nevertheless, the following pointers are highly suggestive. First, as has been seen, the *Grammar of Plainsong* had been commissioned by the archdiocese of Birmingham and had already run through three editions by the late 1930s. Second, because *Plainsong for Schools* was originally intended for use in the Liverpool archdiocese, it almost certainly swung that whole region onto Mocquereau's side. Likewise, Raymond Dixon, choirmaster at Lancaster Cathedral, switched from the Vatican editions in the late 1920s, pushing that diocese, created from Liverpool in 1925, into the Mocquereau camp. For instance, its official list of approved music recommended Gatard's *Manual of Plainchant*. At Stonyhurst the *Cantionale* produced by Driscoll in 1936 included a supplementary 'Kyriale' printed by Desclée equipped with rhythmical signs. Given Driscoll's similar work at Wimbledon, Beaumont and the seminary at Manresa this suggests that the English Jesuits fell into line too. Meanwhile, in the North East, from the 1920s students at

81 F.X. Mathias, *Organum Comitans ad Kyriale seu Ordinarium Missae* (Ratisbon, Rome, New York, Cincinnati, 1910). McLachlan to Bewerunge, 2 March 1913; 1 November 1909 (for her dissatisfaction with Matthias); 27 October 1904, 1 November 1905, 15 September 1905, 18 September 1905 and 25 November 1914 (discussion of Guilo Bas's accompaniments); 18 December 1905, 19 January 1906, 29 January 1906, 15 February 1906, 26 February 1906, 9 March 1906, 26 March 1906, 6 April 1911, 14 October 1911, 15 November 1905, 9 March 1912, 28 May 1912, and 25 November 1914 (requests for Bewerunge's accompaniments). For Bewerunge's replies see 14 December 1905, 9 July 1906, 19 October 1906, 5 March 1907, 14 October 1907, 26 October 1907, 11 November 1907, 28 January 1908, 21 February 1908, 20 May 1909, 20 December 1909, 4 December 1910, 17 February 1911, 3 March 1911, 4 April 1911, 19 October 1911, 18 May 1912, 2 September 1912, 17 March 1913, 18 March 1913, 12 April 1913, 18 April 1913, 11 January 1917 and 3 December 1917. SAA, W1219 and W1914.

82 Letter from McLachlan to Bewerunge, 8 October 1912. SAA, W1219.

Example 10.5a Extract from Terry's accompaniment to the 'Gloria' from the *Missa 'Cum Jubilo'* (London, 1933), p. 2

Example 10.5b Extract from H.P. Allen's accompaniment to the *Missa 'Cum Jubilo'*. Taken from *Plainsong for Schools Part 1*: 67

Example 10.6a H.J. Biton's accompaniment for *Pange Lingua* (1914):[83]

Example 10.6b H.P. Allen's accompaniment to *Tantum Ergo*, using the same melody as
           for *Pange Lingua*. Taken from *Plainchant for Schools. Part 1* (1930): 50

Ushaw used *Liber Usualis* equipped with the same signs. The position was further
reinforced by two sets of recordings; one by the monks of Solesmes, directed by
Joseph Gajard (c.1930); the other by the monks of Ampleforth, directed by Bernard
McElligott (1928).[84]

Against this, however, it should be noted that Terry's realisation of plainchant,
which followed the Vatican edition, remained in use through his publications of
Holy Week music, and these were on the official list of music recommended by the
diocese of Lancaster.[85] Terry's realisations also appear in *The Benediction Choir
Book*.[86] Likewise, as has been seen, Cistercians and Dominicans, despite the work
by Field and Harrison, continued to use Vatican style editions of their own. Stray
elements of Medicean style chant also crop up here and there. For example, Hall's
Evening Service for Sundays and Festivals is on Lancaster's diocesan list of music,
and the revised 1931 edition of Tozer's *Complete Benediction Manual* includes other
examples.[87]

83 A.J. Biton, *Vade Mecum Paroissial* (Paris, Rome, Tournai, 1914), p. 109.

84 *Gregorian Chant: The Choir of the Monks of Saint Pierre de Solesmes*, Dom Joseph
Gajard OSB (dir. and author of the accompanying critical introduction. HMV Album Series
120. DM 71-82 c.1930. For McElligott's recording see HMV C2087/8. Mary Berry, 'The
restoration of the chant and seventy-five years of recording', *EM*, 7 (1979): 197–217.

85 Richard Terry (ed.), *Music for the Morning Office on Palm Sunday, Music for the
Morning Office on Good Friday* (London, 1909).

86 Richard Terry (ed.), *The Benediction Choir Book* (London, 1937).

87 Albert E. Tozer (ed.), revised by Robert Hasberry, *New and Complete Benediction
Manual* (London, 1898/1931R), *Tantum Ergo* setting no. 41 and *Adoremus* setting no. 12.

Thus, despite the strong drive towards uniformity, a good deal of variety survived in early twentieth-century plainchant performance practice, and this is especially noticeable when accompaniments are examined. Bewerunge is an extreme instance. His use of very few chords drove him to conceive of the melodic line as a sequence of note clusters, each forming what was really a broken chord (see Example 10.7[88]). He was, in effect, anticipating the concept of 'Coupure' developed by Cardine in the 1950s. It was also very much an open question whether congregations could be persuaded to sing plainchant *en masse*. This was not simply because of the conflicting – and often arcane – messages sent out to the English Catholics by plainchant specialists. Its notation was obscure and complex, and its pseudo-Medieval and predominantly *monastic* style alien to contemporary musical culture. Above all, in practice plainchant often proved too difficult for congregations to learn. This point was clearly recognised by Dom Gregory Murray, after two decades of proselytising the plainchant cause, in the preface to his *First People's Mass*, published in 1950.

> In parish churches it would seem desirable for the congregation to take an active part in the singing of the Mass. Hitherto efforts to encourage the practice have largely failed because it has been assumed that plainsong Masses of the Kyriale were within the capacity of unskilled singers. The simple fact is that these plainsong Masses were never intended for congregational use; they were composed for highly trained choirs and their worthy performance demands long hours of practice and a vocal technique far beyond the powers of an ordinary congregation. If our people are to sing at Mass, they must be provided with music which they can readily grasp, learn by heart and sing with ease: music which presents no greater difficulty than an ordinary hymn tune. *A People's Mass* is an attempt to supply this need.[89]

The challenge to Solesmes and all it stood for is unmistakable. Murray, in effect, declared that attempts to promote congregational singing in England had failed because the wrong sort of music was being used. Four-part hymnody, not plainchant, was the answer; and by saying this Murray condemned the Ultramontane use of plainchant to create a closed musical-liturgical culture separated from contemporary secular reality. He reasserted the importance of reaching out to, and connecting with, contemporary lay concerns and values.

---

88 Extract from the 'Gloria Dei' of the Mass '*In Dominicis*' taken from a letter by Bewerunge to McLachlan 11 January 1917. SAA, W1914. This is the only surviving sample of the dozens of accompaniments he prepared for the nuns.

89 Anthony Gregory Murray, *First People's Mass* (London, 1950).

Example 10.7   Bewerunge's approach to plainchant accompaniment

Laurentia McLachlan's proposed amendments.

Chapter 11

Renaissance Polyphony with an English Inflexion: The Work of Sir Richard Terry

Terry's early career at Downside and Westminster

As has already been noted *TLS* placed Renaissance polyphony second only in importance to plainchant in the canon of church music. So, given that *TLS* was in many ways the culmination of some 30 years' lobbying by Cecilians, it is no surprise to find that there was a considerable spurt of interest in the revival of the genre. In England the leading figure associated with the movement was Sir Richard Terry (1866–1938). Terry, of course, did not create the Renaissance polyphonic revival. He built on work already undertaken by British Cecilians and their predecessors, such as John Moore Capes and James Burns. Even in his own day others, for example Edwin Bonney at Ushaw or William Sewell and Henry B. Collins at the Birmingham Oratory, promoted such music alongside him. However, his position at Westminster gave him a much higher profile, and this helped him give the movement a distinctively English Catholic twist.

Born at Ellington, Northumberland, he was educated and later served as an assistant master at Battersea Grammar School, where his uncle was headmaster. In 1886 he won an organ scholarship to Oxford, and in 1887 he obtained a choral scholarship at King's College, Cambridge, where he was taught by Charles Stanford. At this stage he was a High Church Anglican. In 1890 he became organist and choirmaster at Elstow School, Bedford, after which between 1892 and 1894 he worked at St John's Cathedral, Antigua. He then returned to work at Thanet College, Margate and St John's College, Leatherhead. However, in 1895 he was converted to Catholicism by Fr Bowden of the London Oratory and obtained a temporary post at St Dominic's Church, Newcastle. His first breakthrough was his appointment as an assistant music master by Abbot Ford at Downside.[1]

As first abbot of Downside, Ford was a key figure in the 'Downside Movement' that did so much to prepare the way for developments in plainchant. He was also something of a musician himself, since later he chaired the musical committee for the preparation of the *Westminster Hymnal*. Moreover, Downside's monastic library has copies of Proske's *Musica Divina*, and this may well have triggered Terry's interest in Renaissance polyphony. In 1897 Terry directed a performance of Palestrina's *Missa 'Aeterni Christi Munera'*. The following year, at Holy Week, Terry produced

---

1 Hilda Andrews, *Westminster Retrospect: A memoir of Sir Richard Terry* (London, 1948), pp. 1–19.

works by Arcadelt, Tye and Victoria.[2] Such performances were quickly followed up by his publication of the *Downside Masses* and *Downside Motets* series of music. Initially they were privately produced as dyeline copies by the Abbey, but from 1905 they were printed by Cary and Co. It is important to note though that at this stage Terry was not averse to modern styles of music, as his *Mass of St Gregory (No. 1)* (1896), dedicated to Ford, and his *Mass of St Dominic (No. 2)* show.

The *Downside Masses* consisted of the following works: Casciolini: *Mass for Four Voices*, Hasler: *Mass 'Dixit Maria'*, Heredia: *Mass for Four Voices*, Lassus: *Mass 'Quinti Toni'*, Lotti: *Simple Mass for Four Voices*, and Viadana: *Mass 'L'Hora Passa'*. All are works by Continental composers, three of whom are 'Roman'. In this respect Terry followed well-worn Cecilian policy, yet the presence of Casciolini and Lotti among them shows that, even at this late date, Renaissance polyphony could still be interpreted to include some mid-seventeenth- and eighteenth-century compositions. After all, such composers continued to use the *stila antiqua*. Their practical purpose is also manifest, as shown by some of their titles and the fact that they are all for four voices. The *Downside Motets* break new ground, however, by offering a mixture of English and Continental works. For example, volume 4 contains Byrd: *Civitas Sancti Tui*, Carissimi: *Ave Verum*, Palestrina: *Salvator Mundi*, Tallis: *Bone Pastor* and *Veni Creator Spiritus*, Tye: *Si Ambulem in Medio*. Terry was not the first to do this. For example, in 1890 Novellos published W.S. Rockstro and William Barclay Squire's edition of Byrd's *Missa Quatuor Voci*. Terry himself collaborated with Barclay Squire in an edition of Byrd's *Missa Quinque Voces*, published by Breitkopf and Härtel, and in 1898 Charles Gatty included Byrd's Three Part Mass in *Arundel Hymns*. However, Terry's underlying purpose was distinctive – namely to reclaim a forgotten English Catholic heritage. In the preface to volume 5 he states:

> Many such compositions have been adapted (since the havoc caused by the Reformation) to English words for the use of the Established Church till all memory of their Catholic origin has gradually died out. It will be the object of this publication to give in each issue some one or more acknowledged masterpieces, but with the original Latin text restored. Each issue will also contain some hitherto unpublished piece or pieces by English composers. The English school will thus occupy the foremost place in the collection but the great polyphonic schools of Italy, Spain and the Netherlands will be drawn upon to no small extent.

Second, Terry argued that such English composers belonged to an international Catholic scene. It was possible, then, to be both English and Roman. The theme is fully developed in his book *English Catholic Music*, published in 1907.[3] Here he presents the idea that Renaissance polyphony began with John Dunstable, an English composer, and was then transmitted to Rome via Flemish composers. Palestrina's musical style therefore had English roots, and there is an unmistakable parallel with similar ideas about how Gregorian plainchant was transmitted to Anglo-Saxon England by St Augustine and then back again to Rome via Alcuin and other scholars of the Carolingian Renaissance. Terry could thus claim that England would have

---

2 Ibid., pp. 36 and 39.
3 Richard Terry, *Catholic Church Music* (London, 1907), pp. 59, 178–9, 183 and 192.

remained a great musical nation were it not for the Reformation, which cut it off from international Catholic culture. This in itself is a musical application of Gasquet's claims about the deleterious cultural effects of the dissolution of the monasteries; something Terry might have picked up at Downside where Gasquet had been prior.[4] Terry then sought to show that the great English Renaissance polyphonists were Catholics, citing Blytheman, Byrd, Redford, Phillips, Tallis and Whyte. Tye, he admits, was a Protestant, but Terry blunted the implications of this by praising Tye's pre-Reformation settings of Latin texts. As for Orlando Gibbons, Terry comes close to arguing that he was a Catholic in all but name. For instance he states that 'with "Hosanna" I have no hesitation in describing it as an adaptation of the Palm Sunday antiphon *Hosanna Filio David*'.[5] Terry concludes his book by stating that the Catholic music performed in Anglican Cathedrals was 'written by Catholics for the services of the Catholic Church. It is our heritage – our birthright; and the fact that our claims have lain so long in abeyance does not make it any the less ours, or its revival any the less a duty which we owe to the memory of our Catholic forefathers. Its possession is one more link with our national past – that glorious past when this England of ours was undivided in her loyalty to the See of Peter.'[6]

Terry's work at Downside helped secure him the post of Master of Music at Westminster Cathedral in 1901. At that time the building was still under construction, and the consecration did not take place till 1910. Services were initially conducted in the Cathedral hall from June 1902. Terry owed his appointment in part to the impression made by Downside's choir at the opening of Ealing Abbey on 25 November 1899 in the presence of Cardinal Vaughan;[7] but he also benefited from a chapter of accidents. Vaughan had planned for a monastic chapter staffed by monks from Downside residing at Ealing. When this scheme fell through he turned to the Benedictines at Farnborough and the exiled Solesmes community at Appuldurcombe. Only after these plans had also failed did he fall back on a community of secular canons supported by a non-monastic choir, giving Terry his opportunity.

Terry began with a virtual *tabula rasa*. Moreover, he benefited from the fact that he could work with 28 choirboys trained in a choir school supported by 16 salaried singing men, although the latter were cut to 14 in 1901 and 6 in 1912. The result was a very different repertoire from that offered by other English Catholic establishments, dependent as they often were on amateur resources. An almost exclusive diet of plainchant and Renaissance polyphony was offered. Theoretically, this was similar to that projected 50 years before by Hardman and Lambert at St Chad's, Birmingham, but the scale was altogether different. For instance, as regards works by Palestrina, Edward Hutton estimated that during Terry's tenure in office (1901–1923) 27 Masses, 60 motets, 27 offertories, 35 Magnificats and the *Improperia* were performed.

---

4   Aidan Gasquet, *Henry VIII and the English Monasteries: An attempt to illustrate the history of their suppression* (2 vols, London, 1889), pp. 519–21. Terry, *Catholic Church Music*, p. 192.

5   Ibid., p. 196. He then performs the same trick with Tye's *I Will Exalt* and Redford's *Rejoice in the Lord*.

6   Terry, *Catholic Church Music*, p. 192.

7   Andrews, p. 50. See also pp. xii and 41.

Indeed, ten Masses were already in the repertory by 1910, emphasising the fact that Palestrina formed the bedrock of Westminster's repertoire in the 1900s.[8] His output was supplemented by a systematic programme of performances of works by other composers. For example, in 1907 the entire *Cantiones Sacrae* by Peter Phillips was performed; in 1909 the contents of Jakob Handl's *Opus Musicon* Book 4 were sung; and 1911 was dominated by Spanish Renaissance composers, with Terry drawing on recent editions by Pedrell. As a result, under Terry's successors Victoria's *Tenebrae* settings became a standard feature of Holy Week celebrations at Westminster up to the mid-1950s. However, on this liturgical occasion Terry also frequently turned to other composers. For instance, in 1918, following studies of the Eton Choir Book and Old Hall Manuscript, discovered in 1898, Holy Week was dominated by the works of Nicholas Ludford and Robert Fayrfax. Likewise, during Holy Week in 1921, eight Masses by John Taverner were performed.[9] Westminster Cathedral thus became a showcase for Renaissance polyphony. 'Palestrina for Tuppence' was Stanford's cry to his students at the Royal College of Music. By this he meant that, for the price of a bus fare, they could go down to Westminster Cathedral and hear the latest rediscoveries of the Renaissance repertory. Westminster's status, moreover, was boosted by the publication of regular press reports and programmes in the *Daily Telegraph* from 1907, as well as sometimes in *The Tablet* and the *Westminster Cathedral Chronicle*.[10]

Like other Cecilians, Terry did not hesitate to place his own compositions alongside a genuine plainchant and Renaissance polyphonic repertory. Table 11.1 shows the resulting combination in his booklet *Music for Palm Sunday*, originally prepared for Westminster and later published by Cary and Co. in 1909. Similar collections were prepared for Maundy Thursday and Holy Saturday. The practical concessions to the limited capacities of the average parish choir should be noted.

The bedrock of Terry's compositional output was his Masses, which were widely circulated and frequently reprinted. These show how, beginning with a fairly modern musical language, Terry came to be influenced by plainchant and Renaissance polyphony. In this respect, his approach is similar to other Catholic composers, such as Sewell and Zulueta. Surprisingly, the *Mass of St Gregory*, his first Mass, has no traces of plainchant, despite the dedication to Abbot Ford of Downside.[11] It is, for its day, a modern composition, characterised by wide dynamic ranges (*p* to *ff*), diatonic language and, in places, the deployment of sophisticated harmonic techniques (Example 11.1). The grandiloquent strokes in the organ part for the 'Gloria' should also be noted. On the other hand, as a concession to Cecilian tastes, in its revised

---

8   Edward Hutton: Obituary Letter to the *Tablet*, 171 (January–June 1938): 579. Andrews, p. 84.

9   Ibid., pp. 84, 89, 104,107, 118, 124–5, 127 and 129. See also Robertson, *Music of the Catholic Church* (London, 1961), pp. 72, 115–16.

10   Andrews, pp. 75 and 133. Full details of the Holy Week programme began to be published by the *Westminster Cathedral Chronicle* in 1913.

11   Richard Terry, *Mass of St Gregory No. 1 (Revised Edition)* (London, n.d). The date 1896 at the end of the 'Agnus Dei' almost certainly refers to the time of its composition, rather than its publication.

Table 11.1   The contents of Richard Terry (ed.), *Music for Palm Sunday*

Anon:	'Hosanna Filio David' (SATB)
Anon:	'Collegereunt Pontifices' (text for the Gradual) (SATB)
Anon:	'In Monte Oliveti' (SATB)
Responses:	Vatican Plainchant: 'Pueri Hebraeorum' (solo voice)
	'Portuguese': 'Pueri Hebraeorum' (solo voice)
	Palestrina: 'Pueri Hebraeorum' (SATB and segue organ)
Antiphons (for the Palm Sunday procession):	'Old Hymn Melody': 'Cum Appropinquaret' (SATB)
	Harmonised plainchant, Mode VIII: 'Cum Audisset Populus' (SATB)
	Terry: 'Occurrent Turbae' (SATB)
	Terry: 'Cum Angelis' (SATB)
	Vatican plainchant: 'Gloria, Laus et Honor' (Unison voices)
	'Old Welsh Air' arr. Terry: 'Ingrediente Domino' (SSATB)
	Viadana: 'Ingrediente Domino' (SATB)

form all the movements except the 'Gloria' could be sung unaccompanied. A practical feature is the fact that the treble part does not rise above a g″.

The first signs of change appear in the *Mass of St Dominic*, composed in 1899 and dedicated to St Dominic's Church, Newcastle.[12] 'Modern' features still predominate, with dynamics ranging from *pp* to *ff*, the use of diatonic harmony – often in a sophisticated manner (see Example 11.2) – and the requirement for a full organ equipped with pedal board and preferably several manuals, as pencil annotations on the organist's copy from St Dominic's Church in my possession illustrate.[13] Elsewhere, however, the vocal writing is restrained, such as at the start of the 'Kyrie' (Example 11.3), and boys' rather than women's voices are assumed. The most striking feature is the adoption of a chant-like approach to the 'Credo', producing something very different from the florid grandiloquence of such a movement in a mass by Gounod or J.E. Turner (see Example 11.4). From a technical standpoint this shows Terry's attempt to reach a compromise between Pothier's plainchant principle of following the rhythm of the text and the use in music of a regular metrical beat. In the preface singers are instructed to regard the breves as reciting notes without a uniform time value, and up to the syllable in capitals they are to be sung 'at the same pace as good reading'. Thereafter the basic pulse was ♩ = 88, and the time value to the next bar would be worth two beats. If there is a single succeeding syllable then the rhythm would be a dotted minim plus a crotchet; if there are two succeeding syllables the rhythm would be a minim plus two crotchets; and if there are three succeeding syllables then a dotted crotchet, quaver and two crotchets would be used.

The real change, however, occurs with the next work, Terry's *A Short and Easy Mass (No. 3) on the theme 'Veni Sancte Spiritus'*, composed at Westminster and

---

12 Richard Terry, *Mass of St Dominic* (London, 1899), dedicated 'To the Very Rev. Edmund Buckler OP (Prior) and the Choir of St Dominic's Newcastle-on-Tyne'.

13 For example, on the first page there are pencilled references to 'Great' and 'Swell'.

Example 11.1   Opening of the 'Kyrie' from Terry's *Mass of St Gregory*

Example 11.2   Terry's progression from a second-inversion G major chord to
                C major in the 'Kyrie' of his *Mass of St Dominic* (an example of
                'modern' diatonic harmony – note the chromatic touch)

published in 1904.[14] First, the title betrays a plainchant basis, something not seen in
his previous Masses. Thus Example 11.5 shows that the opening of the 'Kyrie' is a
straight metrical version of the start of the plainchant hymn, while Examples 11.6
and 11.7 show the relationship between other parts of the melody and elements in the
'Sanctus' I and II as well as in the 'Agnus Dei'.

---

14 Richard Terry, *A Short and Easy Mass (No. 3) on the theme 'Veni Sancte Spiritus' for
four voices with or without organ'* (London, 1904).

Example 11.3   Opening of the 'Kyrie' in Terry's *Mass of St Dominic*

Example 11.4   Opening of the 'Credo' in Terry's *Mass of St Dominic*

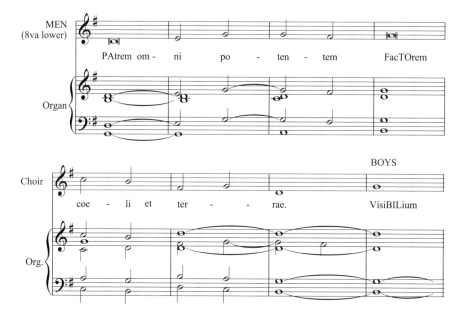

Second, as in the *Mass of St Dominic* and in his Holy Week Music, Terry uses what he now called 'harmonised inflexions' in the 'Credo' and 'Gloria'.[15] The pulse is set at ♩ = 96, which is somewhat faster than in the *Mass of St Dominic*, and therefore betrays the growing influence of the more rapid method of chanting recommended

---

15 The latter is directly referred to in the Preface, suggesting that Terry prepared his Holy Week music collection sometime between 1901 and 1904, some time before its general publication by Carys after 1907.

Example 11.5a Opening of the plainchant melody *Veni Sancte Spiritus*

Ve- ni sanc- te Spi- ri- tus.

Example 11.5b Terry's version of this in the opening of his *Mass on the theme 'Veni Sancte Spiritus'*

Example 11.6a Extract from the plainchant melody *Veni Sancte Spiritus*

Flec- te quod est ri- gi- dum.

Example 11.6b Terry's adaptation of the melody in the 'Sanctus I' of his *Mass on the theme 'Veni Sancte Spiritus'*

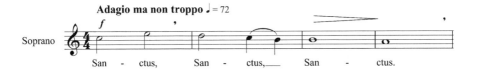

Example 11.7a Extracts from the melody *Veni Sancte Spiritus*

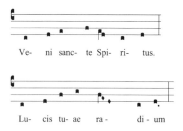

Example 11.7b Terry's adaptation of these extracts in the 'Sanctus II' and 'Agnus
Dei' of his *Mass on the theme 'Veni Sancte Spiritus'*

by Solesmes. The overall effect on the mood of the Mass then is much greater than
in the *Mass of St Dominic*, despite the wide range of dynamic levels (*p* to *ff*). This is
because a form of chant is used in the largest two movements of a Mass whose tempi
are relatively slow, producing a more restrained effect.[16]

Third, Terry acknowledges the influence of Renaissance composers. Indeed,
in the Preface he justifies the chord progression that concludes the 'Sanctus I' by
reference to Thomas Morley. However, he admits that elsewhere modern diatonic
harmony is used.

---

16 The tempi in the other movements are: Kyrie, Larghetto ♩ = 80; Sanctus I, Adagio ma
non troppo ♩ = 72; Sanctus II, Andante ♩ = 92; Benedictus, Adagio: ♩ = 72; Agnus Dei, Andante
Moderato: ♩ = 76.

Such features are picked up and modified in Terry's next two Masses (Examples 11.8a and 11.8b). The *Short Mass in C*, also composed in 1904, is a unison mass, but the repetitions of the text preclude its singing by congregations. Clearly, then, it was designed for the limited capacities of many Catholic parish choirs.[17] As such, it fitted in with Terry's policy, inaugurated in 1907, of finding time to perform simple modern masses at Westminster. The preface states that the 'Credo' is based on a fragment from Luther's hymn melody 'Ein' feste Berg'. At that time, then, Terry did not disdain Protestant melodies; something that he attacked in the preparations for the *Westminster Hymnal* of 1912. The rest of the mass is built out elements from the opening of the plainchant *Missa 'De Angelis'*, giving a unified feel to the whole work.

Example 11.8a Opening melody from the 'Kyrie' of Terry's *Short Mass in C*

Example 11.8b Opening phrase of the 'Kyrie' in the *Missa 'De Angelis'*

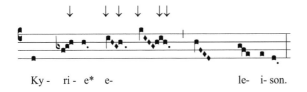

Terry's *Short and Easy Requiem Mass (No. 5)*, published in 1907, is dominated by chanted 'harmonised inflexions'.[18] However, it also throws an interesting light on Terry's understanding of plainchant at that time (Example 11.9). The 'Kyrie' is a harmonisation of the melody given in the Gregorian plainchant *Mass No. XV*. In the preface Terry states that when plainchant is harmonised it ceases to be plainchant. This apparently justifies the use of diatonic language in the 'Kyrie', while using modes in the 'Sanctus' and 'Benedictus'; he adds that 'the question of what "plainchant Edition" he [the composer] has used is irrelevant'. The most curious effect can be seen in the rhythm. It is not clear whether Terry means what he writes in the score, but if it is literally interpreted then each bar is of equal length, and therefore the triplet minims move more quickly than the duplets. This is something that neither Pothier nor Mocquereau would have been likely to accept.

---

17 Richard Terry, *Short Mass in C* (London, 1909). Terry's *Mass of St Bruno (No. 6)* (London, 1907) is another unison setting of the same type.

18 Richard Terry, *Short and Easy Requiem Mass (No. 5)* (London, 1907).

Example 11.9   Extract from the 'Kyrie' of Terry's *Short and Easy Requiem Mass*

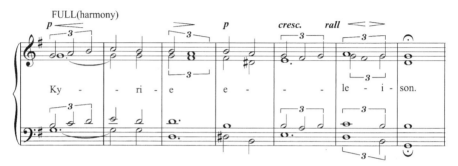

Terry was not content solely to promote his own music. He also used Westminster Cathedral as a forum for music by his English contemporaries, notably works by Vaughan-Williams, Holst, Howells, Oldroyd and Stanford. This fitted in with his Catholic musical ideology: if the Reformation had led to the decay of English music, then the Catholic revival should restore it to its former vigour. However, two points immediately stand out. None of these composers were Cecilians, reflecting Terry's poor opinion of most works from that source. However, Vaughan-Williams's *Mass in G Minor*, performed at Westminster in 1923, clearly betrays the effects of that composer's interest in Tudor music. Second, several of these composers were not Catholics, undermining Terry's ideological logic. Here again Terry broke his own rule, set out in the *Westminster Hymnal*, that only music by Catholic composers should be performed in Catholic services. For example, Vaughan-Williams's Mass was first performed by Holst's choir at Morley College, showing how the work straddled the boundary between concert and liturgical use. In turn, this is symptomatic of the fact that, frequently, the vocal skills within working Catholic church choirs had not kept pace with the rising technical demands of more modern works. Thus, when Terry introduced it at Westminster, because there were only four men still on the regular payroll, he had to solicit the services of John Driscoll's choir from the Sacred Heart church, Wimbledon;[19] and, according to the *Times*, the main load was carried by that body. Not surprisingly then, the performance of new modern works formed only a small part of Westminster's total workload. For example, 88 out of 127 works

---

19 Andrews, pp. 132–4. H.W.R. Lillie, Obituary of John Driscoll, *LN:Our Dead 1939–45* (1947–48): 119–37.

performed at Holy Week during 1913 were composed before 1650, only one from
the period 1651–1750 and seven from the period after 1851.

The spread of Renaissance polyphony in the early twentieth century: a flawed achievement

The Motu Proprio *Tra le Sollectudini*, with its endorsement of plainchant and
Renaissance polyphony, appeared to vindicate Terry's cause. Immediately he followed
it up in two ways: first through new publications, second by influencing the content
of diocesan lists of officially approved music. In addition to the *Downside Masses*,
Downside Motets and his own compositions Terry also took over from Tozer and
J.E. Turner the editing of Cary's *Motets Ancient and Modern* series. Later, in 1931,
he edited 16 works in Cary's *Polyphonic Motets* series, and in 1934 he produced
20 works by English composers in Novello's *Tudor Motets* series. Alongside Terry
the work of Henry Collins, editor of J. and W. Chester's *Latin Church Music of the
Polyphonic Schools*, should also be observed. Many of these items originated in
dyeline copy editions Collins prepared during and immediately after the First World
War for the Birmingham Oratory, copies of which still survive in the choir loft at
Oscott College chapel.

The diocesan lists of officially approved music were a Cecilian idea. Indeed,
as already observed, some attempts had already been made to produce such lists in
England. *TLS* gave it official endorsement. Terry and his allies seized control of the
relevant committees. For example Salford's list of 1904 was drafted on the instructions
of bishop Casartelli by a team that included Herbert Allen (the secretary and
Casartelli's personal music advisor), W.A. Norris (choirmaster at Salford Cathedral),
F. Ambrose Turner (choirmaster at Upholland Seminary), Bewerunge (Maynooth
College, Dublin), J.J. Dunne (choirmaster at Holy Cross College, Cunliffe, Ireland),
Henry Parkinson (Rector of Oscott), and Terry himself.[20] All of them were plainchant
or Renaissance polyphonic specialists; and the Irish Cecilian contribution should be
observed. Terry also helped prepare the Liverpool and Westminster Archdiocesan
lists as well as producing his own set of recommendations in his books *Catholic
Church Music* and *Music of the Roman Rite*.[21]

These lists, then, were Cecilian in spirit. For example, male voice choirs are
assumed in the Salford List; and, despite Terry's reservations, they are packed with
works by modern Cecilian composers. Salford's list names at least 31 of them,
including Blied, Diebold, Drobisch, Ebner, Filke, Forrester, Greisbacher, Greith,
Gruber, Haller, Hanisch, Jaspers, Kaim, Kerbusch, Koenen, Mitterer, F. Molitor,
J. Molitor, H. Oberhoffer, Perosi, Piel, Plag, De Prins, Quadflieg, Sechter, Seymour,
Singenberger, Tanner, Witt, Zangl and Terry himself. Indeed, earlier drafts of the
Salford booklet make direct reference to the Irish Cecilian list and incorporate sections

---

20 The other members were Francis Daniel (Canon and parish priest at Ribchester) and
Alfred Anselm Poock (of St Augustine's Church, Manchester).

21 See the Bourne Papers Box 1/87 'Music-Church 1904–1910', Westminster Archdiocesan
Archives, for the membership of the Liverpool Commission (H. Worth, C.E. Brown, C.A. Cox,
James Butler OSB, John Nicholson, Charles Nicholson SJ, and F. Bamber).

giving the names of inappropriate works or composers, including compositions by
Cherubini, Dvořák, Farmer, Gounod, Haydn, Kalliwoda, Mozart, C. Murphy, J.P. Murphy,
Niedermeyer, Schmid, Silas, Spohr and Van Bree.[22] It is a tribute then to the enduring
popularity of the Classical Viennese and 'Modern' styles that the Salford list not only
retains works by Webbe and Newsham but also compositions by Paxton, Butler and
J.E. Turner.[23]

On the surface, such patterns continued after the First World War. For example,
Lancaster's diocesan list of approved music, issued in 1929, recommends works
by most of the Cecilians mentioned in the Salford list plus works by Barrat, De
Falconara, Hohnerlein, Klein, Lipp, Sephner, Seymour, Stehle, Tinell and Turton. It
also refers to works by Baini and Bordes, as well as Potiron's plainchant imitations.
Likewise, a shorter list prepared in 1927 for the diocese of Southwark lists 22 motets
and 5 Masses by Ebner, 5 motets and a Mass by Goller, 5 motets by Mitterer, 1 motet
and 7 Masses by Perosi, 4 motets and 7 Masses by Ravanello and 8 motets by Stein.[24]

Nevertheless, the achievement was flawed in several respects. First, as already
noted, Solesmes's revision of plainchant, by exalting Medieval over Renaissance
sources, undermined the alliance between this sort of music and Renaissance
polyphony, although that had been a central premise in *TLS*. Second, as the Salford
list had shown earlier, Classical Viennese and 'Modern' compositions were not
completely eliminated. For example, Lancaster's list contains non-Cecilian works
by Butler, Cary, Cherion, Crookall, Danby, Dumont, Haydn, Kalliwoda, Lutz,
Manners, Mozart, Moorat, Niedermeyer, Novello, Rheinberger, Richardson,
Romberg, Schulthes, Sewell, Silas, Stadler, J.E.Turner, Tozer, C. Vaughan, Vico,
Webbe, Westlake, Winter and Zulueta. In most cases such compositions appear
to survive either because they were simple and practical or because, stylistically,
they straddled the Renaissance and 'Modern' idioms. Even so, this does not fully
explain the presence of Rheinberger, who was critical of the Cecilian movement, or
Silas, whose *Mass in C* is large and complex. Third, performances of Cecilian works
must have been hit by the deleterious effect of the First World War on the German
publishing industry. For example, at Ushaw surviving publications from Ratisbon,
the centre for the dissemination of German Cecilian music, collapsed from 70 in the
period 1850–1900 to 20 in 1901–1950.

Third, in practice English Catholics were not offered the full gamut of the
Renaissance polyphonic repertoire. The biggest example concerns Palestrina, 800 of
whose works appear in Haberl's collection.[25] This gives a good idea of the state of
knowledge about Palestrina among Catholic musical scholars at the time. However,

---

22 Salford's *List of Approved Church Music* (Salford, 1904), pp. 1 (all male choirs) and
25 (Irish influence by reference to the musical supplement of *Lyra Ecclesiastica*). For a list
of works by banned composers see Louis Casartelli: 'Episcopal Notices: Church Music. 1st
List', *The Harvest* (December 1903): 299–300.

23 Salford *List of Approved Church Music*, pp. 18–19.

24 See *Approved List of Church Music for the Diocese of Lancaster* (Preston, 1929).
Ernest Jenner, *Our Church Music*, 'List III: Modern Masses and Motets' (Southwark, 1927).

25 Two items, a collection of 52 motets, referred to the Salford Diocesan List, and *Salva
Nos*, which is mentioned in the *Stonyhurst Magazine* but whose authenticity is dubious, have
not been included in this total.

the number of Palestrina's works specifically referred to in diocesan lists of approved music is much smaller, although some mention the big editions by Proske and Haberl (Table 11.2).

Table 11.2   The number of Palestrina's compositions recommended in lists of approved church music

List	Date	Number of Palestrina's works
Salford	1904	9 (excluding the reference to Haberl's edition)
Westminster	1906	97
Liverpool	1906	7
	1911	<u>15</u>
		<u>22</u>
Lancaster	1929	24
Terry: *Catholic Church Music*	1907	73
Terry: *Music of the Roman Rite*	1931	<u>76</u>
Terry: Total number of pieces listed in the two books (most appear in both)		79

The same picture emerges in published catalogues and through analysis of works performed in different places. For example, an undated inter-war list produced by Cary gives only one work by Palestrina, and a 1938 list produced by J. and W. Chester has just 37. Likewise, in a discussion of published Palestrina repertoire from the early 1930s H.B. Collins mentions 23 works. Surprisingly, considering their reputation for loyalty to the Papacy, major Jesuit establishments often displayed limited or no interest. For example, at Beaumont College, Old Windsor between 1918 and 1940 there were no performances of Palestrina. The same was true at Corpus Christi church, Bournemouth in 1926–27; although in this case this is the one year when music was listed here. There are nine works in the 1938 list of performances at the Sacred Heart church, Wimbledon, eight on lists for 1928, 1938 and 1961 relating to Farm Street Church, and seven in reports in the *Stonyhurst Magazine* between 1904 and 1938. Outside the Jesuit orbit, the *St Dominic's Parish Bulletin* (from Newcastle) between 1930 and 1939 mentions six works by Palestrina. On the other hand, at Salford Cathedral 10 works by Palestrina out of 115 were performed during Holy Week in 1904, and of course Westminster under Terry gave due prominence to his output, as has been seen.[26]

---

26 Henry Collins, 'The Polyphonic Motet', *ML*, 2/4 (October 1931): 84–6; 3/1 (January 1932): 4–6; 3/2 (April 1932): 58–60; 3/3 (July 1932): 62–4; 3/4 (October 1932): 86–9. *Beaumont Magazine*, St Stanislaus College, Beaumont, Old Windsor. *Farm St Journal*, Farm St Church, London. *Bournemouth Catholic Record*, Corpus Christi Church, Bournemouth. *St Dominic's Parish Bulletin*. Cuthbert Cary Elwes, List of music performed at the Church of the Sacred Heart, Wimbledon, *LN*, 54 (1938): 195–6. *St Dominic's Parish Bulletin*, St Dominic's

This phenomenon is hard to explain. However, there are two possibilities. First, choirs were used to singing a repertoire either for an SATB combination voices, or, in places like Convents and Seminaries, for upper or lower voices only. Yet Palestrina and his contemporaries often wrote for combinations other than these, so a choir might well balk at tackling music for 6, 7 or 8, let alone 12, voices. Second, there are limits to what any choir can master. For example, in 1938 Wimbledon's choir performed 203 pieces – an exceptionally high figure; yet Palestrina's known output is four times the size of this. It was simply unrealistic for publishers to print more than a fraction of his music for this mass market, especially in the face of competing claims from other composers.

The nature of Renaissance polyphony in early twentieth-century Catholic England: issues of performance environment, performance practice, and the editing of music

The failure to offer the full Renaissance polyphonic repertoire therefore has much to do with the problems of planting it in a twentieth-century parish environment, and one moreover that was often proletarian or lower middle class, given the social balance of the English Catholic community. This was completely different from the locations and audiences for which much of this type of music was originally composed. What is more, when it came to performances there was a tendency to lump all Renaissance composers together without much regard for the fact that individually they themselves wrote for different audiences. Thus Palestrina wrote most of his music for the Sistine Chapel, St Maria Maggiore or St Peter's, Rome – major ecclesiastical establishments with trained salaried choirs. Their only equivalents in early twentieth-century Catholic England were at places such as Westminster Cathedral, the London Oratory, and St Chad's, Birmingham. On the other hand Lassus, although he worked in the Sistine Chapel, spent most of his career in the Bavarian ducal chapel. This was a smaller, more intimate location, and here Lassus was catering for the personal tastes of a court, not a parish or a cathedral. Byrd represents an interesting variation on this. His religious output was intended for Lincoln Cathedral, Elizabeth I's Chapel Royal and aristocratic Recusant households. The first two were Anglican, although a Latin version of the Book of Common Prayer was used in the Chapel Royal; however, the third, for which his three Masses were composed, was even more restricted and intimate than a court chapel. Yet choirmasters like Terry did not hesitate to perform such works in large buildings like Westminster Cathedral. Meanwhile, Peter Phillips was at a halfway point between Byrd and Lassus. He was English, but, after a spell in Elizabeth's Chapel Royal, he worked in the court chapel of Archduke Albert and Archduchess Isabella in the Spanish Netherlands.

Such distinctions underline the fact that the nineteenth and twentieth centuries were completely different eras from the Renaissance period, and some Catholic

---

church, Newcastle. *Holy Week at Salford Cathedral 1904*, Spirit Duplicated copy amongst the Casertelli Papers, Salford Diocesan Archives.

commentators recognised the implications of this for the revival of older musical styles. As early as 1846 the anonymous author of the article 'Sacred Music and Palestrina', discussing the religious ethos Palestrina's music was supposed to promote, noted that 'the artist of today, who tries to emulate this style, will feel, however high he can raise himself, that the writer's mind was pitched at a point of devotional earnestness, which is perhaps, impossible of attainment in times like our own'. Thus 'the traditional manner of performance is lost, or its echoes only faintly linger in the Papal Chapel at Rome'.[27] Some 50 years later, in 1907, Terry remarked the same thing, adding that people in his day thought diatonically, not in modes.[28] Such opinions have been endorsed and developed by modern commentators. For example, Mager notes the growing divide in the nineteenth century between music performed in churches and that produced in concert hall.[29] Even when the work was the same, the interpretation could be different. A classic instance is Otto Goldschmidt's 1881 edition of Palestrina's *Missa Papae Marcelli*, copies of which appear occasionally in Catholic church collections, some in reprints from the 1920s and 1930s. This was prepared for a concert performance by the London Bach Choir using early–mid-nineteenth-century editions prepared by Capes, Niedermeyer and Proske. Instead of retaining Palestrina's SATTBB scoring, Goldschmidt converted it to an SSAABB or SSATBB combination; presumably because the London Bach Choir had female upper voices.[30] Two other aspects have been observed by Frederick Neumann. The first was the effect of nationalism, which can be illustrated by Terry's attempts to show that English Renaissance polyphonists were loyal Catholic Englishmen working in an international Roman environment. The second is the fact that up to the nineteenth century, composers wrote for the day, so their works had a short life expectancy. Such practices were in sharp contrast with the modern development of a canon of enduring masterpieces without which the idea of recovering a past cultural heritage would be virtually inconceivable.[31]

In turn, as Bernard Sherman points out, this contrast highlights the tension between creating an authentic historical performance and the desire to update a work for modern consumption, as Goldschmidt did. One aspect concerns the way such music was presented to performers, especially when compared with plainchant. Solesmes, it will have been noted, had no qualms about offering plainchant in printed versions of fourteenth-century neums. The same thing did not happen with Renaissance polyphony. Nor, except with some Cecilian imitations, were individual voice parts provided, as had been the custom in Renaissance times; instead, every singer had a full vocal score. Yet, as has been seen, in the early–mid nineteenth century Catholic choirs had often been expected to use individual voice parts copied in manuscript from the printed full score. Many also became familiar with the sixteenth-century style notation used in the measured plainchant editions published from Mechlin

---

27 Anon., 'Sacred Music and Palestrina', reprinted in the *Catholic Weekly Instructor* from the *New Quarterly Review*, London, Derby, Dublin (1846) 3: 102–104.

28 Terry, *Catholic Church Music*, p. 50.

29 Mager, *The Debate over the Revival of Ancient Church Music*, pp. 64–5.

30 Otto Goldschmidt (ed.), Palestrina: *Missa Papae Marcelli* (London, 1881).

31 Frederick Neumann, *New Essays on Performance Practice* (Rochester, NY 1989), pp. 6–7.

and Ratisbon, which is very similar to that used in original manuscript and printed copies of Renaissance polyphony. Terry, for one, must have known this. In an article entitled 'Early Belgian Composers' he provides a table of just such symbols.[32] So, in theory there should have been no greater difficulty persuading Catholic choirs to sing from 'authentically' notated music in this style than in getting them to read from fourteenth-century style plainchant neums.

Yet this was not done. To a man editors 'translated' Renaissance notation into a modern format. It is interesting, then, to speculate why this happened. Undoubtedly, for the purposes of promoting the repertoire amongst what were mainly amateur volunteer groups, this was more convenient. A distinction might also be drawn between monastic communities, with the time and motivation to learn plainchant from fourteenth-century plainchant neums, and lay choirs who might not be prepared to do the same thing with Renaissance polyphonic notation. Against this it might be countered that, in the 1930s especially, some progress *was* made persuading such choirs to master plainchant neums. On the other hand this was only achieved after the most forceful official representations backed by a concerted programme of fairly mechanical training within Catholic schools. When all was said and done, Renaissance polyphony did not enjoy the same official liturgical status as plainchant; and, if training people to sing plainchant *monody* from neums was hard, then trying to get them to perform Renaissance *polyphony* – especially if unaccompanied – from archaic forms of notation might have seemed well-nigh impossible.

It should come as no surprise then to discover deficiencies in Catholic early twentieth- century editorial and performance techniques by Terry and others. For, if the notation is 'translated', inevitably the music will be subtly changed. This is because different notational systems reflect different approaches to the way the music is conceived and performed. Thus, as regards performances of Palestrina, Frances Cameron noted in 1962 that 'on many sides we are hedged about with false traditions – traditions which often go back no further than the nineteenth-century interest in his compositions'.[33] Such deficiencies were further complicated by ideological considerations. One is the idea that Renaissance polyphony should be performed *a cappella*. This represented a marriage between ideology, history and practicality. It would be convenient if it was historically true because such works, unlike many more modern compositions, could be performed at Lent and Advent, when organs were discouraged, and it fitted in with the drive against the use of instruments in church. For instance the anonymous author of 'Sacred Music and Palestrina' declared that 'purely vocal composition offers the most decent and appropriate form in which art can be employed in public worship. There is an appearance of spontaneity and sincerity in the union of many voices, which is dissipated by the intrusion of instrumental adjuncts'. The trouble is that recent modern scholarship has revealed a more ambivalent picture. As already noted, the German College in sixteenth-century Rome used musical instruments. In addition, Graham Dixon, citing works by Viadana, argues that by the late sixteenth and early

---

32 Richard Terry, 'Early Belgian Composers' in Richard Terry (ed.), *A Forgotten Psalter and other Essays* (London, 1929), p. 195.

33 Frances Cameron, 'Only for Devotees', *Church Music*, 22 (October 1962): 9–13.

seventeenth centuries the shift to monody and continuo was already well under way, especially if due allowance is made for the fact that at that time publishers were generally about twenty years behind the times and that a good deal of improvisation took place in the Sistine Chapel. Dixon's observations are confirmed by the contents of the *Liber Primi Albori Musicali*, by Lorenzo Penna, published from Bologna in 1590, a copy of which survives at Stonyhurst College. Part 3 is devoted exclusively to the techniques of converting a figured bass into a full vocal score and back again. Such practices therefore put into context the adaptation of several Palestrina works, most notably the *Missa Papae Marcelli* by Anerio and Soriano, to fit the new style. It is interesting, then, to note that Haberl published these adaptations in his edition of *Palestrina's Werke*. Does this mean that he was aware of the change of style that Dixon supposed this to represent? The answer is that we do not know. Certainly it was not something picked up by English Catholic musicians at the time, perhaps because the focus was on recovering Palestrina's *oeuvre*; and anyway it was assumed that he stood at a peak of compositional excellence after which there could only be a decline. In this way a mentality based on a canon of 'great composers' may have been a barrier to authentic interpretation.[34]

Another aspect concerned the size of the choir. Modern research, taking account of the chronic absenteeism noted by Sherr, suggests that one voice to a part could often have been the norm in the Sistine Chapel.[35] Late nineteenth- and early twentieth-century choirs though were generally larger. Thus the reduction in the size of Westminster Cathedral's choir during the First World War would have inadvertently produced – by modern standards – a more authentic performance. Indeed, people at that time noted – with some surprise – that such performances actually worked.[36]

A further feature concerned the relationship between text and music. This had been extensively discussed by Mocquereau in the 1901 issue of *Paléographie Musicale*.[37] At that time though (unlike later) Mocquereau still subscribed to Pothier's interpretation of plainchant rhythm derived from the text. Moreover, he was concerned to show how Renaissance polyphony had grown out of plainchant. He therefore argued that the rhythmic patterns in the melodic lines used by sixteenth-century Renaissance polyphonists up to Palestrina were derived from rhythms in the text in exactly the same way as Pothier had argued with monodic plainchant. Indeed, he asserted that Palestrina took a more 'modern', and therefore debased, approach to the relationship between musical and textual rhythms. What hardly anyone noticed at that time though was the implications of revisions to liturgical texts in different historical periods. A stray example occurs in a copy in the Church Music Association collection of Edmund Fellowes's edition of Byrd's *Ave Verum Corpus*, published by Stainer and Bell in 1938 and formerly belonging to Patrick Morrison, of Mount St Mary's College, Derbyshire. At the bottom of the first page Morrison noted the

---

34 Graham Dixon, 'The Performance of Palestrina: Some questions, but few answers', *EM*, 24 (1994): 667–75 esp. 668–9 and 671–2.

35 Richard Sherr, 'Competence and incompetence in the Papal choir in the age of Palestrina', *EM*, 24 (1994): 607–629.

36 Andrews, p. 124.

37 *PM*, 7(1901): esp. 91–105.

differences between the text and that given in his copy of the *Liber Usualis*. Earlier the same issue had been investigated by Bewerunge. In a letter to McLachlan dated 28 June 1916 discussing his study of five Palestrina Offertories he states:

> I forgot if I mentioned that in my study of Palestrina I came across some peculiar readings (which the editor has reduced to the readings of the post-Tridentine Missal). Thus in the Off. *Justiciae Domini* (Dom. 3. Quadr.) Palestrina had composed the words et duliciana, and the editor made a mess of it by substituting the reading et judicia ejus dulciana.

Bewerunge then proceeded to give other examples from Palestrina's *Confitebor*, *Populem Humilem* and *Sicut in Holocaustis*. In subsequent letters he then reports further research by an anonymous assistant in the Royal Library of Berlin confirming such conclusions.[38]

All of this had practical consequences for editions. First, there was the emerging divide between scholarly and performance publications, something noted by Collins in the early 1930s. Indeed, apropos the latter, he observed that 'these editions vary, of course, greatly in value'.[39] There is a fundamental difference between, for instance, Haberl's *Palestrina's Werke* and Terry's *Downside Motets* series. The former is designed for study in a library, the latter for practical performance by a choir. This is very different from the scene in 1811, when Novello produced his *Collection of Sacred Music*. This *looks* like a de-luxe edition, but in fact it was intended to be a master copy from which manuscript voice parts would be copied. Second, the music was frequently transposed. For example, Haberl published an edition of Palestrina's *Missa 'Aeterni Christi Munera'* with the parts taken down by a third.[40] Third, editors added extra directions; and they were not always scrupulous in showing where they had done this. For example, Terry, in his 1905 *Downside Masses* edition of Lassus's *Missa 'Quinti Toni'*, adds dynamics, tempi, accentuation markings and instructions as to when sections should be sung by solo voices (see Figure 11.1). As a result such directions may tell us more about how the music sounded as directed by Terry at Downside or Westminster than in Lassus's own day.

The most fundamental aspect of such changes concerned the conversion of music from part books to full vocal scores. As noted before, in the former singers have to sing linearly; with the latter, they can 'find their notes' by reference to the other parts, leading them to think more in terms of chords. Rhythm in Renaissance music would also be affected by the positioning of bar lines in more modern vocal scores. When these vertically cut across all the parts, any semi-independent rhythmic interplay between them may be obscured, given that – rhythmically speaking – they are all forced into the same vertical straitjacket. Even if this is set to one side, the variations between different editions can be striking, as comparisons between Terry's *Downside Motets* (1901/R1905) and *Tudor Church Music* (*TCM*)(1921) editions of Byrd's *Ave Verum* illustrate (Figures 11.2 and 11.3). In the *Downside Motets* edition

---

38 Bewerunge to McLachlan. Letters dated 28 June 1916, 19 October 1916, 11 January 1917 and 6 May 1917, SAA. The edition in question is almost certainly that produced by Haberl. A projected article reporting these discoveries appears to have been rejected for publication.

39 Henry Collins, 'Ecclesiastical Polyphony', *ML*, 2/2 (April 1931): 28–31, esp. 31.

40 Franz X. Haberl (ed.), Jo. Petraloysius Praenestina: *Missa 'Aeterna Christi Munera'* (Leipzig, n.d.).

Figure 11.1   The opening page of Terry's edition of Lassus, *Missa 'Quinti Toni'*
(London, Cary and Co., *Downside Masses*, 1905)

Figure 11.2   The opening page of the *Downside Motets* edition of Byrd, *Ave Verum Corpus* (ed. Richard Terry, London, 1905)

Figure 11.3   The opening page of the *Tudor Church Music* edition of Byrd, *Ave Verum Corpus* (ed. Richard Terry, London, 1921)

the imposition of a rigid 2/2 time produces a 'square' and 'chunky' effect. *TCM* undermines this by interpolating 2/4 and 3/4 bars within the basic 4/4 framework, by using an 'off beat' entry with the opening 'A-ve', and by placing the first syllables of 'MA-ri-ae' and 'VIR-gi- ne' on the weaker third (as opposed to the first) beats of the bar. Likewise, a basic minim pulse is adopted in the *Downside Motets* edition, whereas the *TCM* edition uses crotchets, thereby enhancing the linear aspect of the work and possibly speeding up the tempo.[41] It also means that in the *TCM* edition the bar lengths are longer, emphasising the coherence of each phrase and even individual words. For example, in the *Downside Motets* edition the syllables of 'Ver-um' and 'Cor-pus' are separated by bar lines, whereas the integrity of these words is retained in the *TCM* edition. Indeed, such differences may even be symptomatic of changes to plainchant understandings. The syllabic approach in *Downside Motets* may be a hangover from the days of slow measured plainchant, whereas the *TCM* edition twenty years later reflects the impact of the faster-moving linear approach to plainchant advocated by Solesmes.

Finally, it will be observed that, officially at least, both publications were edited by Terry. Nevertheless, Richard Turbet has shown that such differences reflect clashes of opinion within the editorial board of the *Tudor Church Music* series. Essentially this had two aspects: the first, as already noted, concerns issues of scholarship and taste; the second was about matters of efficiency and care. Terry's sloppiness editorially and in performance practice was proverbial, and noted even by his eulogist Hilda Andrewes. According to Turbet, he may also have been on the verge of a nervous breakdown.[42] As a result, in the *Tudor Church Music* project he was unseated as chief editor through the machinations of his sub-editors – Percy Buck, Edmund Fellowes, A. Ramsbotton and Susan Townsend Warner, all of whom were Anglicans. The long-term effects were profound, given that the *TCM* series became a major pillar in the Anglican Renaissance polyphonic choral repertoire. From a Catholic perspective a great opportunity had been lost. Had Terry remained in charge it is possible that his Catholic ideological vision of the place of such music might have been extended to this constituency; and from there it could have become an accepted orthodoxy in the British musical circles.

---

41 This type of argument is presented by Cameron, pp. 10–11.

42 Richard Turbet, 'An affair of honour: "Tudor Church Music": the ousting of Richard Terry, and a trust vindicated', *Mlet*, 76 (1995): 593–600. 'A monument of enthusiastic industry: further light on "Tudor Church Music", *MLet*, 81/3 (August 2000): 433–7. Andrews, pp. 129–30 and 142. Peter Doyle, *Westminster Cathedral 1895–1995* (London, 1995), pp. 51–69, esp. 53.

Conclusion
Catholic Church Music in the
Early Twentieth Century:
Visions of Uniformity – Diverse Reality

The threat of atrophy

To sum up, the campaign to promote plainchant and Renaissance polyphony spearheaded by *TLS* produced only mixed success. Nevertheless, its achievements and limitations throw light on the nature of Catholic musical culture and the environment in which it operated. At its heart lies the difference between the vision of what was supposed to be happening, and the actual reality on the ground.

Certainly, as has been seen, progress was made, not just in the more widespread performance of both genres, but in the rediscovery and editing for publication of largely forgotten or hitherto unknown repertoire. Such developments were underpinned by significant changes in scholarly method, performance technique and aesthetic appreciation. In turn these can be contextualised in the light of parallel developments in liturgical, biblical and religious-historical studies.

Potentially, the implications were quite startling. For example, during Holy Week in 1925, the choir at Ampleforth, under the direction of Bernard McElligott, the future founder of the Society of St Gregory, performed 48 works. Nineteen of these were plainchant, 28 belonged to the Renaissance polyphonic genre, one was late medieval, two were by J.S. Bach and ten, including a 'Cologne tune', were classified as 'traditional'. In other words there was nothing from the nineteenth and twentieth centuries. Yet, only a few decades before, the Ampleforth community had produced practicing composers, such as Burge, Hedley and J.E. Turner.[1]

Similar phenomena can be observed elsewhere. In 1932 the choir at St Mary's Church, Poplar, in London, congratulated itself on the performance of programme entirely made up of plainchant and Renaissance polyphony on the first and second Sundays of Pentecost. The only exception was an arrangement of the early eighteenth-century tune 'Dwyfer' by Terry.[2] Likewise, reports in the *Upholland Magazine* between 1936 and 1942 refer to the performance of 67 compositions, in addition to a basic diet of plainchant. Of these, 51 were composed between 1501 and 1650, one between 1451 and 1500, and three between 1701 and 1800. Aside from three undated items, only six were composed after 1851.[3]

---

1 Anon report, *AJ*, 30/111 (Summer 1925): 198–9.

2 'Our members' activities', *ML*, 3/3 (July 1932): 68.

3 Thomas Muir, *Full in the Panting Heart of Rome:Roman Catholic Church Music in England: 1850–1962* (Durham, PhD thesis, 2004), p. 563.

Vigorous promotion of plainchant and Renaissance polyphony therefore had the potential to reduce Catholic church music to a state of atrophy. The career of Edward Elgar illustrates the impact this could have, not just on the output but on the religious state of mind of a major composer with apparently strong 'Catholic' credentials. For a start, some might argue that Elgar's melodies owe something to the supple lines of Solesmes plainchant. Yet there is no sign that Elgar had any connections with Stanbrook Abbey, just outside his native Worcester, although this was a major centre for promoting this kind of chant. Elgar's Catholic links were with St George's Church, Worcester, which was run by Jesuits. Judging by English Jesuit tastes elsewhere the chant he would have encountered there before 1903 would almost certainly have been in the measured Renaissance style. True, Elgar dedicated his setting of *Ave Maris Stella* to the Benedictine Canon Dolman of Belmont, but at that time Belmont too was clinging to the measured style. Elgar's Jesuit connections may also explain the similarity between his style and those propounded by such Jesuits as Maher and Zulueta – his almost exact contemporary. In short Elgar was a proponent of 'modern' Catholic styles, as opposed to Cecilian imitations of Renaissance polyphony, a style in which he never displayed much interest.

Another striking feature is the limited quantity and scale of Elgar's music for Catholic *services*, as opposed to oratorios with a religious subject intended for the concert hall. What is more, almost all of it was composed before 1902, although some items were published after that date, the year when his *Ave Verum* came out. It surely is not coincidental that Elgar ceased attending Mass after the composition of his oratorio *The Dream of Gerontius* in 1900. It is significant that the text was compiled by John Henry Newman who, despite his elevation to the Cardinalate, was well known for his ambivalent relationship with the strongly Ultramontane temper prevalent in Rome and amongst the senior English hierarchy. Elgar's religious doubts therefore overlap with the fact that the restrictive Ultramontane approach to church music limited the scope for his wider ambitions as a composer.[4] Symptomatic was Elgar's well-known dissatisfaction with his job as choirmaster at St George's.

In turn this highlights a wider truth. Even when, as was probably the case at Worcester, there was no intention of restricting repertoire to plainchant and Renaissance polyphony, the promotion of such styles automatically could have an atrophying effect. It was simply a matter of capacity. With any choir there is a limit to the number of performance opportunities and the amount that can be learnt within the time available for rehearsal, especially if the group consists of amateurs with variable musical skills, as was usually the case in Catholic circles. So, attempts to extend repertoire 'backwards' in time necessarily diverted attention from new music. Worse, the problem would be compounded if choirs tried to retain the Classical Viennese and Embassy Chapel repertoires, and in any case by the 1920s such music had ceased to be 'modern'.

In such circumstances a choir could all too easily get locked into a treadmill of repeating more or less the same repertoire year by year. For example, the choir at St Dominic's, Newcastle is reported to have sung 85 compositions in 878 performance slots between 1930 and 1939. This means that a work was repeated on 793 occasions

---

4   Stephen Hough, 'Enigmatic Catholic'. *Tablet*, 6 June 2007 (no volume number): 10–11.

– 90 per cent of the time! The same phenomenon occurred at Stonyhurst, though to a lesser degree. Between 1904 and 1923 *The Stonyhurst Magazine* reported the singing of 221 works in 836 performances; so items were repeated on 615 occasions, or 73.5 per cent of the time. Between 1926 and 1938 the figures fell to 36 works on 128 occasions, since during that time *The Stonyhurst Magazine* confined most of its music reports to Holy Week, but the proportion of repeated works is roughly the same – 70 per cent.[5]

However, records of performances at the Jesuit church in Farm St, Mayfair show that such dangers could be resisted, but only as a result of increasing the work rate. Monthly music programmes in the *Farm St Journal* for 1928 show that 234 compositions were performed on 444 occasions. So here a composition was repeated only 47 per cent of the time (210 out of 444). Clearly, one factor was the greater number of performance opportunities; another was the fact that this choir was directed by John Driscoll, one of the most proficient and ruthless choirmasters of the age. The figures for 1938 show the consequence of a reduction in tempo, although the choir still enjoyed a high reputation under the direction of Fernand Laloux and Guy Weitz. In that year 148 works were sung on 354 occasions. Works were therefore repeated on 206 occasions, or 58 per cent of the time.[6]

It is significant that, both at Stonyhurst and Farm St, efforts were made to maintain a balance between different repertories. Yet, as has been seen, this meant that, when the number of performances was reduced, hard choices had to be made. Table 12.1 shows that in both cases music from the eighteenth and early nineteenth centuries was squeezed, but not to the point of extinction. The difference in work rate between the two institutions, though, meant that, whereas at Farm St a strong interest in 'modern' repertoire was maintained, at Stonyhurst the net effect was a very thin spread of works from all periods.

Market forces

Such potential for atrophy was enhanced by developments in the printing and publishing industries noted earlier. Mass production of smart-looking printed copies reduced the local incentive to make hand-copied arrangements, let alone perform newly composed local music. This is the true significance of the centralisation of much of the publishing industry on London. Of the repertoire listed in Table 12.2 below, 50.6 per cent was produced there; much of the rest came from abroad, leaving very little scope for provincial firms. This was an age with no photocopiers or Gestetner machines, let alone computerised music-writing programs. To be fully economic, lithography or musical type required long print runs. Such mass

---

5   Muir, *Full in the Panting Heart of Rome*, pp. 563, 565 and 425–72 (describing the nature of the source material. Note that the issues of *St Dominic's Parish Bulletin* used were those stored at the Dominican Priory next door. The volumes for 1936 and 1938 are missing. Data relating to Stonyhurst has been extrapolated from articles entitled 'Choir notes', 'Music Notes' or 'Music for Holy Week'. No such articles appear in *The Stonyhurst Magazine* issues during 1916, 1924, 1927–29 and 1931.)

6   Ibid., p. 564.

Table 12.1   Categorisation of repertoire by period of composition as reported in *The Stonyhurst Magazine* and *Farm St Journal**

Period of composition	Stonyhurst		Farm St	
	1904–23	**1926–38**	**1928**	**1938**
No. of works	221	37	234	148
No data (mainly Plainchant)	88	19	11	17
1451–1650	18	5	41	27
1651–1800	10	2	26	6
1751–1800	36	3	26	7
1851 onwards	29	5	80	78
In addition some works belong to the following overlapping periods				
1601–1700	6	0	9	2
1801–1900	35	4	41	9

*   Muir, *Full in the Panting Heart of Rome*, pp. 577–8. See pp. 425–72 for a description of the methods of database construction and analysis used to obtain these figures. Pp. 439–40 deal with the methods used to categorise works by their period of composition.

production made it not just worthwhile, but essential for publishers to extend and enforce the law on copyright. For the first time they had the capacity to supply the entire mass market and reap the rewards consequent upon establishing monopolies over it. In this respect the passage of the 1911 Copyright Act was a major milestone, especially when reinforced by reciprocal copyright treaties and agreements with other countries.[7]

The result was that Catholic musicians usually faced a 'take it or leave it' situation. Copyright law, plus a natural reluctance to make hand copies when cheap smart editions were available, meant that they had to perform the music more or less exactly as it was printed. In this way a standardised version and method of performance of any item across the whole country became a real possibility. As has been seen, this was particularly true with plainchant, thanks to the introduction of the Mechlin, Pustet, Solesmes and Vatican Typical editions of chant books.

---

7   Victoria Cooper, *The House of Novello: Practice and Policy of a Victorian Music Publisher, 1829–1866* (Aldershot, 2003), pp. 103–4. James Coover, *Music publishing. Copyright and copyright piracy in Victorian England. A twenty-five year chronicle 1881–1906 from the pages of the 'Musical Opinion and Musical Trade Review' and other English music journals of the period* (London and New York, 1985), pp. 13–37, 51–2 and 78–82. 'Ch 46: An Act to amend the Law of Copyright, 16 Dec, 1911' in *The General Public Acts passed in the first and second years of the reign of his majesty King George the Fifth* (London, 1911–12), pp. 182–205.

What is more, because copyright created monopolies, and therefore safe markets for sales, publishers had less incentive to add new compositions to their existing portfolios of music, once these had been established. Why go to the trouble and expense of publishing new music when you can continue selling the old to a captive market? Furthermore, if you decided to add to your portfolio, it was much safer to produce editions of 'ancient' music. No royalties had to be paid to the composer, the cachet attached to old music guaranteed sales, and you could use the services of your 'in house' editor. The work of Henry Collins and his successors Henry Washington and Bruno Turner on the *Latin Church Music of the Polyphonic Schools* series published by J. and W. Chester is a classic example. From a publisher's point of view reliable scholarly editors were potentially more valuable than composers with their alleged reputation for individuality and mercurial temperaments. It is no accident that men such as Collins, Terry and Tozer sacrificed composing for editing.

At the same time long print runs meant that particular editions could remain in circulation for decades. One of the most remarkable phenomena of the 1950s and 1960s was the way publishers continued to reprint editions using the typefaces and formats originally set up before the First World War (see Table 12.2). In this way performance styles current in the 1900s could retain their grip on Catholic musicians long after they had been superseded by scholarly advances and changes in performance fashions that had occurred elsewhere. This applied not just to Renaissance polyphony and plainchant, it extended to the Viennese Classical repertoire and its successors, especially as presented by Novello and Co. in editions originally prepared for the Choral Society market by Berthold Tours, Joseph Barnby and – behind them – Vincent Novello himself.

Local realities

All this was music to Ultramontane ears. For them 'atrophy' was not a vice, it was a pejorative word for 'unchanging uniformity' – a positive virtue! As has been seen plainchant and Renaissance polyphony formed part of the strategy to insulate Catholics from pernicious outside modern influences. Yet, paradoxically, such isolationism did not seem to discourage the flow of converts – 746,000 between 1900 and 1960![8] Indeed, taking refuge within alleged past certainties appeared to be an attraction, especially amongst High Church Anglicans and the middle-class intelligentsia exemplified by Terry and Edmund Rubbra. Looked at this way, the Catholic Church did not need to dress itself up in modern garb, as Hemy had assumed. People would come to it and accept its uncompromising terms as it stood.

For these reasons the interests of publishers and Ultramontanes appeared to coincide. The result, then, should have been a surge of publishing activity before the First World War as repertoire was redefined according to Ultramontane criteria, followed by decades of relative stagnation, both in terms of output and receptivity to

---

8   Sheridan Gilley, 'The Years of Equipoise: 1892–1943', in Vivian McClelland and Michael Hodgetts (eds), *From without the Flaminian Gate: 150 years of Catholicism in England and Wales: 1850–2000* (London, 1999), p. 41.

modern musical styles. To some extent, this was what happened. Local reality on the ground, though, shows the situation to be more complex.

Table 12.2 gives data from 9,045 printed and engraved publications (including later editions) containing 7,898 compositions found in 23 centres.[9] The figures do not include the contents of liturgical chant books, hymnals or Benediction manuals. This is because such sources are fundamentally different in character. They are standard compilations found all across the Catholic Church in England, and as such they were available to officiating clergy and, in theory at least, to congregations. The statistics therefore show what repertoire was published for the almost exclusive use of choirs. This means they emphasise the degree of diversity within it. Indeed, virtually every collection has items that cannot be found elsewhere, and it stands to reason that, as more collections are examined, the extent of diversity will expand, albeit at a diminishing rate.

Overall the data shows that the number of publications and compositions nearly quintupled between 1801–49 and 1850–1900, but then fell by about two-fifths thereafter. Moreover, it should be remembered that the survival of older publications shows that they were still available for use in later periods. So far, then, this squares with the pattern of vigorous growth in the nineteenth century followed by early twentieth-century atrophy, as theoretically sketched out earlier. However, when the dates of composition are examined there are significant differences. As expected, there was a decline in the proportion of contemporary or near contemporary works (that is, music composed up to 50 years before publication) from 46.6 per cent in 1801–1849 to 23.3 per cent in 1850–1900; but, after 1900 there is a recovery to 49.3 per cent – slightly more than the equivalent proportion a century before. This suggests that campaigns to promote plainchant and Renaissance polyphony did not prevent Catholic church music in England from keeping up to date. Rather, it confirms the continued interest in contemporary works revealed by the statistics of performances at Stonyhurst and Farm St. Indeed, other Jesuit centres display the same phenomenon. At Beaumont College, Old Windsor the *Beaumont Review* reported that 65 works were performed between 1918 and 1940. Of these, 17 were composed after 1851. Similarly, reports in the *Bournemouth Catholic Record* show that 35 out of 79 compositions fall into this category at Corpus Christi church, Bournemouth in 1926–27, whilst at the Sacred Heart church, Wimbledon the proportion was 49 out of 203. Elsewhere, at St Dominic's, Newcastle the figure between 1930 and 1939 is 21 out of 85.[10]

Against this it might be contended that some of the compositions were by Cecilians. Thus, even if they were contemporary, they were written in a deliberately archaic style. However, the data shows that, when isolated, these constitute only 184 out of 3,553 works in 1850–1900 and 79 out of 2,103 works after that. On the other hand a more serious objection stems from the exclusion of data found in chant

---

    9   See Appendix B in the Bibliography for a list of the sources used for compiling Table 12.2. Methods of database construction and analysis are the same as those used in Muir, *Full in the Panting Heart of Rome*, pp. 425–72.

    10 Muir, *Full in the Panting Heart of Rome*, pp. 576–7.

Table 12.2   Analysis of published compositions from 23 collections of Catholic
              music in England

General figures	
Total no. of publications	9189
Total no. of London publications	4651
Total no. of compositions	7509
Period of publication: 1801–49	
Total no. of publications	898
Total no. of compositions	751
No data	233
Post-1751	350
Plus, in addition, compositions for the period 1701–1800	48
Period of publication: 1850–1900	
Total no. of publications	4053
Total no. of compositions	3552
No. of identifiable Cecilian compositions	184
No data	530
Post-1801	829
Plus, in addition, compositions from the period 1751–1850	261
Period of publication: 1901–50	
Total no. of publications	2307
No. of reprints produced after 1945 using a pre 1914 typeface	380
Total no. of compositions	2103
No. of identifiable Cecilian compositions	79
No data	328
1851 onwards	1038
Plus, in addition, compositions from the period 1801–1900	86

books, hymnals and Benediction manuals. The former, if included, would definitely push all Catholic repertoire in an archaic direction, since they contain nothing but plainchant. With hymnals and Benediction manuals the position is somewhat different. As has been seen, the nineteenth century witnessed a substantial increase in new music for both these forms, followed by a consolidation of repertoire accompanied by rising interest in Early Modern chorales and the abandonment of most Classical Viennese material in the early twentieth century. This then fulfils the patterns of development one might expect from an alliance between Ultramontanes and publishers.

An Ultramontane failure?

There appears then, to be a divide between repertoire found in chant books, hymnals and Benediction manuals, and that exclusively intended for choirs. With the latter the Ultramontane dominance was not as complete as its protagonists might have liked, hence the efforts to bring them under more clerical control noted earlier. There are several possible reasons for this limitation. One may simply be personal taste. People *liked* the Classical Viennese style and subsequent modern developments. Conversely, plainchant does not always seem to have aroused much enthusiasm. Symptomatic is Pius XI's reiteration of the principles of *TLS* in the encyclical *Divini Cultus* of 1928. In England this inspired Bernard McElligott to found the Society of St Gregory, specifically to promote plainchant.[11] Both events suggest that many believed that the impetus given by *TLS* had been lost during or immediately after the First World War.

Second, whatever Ultramontanes might say, in practice it was impossible to exclude outside modern influences, especially in a society where Catholicism was not the official state religion and where the principles of religious toleration were generally accepted. The flow of converts alone ensured the transfusion of different ideas, however indirectly they might operate. Despite high-profile conversions amongst the intelligentsia most changes of faith occurred as a result of 'mixed' marriages. In 1939, for instance, these accounted for 31.1 per cent of all Catholic marriages. In this respect the Catholic Church grew, not as a result of Ultramontane insulation, but because people defied it.[12]

Third, there were the inherent tensions and inconsistencies already observed in the plainchant and Renaissance polyphonic causes. Solesmes's redefinition of plainchant did not just weaken the connection between the two genres; attempts to promote it as a vehicle for congregational participation highlighted the fact that Renaissance polyphony was designed for performance by choirs only. Another aspect was the attempt to incorporate English samples of plainchant and Renaissance polyphony within the musical canon of an international musical culture. Ideologically this was a reaction against the claim that the Catholic Church in England was 'Roman', and therefore foreign. This suggests that, subconsciously at least, people such as Shebbeare and Terry felt the tension between the rival claims of an international religious body and English nationalism.

In addition, there was the divide between Ultramontane and scholarly approaches to authenticity. For Ultramontanes, research was fine so long as its results fitted in with their preconceived notions about the nature of the Catholic Church. Moreover, in the interests of uniformity based on continuity with the past, they expected research to produce 'once and for all' solutions. Consequently, they were unlikely to appreciate the potential for unexpected conclusions and perpetually changing results that follow from unfettered academic research and debate in arts subjects. Solesmes's emphasis on the differences between plainchant and Renaissance polyphony was bad enough, since this undermined the musical continuity between the Medieval and Counter-Reformation Church. This was one reason why Rome was slow to abandon the measured chant encapsulated in the Pustet editions. What was worse was the clash between rival theories concerning plainchant rhythm advocated by Pothier and Mocquereau. As has been seen, these lay at the heart of the debates over the Vatican

---

11 Richard Terry, *Music of the Roman Rite: A manual for choirmasters in English speaking countries* (London, 1931), pp. 285–303. Alberic Stacpole, 'Fr Bernard McElligott. II: The Liturgical Years', *AJ*, 77/3 (1972): 86–97.

12 Gilley, p. 39.

Typical editions. The end result, namely the 'toleration' of Mocquereau's rhythmical signs in rival editions, shows that the Vatican accepted the situation with bad grace. The confusion that followed as rival protagonists for each side fought for dominance cannot have helped the plainchant cause in England.

Any drive for uniformity had also to be accommodated to practical contemporary realities. As has been suggested, limitations on the number of performances and the musical capacities of Catholic choirs restricted the number of Renaissance polyphonic compositions companies might be willing to publish. Plainchant was easier for people to sing if accompanied on the organ following the principles of 'modern' four-part harmony, albeit with a nod in the direction of modality. Similarly, Renaissance polyphony was laid out using 'modern' notational symbols in the full vocal score editions to which choirs had become accustomed. Beyond that, any attempt to mass-produce 'authentic' editions of 'ancient' music was essentially an artificial exercise, since it produced an ideal that had never existed in the first place. In the Middle Ages there was no printing press; and during Renaissance times such technology, although available, lacked the late nineteenth-century capacity to serve mass lower- and middle-class markets. This means that diversity of performance must have been the rule in Medieval and Early Modern times. You do not have to accept Peter Jeffrey's ideas about the nature of oral transmission with plainchant. The fact that Solesmes's 'palaeographic workshop' was designed to distil a 'master' version of each plainchant melody is a confession of the diversity that developed in the Middle Ages.

In the end, though, the most basic factors behind the failure of plainchant and Renaissance polyphony to gain complete dominance in the early twentieth century were not to do ideological shortcomings but were the consequence of structural phenomena. Despite the superficial appearance of monolithic uniformity the Catholic Church in England was inherently diverse. Such diversity was expressed institutionally, through the variety of clergy that served these institutions, and liturgically. Institutional diversity is instantly recognisable in the distinctions between, for example, cathedrals, parishes or missions, seminaries, schools and monasteries. Within each there are several subcategories: between rural and urban missions, between communities of monks and nuns, and between the variety of schools for boys and schools for girls (most of them run by convents). Institutional diversity inevitably results in clerical difference, for example the basic divide between secular priests and Regulars. Within the latter further distinctions can be drawn between 'active' orders, such as Jesuits, Oratorians, Dominicans or Sisters of Notre Dame, and more 'contemplative' and enclosed communities, such as Benedictines, Augustinians or Cistercians. In addition, of course, each religious order had its own distinct ethos. There were also numerous hybrids overlapping these different categories, and in each case the balance between different elements was subject to change. Until 1926 Stonyhurst was a Seminary as well as a school. The same was true – in reverse – of Ushaw up till the 1960s, and in both cases staff served the local community as parish priests. In Stonyhurst's case St Peter's Church is still the parish church. In similar fashion St Dominic's Church, Newcastle and St Dominic's Church, Stone served the parish, as well as the monastic communities. The EBC illustrates such duality on a large scale. Despite the 'Downside Movement' many English Benedictines still served – and serve – in many parishes up and down the country. Thomas Anselm Burge was a classic example. Between 1885 and 1898 he was Prior at Ampleforth, where he was a leading proponent of ideas associated with the 'Downside Movement'. Ironically, from 1899 till his death in 1929, he then worked as parish priest on St Austin's mission, Grassendale, on the outskirts of Liverpool. His 'St Austin's Log' shows how much a monk who had taken vows of stability could get about. In March 1901 he visited Pothier at Wandeville. As a result he became a major protagonist of Pothier's method for singing plainchant. In June he was 'invited by Monsignor Corbishley to Ushaw to lecture and convert the House to love of plainchant'. In August 1905 he attended the Strasbourg Conference on plainchant, where 'Dom Mocquereau's strange theories and pretensions' were debated.[13]

Institutional and clerical difference is reflected in the liturgical diversity outlined in Chapter 2. The distinction between the Roman and the various different monastic rites is an obvious example. Another aspect was the relative importance attached by different institutions to each type of service. This was inevitable, given the different objectives of the clergy who served them. In enclosed religious orders everything revolves around the Office, which in turn gives particular significance to the Mass. In parishes, the basic relationship – and distinction – was between the Mass and extra-liturgical services. The former was for the parish community as whole, whereas the latter often grew up to serve the needs of particular guilds and confraternities. In addition the division between outdoor public occasions, such as processions, and more personal indoor devotions, such as Benediction, should be noted. In each case the nature of the service was shaped by its function and the needs of the organisation or group it was supposed to serve.

Liturgical variety, stemming from institutional and clerical divisions, is inherently likely to produce musical difference. In this respect music really was 'the handmaid of the liturgy', but not in the sense envisaged by *TLS*. Music had to cater for a wide variety of different needs. It *had* to be diverse, in style as well as in textual content. An exclusive focus on plainchant and Renaissance polyphony was therefore inadequate. This was something even *TLS* admitted with its highly circumscribed acceptance of more recent music. Moreover, if music had to be diverse, then, for commercial reasons, publishers were likely to respond. As has been seen, not only did they continue to print editions of Viennese Classical and Embassy Chapel repertory, they continued to publish more modern works. In this respect their interests did not necessarily coincide with those of Ultramontanes.

Such diversity was enhanced by the expansion of the Catholic Church in England, not just numerically, but in its infrastructure, as new missions, seminaries, schools and monasteries were established across the country. Diverse expansion of this sort therefore counteracted the tendency towards atrophied uniformity inherent in Ultramontane attitudes and a commercial logic shaped by the need for long print runs protected by copyright. Viewed in this light, the Ultramontane stress on uniformity, preferably focussed on 'ancient' musical styles, looks very like a reaction against the often unspoken, but nonetheless powerful centrifugal tendencies within the burgeoning English Catholic community.

---

13   John A. Davies (ed.), *St Austin's Log 1899–1929* (Liverpool, 1999), pp. 5–6, 14–15 and 19.

Select Bibliography

Books and articles

Almond, Thomas Leo, 'The opening of the new choir', *DR*, 24 (1905): 262–4.

Andrews, Hilda, *Westminster Retrospect: A Memoir of Sir Richard Terry* (London: Oxford University Press, 1948).

Anon., 'A Memoir' [of William Eusebius Andrews], *OJ*, 4 (January–June 1837): 244–6.

Anon., Obituary: 'John Driscoll', in *LN: Our Dead 1939–45* (1947–48): 119–32.

Anon., 'Legislation on Church Music', *DR*, 20 (1901): 47–58.

Anon., 'Music as a part of education', *The Rambler*, 3/13 (January 1849): 311–17.

Anon., 'Religious Festival at Grace Dieu, Leicestershire', *OJ*, 5 (July–December 1837): 30.

Anon., Report of the St Cecilia Festival at Oscott College, *Tablet*, 72 (3 December 1904): 911.

Anon., Report of the opening of the new Choir and Chancel at Downside Abbey, 23 Sept. 1905, *Tablet*, 74 (July–December 1905): 492–5.

Anon., 'Sacred Music and Palestrina', reprinted from the *New Quarterly Review* by the *Catholic Weekly Instructor*, 3 (1846): 103–104.

Anon., trans. Joseph Gallagher, 'Sacrosanctum Consilium: Constitution on the Sacred Liturgy', in Walter M. Abbott, *The Message and Meaning of the Ecumenical Council. The Documents of Vatican II with notes and comments by Catholic, Protestant and Orthodox authorities* (London and Dublin: Geoffrey Chapman, 1966).

Anon., 'St Chad's Cathedral, Birmingham: Consecration and dedication', *OJ*, 12 (26 June 1841): 400–402.

Anon., 'The Four Aims' (of the Society of St Gregory), *ML*, 1/1 (October 1928): 1.

Anon., 'The true method to learn the Church's plainsong', in 'The Pious Association', incorporated into *The Evening Office of the Church* (London: James Marmaduke, 1778).

Anon., *Tractatus De Cantu Ecclesiasticae ad Usum Seminarii Mechlinensis* (Mechlin: H. Dessain,1864).

Apel, Willi, *The Notation of Polyphonic Music 900–1600* (Cambridge, MA:The Medieval Academy of America, 1953; 4th edn revised).

Arx, Jeffrey van, 'Archbishop Manning and the *Kulturkampf*', in *Henry Edward Manning (1808–1892)*, *RH*, 21/2 (October 1992).

Arx, Jeffrey van, 'Ultramontanism and the Catholic Church in British politics', *RH*, 19/3 (May 1989): 322–47

Bainbridge, William S., 'Sir Richard Terry', *WCC*, 33 (1938): 137–8.

Beales, Derek, *Prosperity and Plunder. European Catholic Monasteries in the Age of Revolution 1650–1815* (Cambridge: Cambridge University Press, 2003).

Beck, George (ed.), *The English Catholics 1850–1950: Essays to commemorate the centenary of the restoration of the hierarchy in England and Wales* (London: Burns and Oates, 1950).

Bellenger, Aidan, 'Sir Richard Terry and Downside', *The Raven* (1995): 53–7.

Bellenger, Aidan, 'The English Benedictines: the search for a monastic identity' in Judith Loades (ed.), *Monastic Studies: The Continuity of Tradition* (Bangor: Headstart History, 1990).

Bellenger, Aidan, *The French Exiled Clergy in the British Isles after 1789: A Historical Introduction and Working List* (Bath: Downside Abbey, 1986).

Bellenger, Aidan (compiler), *English and Welsh Priests 1558–1800: A working list* (Bath: Downside Abbey, 1984).

Bénédictins de Solesmes [Mocquereau, André] (ed.), *PM*, 1 (1889), containing the St Gall Codex 339 in photographic facsimiles. Solesmes: Imprimerie St Pierre.

Bénédictins de Solesmes [Mocquereau, André] (ed.), *PM*, 2 (in 2 parts) (1891–92), containing a study of many mss and printed illustrations of the *Justus Ut Palma* chant with an extended commentary and the article 'De L'Influence De L'Accent Tonique Latin Et Ou Cursus Sur La Structure Mélodique Et Rythmique De La Phrase Grégorienne' (pp. 7–77).

Bénédictins de Solesmes [Mocquereau, André] (ed.), *PM*, 4 (1894), containing the Einsiedeln Codex 121 in photographic facsimiles.

Bénédictins de Solesmes [Mocquereau, André] (ed.), 'Du Role Et De La Place De L'Accent Tonique Latin Dans La Rythme Grégorien', *PM*, 7 (1901): 21–334.

Bénédictins de Solesmes [Mocquereau, André] (ed.), *PM*, 10 (1909–12) containing articles on 'Les Signes Sangalliens Et Solesmiens' and 'Aperçu Sur La Notation Du Manuscrit 239 De Laon. Sa Concordance Avec Les "Codices" Rythmiques Sangalliens' pp. 65–89, 90–176 and 177–211.

Benedictines of Solesmes [actually Mocquereau, André], *Petit Traité de Psalmodie* (Solesmes: Imprimerie Saint-Pierre, 1897).

Benedictines of Stanbrook [actually Corrigan, Felicitas K.], *In a great tradition: tribute to Dame Laurentia McLachlan* (London: John Murray, 1956).

Benedictines of Stanbrook [actually McLachlan, Laurentia], *Grammar of Plainsong* (Worcester, Stanbrook Abbey and London, Burns and Oates Ltd; New York, Art and Book Co. and Cincinnati: Benziger Bros. 1905. In two parts. 2nd and 3rd revised edns Islington and Liverpool: Rushworth and Dreaper, 1924 and 1934).

Benedictines of Stanbrook Abbey [actually Laurentia McLachlan], *Rules of Psalmody adapted from the second edition of the 'Petit Traité de Psalmodie'* (Tournai, Rome: Desclee, Lefebvre et Cie., 1904).

Benedictines of Stanbrook Abbey [actually Laurentia McLachlan], *Gregorian Music: An outline of musical palaeography illustrated by facsimiles from ancient manuscripts* (London and Leamington: Art and Book Co., 1897).

Benedictines of Stanbrook Abbey [actually Laurentia McLachlan], *Handbook of Rules of singing and phrasing Plainsong* (London: Art and Book Co, 1897; 5th ed., Worcester, Stanbrook Abbey, 1957).

Bergeron, Katherine, *Decadent Enchantments: The Revival of Gregorian Chant at Solesmes* (Berkeley, Los Angeles, London: University of California Press, 1998).

Berry, Mary, 'The restoration of the Chant and seventy-five years of recording', *EM*, 7 (April 1979): 197–216.

Bewerunge, Henry, 'The Vatican Edition of Plainchant. Part I', *IER* (4th series) 19 (1906): 44–63.

Bewerunge, Henry, 'The Vatican Edition of Plainchant. Part II', *IER* (4th series) 20 (1906): 414–28.

Blom, Joannes Maria, *The Post-Tridentine Primer* (n.p.: Krips Repro B.V. Mappel, 1979).

Blom, Joannes Maria, Blom, J., Korsten, F. and Scott, Geoffrey (compilers), *English Catholic Books 1700–1800: A bibliography* (Aldershot: Scolar Press, 1996).

Borromeo, St Charles (ed.), trans. John A. McHugh and Charles J. Callan, *Catechism of the Council of Trent for Parish Priests* (Rockford, IL: Tan Books and Publishers Inc., 1982).

Bossy, John, *The English Catholic Community 1570–1850* (London: Darton, Longman and Todd, 1975).

Boylan, Anthony, 'Renewing the Renewal I: The new General Instruction of the Roman Missal', *ML*, 31/2 (No. 315) (Summer, 2005): 11–12.

Boylan, Anthony, 'Liturgiam authenticam – Is this Liturgical Renewal?', *ML*, 28/3 and 4 (Autumn and Winter, 2002): 10–15.

Britten, James, 'Letter to the Editor' (about the *Westminster Hymnal*), *Tablet*, 88 (6 July, and 10 August 1912): 27 and 222–3.

Butler, Cuthbert, *The Vatican Council 1869–1870* (London: Collins, 1930/1962R).

'C.R.', 'Roman Catholic Church Music Notes', *OC*, 20 (1912–13): 229–30, 274–5, 291, 342–3, 380–81. 22 (1914–15): 36–7, 78–9, 132–3, 178–9, 209, 433–4.

Cabrol, Fernand, trans. C.M. Anthony, *The Holy Sacrifice: A Simple Explanation of the Mass* (London: Burns Oates and Washbourne Ltd, 1937).

Cabrol, Fernand, trans. C.M. Anthony, *The Mass of the Western Rite* (London: Sands and Co., 1934).

Cagin, Paul and Mocquereau, André, *Plainchant and Solesmes* (London: Burns and Oates Ltd., internal references date its publication to 1904).

Cagin, Paul, 'The work of Solesmes in the restoration of Plainchant', *Tablet*, 72 (5 November 1904): 722–4.

Cardine, Eugene, trans. Herbert M. Fowells, *Gregorian Semiology* (Solesmes: 1982).

Casartelli, Louis C., 'A Letter on Church Music', *The Harvest* (26 January 1906): 5–8.

Casartelli, Louis C., 'Episcopal Notices', *The Harvest* (December 1903): 299–300.

'The Cathedral Clergy'(compilers), *A History of St Chad's Cathedral, Birmingham* (Birmingham, Cornish Bros. Ltd., 1904).

Champ, Judith, *A Temple of Living Stones: Oscott College Chapel* (Oscott: St Mary's College, 2002).

Champ, Judith (ed.), *Oscott College 1838–1988. A volume of commemorative essays*. (Oscott: St Mary's College, 1988).

Clifford, C.G., 'The Choir', *UM*, 95 (July, 1935): 106–12.

Collins, Henry B.,'Ecclesiastical Polyphony', *ML*, 2/2 (April, 1931): 28–31.

Collins, Henry B., 'The Polyphonic Motet', *ML*, 2/4 (October 1931): 84–6; 3/1 (January 1932): 4–6; 3/2 (April 1932): 58–60; 3/3 (July 1932): 62–4; 3/4 (October 1932): 86–9.

Combe, Pierre M., 'La Restauration du Chant Grégorien. III: L'Oeuvre de Saint Pie X', *EG*, 8 (1967): 139 221.

Combe, Pierre M., 'Préliminaires de la Réforme Grégorienne de S. Pie X' [in three parts], *EG*, 7 (1967): 66–139.

Combe, Pierre M., 'La Réforme du Chant et des Livres du Chant Grégorien à L'Abbaye de Solesmes 1833–1883', *EG*, 6 (1963): 186–234.

Congregation for Divine Worship and the Sacraments, 'Liturgiam Authenticam' (Latin text) *Notitiae*, 37/3–4 (2001): 120–74.

Connelly, Joseph, "One in voice and heart": The Motu Proprio of Pius X after fifty years', *Tablet*, 202 (21 November 1953): 495–6.

Coppa, Frank, *The Modern Papacy since 1789* (London and New York: Addison Wesley Longman, 1998).

Cooper, Victoria L., *The House of Novello. Practice and Policy of a Victorian Music Publisher 1829–1866* (Aldershot: Ashgate, 2003).

'Gathered' by Coover, James, *Music Publishing. Copyright and Piracy in Victorian England. A twenty-five year chronicle. 1881–1906 from the pages of the 'Musical Opinion and Music Trade Review' and other English music journals of the period* (London and New York: Mansell Publishing Ltd., 1985).

Corp, Edward, 'The Court as a centre of Italian music', in Edward Corp et al., *A Court in exile: the Stuarts in France 1689–1718* (Cambridge: Cambridge University Press 2004).

Corp, Edward, 'Music at the Stuart Court at Urbino 1717–1718', *Mlet*, 81/3 (August 2000): 351–63.

Crichton, James D., 'The Liturgy of the Roman Catholic Church over one hundred years – an interview with Monsignor James D. Crichton', *ML*, 27/1 (No. 302) (Summer, 2001): 10.

Crichton, James D., *As it was: Reminiscences and Prophecies* (Mildenhall: Decani Press, 1991).

Crichton, James D., *Worship in a Hidden Church* (Blackrock: The Columba Press, 1988).

Crichton, James D., Winstone, Harold, and Ainslie, John (eds), *English Catholic Worship. Liturgical Renewal in England since 1900* (London: Geoffrey Chapman, 1979).

Crocker, James D., 'Gregorian Studies in the twenty first century', *PMM*, 4/1 (April 1995): 33–81.

Cross, Tony, 'Robert Rudolph Suffield's Dominican Decade (1860–1870)', *RH*, 28/1 (May, 2006): 103–128.

Daly, Kieran Anthony, *Catholic Church Music in Ireland 1878–1903: The Cecilian Reform Movement* (Dublin: Four Courts Press, 1995).

Danjou, F. (with comments at the end by 'A.J.P.'), 'Discovery of a complete and authentic copy of the original antiphonary of St Gregory', *The Rambler*, 3 (November 1848): 174–80.

Darby, Rosemarie, *The Music of the Roman Catholic Embassy Chapels in London. 1765–1825* (University of Manchester (John Rylands Library): MMus thesis, October 1984).

Davies, John A. (ed.), *Thomas Anselm Burge. St Austin's Log 1899–1929* (Liverpool: St Austin's, Grassendale, 1999).

Dawney, Michael, 'Richard Terry: A Pioneer in Church Music', *ML*, 14/2 (April, 1988): 39–42.

Day, Timothy, 'Sir Richard Terry and 16th Century Polyphony', *EM*, 12/2 (May, 1994): 297–309.

Dixon, Graham, 'The Performance of Palestrina: Some questions, but few answers', *EM*, 22 (November 1994): 667–75.

McClelland, Vivian, A. and Hodgetts, Michael (eds), *From without the Flaminian Gate: 150 Years of Catholic History in England and Wales 1850–2000* (London: Darton, Longman and Todd, 1999).

Doyle, Peter, *Westminster Cathedral 1895–1995* (London: Geoffrey Chapman, 1995).

Durkin, Margaret, *A Short History of St Mary's, Burnley* (Burnley: Private publication, n.d.).

Eaton, Robert, 'At Ratisbon in 1894', *ML*, 3/3 (July, 1932): 60–61.

Edwards, Eanswythe, 'The influence of the EBC on Stanbrook Abbey. Dom Gueranger's revival', *EBC History Symposium* (1985): 31–6.

Edwards, Eanswythe and Truran, Margaret, 'Dom Laurence Shepherd', *EBC History Symposium* (1985): 37–59.

Egerton, F. Clement, *A Handbook of Church Music* (London: R. and T. Washbourne Ltd, 1909).

Eudine, A., 'Letter to the Editor: The Solesmes Plainsong', *Tablet*, 72 (July–December 1904): 170.

Fellerer, Karl Gustav, 'Church Music and the Council of Trent', *Musical Quarterly*, 39 (1953): 576–94.

Ferrarri, Gustave, 'Karle Proske', in J.A. Fuller Maitland (ed.), *Grove's Dictionary of Music and Musicians* (London: Macmillan and Co. Ltd., 1907) 3: 826–7.

Field, Justin, *The Simplicity of Plainsong* (New York: J. Fischer and Bros., 1931).

Fillion, L.C., *The New Psalter of the Roman Breviary* (London/St Louis: B. Herder 1915; original edition published from Paris in 1912).

Flon, Nancy Marie de, *Edward Caswall, Newman's brother and friend* (n.p.: Gracewing, 2005).

Foley, B.C., *Some Other People of the Penal Times: Aspects of a unique social and religious phenomenon* (Lancaster: Cathedral Bookshop, 1991).

Fortescue, Adrian, *The Ceremonies of the Roman Rite Described* (London: Burns and Oates, 1918. A fourth revised edition was prepared by J.B. O'Connell in 1932).

Fortescue, Adrian, *The Mass: A study of the Roman Liturgy* (London: Burns and Oates, 1932).

Fortescue, Adrian, 'Liturgy', in *The Catholic Encyclopaedia* (London: The Encyclopaedia Press, 1914) 9: 306.

Frere, Walter H., Briggs, H.B., Stainer, John and Shebbeare, Wilfrid.G. Alphege, *A Manual of Plainsong* (London: Novello and Co., 1902).

Fuller, R.C., *'Steadfast in loyalty': A short history of Warwick St Church formerly the Royal Bavarian Chapel with a brief guide for visitors* (London: Church of Our Lady of the Assumption and St Gregory, 1973).

Gajard, Joseph, trans. R. Cecile Gabin, *The Solesmes Method* (Collegeville, MN: The Liturgical Press, 1960).

Gasquet, Aidan, 'Revising the Vulgate', *DubR*, 143 (July–October 1908): 264–73.

Gasquet, Aidan and Bishop, Edmund (eds), *The Bosworth Psalter: An account of a manuscript formerly belonging to O. Turville-Petre esq. of Bosworth Hall, now Add Mss 37517 at the British Museum* (London: George Bell and Sons, 1908).

Gasquet, Aidan, *The Monastic Life* (London: 1904).

Gasquet, Aidan, *Henry VIII and the English Monasteries: An attempt to illustrate the history of their suppression* (London: John Hodges, 1889, 2 vols).

Gatard, Augustin, 'Letter to the Editor', *Tablet*, 69 (6 June 1903): 899.

Gatard, Augustin, 'Gregorian Music: Its nature and history', *Tablet*, 69 (21 March 1903): 464–6.

Gillow, Joseph, *A Literary and Biographical History or Bibliographical Dictionary of English Catholics from the Break with Rome, in 1534, to the present time* (London: Burns and Oates, 1885, 5 vols).

Gladstone, Francis Edward, 'Letter to the Editor' (about *The Westminster Hymnal*). *Tablet*, 88 (20 July 1912): 104.

Gray, Freddy, 'Bad Church music to be outlawed', *The Catholic Herald*, No. 6210 (29 January 2005): 1.

Green, Bernard, 'Cuthbert Hedley: 1837–1915', *AJ*, 93 (1988): 21–8.

Guy, Robert (arranger, under the supervision of Hedley, Bishop Cuthbert), *The Synods in English being the text of the Four Synods in English translated into English* (Stratford on Avon: St Gregory's Press, 1886).

Gueranger, Prosper, trans. Laurence Shepherd, *The Liturgical Year* (Worcester: Stanbrook Abbey, 1867/R1895).

Haberl, Franz Xavier, trans. N. Donnelly, *Magister Choralis: A theoretical and practical manual of Gregorian Chant* (Ratisbon: Pustet, 1877 (4th edition); a revised Italian translation prepared by De Santi, Angelo in 1888 and a French translation appeared in 1896).

Haigh, Christopher, *The English Reformations: Politics and Society under the Tudors* (London: Oxford University Press, 1993).

Haigh, Christopher, 'The continuity of Catholicism in the English Reformation', *PP*, 93 (November 1981): 37–69.

Halsbury's Statutes of England and Wales (London: Butterworths, 1989/R2000, 4th edition, vol. 11).

Hall, Martin, 'An interview with J.D. Crichton', *ML*, 27/2 (Summer 2001): 15–29.

Hameline, Jean-Yves, 'L'intérêt pour les chants des fidèles dans la catholicisme français d'Ancien Régime et le premier mouvement liturgique en France', *La Maison Dieu*, 241 (2005): 29–75.

Harlay, John, *William Byrd: Gentleman of the Chapel Royal* (Aldershot: Scolar Press, 1997).

Harper, John, 'Gothic revivals: Issues of influence, ethos and idiom in Nineteenth-century English monasteries', in Dibble, Jeremy and Zon, Bennett (eds), *Nineteenth-Century British Music Studies Vol. 2* (Aldershot: Ashgate, 2002): 15–31.

Harper, John, *The Forms and Orders of Western Liturgy from the Fourth to the Eighteenth Century. A historical introduction and guide for students and musicians* (London: Oxford University Press, 1991).

Harrison, James, *How to Sing Plainchant. Chiefly for the use of Dominican Choirs* (Ditchling: St Dominic's Press, 1920).

Harwood, Thomas, 'Public opinion and the 1908 Eucharistic Congress', *RH*, 25/1 (May 2000): 120–33.

Haskell, Harry, *The Early Music Revival: A History* (London: Thames and Hudson, 1988).

Hastings, Adrian, *A History of English Christianity 1920–85* (London: Collins, 1986).

Hayburn, Robert F., *Papal Legislation on Sacred Music 95AD to 1977AD* (Collegeville, MN: The Liturgical Press, 1979).

Heyer, Friedrich, trans. D.W.D. Shaw, *The Catholic Church from 1648 to 1870* (London: A. and C. Black, 1963/R1969).

Higgins, P.V., 'The Psalms of the Vulgate', *IER* (4th series), 22 (1907): 372–9.

Hedley, Cuthbert, *Church Music: A Pastoral Letter* (London: CTS, 1897).

Hedley, Cuthbert, 'The Monastic Office'. *Tablet*, 106 (July–December 1905): 492–4.

Heimann, Mary, *Catholic Devotion in Victorian England* (Oxford: Clarendon Press, 1995).

Hiley, David, *Western Plainchant: A Handbook* (Oxford: Clarendon Press, 1993).

Hodgson, B., 'The Dominicans in Newcastle Part II 1539–1992', *NCH*, 33 (1992): 31–8.

Hodgson, Gill, *St Mary and St Everilda* (Everingham: private publication, 1988).

Holmes, J. Derek, *The Triumph of the Holy See. A short history of the Papacy in the nineteenth century* (London: Burns and Oates/Patmos Press, 1978).

Hurd, Michael, *Vincent Novello and Company* (London: Granada, 1981).

Hutchings, Arthur, *Church Music in the Nineteenth Century* (London: Herbert Jenkins, 1967).

Hutton, Andrew, Letter of Obituary about Richard Terry, *Tablet*, 171 (January–June 1938): 579.

Jansen, N.A., *Les Vrais Principes du chant Grégorien* (Mechlin: P.J. Hanicq, 1845).

Jeffrey, Peter, *Re-envisioning Past Musical Cultures: Ethnomusicology in the study of Gregorian chant* (Chicago: University of Chicago Press, 1992/R1995).

Jeffrey, Peter, 'A Chant historian reads *Liturgiam Authenticam: The Latin Liturgical Translation*', *Worship*, 78/1 (January 2004): 2–24.

Johner, Dominic, trans. W.H. Hoffer, *A New Manual of Gregorian Chant* (Ratisbon: Pustet, 1914).

Joncas, Jan Michael, *From Sacred Song to Ritual Music. Twentieth-Century Understandings of Roman Catholic Worship Music* (Collegeville, MN: The Liturgical Press, 1997).

Julian, John, *A Dictionary of Hymnology* (London: John Murray, 1992).

Jungmann, Joseph, trans. Francis Bonner, *The Mass of the Roman Rite: Its Origins and Development* (New York, Boston, Cincinnati, Chicago, San Francisco: Benziger Bros. Inc., 1950, 2 vols).

Kassler, Michael (ed.), *The English Bach Awakening: Knowledge of J.S. Bach and his music in England 1750–1830* (Aldershot: Ashgate, 2004).

Kirk, John, ed. John Pollen and Edwin Barton, *Biographies of English Catholics in the Eighteenth Century* (London: Burns and Oates, 1909).

Kleiner, Peter, Shore, E.P., McFarlane, James and Gavin, Melville, 'Copyright' in Sadie, Stanley (ed.), *The New Grove Dictionary of Music and Musicians* (London: Macmillan, 2nd ed, 2000) 6: 421–5.

Knuckley, T.H., 'Letter to the Editor', *Tablet*, 87 (January–June 1912): 1022.

Knuckley, T.H., 'Letter to the Editor' (about *The Westminster Hymnal*), *Tablet*, 88 (29 June 1912): 1022.

Kollar, René, *Westminster Cathedral: From Dream to Reality* (Edinburgh: Faith and Life Publications Ltd, 1987).

Lambillotte, Louis, ed. P.J. Dufour, *Esthetique théorie et pratique du chant Grégorien restauré d'après la doctrine des anciens et les sources primitives* (Paris: Librairie d'Adrien Le Clerc et cie, 1855).

Landon, Howard Robbins, *Haydn: Chronicle and Works: The Years of The Creaton 1796–1800* (London: Thames and Hudson, 1977).

Landon, Howard Robbins and Wyn Jones, David, *Haydn: His life and music* (London, Thames and Hudson, 1988).

Leichtentritt, Hugo, 'The Reforms of Trent and its effect on music', *MQ*, 30 (1944): 319–28.

Le Mée, Katherine, *Chant: The Origins, Form, Practice and Healing Power of Gregorian Chant* (London: Random House Ltd, R1994).

Lewis, Anthony, 'English Catholic Music' in Spink, Ian (ed.), *The Blackwell History of Music in Britain: The seventeenth century* (Oxford: Blackwell, 1992).

Little, Bryan, *Catholic Churches since 1623* (London: Robert Hale, 1966).

Little, Vilma, *The Chant: A Simple and Complete Method for Teachers and Students* (London: Herder Book Co. and Tournai: Desclee et Cie., 1938).

Little, Vilma, *The Sacrifice of Praise: An introduction to the meaning and use of the Divine Office* (London: Longman, Green and Co., 1957).

Mager, Sybille, *The Debate over the Revival of Ancient Church Music in Victorian England* (Cambridge: PhD thesis, 2000).

Mager, Sybille, '*Music becomes a prayer*': The movement for the reform of Catholic Church music in late nineteenth-century Germany and Austria (Cambridge: MPhil thesis, 1994).

'Magister Choralis': 'From Our Roman Catholic Correspondent', *OC*, 8 (1900–1901): 6–7, 74, 226–7, 300; 9 (1903–1904): 75, 127–8, 135, 161, 180, 227; 12 (1904–1905): 21, 55, 93, 131, 153–4, 164, 257; 13 (1905–1906): 11, 44, 70, 130, 298; 14 (1906–1907): 10, 36, 187, 222, 229, 260, 283.

Malcolm, Joan, 'The Ampleforth Fragments: A preliminary survey', *PMM*, 7/2 (1998): 129–40.

McClelland, Vivian A. and Hodgetts, Michael (eds), *From without the Flaminian Gate: 150 Years of Roman Catholicism in England and Wales 1850–2000* (London: Darton, Longman and Todd, 1999).

McLachlan, Laurentia, 'Dom André Mocquéreau, 1849–1930', *ML*, 1/2 (January 1930): 74–5.

McLachlan, Laurentia (ed.), 'Antiphonaire Monastique XIIIeme Siècle F. 160 de la bibliothéque de la Cathédrale de Worcester' in *PM*, 12 (Paris, Rome, Tournai: Desclée et Cie, 1922–25).

McSwiney, James, *Translation of the Psalms and Canticle with Commentary* (London/Dublin: Sands and Co., 1901).

Milburn, David, *A History of Ushaw College* (Durham: Ushaw College, 1964).

Millar, Francis, 'Church Music', *OJ*, 19 (June–December1844): 202.

Millar, Francis, 'Choral Music in St Chad's Cathedral, Birmingham, *OJ*, 15 (22 October 1842): 271–2.

Miller, John, *Popery and Politics in England 1660–1688* (Cambridge: Cambridge University Press, 1973).

Mitchell, W.H., 'The first fruits of the Gregorian Commission', *Tablet*, 74 (July–December 1905): 900.

Mocquereau, André, trans. Tone, Aileen, *Le Nombre Musical Grégorien: A Study of Gregorian Musical Rhythm*. Vol. 1, part 1 (Paris, Tournai, Rome: Desclée and Co., 1932).

Mocquereau, André and Gajard, Joseph. Approved translation by Laurence Bevenot, *The Rhythmic Tradition in the Manuscripts* (Paris, Tournai, Rome: Desclée and Co., 1952).

Mocquereau, André, 'The Solesmes School of Plainsong. Part I. Its Critical Method', *Tablet*, 72 (5 November 1904): 763–5.

Mocquereau, André, 'The Solesmes School of Plainsong. Part II. The history of a neum', *Tablet*, 72 (19 November 1904): 804–806.

Mocquereau, André, 'The Solesmes School of Plainsong. Part III. Evolution in taste and tradition', *Tablet*, 72 (26 November 1904): 883–4.

Moloney, Michael, 'Gregorian Music. 1. The work of restoration', *UM*, 15 (March, 1905): 25–54.

More, Sr. Thomas (alias Berry, Mary), *The performance of Plainsong in the later Middle Ages and the sixteenth century* (Cambridge: PhD thesis, 1968).

Morrisroe, P., 'The character of music at Low Mass', *IER* (4th series), 21 (1907): 201–202.

Moynihan, Paul (ed.), 'From the archives: An English St Gregory Society' (supplies the original text of Bernard McElligott's letter to *The Universe* advocating the foundation of an English Society of St Gregory), *ML*, 30/3 (no. 315) (Autumn, 2004): 10.

Muir, Thomas E., *Stonyhurst* (Cirencester: St Omers Press, R2006 (revised ed.)). For the original edition, see *Stonyhurst College, 1593–1993* (London: James and James, 1992).

Muir, Thomas E., 'Charles Newsham, Henry Hemy, John Richardson and the rise of Benediction Music in Nineteenth-century Catholic England', *NCH*, 47 (2006): 10–22.

Muir, Thomas E., 'Music at the church of Our Lady and St Michael, Alston Lane, near Preston', *NWCH*, 33 (2006): 71–80.

Muir, Thomas E., 'The reception of Joseph Haydn's Music in the English Roman Catholic Community', *Haydn Society of Great Britain*, 24 (2005): 3–18.

Muir, Thomas E., 'Music for St Peter's Church 1811–1940', *SM*, 52 (no. 498) (2002): 277–91.

Muir, Thomas E., 'Vision and reality: Edward Hansom's work at Stonyhurst and Downside' (*EBC History Symposium*: Private publication, 1996: 34 53).

Nocent, Adrian, 'The Mass from Pius V to Vatican II', *Liturgy*, 8/3 (February–March, 1984): 94–112.

Norman, Edward, *The English Catholic Church in the Nineteenth Century* (Oxford: Clarendon Press, 1984).

Oates, D., Hemy, R.A. and Thomas, D.H., 'Henri Frederick Hemy (1818–1888) and his descendants', *NCH*, 36 (1995): 31–41.

Oberhoffer, Heinrich, 'Desiderata, In connection with the official Ratisbon edition of the Choral Books. Part I', *AJ*, 2 (1896): 195–202.

Oberhoffer, Heinrich, 'Desiderata: In connection with the official Ratisbon edition of the Choral Books. Part II: The inaccuracies of the edition', *AJ*, 2 (1896): 318–37.

O'Connell, James, *The Celebration of Mass: A study of the rubrics of the Roman Missal* (London: Burns Oates and Washbourne Ltd., 1940).

O'Keefe, Dunstan, 'Gregory the Great: Past legend and present interpretation', *ML*, 30/1 (no. 313) (2004): 10–14, and 30/2 (no. 314) (2004): 23–5.

O'Regan, Noel, 'The performance of Palestrina: some further observations', *EM*, 24 (February 1996): 145–54.

O'Shea, William J., *The Worship of the Church: A companion in liturgical studies*. (London: Darton, Longman and Todd, 1957/R1960).

Oldmeadow, Ernest, 'The Catholic Church and Music: A Hundred Years of Catholic Music', in (introduced by) Bourne, Francis, *Catholic Emancipation 1829–1929. Essays by various writers* (London: Longmans, Green and Co., 1929: 121–40.)

Olleson, Philip and Palmer, Fiona, 'Publishing music from the Fitzwilliam Museum, Cambridge: The work of Vincent Novello and Samuel Wesley in the 1820s', *Journal of the Royal Musicological Association*, 130/1 (2005): 38–73.

Olleson, Philip, *Samuel Wesley, the man and his music* (Woodbridge: Boydell and Brewer, 2003).

Olleson, Philip, 'The London Embassy Chapels and their music in the eighteenth and early nineteenth centuries' in Wyn Jones, David (ed.), *Music in Eighteenth Century Britain*) (Aldershot: Ashgate, 2000).

Olleson, Philip, 'Samuel Wesley and the *Missa De Spiritu Sancto*', *RH*, 24/3 (May, 1999): 309–319.

Palmer, Fiona, *Vincent Novello (1781–1861). Music for the Masses* (Aldershot: Ashgate, 2006).

Pereiro, James, '"Truth before peace": Manning and Infallibility', in *Henry Edward Manning (1808–1892)*, *RH*, 21/2 (October 1992): 218–53.

Phelan, Helen, 'Gregorian Chant and contemporary liturgy', *ML*, 28/1 (no. 305) (Spring, 2002): 20–22.

'Philalethes', 'Consecration of churches at Grace Dieu, Whitwick and Mount St. Bernard', *OJ*, 5 (July–December 1837): 283–4 (reprint from the *Staffordshire Examiner*).

'Philharmonicus', 'Père Lambillotte queries on Ecclesiastical Music', *The Rambler*, 3 (1849): 536.

Plumb, Brian, 'A Victorian Monk Musician. Fr. J.E. Turner at Ampleforth', *AJ*, 79: 61–4.

Plumb, Brian, 'Dead, Buried and Scorned? Catholic Church Music 1791–1960', *NWCH*, 26 (1999): 70–95.

Plumb, Brian, 'Hymnbooks revisited', *NWCH*, 27 (2000): 68–91.

Pouderoijn, Kes, 'Work on the new *Antiphonale Romanum*', in Hartley, Mark (ed.), *Panel of Monastic Musicians Conference (full texts and summaries). Ampleforth Abbey 14–18 October 2002* (Panel of Monastic Musicians, 2003).

Pothier, Joseph, *Les Mélodies Grégoriènnes d'après la tradition* (Tournai: Desclée, Léfebvre et Cie., 1881).

Potiron, Henri, 'The aesthetics of Gregorian accompaniment', *ML*, 1/4: 97–100.

Pugin, Augustus Welby, *An Ernest Plea for the Revival of the Ancient Plainsong* (London: Charles Dolman, 1850).

Rayburn, John, *Gregorian Chant: A history of the controversy concerning its rhythm* (Westport, CT: Greenwood Press, 1964).

Reid, Alcuin, *The Organic Development of the Liturgy: the principles of liturgical reform and their relatonship to the twentieth-century liturgical movement prior to the Second Vatican Council* (Farnborough: St Michael's Press, 2004).

Report of the Archbishops' Commission on Church Music, *In Tune with Heaven* (London: Church House Publishing/Hodder and Stoughton, 1992).

Reynolds, E.E. (ed.), *The Mawhood Diary*, CRS, 50 (1956).

Richards, Michael, 'Prelude: 1890s to 1920', in Crichton, James D., Winstone, Harold and Ainslie, John (eds), *English Catholic Worship: Liturgical Renewal in England since 1900* (London: Geoffrey Chapman, 1979).

Riley, Emma, 'John Lingard and the liturgy', in Philipps, Peter (ed.), *Lingard Remembered: Essays to mark the sesquicentenary of John Lingard's death*, CRS (2004).

Robertson, Alec, *Requiem: Music of Mourning and Consolation* (London: Cassell, 1967).

Robertson, Alec, *Music of the Catholic Church* (London: Burns and Oates, 1961).

Robertson, Alec, *The Interpretation of Plainchant: A preliminary study* (London: Oxford University Press, 1937).

Roche, Jerome, '"The praise of it endureth for ever": The posthumous publication of Palestrina's music', *EM*, 22 (November 1994): 331–8.

Rock, Daniel, rev. Weale, W.H. James, *Hierugia or the Holy Sacrifice of the Mass with notes and dissertations elucidating its doctrines and ceremonies* (London: John Hodges, 1892, 2 vols).

Rottmann, Alexander, *London Catholic Churches: A historical and artistic record* (London: Sands and Co., 1926).

Routley, Eric (with a concluding chapter by Dakers, Lionel), *A Short History of English Church Music* (London: Mowbray, 1977/R1997).

Rowntree, John, 'Lulworth Chapel and a missing Arne Mass', *MT*, 128 (1987): 347–9.

'Sacerdos', 'Article IX – Plainchant', *DubR*, 2/2 (1874): 172–204.

Sacred Congregation of Rites, trans. Howell, Clifford, *An instruction by the Sacred Congregation of Rites on Sacred Music and Liturgy in the spirit of the Encyclical Letters 'Musica Dacra Disciplina' and 'Mediator Dei' of Pope Pius XII* (London, Herder, 1959).

Schmitt, A., *Méthode pratique de chant Grégorien. Leçons données aux Bénédictins du temple* (Paris: Charles Chauvin/Blanc-Pascal, 1885).

Scott, Geoffrey, 'Bishop Austin O'Neill OSB 1841–1911', *DM*, 163 (2000): 2–7.

Scott, Geoffrey, 'Bishop Austin O'Neill OSB: 1841–1911, An Edmundian enduring *Diu Quidem*' (EBC History Conference, 1999).

Shebbeare, Wilfrid, G. Alphcge, *The Music of the Liturgy* (Beaconsfield: Society of St Gregory Pamphlets, 1959).

Shepherd, Lancelot C., *The Mass in the West* (London: Burns and Oates, Faith and Fact Books 114, 1962).

Sherr, Richard, 'Competence and incompetence in the Papal Choir in the age of Palestrina', *EM*, 22 (November 1994): 607–29.

Simpson, Mary, 'Letter to the Editor' (concerning *The Westminster Hymnal*), *Tablet*, 88 (27 July 1912): 146.

Stephen, John, *The Adeste Fideles. A study of its origin and development* (Buckfast Abbey: Buckfast Abbey Publications, 1947).

Sutton, Edward S., 'The Benedictine Abbey of Quarr', *WCC* (November 1922): 210–12.

'T.F.C.F.', 'From Our Roman Catholic Correspondent', *OC*, 23 (1915–16): 76, 116, 158.

Terry, Richard, *Music of the Roman Rite: A Manual for Choirmasters in English Speaking Countries* (London: Burns Oates and Washbourne Ltd., 1931).

Terry, Richard, *A Forgotten Psalter and other essays* (London: Oxford University Press, 1929).

Terry, Richard, 'Congregational Singing', *WCC*, 1922: 195–6.

Terry, Richard, 'Church Music and the 'Motu Proprio' (text of an address delivered at a CTS conference held in Preston), *Tablet*, 78 (July–December 1907): 617–22.

Terry, Richard, *Catholic Church Music* (London: Greening and Co., 1907).

Thurston, Herbert, 'Our Catholic Music a Century Ago', *WCC*, 1926: 108–114.

Thurston, Herbert, 'Our Benediction Service', *The Month*, 1905: 45–9.

Truran, Margaret, 'Chant from a historical perspective', *PMMN*, 1998: 3–4.

Truran, Margaret, 'Music and Liturgy in Stanbrook's tradition', *PMMN*, 1985. n.p.

Turbett, Richard, 'An affair of honour: "Tudor Church Music," the ousting of Sir Richard Terry, and a trust vindicated', *MLet*, 76/4 (1995): 593–600.

Turbett, Richard, 'A monument to enthusiasm and industry: Further light on "Tudor Church Music", *MusLet*, 81/3 (2000): 433–7.

Turner, Joseph, F., 'The Liverpool School of Plainsong', *ML*, 1/2 (January 1930): 78–81.

Turner, Joseph, F., 'The Plainchant: A note for the editor' in Ibison, James and Maxwell, John (eds), *Upholland College: A record of the new buildings 1923–30* (Upholland: 1930: 41–3).

Turner, Joseph, F., 'Plainsong Progress', *ML*, 2/2 (April 1931): 38–46.

Tweedy, J.M., *Popish Elvet. The History of St Cuthbert's, Durham* (Durham: Private publication, n.d., in two parts).

Ullathorne, William, *A discourse given at St Chad's Cathedral on the half jubilee of its choir by Bishop Ullathorne* (London: Burns and Oates, 1882).

'Viator', 'From Our Roman Catholic Correspondent', *OC*, 18 (1910–11): 116.

Walsh, Barbara, *Roman Catholic Nuns in England and Wales 1800–1937: A Social History* (Dublin: Irish Academic Press, 2002).

Ward, Bernard, *The Sequel to Catholic Emancipation 1829–1850* (London: Longmans and Co., 1915, 2 vols).

Ward, Bernard, *The Eve of Catholic Emancipation 1803–1829* (London: Longmans and Co., 1911, 3 vols).

Ward, Bernard, *The Dawn of the Catholic Revival in England 1781–1803* (London: Longmans and Co., 1909, 2 vols).

Wareing, E. Vincent, 'Tenebrae in Westminster Cathedral', *WCC*, 1907: 22–6.

Washington, Henry, 'The Oratory Musical Tradition' in Napier, M. and Laing, A. (eds), *The London Oratory Centenary. 1884–1984* (London:Trefoil Books, 1984: 153 onwards).

Watt, Philip, Obituary, 'Fr Francis Zulueta', *LN*, 52: 155–7.

Whelan, Basil, *The History of Belmont Abbey* (London: Bloomsbury, 1956).

Wilson, John, *The Life of Bishop Hedley* (London: Burns Oates and Washbourne, 1930).

Wiseman, Nicholas, Letter, *OJ*, 13 (July–December 1841): 67.

Wiseman, Nicholas, *Four Lectures on the Office and Ceremonies of Holy Week as performed in the Papal Chapel delivered in Rome in the Lent of 1837* (London: Charles Dolman, 1839).

Zon, Bennett, *Music and Metaphor in Nineteenth-Century British Musicology* (Aldershot: Ashgate, 2000).

Zon, Bennett, *The English Plainchant Revival* (London: Oxford University Press, 1999).

Zon, Bennett, 'Plainchant in Nineteenth-Century England: A review of some major publications of the period', *PMM*, 6/1 (1997): 53–74.

Zon, Bennett, *Plainchant in the Eighteenth-Century Roman Catholic Church in England (1737–1834). An examination of surviving printed and manuscript sources with particular reference to the work of John F. Wade* (Oxford: DPhil thesis, 1993).

Zon, Bennett, 'Plainchant in the Eighteenth-Century English Catholic Church', *RH*, 21/3 (May 1993): 361–80.

Internet sources

www.latin-masssociety.org/canon.htm: 'The Glory of the Silent Canon. A homily preached at the launch of CIEL UK at St James', Spanish Place, London by a priest of the Oratory' (1 March 1997).

www.latin-mass-society.org/canon.htm: Hildebrand, Dietrich, 'The case for the Latin Mass' (reproduced from the October 1966 issue of *Triumph*).

www.bios.org.uk: British Institute of Organ Studies. This includes the National Pipe Organ Register (NPOR).

www.puericantors.org

www.vatican.va/roman_curia/congregations/ccdds/documents/re_com_ccdds_doc_ 20010507-liturgiam-authenticam_en.html Congregation for Divine Worship and the Sacraments: *Liturgiam Authenticam* (English translation).

www.vatican.va/holy_father/John_Paul_ii/letters/2003/documents/hf_jp-ii_let_2 *Chirograph of the Supreme Pontiff John Paul II for the centenary of the Motu Proprio 'Tra Le Sollectudin' on sacred music.*

Selected recordings

Gregorian Chant: The Choir of the monks of Saint Pierre de Solesmes conducted by Joseph Gajard OSB. (Decca LP LX3119 (8 sides): 1956).

Gregorian Chant: The Choir of the monks of St Pierre de Solesmes. Dom Joseph Gajard OSB (Dir.) (HMV Album Series 120 (78 RPM records) DM 71–82, c.1930).

The Gregorian Congress of 1904. Plainchant and speeches recorded in Rome by the Gramophone Company. Transfers made by Howell, Anthony and EMI. Cover notes by Berry, Mary (Discant Recordings, Mono LP (2 records), no numbers supplied, 1982.

Queen of heavenly virtue: Sacred music for Henrietta Maria's chapel in Oxford. Concertare, Wainwright, Jonathan P. (dir.) (Isis Records, CD023, 1997).

Plainchant: Cathédrale D'Auxerre XVIIIe Siècle (Ensemble Organum, Marcel Peres (dir.) (Harmonia Mundi, CD 901319, 1990).

Plainsong to Polyphony Vol. 1. Choir of the Carmelite Priory, John McCarthy (cond.). (HMV CLP1895, 1961). This contains a selection of Renaissance polyphonic works with the matching plainchant compositions on which they are based. The style of plainchant singing is that of Solesmes according to Mocquereau's rhythmic principles.

The Choir of 1966: St Albans, Church choir of St Albans, Blackburn, directed by 'Mr Tolman' on the occasion of his retirement (Lancaster: 'Deroy' Sound Service, LP (no number), 1966). A unique example of a pre-Vatican II style provincial Catholic choir singing in rehearsal conditions without the conductor knowing they were being recorded.

Select list of liturgical books, hymnals, Benediction manuals and other musical collections

Alfieri, Pietro (ed.), *Raccolta di musica sacra* (Rome, n.p., 1841–47).

Allen, Herbert P., *Accompaniments to 'Plainsong For Schools'* (Liverpool: Rushworth and Dreaper, 1930).

Anon. (ed.), *Convent Hymns and Music used by the Pupils of the Sisters of Notre Dame* (Liverpool: Printed by Rockliff Brothers Ltd., 1891).

Anon. (ed.), *Graduale Juxta Missale Romanum* (Lyons: J.M. Boursy, 1816).

Anon. (ed.), *Kyriale Simplex* (Rome: Vatican Press, 1965, Typical Edition).

Anon. (ed.), *Hymns for the Ecclesiastical Year with accompanying tunes and six Benediction services* (London: Art and Book Company/CTS, 1895).

Anon. (ed.), *St Dominic's Hymn Book* (London: R. and T. Washbourne, 1881).

Anon. (ed.), *St Winifrid Hymn Book* (London: R. Butler, n.d.).

Anon. (ed.) [probably Police, F.], *The Parochial Hymn Book* (London: Burns and Oates, 1883).

Bainbridge, William S. (ed.), *The Westminster Hymnal* (London: Burns Oates and Washbourne, 1940).

Barton, Edwin and Myers, Edward (eds), *The new Psalter and its use* (London, New York, Bombay: Longman, Green and Co., 1913).

Bas, Julius (ed. and realiser of the accompaniments), *Commune Sanctorum* (based on the Vatican Edition) (Tournai, Paris, Rome: Desclée et Cie., 1921).

Bas, Julius (ed. and realiser of the accompaniments), *Kyriale Seu Ordinarium Messe* (based on the Vatican Edition) (Tournai, Paris, Rome: Desclée et Cie., 1921).

Bas, Julius (ed. and realiser of the accompaniments), *Proprium De Tempore Pro Gradualis Romani Adventus, Nativitatis, Epiphaniae, Quadragesimae usque ad Pascha* (Tournai, Paris, Rome: Desclée et Cie, 1921/1925).

Bas, Julius (ed. and realiser of the accompaniments), *Proprium Sanctorum* (based on the Vatican Edition) (Tournai, Paris, Rome: Desclée et Cie., 1927).

Benz, Johann, *Cantica Sacra, or Gregorian Music* (London, Derby and Dublin: J. Richardson and Son/J.A. Novello, 1846/R1849).

Birtchnell, Frank and Brown, Moir (comp. and arr.), *The Notre Dame Hymn Tune Book* (Liverpool: Rockcliff Bros. (printers), 1905).

Biton, L.-J. (ed.), *Cantus ad Processiones et Benedictiones Ssmi Sacramenti* (following the Vatican edition) (Tournai, Paris, Rome: Desclée et Cie., 1927).

Biton, L.-J. (ed.), *Vade Mecum Paroissial* (Paris, Rome, Tournai: Desclée et Cie., 1914).

Diocese of Lancaster, *Approved List of Church Music* (Preston: 1929).

Diocese of Liverpool, *Approved List of Church Music* (Liverpool: Rockcliff Bros. (printers), 1906).

Diocese of Liverpool, *Supplementary List of Approved Church Music* (Liverpool: Rockcliffe Bros. (printers), 1911).

Caswall, Edward (trans.), *Lyra Catholica, containing all the Breviary and Missal hymns with others from various sources* (London: James Burns, 1849).

Caswall, Edward, *Hymns and Poems* (London: Burns and Oates, 1873).

Coghlan, James P. (ed.), *Divers Church Chants* (London: 1790).

Coghlan, James P. (ed.), *The Evening Office of the Church* (London: 1790).

Coghlan, James P. (ed.), *Plainchant for the Chief Masses* (London: 1787).

Driscoll, John (ed.), *Accompaniments to The Catholic Schools Hymn Book* (London: CTS, 1920).

Driscoll, John (ed.), *The Catholic Schools Hymn Book* (London: CTS, 1920).

Driscoll, John (ed.), *Wimbledon Cantionale* (with supplements for Stonyhurst and Beaumont Colleges) (Wimbledon: Sacred Heart Church, 1918/R1920).

[Duval (ed.), revisions by Voght, P.F. De and Bogaerts, P.C.C.], *Vesperale Romanum* (Mechlin: H.J. Hanicq, 1854, 2nd ed.).

Ett, Caspar and Hauber, J. Michael (eds), *Cantica Sacra in usum Studiosae Juventutis* (Monarchii, 1854).

Faber, Frederick, *Hymns by Frederick William Faber DD.* (London: Burns and Oates, 1861/R1890).

[Faber, Frederick (ed.)], *The Oratory Hymn Book* (London: Thomas Richardson and son, 1854).

[Groom, Alban, Palmer, Raymund and Suffield, Robert (eds)], *The Crown of Jesus: A Complete Catholic Manual of Devotion, Doctrine and Instruction* (London, Dublin and Derby: Thomas Richardson and Son, 1862).

Guidetto, A. John, rev. Pelichiari, Francis, *Directorium Chori* (Rome: Vatican Press, 1582/R1737).

[Haberl, Franz Xavier ed.], *Epitome ex editione typica Gradualis Romani* (Ratisbon, New York, Cincinatti: Pustet, 1890) (copyright note for 1886). This contains an appendix listing the Proper Offices for English saints, showing that it was intended for the British market.

[Haberl, Franz Xavier (ed.)], *Graduale* (Ratisbon: Pustet, 1871).

[Haberl, Franz Xavier (ed.)], *Officium Hebdomadae Sanctae* (Ratisbon: Pustet, 1875).

[Haberl, Franz Xavier (ed.)], *Officium Majoris Hebdomadae* (Ratisbon, New York and Cincinnati: Pustet, 1876).

[Haberl, Franz Xavier (ed.)], *Vesperale Romanum* (Ratisbon, New York and Cincinnati: Pustet, 1887).

[Haberl, Franz Xavier (ed.)], *Officium Majoris Hebdomadae* (Ratisbon, New York, Cincinnati: Pustet, 1895).

Hemy, Henri (ed.), *Crown Of Jesus Music* Parts I, II, III and IV (London: Burns Oates and Washbourne, N.d. Parts I, II and III originally published in London, Dublin and Derby by Thomas Richardson and son, 1864).

Howard, Henry, Duke of Norfolk and Gatty, Charles (eds), *Arundel Hymns* (London: Boosey and Co./ R. and T. Washbourne , 1898 (Part 1 only)/1901/R1905).

Jenner, Ernest, *Our Church Music. III:* Lists of Modern Masses and Motets (Diocese of Southwark, 1927).

Lambert, John (ed.), *Ordinarium Missae e Graduale Romano: A complete Organ accompaniment for the Ordinary of the Mass from the Roman Gradual* (London: Burns and Lambert, 1850).

Little, Vilma G. (ed.), *Cantate Domino: A Collection of Supplementary Hymns* (Liverpool: Rushworth and Dreaper, 1932/1941).

Little, Vilma G. (ed.), *Laudate Dominum; A Benediction Manual compiled chiefly from English MSS* (Liverpool: Rushworth and Dreaper, 1936 and 1947).

Matthias, Franz Xavier, *Organum Comitans ad Kyrieale seu Ordinarium Missae* (Ratisbon, Rome, New York, Cincinnatti: Pustet, 1910).

Monks of Solesmes (eds), *Antiphonale Monasticum pro diurnis horis* (Tournai, Paris, Rome: Desclée et Cie., 1933 and 1934) (no. 818). Equipped with rhythmic signs.

Monks of Solesmes (eds), *Cantus Missae In Festis Solemnioribus* (Paris, Tournai, Rome: Desclée et Cie., 1920). Equipped with rhythmic signs.

Monks of Solesmes (eds), *Graduale Romanum* (Tournai, Paris, Rome: Desclée et Cie., 1909, also 1924). Equipped with rhythmic signs.

Monks of Solesmes (eds), *Graduale Romanum* (Tournai, Paris, Rome: Desclée et Socii, 1910). This is laid out in modern notation.

Monks of Solesmes (eds), *Kyriale seu Ordinarum Missae cum Cantu Gregorionis* (Rome, Tournai: Desclée et Cie., 1904).

Monks of Solesmes [Pothier, Joseph (ed.)], *Liber Gradualis* (Solesmes: Imprimerie Saint-Pierre, 1895).

Monks of Solesmes (eds), *Liber Responsorialis Pro Festis I. Classis Et Communi Sanctorum Juxta Ritum Monasticum* (Solesmes: Imprimerie Saint-Pierre, Solesmes, 1895).

Monks of Solesmes (eds), *Liber Usualis* (Tournai, Rome: Desclee et Cie, 1913). Equipped with rhythmic signs.

Monks of Solesmes (eds), *Manuale Missae et Officiorum ex Libris Solesmesibus Excerptum* (Tournai, Rome: Desclée, Lefébvre et Soc., 1903).

Monks of Solesmes (eds), *Notes des Vêpres et de l'Office pour tous les dimanches et fêtes doubles: Chant Grégorien* (Solesmes: Imprimerie Saint-Pierre, 1898).

Monks of Solesmes (eds), *The Liber Usualis with Introduction and Rubrics In English* (Tournai: Desclée and Co., 1950). Equipped with rhythmic signs.

Newman, John Henry (ed. and trans.), *Hymni Ecclesiae* (London: Alexander Macmillan, 1838/1865R).

Novello, Joseph Alfred (ed.), *Cantica Vespera: The Psalms chanted at Vespers and Compline adapted to the Gregorian Songs* (London: J.A. Novello, 1841).

'F.O.' [Oakeley, Frederick] (ed.), *Lyra Liturgica: Reflections In Verse For Holy Days and Seasons* (London: Burns, Lambert and Oates, 1865).

Ould, Gregory, and Sewell, William (eds), *The Book of Hymns with Tunes* (London: Cary and Co./ Edinburgh: A. Harkins and Bros., 1913).

Pitts, William (ed.), *Oratory Hymn Tunes* (London: Novello and Co., n.d).

Pothier, Joseph (ed.), *Le Livre de saluts* (Paris: A L'Art Catholique, n.d.)

[Pothier, Joseph (ed.)], *Graduale Romanum* (Tournai: Desclée, Lefébvre et Socii, 1883).

Potiron, Henri, *Accompagnement du Chant Gregorien par les Benedictions du T.S. Sacrement d'apres 'Cantus Selecti' et les 'Varii Cantus'* (Tournai, Paris, Rome: Desclée et Cie, 1934).

Potiron, Henri, *Gradual Paroissial contenent l'accompagnement du chant Grégorien pour les messes des dimanches et principales fêtes* (Paris, Tournai, Rome: Desclée et Cie., 1933).

Sacred Congregation of Rites (ed.), *Directorum Chori Omnium Ecclesiarum* (Rome: 1889).

[Shebbeare, Alphege] (ed.), *Hymnale* (English Benedictine Community, 1905).

Read, William, and Knight, Gerald (eds), *A Treasury of English Church Music* (London: Blandford Press, 1965).

Sandberger, Adolf (ed.), *Orlando di Lasso' Werke. Kompositionen mit Deutschen Text. Kompositionen mit Franzoschichen Text* (Leipzig: Breitkopf and Härtel, 1895 onwards).

Sisters of Notre Dame (eds), *New Hymns by the Sisters of Notre Dame* (London: Cary and Co., 1925).

Storer, John (ed.), *The Catholic Tune Book containing a complete collection of tunes in every metre to all English Hymns in general use, and also settings of the Latin Vesper Hymns* (London: Alphonse Cary and R. Washbourne, 1892).

Terry, Richard (ed.), *The Benediction Choir Book* (London: Burns Oates and Washbourne, 1937).

Terry, Richard [Hedley, Cuthbert and others] (eds), *The Westminster Hymnal* (London: R. and T. Washbourne, 1912, R1916, R1919, R1924).

'The Catholic Hierarchy' (ed.), *The new (complete) Catholic Hymn Book containing the hymns prescribed and arranged by the Catholic Hierarchy: with Latin hymns and Benediction service* (London: R. and T. Washbourne, 1910).

Trappes, Francis and Maher, William J. (eds), *Liturgical Hymns for the Chief Festivals of the Year selected from the Office of the Catholic Church and so translated into English as to be adapted to Old and New Music* (London: R. Butler, n.d.).

Tozer, Albert E. (ed.), *Catholic Church Hymnal* (London: Cary and Co., 1906).

Tozer, Albert E. (ed.), *St Dominic's Hymn Book* (London: R. and T. Washbourne, 1901).

Tozer, Albert E. (ed.), *Catholic Hymns: Original and Translated with accompanying tunes* (London: Cary and Co./Burns and Oates, 1898).

Tozer, Albert E. (ed.), *New and Complete Manual for Benediction* (London: Cary and Co., 1898).

Tozer, Albert E. (ed.), *Catholic Hymns with accompanying tunes being a musical edition of S. Dominic's Hymn Book* (London: Burns and Oates/Novello, Ewer and Co., 1886).

Tozer, Albert E. (ed.), [revised Hasberry, James] *Complete Benediction Manual* (London: Cary and Co. 1931).

[Vatican Commission headed by Pothier, Joseph] (eds), *Antiphonale Sacrosanctae Romanae Ecclesiae Pro Diurnis Horis* (Rome: Vatican Press, 1912).

[Vatican Commission headed by Pothier, Joseph] (eds), *Graduale* (Rome: Vatican Press).

[Vatican Commission headed by Pothier, Joseph] (eds), *Kyriale* (Rome: Vatican Press, 1905).

Wagner, Peter, *Accompaniment by Dr P. Wagner to the Selection of Gregorian Music contained in the Holy Ghost Hymnal* (Paris: Procure de la Musique Religieuse/ Dublin: The Holy Ghost Fathers, n.d.).

[Willson, Dominic] (ed.), *Plainsong For Schools Part One* (Liverpool: Rushworth and Dreaper, 1930/R1940) (rhythmic signs used).

[Willson, Dominic] (ed.), *Plainsong For Schools Part Two* (Liverpool, Rushworth and Dreaper, 1934) (rhythmic signs used).

Witt, Franz Xavier (transposed and harmonically ornamented) ed. A.J. Quadflieg, *Organum Comitans ad Ordinarium Missae quod ut partem Gradualis Romani curavit Sacrorum Rituum Congregatio* (Ratisbon, Rome, New York: Pustet, 1872/ R1901, 7th edn).

Young, William (ed.), *The Catholic Choralist for the use of the Choir, Drawing Room, Cloister, and Cottage harmonised and arranged for the voice, band, piano-forte and organ* (Dublin/Penzance: The Choralist Office/The Catholic Library, 1842).

Contemporary reference works not listed elsewhere

The Catholic Directory (London: Burns and Oates). 1850–present.
The Laity's Directory (London: Keating, Brown and Keating) 1805–1839.

Manuscript collections and archives

Belmont Abbey, Hereford, HR2 9RZ: library and archives, esp. Weg Prosser Correspondence. Envelope MS 39–73 and the Mss. 'History of Belmont' by Dr Newlyn Smith MS754.

Canonesses of the Holy Sepulchre : 48, Priory St, Colchester, Essex, CO1 2QB (formerly living at New Hall, near Chelmsford, Essex): archives.

Douai Abbey, Woolhampton, Reading, RG7 5TQ: library and archives. Esp. Wade Mss. Chant books and correspondence between Cecila Heywood, abbess of Stanbrook and Austin O'Neill (File A O'Neill).
Downside Abbey, Stratton on the Fosse, Bath, Somerset, BA3 4RH: library archives. Esp. the Gatty Papers relating to the production of *Arundel Hymns*. Boxes 1268, 1269, 1275, 1276 and numerous Mss. copies of works by Fabouillier and other late eighteenth- and early nineteenth-century composers (Edmund Bishop annexe).
Mount St Bernard Abbey, Coalville, Leicester, LE67 5UL: library.
Rawtenstall, Lancs. Public library: Mss transcript copied in 1904 of Heap, Moses, *My life and times – Moses Heap of Rossendale 1824–1913*.
Salford Diocesan Archives, St Mary's Presbytery, Burnley, Lancs., BB10 4AU, esp. Box 193 (Bishop Casartelli's Letters), folder marked 'Church Music: 1903–1905'.
Stanbrook Abbey, Callow End, Worcester, WR2 4TD: archives, esp. the Box marked 'D. Laurence Shepherd and Guéranger', the McLachlan–Mocquereau and McLachlan–Bewerunge correspondence, correspondence connected with the establishment and work of the Society of St Gregory (Box marked 'D.L. McL to Allen/Holland, Edeson and J.F.Turner'), correspondence relating to the production of the *Stanbrook Hymnale*, and a small collection of late eighteenth- and early nineteenth-century manuscript and printed music. See also some manuscript music in the organ loft.
Stonyhurst College, Blackburn, Lancs, BB7 9PZ: Arundell Library and annexe known as 'Cacus', esp. rare Wade chant books and 'The Diary of John Gerard. 1868–1869: Log of Ye Corpus Doctum of ye doings thereof with some notice of contemporary history' (E/III/2).
St Dominic's church presbytery, Newcastle, NE1 2TP: library.
St Mary's Abbey, Oulton, Nr Stone, Staffs., ST15 8UP: archives.
Talbot Library, St Walburge's Church, Preston.
University of Durham Library, Palace Green, DH1 3RL: Pratt Green collection.
Westminster Archdiocesan archives, Abingdon Rd, Kensington, London, W8 6AF, esp. the Bourne papers and Low Week documents.

Collections of music used to compile the statistical data in Table 12.2

Parish/mission churches

Our Lady and St Michael, Alston Lane, Longridge, Lancs., PR3 3BJ.
Our Lady of Lourdes, Leigh on Sea, Essex, SS9 1NG: list of music stored kept by the Latin Mass Society, 11–13 Malkin St, London, WC28 5NH.
Our Lady of Mount Carmel, 27 High Park St, Liverpool, L8 8DX.
St Augustine, St Austin's Place, Preston, Lancs., PR1 3YJ: collection transferred to the Talbot Library, listed and then dispersed or incorporated into the main music collection there.
St Cuthbert, Old Elvet, Durham, DH1 3HL.

St Gregory the Great, Blackpool Rd, Preston, Lancs., PR1 6HQ: most of the collection was transferred to the Talbot Library, listed and dispersed. Items left in the choir loft have been incorporated into the statistical data.

St Mary of the Angels, Bolton Le Sands, Carnforth, Lancs., LA5 8DN: collection transferred to the Talbot Library, where it was listed before dispersal or incorporation into the main music collection there.

St Mary, School Lane, Chipping, Preston, Lancs., PR3 2QD.

St Mary, Todmorden Rd, Burnley, Lancs., BB10 4AV.

The 'Frank Hickey' collection, containing music formerly belonging to St Wilfrid's Church, Hexham St, Bishop Auckland, Co. Durham, DL14 7PU, where he had been organist in 1939 and between 1950 and 1977. The collection is held by him at 6, Everley Lane, Bishop Auckland, Co. Durham, DL14 7QR.

The 'Miss Oldfield' collection, formerly belonging to St Ignatius, Preston, PR1 1TT, then transferred to the Talbot Library, where the items were listed before incorporation into the main music collection there.

Private chapels

Chapel of the Sacred Heart, Broughton Hall, Skipton, North Yorks., BD23 3AE.

Croxdale Hall, Tudhoe, Nr Durham, DH6 5JP.

St Mary and St Everilda, Everingham, East Yorks., YO43 3DB: music currently stored at the Bar Convent, York.

Monasteries/convents

Bar Convent, Blossom St, York, YO24 1AQ.

Bryn Mair Convent (Order of Our Lady of Charity), Monastery Rd, Pantasaph, Holywell, Flintshire, CH8 8PN: collection transferred to the Talbot Library, where it was listed before dispersal or incorporation into the main music collection there.

Douai Abbey, Upper Woolhampton, Reading, Berks, RG7 5TQ: library and John Rowntree collection.

Downside Abbey, Stratton on the Fosse, Bath, Somerset, BA3 4RH: Tower Music Room and the monastic library.

Seminaries and schools

St Cuthbert's College, Ushaw, Durham, DH7 9RH: old music room; some items in the dormitories.

St Mary's College, Oscott, Chester Rd, Sutton Coalfield, West Midlands, B73 5AA.

Stonyhurst College, Blackburn, Lancs., BB7 9PZ: music basement, with some items transferred to the Arundell Library archives.

Miscellaneous collections

Church Music Association (CMA) Collection: The CMA was a group that evolved away from the SSG in the 1950s and then reunited with it in 1977. Items incorporated in the statistics presented here all date from before 1962 and many date back to the 1900s. The collection was until recently kept at the Franciscan Study Centre, Giles Lane, Canterbury, Kent, CT2 7NA. It is now (2007) held by the Society of St Gregory at The Talbot Library in Preston (see below).

Royal College of Music, Prince Consort Rd, London, SW7 2BS: music by Henry George Nixon, File HYGeorge 10 and 7.

The Talbot Library, St Walburghe's Church, Preston, PR2 2QE: general collection of old music. The statistics here distinguish between these items and those formerly belonging to the other collections listed above.

Index